Federalism:
The Multiethnic Challenge

Federalism: The Multiethnic Challenge

edited by
GRAHAM SMITH

LONGMAN
London and New York

Longman Group Limited,

Longman House, Burnt Mill,
Harlow, Essex CM20 2JE, England
and Associated Companies throughout the world.

*Published in the United States of America
by Longman Publishing, New York*

© Longman Group Limited 1995

First published 1995

ISBN 0 582 225795 CSD
ISBN 0 582 225787 PPR

British Library Cataloguing-in-Publication Data

A catalogue record for this book is
available from the British Library

Library of Congress Cataloging-in-Publication Data

Set by 7 in 11/12pt Garamond

Produced by Longman Singapore Publishers (Pte) Ltd.
Printed in Singapore

For Alexander

Contents

Preface

In the period between the conception and completion of this book, the relationship between federalism and ethnoregionalism has moved towards occupying a more prominent place within the arena of post-Cold War politics. The socialist ethno-federations of the Soviet Union, Yugoslavia and Czechoslovakia all disappeared from the geopolitical map in the early 1990s, while in both South Africa and Ireland the federal question is back on the political agenda. The 1994 election in Quebec of the *Parti Québécois* has again shown how vulnerable the Canadian federation is to the possibility of fragmentation. Yet despite the significance of these events to a late twentieth century world characterised by the simultaneous processes of fragmentation and greater globalisation, federalism, as an object of intellectual enquiry, has slipped from the social science agenda.

This book is designed as a contribution to rectifying this slippage. Its aim is to examine those federal formations where cultural differences – based around race, ethnicity, tribe, language or religion – provide their architectural focus as well as the utility and appropriateness of federation to managing such differences. The book is divided up as follows. A scene-setting chapter introduces the reader to some of the central questions concerning federalism and cultural difference by focusing on the relationship between federation and questions of ideology, political practice and social justice. The rest of the book falls into three parts. In Part I we consider those federations whose very legitimacy is under question from particular ethno-regional communities. Here the underlying reasons for federal crisis are examined and the ability of federation as a strategy of conflict management explored. Part II focuses on the break up of socialist federations and the search in both post-socialist Russia and Bosnia to find a federal solution to their multi-ethnicity. In Part III consideration is given to multiethnic polities where federation is being actively considered as a way of managing multiethnic divisions along more democratic lines. A postscript has been added, signalling in particular how comparative analysis can enrich our understanding of the idea and practice of federations.

As editor, it is a pleasant duty to offer thanks and appreciation to the contributors particularly for their willingness to follow editorial guidelines. I also owe a special debt to John Agnew, Stuart Corbridge, Norberto De Sousa, Gerry Kearns, Benno Werlen and Andrew Wilson for reading parts of the text and for their useful and encouraging comments. As always it has been a pleasure to work with Chris Harrison, publisher at Longman, and with Ian Agnew who drew the maps and diagrams.

GRAHAM SMITH
Cambridge
October 1994

List of Maps and Diagrams

List of Tables

List of Contributors

John Agnew, School of Geography, University of Syracuse, Syracuse, United States.

James Anderson, Faculty of Social Sciences, The Open University, England.

Stuart Corbridge, Department of Geography, University of Cambridge, England.

Martin Dent, Department of Politics, University of Keele, England.

Montseratt Guibernau, Centre for Ethnic Relations, University of Warwick, England.

Robert J. Kaiser, Department of Geography, University of Missouri-Columbia, United States.

Alexander Murphy, Department of Geography, University of Oregon, United States.

Vesna Popovski, Department of Sociology, University of Leicester, England.

Jenny Robinson, Department of Geography, University of Natal, South Africa.

Graham Smith, Department of Geography, University of Cambridge, England.

Colin H. Williams, Department of Welsh, University of Wales College of Cardiff, Wales.

CHAPTER ONE

Mapping the Federal Condition: Ideology, Political Practice and Social Justice

Graham Smith

Federalism has emerged as a major issue on the political agenda of the post-Cold War world. That it has been propelled into occupying a more central place owes much to the resurgence of both nationalist and ethnic tensions which have paralleled, if not taken sustenance from, the end of the Cold War and the accompanying search for how best to organise our national and ethno-regional communities so as they can live with difference. Such world-historical changes have seen the demise of socialist federations and the subsequent but only too painful search by some of their successor states, notably Russia and Bosnia, to experiment with new forms of federation as ways of living (or not) with cultural diversity. In Western Europe, not only is federalism considered as a project for re-negotiating the political boundaries of sovereignty and citizenship but for many ethno-regional communities – like the Catalans, Scots and Flemish – as a way of refocusing a politics of identity by going simultaneously local and continental. For Canadians, long since used to living with federalism, the issue of sovereignty association, first mooted by the Parti Québécois a generation ago, is back on the table questioning not only Quebec's relationship to the rest of Canada but whether a federation living with so many other claims to cultural difference can continue to be defined by its linguistic dualism alone. And in the post-colonial world of the South, where federalism was a belated and often imposed import, ethnic and national differences challenge its utility to manage communities with often limited respect for recognising the rights of others while also offering the possibility, as in post-apartheid South Africa, of constructing more socially just polities.

It would seem that there has never been such a time as the late twentieth century in which the idea and practice of federalism has rendered old certainties about the geopolitical landscape so uncertain. Whether however this constitutes, as Elazar claims, 'a federal revolution sweeping the world' (1991:7) remains debatable.

1

Yet federation and the possibilities and opportunities that it may offer for constructing more democratic and possibly less nation-state-bound communities raises questions about its appropriateness as a form of governance in multiethnic societies to effectively respond to the economic, social and political conditions offered by the late twentieth century. In this regard, three challenges seem particularly apposite.

Firstly, there is the challenge of what can be loosely labelled as globalisation. There is a sense that as a consequence of the impact of globalising processes – the internationalisation of capital, the greater mobility of labour, the growth in continental trading blocs – the territorial boundaries of the nation-state are becoming increasingly blurred and less appropriate. Localities are being reshaped in more direct ways than ever before by these processes, in which the regulatory role of the state has become increasingly marginal to structuring the localities and peoples under its territorial jurisdiction. Thus in a late modern federal democracy like Canada, there is more than just a sense that its provinces have gone simultaneously 'local' and 'global'. On the one hand, such localities have become more autonomous, questioning the centre's capacity to act as the most appropriate arena for expressing and integrating regional views or for defining a national interest that transcends locality. On the other hand, the greater global interdependency of its regions has been accompanied by more globally-conscious and assertive local identities. In the case of Quebec, for instance, provincial elites have been instrumental in redefining its relationship to the global market place, in which 'crucial to such entrepreneurs is their nationalist sense of self, their notion that they have overcome the odds and they can now move internationally, their culture intact' (Breton and Jenson, 1991). Quebec is not unique: both globalisation and the challenges that it represents to the nation-state have prompted other sub-national governments to chart their own particular ways within the global geopolitical economy linked in part to a realisation that such intervention is increasingly central to their provincial well-being (Fry, 1988). Nor are such activities confined to the economic sphere: federated communities have become increasingly engaged in promoting cultural relations with other provincial units within the global arena based often upon their shared limits to sovereignty, contributing to a more general trend in transnational politics which has been labelled 'globalisation from below' (Camilleri and Falk, 1992; Smith, 1994b).

Secondly, there is the challenge of sub-state or locally-based nationalisms to federalism. Nationalism in effect tests the proposition that a federation can actually fashion a sense of identity in which sub-state national identities are not, to use Anderson's (1990) phrase, 'imagined as ultimately sovereign' but rather as possessing multiple and overlapping communities of imagination. Federalism's success in this endeavour necessarily hinges upon whether federations constructed on the basis of ethno-regional markers facilitate the establishment of a dual identity or, as their critics maintain, reinforce, even reify, ethnic, tribal, linguistic and religious divisions, making inter-communal tensions and even fragmentation that much more probable. Judged on these conflicting interpretations, some federations have been successful (Switzerland), others failures (Pakistan, Soviet Union, Yugoslavia), while some still hang in the balance (Canada, India, Nigeria). It may well therefore be, as Habermas (1994) argues, that it is only through constructing our political communities on the basis of 'a constitutional patriotism' that respects all forms of cultural difference and therefore reflects the wishes of all groups within civil society – ethnic, religious, linguistic or gender-based – to live as they wish, and to compete politically by soliciting the voluntary choices of individuals, that federation will act as an antidote to nationalism. Much however will depend upon the nature of the particular federal arrangement and of the symbolic meanings behind the identific boundaries upon which federalism is constructed.

Finally, despite the surprisingly limited reference to federalism among theorists of social justice, federation as a peculiarly territorial and non-majoritarian form of organising the political and cultural life of citizens in multiethnic societies challenges the defensibility of such a form of political organisation. Two such issues are paramount: the idea that citizens have rights to representation on a regionally differentiated basis; and whether ethno-regions have rights to be culturally different through constitutional and other means of public policy protection. Both these components – representation and difference – have implications for social justice, particularly whether federalism so contravenes the rights of the majority as to question its claim to be the handmaiden of democracy. Specifying which citizens are entitled to particular rights, and by what measure, are issues which affect all federal formations, nascent or otherwise.

The purpose of this scene-setting chapter is to examine some of the central questions concerning federalism and its relationship to multiethnic societies whose cultures, politics and identities are undergoing profound change. In keeping with the overall scope of this book, this chapter focuses on political communities whose ethno-regional divisions provide both the template and the strains of federation and on others where federation is viewed as a possible means to managing difference. In so doing the chapter raises basic questions about the politics of ethno-regional identities and rights and of whether such identities and rights can and should be accommodated within a multilayered political architecture designed through spatio-jurisdictional delimitation to facilitate both unity and diversity. The first section explores interpretations of federalism, clarifying in particular the relationship between federalism as ideology and political practice. In the second section we examine the strains and tensions inherent in multiethnic federations, especially the utility of the federal idea as an effective form of conflict management. The final section considers from the standpoint of social justice the implications of federalism for protecting the rights of minorities.

FEDERALISM, IDEOLOGY AND POLITICAL PRACTICE

The term 'federalism' has been subject to differing meanings and applied to many different situational contexts, and identifying its defining features can be as controversial as evaluating them. It is therefore important to begin by distinguishing between federalism as political ideology and as institutional arrangement and to probe the contested nature of these conceptual linkages.

In its most general and commonly conceived form, federalism can be considered as an ideology which holds that the ideal organisation of human affairs is best reflected in the celebration of diversity through unity. Reflected in the attainment and maintenance of such a prescriptive ideal are the values and beliefs of particular interests who see in working towards such a goal recognition of its political validity. Yet beyond this very general conception, it is difficult to defend federalism as a free-standing ideology comparable to or separate from liberalism or socialism. A purely self-referential theory of federalism, unlike that of liberalism or socialism, is unable to answer crucial questions about the human condition: about desire, happiness, justice, value, etc. Rather, federalism as ideology is best considered as an amalgam of doctrines, beliefs and programmatic considerations reflecting the very paradoxes and tensions inherent in thinking about the politics of modernity. So rather than considering it as an ideology that has developed and exists autonomously from the main traditions of political thought or as Burgess and Gagnon note as 'a doctrine which trumpets universal a priori truths' (1993:112), federalism is best treated as traversing a broad range of what we can more usefully call programmatic orientations.

Most straightforwardly, federalism as ideology can be conceived as both universalist and particular in scope. Its universalism is reflected and draws upon a long tradition of normative thought about a desire for ultimate unity of the human condition based upon the assumption that it is only through global democratisation and of working towards embracing world citizenship that the chaotic dangers of political fragmentation and uneven economic development will be overcome. Such universalist thinking is also often found in calls for the creation of larger regional political units as expressed in the notion of European union. More commonly, however, federalism has become bound up with nationally-specific projects in which its advocates have concerned themselves with a particular polity or set of polities. Manifested in calls for the greater devolution of power towards self-governing units, such nationally-specific projects are often linked to pragmatic projects designed to secure, within deeply-divided societies, social unity and political stability.

Federalism has been represented as a centralising and decentralising ideology as well as a doctrine of balance. As a centralising ideology it does not necessarily entail the promotion of centralisation of an unqualified and illimitable kind but it can, particularly when viewed from the localities, invoke the fear of a centralising authority imposing limits on the liberties of its constituent members. Conversely, there is a long established communitarian tradition, represented particularly in the anarchist works of such classical federalist writers as Proudhon, Bakunin and Kropotkin, who were concerned mainly with the state's abolition and replacing it with a form of socio-economic federalism which would secure local autonomy, territorial decentralisation and the greater fragmentation of power. For Kropotkin, whose ideas on federalism formed one of the basic factors in his geographic writings, the state was evil incarnate, equatable with bourgeois interests and xenophobic nationalism; the only path to democracy and to the liberation of the individual lay in the abolition of the state and its replacement by freely federated entities organised along various lines (communities, communes, associations of workers), including that of nationality (Cahm, 1978). More commonly, however, federalism has been conceived as a doctrine of balance. For Proudhon, often described as the founding father of modern federalism, a loose federal state was to provide the only effective solution to the key problem of socio-political organisation: the reconciliation of authority and liberty. Dicey (1908) broadens this in identifying the federal idea as bound up with the goal of finding an equilibrium between forces of centralisation and decentralisation, of reflecting the societal desire for union but not unity. The federal idea, in short, is generally conceived as a compromise, conveyed by the image of checks and balances between unity and diversity, autonomy and sovereignty, the national and regional.

Justifications for federal projects also differ in orientation and emphasis. For many federalists, geopolitical concerns are paramout as in the case of using federalism as a way of preempting inter-communal violence in former multiethnic colonies or simply as a basis for providing an overarching regional security architecture based on mutual self-protection. For Saint-Simon (1814), one of the earliest visionaries of a European Union, it was only through the establishment of common institutions in tandem with preserving the national independence of each of its peoples that the recurrence of European war could be avoided and an enduring peace established. Economic motives also loom large as in the case of the European Union where the benefits of a larger single market are reinforced by a recognition by many Europeans that in the post-Cold War world an enlarged regional trading bloc is central to securing a substantive control of shares in a competitive world economy. For other federalists, emphasis has been placed on its libertarian qualities. For communitarianists, federated communities were thought to be not only compatible with individual liberty but a necessary condition of it. In the federative social contract that Proudhon proposes, rather than the citizen giving up a greater measure of freedom and authority than the part s/he reserves, the citizen retains more power over her/himself than s/he cedes, an end stage, which Proudhon argued, could only be achieved through a federal community (Proudhon, 1863; Hyams, 1979).

Federalism in its orientations can also be conceived as both a territorial and a non-territorial project in multiethnic societies. In the former, ethno-regional communities are considered as most appropriately represented through their spatial compartmentalisation (states, cantons, provinces, communes), predicated on the belief that ethno-regional or national communities should receive due territorial recognition. This is reflected in what is often meant when commentators talk of a federal society (Stein, 1968; Livingston, 1956), in which the boundaries between components of a federation match the boundaries of its ethnic, religious or linguistic communities. Thus for Livingston, without territoriality, a 'society cannot be said to be federalism . . . It becomes functionalism, pluralism, or some form of corporatism' (1956:2). Less commonly, federalism has been conceived as non-territorial, often associated with dispersed ethnic communities. For the Austro-Marxists, Karl Renner and Otto Bauer, who were among the first federalists to address the question of how to reconcile ethnic dispersal with cultural rights, the solution to democratising the multiethnic Austro-Hungarian Empire lay in securing the cultural rights of geographically scattered ethnic groups by providing non-territorial-based institutional supports in combination with a non-territorial form of political representation. In many polities, however, both territorial and non-territorial conceptions of federalism have often been argued for and to varying degrees attained, as in the case of present-day Belgium.

What the foregoing remarks emphasise is the pluralistically programmatic nature of federalism as promulgated by federal visionaries. And despite the often very different projects and philosophies held by federal builders – Lenin's Soviet Union, Nehru's India, Tito's Yugoslavia, Trudeau's Canada or even Delors' European Union – what federalists commonly aspire to is securing and ensuring the reproduction of a particular form of political institutionalisation which reflects and acknowledges diversity. We can refer to this end stage as federation. It is above all an organising principle, containing institutions and structures and legitimised on the basis of providing for and celebrating both unity and difference. Although it is generally acknowledged as a particular type of political formation, federations are not easily distinguishable from other state forms, leading one eminent federal theorist to go so far as to conclude that federation in political practice is a myth (Riker, 1975). Certainly self-ascription offers little in the way of clarification; of the one in ten of the world's present-day polities that claim to be federations, closer scrutiny reveals that it is often difficult to distinguish many of them from unitary state structures. King however provides us with one way out of the self-ascriptive quagmire by defining federation as 'an institutional arrangement, taking the form of a sovereign state, and distinguished from other such states solely by the fact that its central government incorporates regional units in its decision procedure on some constitutionally entrenched basis' (1982:77). In elaborating upon this definition in his 1993 writings he advocates a conception of federation containing four essential features:

1. Its representation is preponderantly territorial

2. This territorial representation is characteristically secured on at least two sub-national levels (which King refers to as 'local' and 'regional government')

3. The regional units are incorporated electorally, or perhaps otherwise, into the decision procedure of the national centre

4. The incorporation of the regions into the decision procedure of the centre can only be altered by extraordinary constitutional measures, not for example by resort to a simple majority vote of the national legislature or by autonomous decision of the national executive.

In distinguishing federation from other forms of state organisation most commentators consider it as a decentralised political system possessing a constitutional government in which constituent territorial units are involved in a politics of accommodation. The nature and scale of the divisions of powers between the centre and the region can be distinguished from other forms of political devolution by virtue of the fact that regional autonomy and representation are not only more devolved but are constitutionally guaranteed. The centre does not have the judicial right to abolish, amend or redefine its territorial units. Thus in federations, regional units are in effect truly local states with local state rights. Citizen representation is also uniquely based on a regional principle which as King further notes is the chief distinguishing feature of federation. Under federations then, citizenship is highly regionalised and the means by which citizens are represented are inextricably bound up with the federalisation of state institutional politics.

Thus King signals what has tended to become an accepted 'given' that federation is a form of state classification equated with particular types of liberal democracies. In this schema only those states whose governments are subordinate to constitutional law and which therefore practice democracy are judged as true federations. According to Burgess and Gagnon (1993), 'toleration, respect, compromise, bargaining and mutual recognition are its watchwords and "union" combined simultaneously with "autonomy" is its hallmark' (p. 7). Such features would exclude what Duchacek (1986) labels 'pseudo-federations' like the Soviet Union, Yugoslavia and Czechoslovakia precisely because the unity of their ethno-regional parts was maintained from above and in which a complex array of techniques of coercion ensured compliance with the centre. So despite clauses in their constitutions which claimed they were federations based on democratic principles, socialist federations could not be considered as true federations. While such federations as measured by liberal democratic criteria may be rightly judged to be imperfect (and for Duchacek the yardstick and ideal measure in which to juxtapose any claims to being a federation is the US model), nonetheless it is important to acknowledge that federal projects take a variety of forms which cannot simply be equated with particular late-modern democracies. To ignore this diversity is to limit our understanding of federations and to impoverish comparative analysis, let alone to ignore the fact that multiethnic polities whose democratic federal credentials are suspect may be capable of moving on to experiment with more democratised forms. Moreover, we should not take as unproblematic the democratic credentials of western multiethnic federations. As Riker (1964) reminds us, it is an ideological fallacy to link federation with guarantees of freedom without interrogating the nature of cultural rights and liberties and how these rights and liberties are both socially and spatially constituted.

FEDERATION AND INTER-COMMUNAL TENSIONS

Much of the academic literature on multiethnic federations has concerned itself with the tensions underlying this particular form of state formation, emphasising the interrelated reasons for their success and failure, stability and legitimacy, resilience and flexibility (Gagnon 1988; Dikshit, 1975; Hicks, 1978; Stewart, 1984). Yet little consideration has been paid to the role of inter-ethnoregional tensions even although such tensions have the potential to result in federal break-up. In taking up this focus it is however only too easy given the character of federal systems to see them as a consequence in perpetual crisis. As King reminds us, '. . . the history of federations is at least as much a history of success as of dissolution' (1993:97). After all, federations, by their very nature, combine elements of duality which at best can only manage the politics of communal particularisms. So while a perpetual state of crisis may be deemed as characteristic of certain multiethnic federations, it often becomes apparent following the break-up of federations that such a form of governance has over generations provided an important and effective means of regulating deep divisions within society and preventing their spillover into inter-communal violence. Yugoslavia is probably the most vivid example of the benefits that federation can bring when juxtaposed with what happens when it gives way to geopolitical fragmentation.

The conditions under which inter-ethnoregional tensions within the federal state arise are multifaceted and complex but in one form or another are reflected in the territoriality of the political party system. Compared to unitary states or even federations based on the 'one nation principle', the impact of 'nationalising processes' such as industrialisation, urbanisation and geographic mobility have had less far-reaching consequences within multiethnic federations in transferring locally-based identities along more nationally organised lines of political affiliation (Gibbins, 1987). Due to the saliency of ethno-regional markers, multiethnic federations rank amongst the least 'nationalised' in their party formations. This carries important consequences: 'Where there is a political party "symmetry" between the federal (central) government and governments of the constitutional units of the federation we can expect the relative particular harmony to have a binding impact upon the federation. Conversely, where there is a notable and resilient "asymmetry" between the actual authorities and the local party elites and organisations the resulting differences of interest may have a centralised effect leading to political mobilisation for decentralist reforms' (Burgess, 1993:107). A notable characteristic of multiethnic federations is the high degree of asymmetry between provincial parties and federal counterparts with national parties often lacking viable affiliates in particular localities. Such enduring asymmetry can be symptomatic of inter-communal tensions and lead to pressures not only for greater autonomy but also for secession from the federation.

Competition between provincial units for scarce resources is characteristic of all federations and need not necessarily be bound up with or lead to demands for greater autonomy or secession. Yet due in part to the constitutive nature of multiethnic federations, where provincial and ethnic boundaries coincide, the politics of nationalism is rarely far removed from the arena of federal politics, feeding into a set of grievances which in one form or another have the potential to mobilise individuals behind calls for the territorial redistribution of power, including independence. As Meadwell writes, 'Federalism . . . is an important source of institutional capacity because it provides a set of political levers and access to resources that make group mobilisation more likely. While often put in place as a means of accommodation and cooption, federal institutions can be quickly turned to new agendas when a coopted leadership is replaced or changes its preferences' (1993:200). With Quebec's so called 'quiet revolution of the 1960s', the province's political elites became less concerned with defending Francophone interests within a federal Canada and more concerned with pushing for radical solutions to protecting Francophone interests through adopting a secessionist position (McRoberts, 1979). Similarly, following the introduction of glasnost throughout the Soviet federation, political elites within the nationality-based union republics moved from a position of trying to secure a greater share of the fiscal budget within the parameters of a permissible federal politics to becoming increasingly supportive of greater economic, political and cultural autonomy for their ethno-regions (Smith, 1990).

Among the multifaceted sources of inter-ethnoregional tensions that have proven to be central to provincial elites seeking a redefinition of sovereign boundaries, four perspectives in particular can be singled out and briefly considered: cultural self-preservation, rectificatory justice, uneven development and the procedures and practices of federation.

Inter-ethnoregional tensions can be linked to fears for the erosion of cultural barriers in which the secessionist region feels that its national culture is imperilled, a condition likely in federal systems dominated by a single hegemonic culture. Such conditions may be bound up with standardising pressures that generate national conformity through the introduction of particular centralist policies (e.g. public education, language); they may also be a consequence of fears generated by more general social changes associated with what Gibbins (1987) calls 'the nationalising character of social change' within federal societies (e.g. greater geographic mobility, the exchange of ideas based on national life and culture) or with the impact on cultural life styles linked to globalising economic and social changes. Such threats to cultural community, that it must be either superseded through assimilation or left behind and its members subject to a subordinate social position, can fuel separatist tendencies but the ability to mobilise support behind the secessionist cause will depend upon whether a sense of common identity is strong enough to overcome identities that crosscut ethno-regional divisions or whether local identity is so diluted by stratification and segmentation as to undermine a shared interest in cultural survivance. Whichever way, individuals and basic class groups are unlikely to mobilise behind the separatist cause, irrespective of the fear of the erosion of national culture, unless it is in their self-defined interests to do so.

Rectificatory justice can in a few instances also provide a powerful source for political mobilisation. Here secessionist demands are linked to claims that membership of the federation was not voluntarily entered into and that the ethno-regional community should therefore have the right to constitute a sovereign state of its own based on the claim, spurious or otherwise, of the ethno-regional group's historic right to sovereignty over its native homeland. Besides often relying on a pre-existing claim to territoriality, justified on the basis of past national sovereignty, such grievances can also involve calls to rectify 'national' borders based on claims that the historic homeland should be congruent with the political community. Such claims remind us that not all federations are voluntarily entered into or even when they are, that support for federal membership is not immune to change. Federal arrangements imposed or negotiated externally, as in the case of many post-colonial states, are especially vulnerable. The Soviet federation is a case in point. Until the late 1980s, federal membership for the Baltic States of Estonia, Latvia and Lithuania was based on a centrally-created myth of voluntary incorporation. The public debunking of this myth by local historicist educators connected with the regions' newly emergent secessionist movements was to provide a powerful weapon for mobilising constituent support for 'a lawful struggle' against 'occupation' by 'a foreign power'. In short, the fledgling secessionist movements could appeal to rectificatory justice and to restoring the statehood that had been denied them as a result of forced incorporation (Smith, 1994a).

Inter-ethnoregional tensions in most federal systems are also bound up with a politics of uneven development. As Simeon notes, 'levels of inter-regional and intergovernmental conflict, cooperation or competition, are not primarily a matter of constitution or of inter-governmental machinery. They are a function of the underlying political economy, the issues that arise, the mobilisation of interests and the ambitions of federal and provincial leaders' (1988:45–46). Not surprisingly, the degree of commitment and effectiveness of redistributive techniques employed by the centre to rectify regional imbalances becomes crucial, drawing issues of redistribution into the arena of nationalist politics. The aggrieved are invariably those ethno-regions – developed or less developed – which feel that they are not benefiting from association. Thus the Yugoslav state's attempts during the last decade of its existence to rectify uneven development succeeded in making its under-industrialised southern republics more pro-centralist only to alienate and make more confederalist the richer northern republics of Slovenia, Croatia and Vojvodina (Denitsch, 1993). In picking up on the possibilities of such linkages, Gourevitch (1979) observes that where the benefits to ethnic peripheries of remaining a part of the core economy are no longer evident or where the potential exists for the periphery to become economically more dynamic, ethno-regional disquiet is more likely to surface in the form of separatist demands.

The costs and benefits of remaining part of a federation are therefore clearly going to play an important part in whether secessionism gains momentum. Rational choice theorists have outlined ways in which ethno-regions are sensitive to fiscal balance sheets and the costs of continued federation. After all, they argue, constituent judgements about the material benefits of remaining part of a particular polity are likely to be pivotal in shaping attitudes towards federation (Polese, 1985; Hechter and Levi, 1985). This may be why some ethno-regions forgo secession in favour of securing greater federal autonomy. Although such an approach is not without its problems, not least because no assumption can be made about actors possessing optimal information regarding the likely success or otherwise of economic alternatives, treating ethno-regions as rational actors does nonetheless provide a useful way of identifying the range of arguments that underpin secessionist debates.

Buchanan's (1991) identification of secessionist scenarios based on rational outcomes can be fruitfully applied to multiethnic federations using the Pareto principle of optimality, where optimality is defined as a system of cooperation that has distributional effects. First, secession can be a strong Pareto improvement. Both the seceding ethno-region and the remaining members of the federation would be better off when secession has been achieved. Here, at least on material grounds, no one is likely to object but it is the least likely of the scenarios. Second, secession is Pareto optimal for both the seceding ethno-region and the rest of the federation but only the secessionist region reaps improvement from secession, while the rest of the federation is neither better nor worse off. Third, secession is not Pareto optimal for either the secessionist region or the rest of the federation, nor is the transition to successful secession a Pareto improvement for the total group. The secessionists are better off following independent statehood, but the rest of the federation is worse off than it was prior to secession. In this situation, the centre is likely to be particularly ardent in its opposition to secession whereas the economic case for secession by the ethno-region is likely to have considerable local appeal. To Buchanan's list, we can add a fourth item. Secession is not Pareto optimal for the federation and its remaining constituents as a result of the ethno-regional unit leaving but the ethno-regional unit is worse off. In this case, the prospect of losing benefits from federal resource transfers may dampen the ethno-regional resolve to advance down the route to secession.

Finally, there is the part that federal institutional procedures and the policies of conflict management adopted by the federal state play in managing inter-communal tensions and conflict. As Burgess and Gagnon rightly remind us, 'the success of federal systems is not to be measured in terms of the elimination of social conflicts but instead in their capacity to regulate and manage such conflicts' (1993:18). One therefore should not consider federation, as Enloe (1977) does, as a means of solving inter-ethnic cleavages. Rather, federation is primarily a territorial strategy of social control designed to secure ethno-regional coexistence.

Two possible strategies can be adopted to prevent disintegration. One is to establish a strong central government to ensure the unity of the federation and to adopt comparable institutional procedures and practices commensurate with such a form of centralised territorial control. The most extreme from of centralisation involves the centre exercising a monopoly or near-monopoly over political party control, a strategy which has often been accompanied by crude but effective policies of divide and rule designed to displace attention from particular social divisions, issues and events. A classic case of such obfuscatory action was Lenin's decision to carve up Soviet Central Asia along ethnic lines as a way of deflecting what was then regarded as likely to prove a politically more problematic pan-regional identity based on Islamic Turkestan, through the artificial creation of nationality-based union republics.

The alternative strategy is to attempt to accommodate the pressures for diversity by instituting increased levels of ethno-regional autonomy. Implementing a strategy which provides sufficient institutional guarantees to enable an appropriate representational base and protection for particular ethno-regions is however not without its problems. A number of federations, for instance, Spain, Canada and Russia, practice a form of asymmetrical federalism whereby certain ethnic regions have been granted more autonomy than other provinces. In taking into account the special character of regions like Catalonia, the Basque lands and Quebec, in part to contain separatist pressures, such arrangements have tended to undermine a sense of common citizenship, giving rise to claims that some provinces and their citizens are 'more equal' than others. The problem facing the Canadian federation, as Milne (1986) notes, is that while asymmetry needs to be acknowledged if the two nationalisms of Canada are not to pull the country apart, the asymmetry of overt special status for Quebec, enshrining provincial and citizen inequality, has not been acceptable to the other Canadian provinces. In order to rectify such asymmetrical imbalances, Watts (1991) raises the legitimate question of whether representatives of more autonomous units should be denied a vote in policy-making on subjects where the jurisdiction of central institutions does not extend to some of the constituent units.

Liberal federal states, however, also employ a variety of other strategies of conflict management designed to secure greater decentralisation. Two such models of non-majoritarian rule in particular often coexist with federation: cantonalism, which involves the multiethnic state being subjected to a micro-partition in which political power is devolved to small scale political units, each of which enjoys mini-sovereignty, and consociationalism, which involves accommodative behaviour on the part of ethnic elites. Neither strategy is necessarily incompatible with federalism or indeed with the other. Moreover, while generally acknowledged as essentially decentralising strategies, there are limits in the extent to which both models delimit power to the ethno-regions.

As a particular form of communalism specifically designed to regionally manage ethnic differences, cantonalism takes as its paradigm the Swiss model. Based upon small-scale territorial units, cantonalism incorporates considerable local sovereignty and the development of asymmetrical relations between different cantons and central government. It is in effect an application of the idea of subsidiarity to ethnic relations in which decision-making power is managed at the lowest appropriate level of a spatio-political hierarchy. Primary powers are therefore invested in the cantons, with each of Switzerland's four major linguistic regions comprising multiple cantons. Such a system therefore encourages the depoliticisation of both political party formations and ethnic politics. And yet 'cantons are usually designed to create ethnically homogenous units where majority rule is practically coterminous with the self-government of the relevant community' (McGarry and O'Leary, 1993:31). Thus linguistic conflict is formally managed under a practice labelled 'rolling cantonalism', whereby existing cantonal units can be partitioned in order to create ethnic homogeneity provided that it is judged by all groups concerned that the experiment has some prospect of success. In the case of demands for greater autonomy from the Swiss Jura, a new canton was established in 1980 out of the Berne canton through an amendment to the federal constitution, something to which the Berne canton consented, albeit reluctantly (Hughes, 1993).

Cantonalism is however not without its problems, not least the drawing up of appropriate levels of government and winning consent for them. In practice, securing such consent has much to do with the way in which local identities overlap in complex ways, thus making ethnic tension that much less likely. Thus the success of cantonalism for the Swiss federation has much to do with the fact that 'the overlapping boundaries of language and religion . . . have weakened both language and religion as divisive forces, for each linguistic group contains representatives of both faiths and . . . vice versa' (Dikshit, 1975:234).

In contrast, consociationalism is a more widely practised form of managing cultural conflict, applicable as much to federal societies (e.g. Belgium, Canada, Switzerland) as it is to societies which are non-federal and where ethnic groups are not geographically concentrated (e.g. Holland). It has also been conceived as a possible model for managing conflict in deeply divided societies where federation might also be a way of managing inter-communal problems, as in Ireland, Bosnia, and Ukraine. It is commonly assumed to be based on four central features: (1) government by ethnic elites in which leaders representing their various ethnic segments come together to settle disputes, (2) proportional representation in government and in public employment, and through the sharing of public expenditure, (3) the right of veto for minorities, and (4) community autonomy for each segment either through a territorial government in a federal system or through institutions (e.g. educational) which confers some self-government on the segment (Lijphart, 1984). If looked at from the integrationist perspective, consociationalism's attraction lies principally in the claim that ethnic depoliticisation can be achieved through the actions of their incorporated elites, despite possible dissension at the mass level. A federation can therefore in principle meet the conditions for consociationalism where a fragmented society combined with a decentralised federal arrangement ensures the autonomy of the various segments. According to McRae, throughout much of the twentieth century Canada's two principal cultural groups, the English and French, have practised a form of consociationalism over certain issues in which the primary arena for elite accommodation has been the federal cabinet and to a lesser extent through meetings between the first ministers on a bilateral and multilateral basis (McRae, 1974). It is however not always clear whether these agreements fall under the rubric of consociationalism if only because the bargaining process has become much more open to public scrutiny and elites have become more sensitive to what their regional electorates think. As Bakvis puts, it 'political elites are finding it more difficult to move away from publicly stated positions or to bridge differences in public opinion' (1987:283).

One of the fundamental doubts that consociationalism raises concerns its democratic accountability. It may have attractions over pure federation in that it allows for less protracted decision-making, but the lack of popular participation implicit in the model and the secrecy invariably surrounding consociational practices may question less its effectiveness to manage ethnic differences than its claim to be commensurate with the process of democracy. But even within the arena of conflict management, the ability of its elites to control members of their ethno-regions, essential to consociationalism's smooth running, is often absent. Moderately-minded autonomous leaders may be faced with opposition from more secessionist-minded constituents which undermines elite authority to speak or negotiate on behalf of the ethno-regional group. Finally, it would be mistaken to infer that the political practices of either consociationalism or cantonalism constitute explanations for the stability of federations. For one thing, even though Switzerland or Canada contains the hallmarks of democratic stability, this does not mean that it is simply a consequence of either consociational or cantonal practices. As critics maintain, as state-initiated managerial devices, there are limits to the degree to which power over economic decisions rests with the state. In the case of Switzerland, for instance, as a consequence of economic power becoming increasingly concentrated in German-speaking Zurich, consociational practices lose some of their effectiveness to ensure that federal decisions are based on the translation of equal cultural decision-taking into policy outputs based on a balanced consideration of ethno-regional interests (Steiner, 1991).

FEDERALISM AND SOCIAL JUSTICE

One of the central questions that federation raises is whether a political system based on non-majoritarian rule is compatible with social justice. Although couched usually in terms of whether regional representation can be legitimately prioritised over citizen equality, it also raises questions within multiethnic federations concerning whether and for whom self-determination is appropriate and if support for certain collectivist rights can coexist with securing the liberty of individuals.

Federalists generally argue that federation functions as a form of empowerment. It in effect creates the opportunities for regional voices to be heard and within multiethnic federations enables ethno-regional issues to take on a greater political saliency. Federations can therefore create regional political elites where they previously did not exist, establish more civil service jobs for local regional groupings, more opportunities for negotiating the territorial distribution of power and more representative institutions. More controversially, it also enables regions to engage in what Trudeau once called 'creative politics' in so much as it can empower localities to tailor economic, social and cultural policies to the specific needs and concerns of their constituents. This greater sensitivity to locality which it is claimed decentralisation provides also ensures that 'federalism possesses the necessary elements to become a social laboratory in order to place new programmes, to experiment' (Gagnon, 1993:37). For localities, empowerment and innovation make federation meaningful.

Federation is also defended on the grounds that it acts as a political device for constraining centralised political power, especially executive power. The retention of ethnic minority group rights through territorial-institutional supports can therefore be defended on the grounds that it protects minority interests against the tyranny of the majority. It in effect decentres sovereignty, re-territorialising it along lines in which ethno-regional ethnoregional voices can be articulated and their interests protected. Whitaker, a proponent of Canadian federation, is however not insensitive to the limits to federal democracy. 'Modern federalism', he writes, 'is an institutionalisation of the formal limitation of the national majority will as the legitimate ground for legislation. Any functioning federal system denies by its very process that the national majority is the efficient expression of the sovereignty of the people: a federation replaces this majority with a more diffuse definition of sovereignty. It does this not by denying the democratic principle, as such, but by advancing a more complex political expression and representation in dual (sometimes even multiple) manifestations which may even be contradictory and antagonistic' (1992:167). Federalists therefore reject the proposition that in ethnically divided societies, majoritarianism is an appropriate conflict-management strategy and that federal politics will necessarily ossify around ethnic issues. Rather, it is argued, as majoritarian rule in multiethnic societies can become an instrument of hegemonic control, the only effective countermeasure is to institute collective rights through providing minorities with the protection to be fairly represented and to be different. Accordingly, 'as ideology, federalism assumes that the retention of some degree of group liberty is a democratic requisite in territorially-fragmented societies and that compound politics are better safeguards against the abuse of political power in general' (Hueglin, 1987:35). Thus federation is about responding to societal demands for group liberty.

Those who question the merits of multiethnic federations are concerned that by structuring the polity along multiethnic lines, federalism enables key policy areas to be hijacked by highly partisan ethno-regional groups who are able to impose their will on others. This fear underlies Riker's (1964) assertion that, at worst, federations have the propensity to secure 'tyranny by a minority' which acts as an 'impediment to freedom for all'. In reasserting his belief in the centrality of individual liberty as the basis of any democracy, he sees majoritarian national government as inherently more democratic. Like many critics, he goes further, in identifying such a fragmentation of political-territorial power as synonymous with greater inefficiency linked in particular to issues of economies of scale. There is however no conclusive evidence that larger jurisdictions are more efficient than smaller ones. As Newton puts it, 'the only thing that we can conclude with confidence is that under certain not well understood conditions, it may or may not, be more, or less, economical to have larger or smaller, local authorities' (1982:193). It is precisely the way in which various administrative functions can be most effectively carried out at particular lowest common denominator scales that underpins the as yet imperfect application of the European Union's notion of subsidiarity (see Hirst, 1994).

The argument against federation as a form of empowerment does not however end there. Commentators have latched on to the way in which in empowering certain ethno-regional groups, other groups and issues are downgraded or hidden from the gaze of federal politics. Because federation tends to deal only with the enabling conditions of striking a balance between representatives of regional units, it does not tackle the corrosive consequences of powerlessness and marginalisation, and the way in which these can inhibit the development of any group identity that differs from the dominant regional norm. This has become particularly evident with the rise and increasing political prominence of new social movements in which the capacity of the federal system and its political parties to represent forms of collective identities other than those of the dominant regional norm is limited. In a late-modern democracy like Canada, it is precisely a new and popular politics of identity – mobilised around aboriginal peoples, women, immigrant groups, church-based communities, as well as the labour movement – that has as Breton and Jenson note ' forced a critique of the politics of representation and a discussion of democratisation onto the agenda' (1991:202). What the politics of 'the new pluralism' tends to highlight is the fact that the most marginalised will be as marginal in a federal system as they are anywhere else; neither the theory nor the practice of federalism is about equalising democratic weight beyond the perimeters of its recognised territorial structures. This becomes especially evident in the increasing multicultural settings of urban metropolises like Toronto, Bombay and Sarajevo where the interests of particular social groupings bare little relation to federal politics. Particularly when combined with consociational practices, federation, in making salient certain concerns, imposes limits on a more genuinely pluralist politics – based on class and other socio-cultural divisions and issues – delimiting plural entry-points and downgrading them to the arena of local provincial politics.

Even if federalism can be justified on the grounds that it fulfils an important function of safeguarding minority interests, this still begs the question of whether federation, as a device designed to preserve cultural difference, can be defended and if so, which cultures have the right to be recognised through federation. Three issues are crucial: whether cultural difference is a social good; if so, which cultures should be supported through territorial recognition; and finally, who should have the right to decide.

According to one line of argument, cultural self-preservation is highly desirable and should be defended. Individuals are, at least in part, essentially constituted and sustained by their cultural identities. We are, as Walzer (1983) puts it, 'all culture producing creatures', creating and inhabiting our own 'meaningful worlds' and non-respect for what that world means to its cultural members would be socially unjust. Thus as an antidote to assimilation, subordinate cultures need to be protected. As their cultural formations cannot be separated from the political or economic sphere in which the ethno-regional group is situated these formations should not be denied legitimacy. So any conception of entitlement should extend to protecting the right to be culturally different. Citizens in multiethnic societies should therefore be entitled to the kind of cultural recognition that goes beyond the basic civil rights of association, speech and toleration. Here cultural protection from unwarranted interference from others is linked to the right of citizens to pursue their conceptions of the good life. Kymlicka (1989) reinforces this point in emphasising that minority cultural self-preservation is of fundamental importance for individuals because belonging to a culture provides them with 'a meaningful context for *choice*'.

Cultural difference, and in particular support of cultures whose existence is in threat, therefore makes it permissible for the polity to intervene in order to secure the promotion of what is deemed to be a social good. In endorsing this position, Taylor (1992) uses the example of the Québécois to explore what he considers to be some of the most important issues raised by the quest for recognition. He examines the collective goals of the Québécois to carry out policies that would enable their cultural survival within the larger context of Canadian society, especially policies that implement French as the official language of Quebec. Seeing to preserve a right of 'survivance' within a liberal polity, he endorses policies which, as Dumm (1994) notes, can in a certain light be seen as infringements upon liberal rights but which might better be seen as immunities. Thus Quebec's language policies, which regulates who can send their offspring to English language schools (not Francophones or immigrants) and which states that businesses with more than fifty employees be run in French, is defended on the grounds that the survival and flourishing of French culture in Quebec is a social good. This can be justified, Taylor argues, so long as the basic rights of citizens who have different commitments or no such commitments at all are protected.

Tackling the question of who qualifies for cultural protection requires recognition of clearcut boundaries upon which to construct a polity based on cultural difference. Any liberal state sensitive to preserving cultural differences is however faced with a task of definition which is politically loaded. The notion of 'historic communities' is considered as one such way forward. Although interpretations vary, it is generally taken to mean a nation whose members are bound together in a historic attachment to territory and by a common culture and who imagine themselves to be different from other nations. The problem, however, is that even on their own terms, 'historic communities' typically overplay their sense of historical sharedness when their cultural identity is threatened, giving the impression of imagined community that may not be as coherently imagined as its self-identifiers claim. Plaid Cymru, for example, vigorously promoted and succeeded in securing greater autonomy for the Welsh language even although many Welsh speakers have subsequently *chosen* to abandon Welsh as their native language. Even in 'communities of fate', where ethnic antagonisms are all-consuming based on what appears as clearcut boundaries of 'them' and 'us', a citizen's sense of 'historic community' is not necessarily the exclusive or even the dominant influence on her/his conception of the good life. It is therefore highly misleading to accept the nationalist view that the rights of a 'historic community' to be culturally different are bound up with the individual liberties of all its members. There are too many grey areas for such claims to be morally justifiable. Consider, for instance, those who have been officially assigned a 'historic community' but who do not imagine themselves as part of that community even although they may, for instance, through inter-ethnic marriage, inhabit part of that community's life world. Nowhere are such practices more problematic than in Bosnia where nationalists claim that the *only* civic links that are relevant are based on three 'historic communities': 'Croats', 'Serbs' and 'Muslims'.

Even if we accept Taylor's argument that cultures can be distinguished on the basis of this right to self-determination, there then emerges the question of whether 'historic communities' are likely to exploit their rights to the detriment of the liberties of others. For cultural protectionists, it is precisely where the state is both centralised and dominated by a particular cultural group that regulation of other cultural groups and their actions is most likely to occur. Dominant cultural groups may seek to control or influence power, threatening to compel others to live in a certain way. Yet it is also conceivable that cultural hegemony may be replicated at the provincial scale in which having won the right to self-protection, the ethno-regional group may seek to have its own chosen objectives made into rights that are detrimental to others who share that same locality. Distinguishing on the basis of intent provides little guidance. If however it can be shown that autonomy would be likely to limit the liberties of other minorities or even through certain cultural practices the liberties of some of its own peoples, then there may be an a priori case for not granting regional autonomy to that group.

If it is accepted that a cultural group wishing autonomy should be granted special status, then we still need to answer the question of who should decide. The crux of the matter is illustrated by Walzer's highly problematic solution to this dilemma. Where historic communities are not coterminous with political community, he argues, then 'we should look for some way to adjust distributive decisions to the requirements of those (collective/historic) units'. The adjustment of distributive decisions to the requirements of communities, he goes on, 'must itself be worked out politically, and its precise character will depend upon understandings shared among the citizens about the value of cultural diversity, local autonomy, and so on. It is to these understandings that we must appeal when we make our arguments' (Walzer, 1983:29). There are however limits to determining cultural rights on such a basis. First, Walzer presumes that all citizens of the political community should constitute the arena for political decision. The problem with this 'nation-state bias' is that hegemonic cultures can prove to be unsympathetic towards providing special privilege, especially when it is envisaged as imperilling their culture and way of life. Second, even if it is accepted that only the 'historic community' should decide, as Kymlicka (1989) observes, is it just that those who live within the ethno-region but who are not members of that 'historic community' be excluded from participating in that decision? If political decision-makers accept that only the wishes of the French speakers of Quebec, the Muslim Bosnians or Russia's Tatars should be treated as definitive concerning the future of their historic communities, then this is hardly likely to appeal to those citizens within the ethno-region who do not share such 'meaningful worlds' but whose well-being, nonetheless, will be either directly or indirectly affected by granting such a 'historic community' special status.

These questions are not irresolvable. However, the major task still confronting the federal project is to find an alternative model of national self-determination to that which up until now has tended to lead to, and has become bound up with, the end stage of the nation-state. Such a project also needs to find ways that allow for mutual recognition of socially significant differences without losing sight of either the right to be culturally different or of safeguarding equity and social justice. As Rosaldo notes, 'Difference need not entail inequality; sameness need not be the condition of equality' (1994:240). It is somewhat paradoxical that the central task now confronting federation and its relationship to multiethnic societies is the same as that formulated by Proudhon well over a century ago: how to combine the right to be different with being a full citizen.

PLAN OF THE BOOK

The rest of this book takes up the central questions raised in this chapter through an examination of particular ethno-federal formations or polities where federation is being considered as a possible way of managing difference. The chapters are divided into three parts.

Part I considers federations that have often been deemed to be in crisis due to their multiethnic character although in many respects federal crisis, when interpreted as a crisis of state legitimation likely to lead to regional fragmentation, has proved to be more chronic than acute. Chapter two considers the case of Canada, the oldest multiethnic federation, which of all the federations considered in this section has perhaps suggested itself to be the most susceptible to break-up. Canada's response to federal crisis has rested mainly on constitutional restructuring designed to ensure that the interests of its provincial parts are harnessed in order to secure a viable sovereign state. While the success of such endeavours in preserving the confederation should not be underestimated, attempts within both formal and informal politics to cultivate the idea of a multicultural society capable of transcending the dual nation concept and of developing structures that enable a celebration of multiple cultural forms have as yet not taken sufficient root in the Canadian imagination to counterbalance linguistic divisions or the possibility of fragmentation along sovereign lines. Belgium, as chapter three also makes clear, while born into existence as a federal state only in 1993, has also had to live with a history of linguistic duality. Because of a long-established, formalised territorial structure based upon linguistic markers and of the saliency that such divisions occupy for Walloons and the Flemish, other issues – linked to regional development, resource allocations and social mobility – become easily ethnicised. Indeed in common with other chapters, what consideration of the Belgian case signals is the need to take on board the significance of the territorial dimension to federalism and of the way in which territory as an arena of both communal identity and conflict is central to comprehending the character of inter-communal tensions, the absence of which has arguably impoverished our understanding of the nature and character of federal systems. What these two late modern federal democracies in their differing ways highlight is not only the problem of replacing essentially binational with multiple forms of identity, but whether in constituting linguistic divisions along territorial lines, territoriality fuels rather than satisfies communal aspirations.

Federal crises linked to multiethnic tensions have also occupied centre stage in the two largest ethno-federations of the third world, India and Nigeria. What is at stake in both polities is not only their ability to manage ethnic, religious and tribal diversity, but whether democracy is capable of coping with a multiplicity of tensions that have periodically manifested themselves in high levels of ethnic violence. The complexity of ethnic and religious federal politics in India, as chapter four illustrates, cannot be adequately understood without comprehending the complex stratification of communities unique to it and the way in which it is overlaid with equally complex identities of language, religion and regionalism. According to chapter four, India is facing a growing federal crisis in part because its founding mythology of federation is coming under attack precisely as threats are being mounted against the other founding myths of independent India: socialism, secularism and democracy. At the same time, India is not likely to fall apart. Its territorial integrity is maintained in part by state coercion and appeals to the threat posed by Pakistan, but also by means of the continuing integration of India's 'economy-in-transition'. The economic liberalisation of India is at once aiding the emergence of regional bourgeoisies and regionalist movements *and* the consolidation of a quasi-national middle class.

In contrast, as chapter five explains, Nigeria has experimented with a particular way of managing ethnic and religious tensions. Based on the idea of creating provinces of roughly equal size and of instigating a policy of equitable division of posts in state government, the Nigerian state has attempted to prevent hegemonic dominance at the federal level by one tribe or region, a policy designed to preempt the conditions that contributed to the 1966 Civil War. Despite its attempt to structure its federation on the basis of territory rather than ethnicity and to manage regional tensions through pursuing from 1960 to 1991 a rolling agenda of new state formations, longstanding regional rivalries not only persist but remain bound up with ethnic politics, something which, as this chapter also notes, is fuelled by differential development.

In Part II we consider those federations in the one-time socialist world whose federal systems eventually proved unable to manage federal crisis and where ethno-regional divisions were crucial to fragmentation. In all three socialist federations, the Soviet Union, Yugoslavia and Czechoslovakia, a particular form of centralisation was practised, based on one party rule, that proved highly effective in managing ethno-regional tensions. However differences did exist in the nature of their federal structures, in part linked to particular national revolutionary traditions. For its part, the Soviet Union became very quickly highly centralised, permitting only limited regional autonomy for its major ethnoregional groupings, whereas in both Yugoslavia and Czechoslovakia attempts were made to pay more attention to renewed pressures for decentralisation and greater autonomy. As chapter six shows, post-Soviet federal Russia faces the task of establishing a new culture of federalism based on assocative democracy, something which, in a civil society where democracy had little more than a foothold before the late 1980s, is proving difficult, especially in a polity facing massive economic and social problems accentuated by moving towards establishing a market-based economy. Whereas the break-up of the Soviet federation was relatively peaceful, as chapter seven shows, the failure of Yugoslavia led to widespread ethnic and religious violence rooted in a polity which increasingly by the late 1980s had become dominated by local nationalist elites. Emerging at the epicentre of this post-federal crisis has been Bosnia-Hercegovina where various forms of ethnic conflict management have been proposed, ranging from strategies of ethnic cleansing and territorial absorption to cantonalism and federalism. In contrast, as chapter eight notes, the rather belatedly established Czechoslovak federation, whose constitution was changed only in 1968 from that of a unitary state to a binational federation, ended peacefully twenty-five years later, despite the fact that what divided the Czech republic and Slovakia contained many of the linguistic, religious and economic ingredients present in Yugoslavia.

In Part III we examine multiethnic polities in which some form of federal arrangement is considered as providing a basis for building upon or replacing other strategies of managing difference. Chapter nine explores the case of Spain and the relative success of the Spanish state in managing ethnoregional demands during its transition from authoritarian to democratic rule. Crucial to managing ethnoregionalism has been the establishment of the so called Autonomous Communities System (ACS) which, in the case of Catalonia and the Basque country, has resulted in considerable regional, ethno-linguistic and economic autonomy. Yet as this chapter also points out, the ACS has also the potential to act as a federalising agent that would not only further transform the Spanish State but provide a building bloc for realising the fulfilment among regionalists in Catalonia and the Basque country of their peoples' connecting up with a grander federal project of a Europe of the regions.

Whether, however, a post-apartheid South Africa can realise a peaceful transition towards democracy through a federal solution, as chapter ten highlights, is even more complex and uncertain. Key arguments in South Africa for federalist solutions have focused primarily on preserving a geographical basis for ethnically-based power and political identity, and with limiting the power of the strong central state. Tensions in particular have been evident between the more strongly centralised African National Congress (ANC), whose electoral support is more geographically spread and even, and the federalist demands of minority parties with a more regional bias (e.g. the Inkatha Freedom Party in KwaZulu/Natal; the National Party in the Western Cape). However, with the end of apartheid, power has shifted substantially to the regions, although fiscal capabilities still lie with the central state. As this chapter argues, the establishment of stronger regional powers will make the scale of political activity between different ethnic and racial groups crucial for a long time to come. Thus while a federalist solution has not been arrived at, what has been negotiated so far has certainly moved South Africa a number of steps closer to a federal arrangement.

The final case study chapter considers Northern Ireland, where multiple cleavages exist along the lines of national identity, religion and, to a lesser extent, socio-economic divisions, and which, as a consequence, make conflict regulation between its two primary communal blocs more difficult. Rather than just focusing on Northern Ireland as the arena for considering conflict regulation, this chapter casts its net more widely, arguing that by situating the province within the broader context of debates over federalisation in Europe, Britain and Ireland, we might well be in a stronger position to work towards a solution to Northern Ireland's problems.

What these case-study considerations of federalism signal is the analytical value of comparative studies, which is taken up in the postscript. Comparative analysis, it is suggested, provides an important basis for understanding the differing practices of federalism and its utility as a form of territorial governance as well as offering the possibility for generalising about the dynamic relationship between federalism and the changing politics of identity in the post-Cold War era.

REFERENCES

Anderson, B. (1990) *Imagined Communities* (London:Verso)

Bakvis, H. (1987) Alternative Models of Governance: Federalism, Consociationalism and Corporatism. In H. Bakvis and W. Chandler (eds), *Federalism and the Role of the State* (Toronto:University of Toronto Press), pp. 279–305

Breton, G. and Jenson, J. (1991) After free trade and Meech Lake: *quoi de neuf? Studies in Political Economy,* vol 34 (Spring), pp. 199–218

Buchanan, A. (1991) *Secession. The Morality of Political Divorce from Port Sumter to Lithuania and Quebec* (Boulder:Westview Press)

Burgess, M. and Gagnon, A. (eds) (1993) *Comparative Federalism and Federation. Competing Traditions and Future Directions* (London:Harvester)

Cahm, J. (1978) Kropotkin and the Anarchist Movement. In E. Cahm and V. Fisera, *Socialism and Nationalism* (Nottingham:Spokesman), pp. 50–68

Camilleri, J. and Falk, R. (1992) *The End of Soveriegnty? The Politics of a Shrinking and Fragmenting World* (Aldershot:Edward Elgar)

Denitch, B. (1993) *Ethnic Nationalism. The Tragic Death of Yugoslavia* (Minneapolis and London:University of Minnesota Press)

Dicey, A. V. (1908) *The Law of the Constitution* (London)

Dikshit, R. (1975) *The Political Geography of Federalism: An Inquiry into its Origins and Stability* (Dehli:Macmillan)

Duchacek, I. (1986) *The Territorial Dimension of Politics. Within, Among, and Across Nations* (Boulder and London:Westview Press)

Dumm, T. (1994) Strangers and Liberals *Political Theory,* vol 22 (No. 1), pp. 167–75

Elazar, D. (1991) Federal democracy in a world beyond authoritarianism and totalitarianism. In. A. McAuley (ed), *Soviet Federalism, Nationalism and Economic Decentralisation* (Leicester:Leicester University Press), pp. 1–12

Enloe, C. (1977) Internal colonialism, federalism and alternative state development strategies *Publius,* vol 7 (No.4), pp. 145–60

Fry, E. (1988) Subnational federal units in an age of complex independence: implications for the international system. In C. L. Brown-John, *Centralising and Decentralising Trends in Federal States* (Langham:University of Arizona), pp. 75–88

Gagnon, A. (1988) Federalism in Multi-Community Countries: A Theoretical and Comparative Analysis. In C. L. Brown-John, *Centralising and Decentralising Trends in Federal States* (New York:University Press of America), pp. 23–37

Gagnon, A. (1993) The Political Uses of federalism. In M. Burgess and A. Gagnon, *Comparative Federalism and Federation.* (Harvester:London), pp. 15–44

Gibbins, R. (1987) Federal Societies, Institutions and Politics. In H. Bakvis and W. Chandler (eds), *Federalism and the Role of the State* (Toronto:University of Toronto Press), pp. 15–31

Gourevitch, P. (1981) The re-emergence of peripheral nationalisms: some comparative speculations on the spatial distribution of political leadership and economic growth. *Comparative Studies in Sociology and History*, vol 21, pp. 303–22

Habermas, J. (1994) Citizenship and National Identity. In B. V. Stanbergen, *The Condition of Citizenship* (London:Sage)

Hannum, H. (1990) *Autonomy, Sovereignty and Self-Determination. The Accommodation of Conflicting Rights* (Philadelphia:University of Pennsylvania Press)

Hechter, M. and Levi M. (1985) A Rational Choice Approach to the Rise and Decline of Ethnoregional Political Parties. In W. Tiryakian and R. Rogowski, *New Nationalisms of the Developed West* (London:Allen and Unwin), pp. 128–46

Hicks, U. (1978) *Federalism. Failure and Successes. A Comparative Study* (New York:Oxford University Press)

Hirst, P. (1994) *Associational Democracy. New Forms of Economic and Social Governance* (Oxford:Polity Press)

Hueglin, T. (1987) Legitimacy, Democracy and Federalism. In H. Bavkis and W. Chandler (eds), *Federalism and the Role of the State* (Toronto:University of Toronto Press)

Hughes, C. (1993) Cantonalism: Federation and Confederacy in the Golden Epoch of Switzerland. In M. Burgess and C. Gagnon (eds) (1993) *Comparative Federalism and Federation* (London:Harvester), pp. 154–67

Hyams, E. (1979) *Pierre-Joseph Proudhon. His Revolutionary Life, Mind and Works* (London:John Murray)

King, P. (1982) *Federalism and Federation* (London:Croom Helm)

King, P. (1993) Federation and Representation. In M. Burgess and A. Gagnon, (eds) *Comparative Federalism and Federation* (London:Harvester), pp. 94–101

Kymlicka, W. (1989) *Liberalism, Community and Culture* (Oxford: Clarendon Press)

Lijphart, A. (1984) *Democracies. Patterns of Majoritarian and Consensus Government in Twenty-One Countries* (Yale:Yale University Press)

Livingston, W. (1956) *Federalism and Constitutional Change* (London:Oxford University Press)

McGarry, J. and O'Leary, B. (eds) (1993) *The Politics of Ethnic Conflict Regulation* (London:Routledge)

McRae, K. D. (ed) (1974) *Constitutional Democracy: Political Accommodation in Segmented Societies* (New Haven:Yale University Press)

Meadwell, H. (1993) Transitions to Independence and Ethnic Nationalist Mobilisation. In W. Booth, P. James and H. Meadwell (eds), *Politics and Rationality* (Cambridge:Cambridge University Press), pp. 191–216

Milne, D. (1986) *Tug of War: Ottowa and the Provinces under Trudeau and Mulroney* (Toronto:Lorimer)

Newton, K. (1982) Is small really beautiful? Is big so ugly? Size, effectiveness and democracy in local government *Political Studies*, vol 30 (No. 2)

Paddison, R. (1983) *The Fragmented State. The Political Geography of Power* (Oxford:Blackwell)

Polese, M. (1985) Economic Integration, National Policies and the Rationality of Regional Separatism. In E. Tiryakian and R. Rogowski, *New Nationalisms of the Developed-West* (London:Allen and Unwin), pp. 109–27

Proudhon, P.-J. (1863) *The Principle of Federation*, E. Denty, Paris. Translated and introduced by R. Venton, (Toronto, Toronto University Press, 1979)

Riker, W. (1964) *Federalism: Origins, Operation, Significance* (Boston:Little Brown and Co)

Riker, W. (1975) Federalism. In F. Greenstein and N. Polsby (eds), *Handbook of Political Science*, vol 5, pp. 93–172

Rosaldo, R. (1994) Social Justice and the Crisis of National Communities. In F. Barker, P. Hulme and M. Iversen (eds), *Colonial Discourse/Postcolonial Theory* (Manchester and New York:Manchester University Press), pp. 239–252

Saint-Simon, C. (1814) *De la Reorganisation de la societe europeenne, ou de la Necessite et des Moyens de rassembler les peuples de l'Europe en un seul corps politique, en conservant a chacun son independence nationale* (Paris)

Simeon, R. (1988) National Reconciliation: the Mulroney Government and Federalism. In A. Gollner and D. Salee (eds), *Canada under Mulroney: An End-of-term Report* (Montreal:Vehicule Press), pp. 45–46

Smith, G. (ed) (1994a) *The Baltic States. The National Self-Determination of Estonia, Latvia and Lithuania* (London:Macmillan)

Smith, G. (1994b) Political Theory and Human Geography. In D. Gregory, R. Martin and G. Smith (eds), *Human Geography. Society, Space and Social Science* (London:Macmillan)

Smith, G. (ed) (1990) *The Nationalities Question in the Soviet Union* (London:Longman)

Stein, (1968) Federal political systems and federal societies. *World Politics* vol 20 (No. 4), pp. 721–47

Steiner, J. (1991) *European Democracies* (London:Longman)

Stewart, W. (1984) *Concepts of Federalism* (Langham:University Press of America)

Taylor, C. (1992) The Politics of Recognition. In C. Taylor and A. Guttman (eds), *Multiculturalism and the 'Politics of Recognition'. An Essay by Charles Taylor* (Princeton:Princeton University Press)

Walzer, M. (1983) *Spheres of Justice: A Defense of Pluralism and Equality* (Oxford:Blackwell)

Watts, R. (1991) The Soviet Federal System and the Nationality Question in Comparative Perspective. In A. McAuley (ed), *Soviet Federalism, Nationalism and Economic Decentralisation* (Leicester:Leicester University Press), pp. 196–207

Whitaker, R. (1992) *A Sovereign Idea. Essays on Canada as a Democratic Community* (Montreal and Kingston:McGill-Queen's University Press)

PART I

Federations in Crisis?

CHAPTER TWO

A Requiem for Canada?

Colin H. Williams

INTRODUCTION

At a time when most political systems appear to be subject to re-evaluation and supra-state processes such as globalisation command our attention, it would be comforting for citizen and academic specialist alike to be able to fall back on the old certainties of tried and tested political formulas. Like Switzerland, Canada has long been heralded as a model federal system which has been tested less by the baptism of fire than by the patience of successive Royal Commissions. But contemporary Canada is once again facing a challenge to its unity, from a reinvigorated Québécois opposition. The Canadian federal experience offers some fascinating insights into the manner in which political forces accommodate a wide variety of diverse interests and claims which periodically call into question the whole political edifice built upon consociational federalism. It could be argued that Canada's national sport is not professional ice hockey, but rather professional constitutional restructuring. Quintessentially moderate, liberal, outward-looking and progressive, Canadian federalism has enjoyed an enviable reputation in the pantheon of political experiments. Yet, in lemming-like fashion, it periodically gives the impression of willing dissolution upon itself, despite, not because of, its political success. We are currently entering one of these dissolution phases, but as this time 'Canada's peril could be mortal' (Walker, 1993), should we be composing a requiem mass?

Canada's great size and immense physical and human diversity pose particular problems because it has yet to come to terms with the basic facts of its geographical heritage. This, of course, is what makes its domestic politics so fascinating and so different from most European examples of federalism. In a comprehensive overview of the geographical features which underlie Canadian politics, Whebell (1983) drew attention to the role that resources, distance, population settlement pattern and communication routes have played in shaping the country. Because of its northerly position and settlement history which hugs the US-Canadian border, Canada is divided into historic regions, which in large measure reflect the regional structure of the immediately adjoining United States. Regionalism is thus a basic tenet of Canadian life and it is perhaps the most intriguing aspect of Canadian historical and political geography. Regional systems, rather than national, have come to characterise social and demographic development. Within each population cluster in the Maritimes, Québec and Ontario, the Prairies and the West Coast, a core–periphery system emerged. 'Thus at each level *"the core tends to provide the political leadership and local source of authority"* for its dependent periphery' (Whebell, 1983:6). As a result of such interaction, the Provinces of Canada reflected a formal recognition of these earlier functional core-oriented regional systems. The construction of a Federal Canada was the means by which the power and energy of these competing regional systems were to be checked and harnessed so as to create a viable, sovereign state. The resulting federal system has provided a flexible arena for dynamic change but is itself periodically challenged in the name of political reform and group rights.

The Dominion of Canada, established in the terms of the British North America Act by the Imperial Parliament in London of 1 July 1867, was a union of three self-governing colonies which became the four Provinces of Québec, Ontario, Nova Scotia and New Brunswick. After Confederation, westward expansion rapidly reached across the continent and British Columbia joined the Dominion in July 1871. By 1905 four more provinces had been added, and in 1949 Newfoundland voted by referendum to become the tenth province. Two territories, the Yukon and the Northwest, administered by the federal government, complete the political components. A third territory, Nunavut, is in the process of being formed as an aboriginal homeland.

The Fathers of Confederation maintained the fundamental principle of parliamentary sovereignty and responsible government within a distinct federal system. Unlike the American experiment, with its written constitution, reliance on its interpretation by the courts, and States' Rights, the Canadian federal system was a re-working of the Old Colonial System of the second British Empire under its sovereign Imperial Parliament and with dependent colonial legislatures (Creighton, 1957:306). This created strong central government with a clear separation of responsibilities between the federal and provincial levels of government. However, a basic *political* fact is that in a federal system *all* members are sovereign to a degree. Thus Québec, as of 1867, received elements of sovereign power (in relation to land, property, its civil code and natural resources) which have merely been enhanced as the federation 'patriated' its full constitution, bit by bit. Since these sovereign powers involved patronage, they would not be given up to a central government by *any* province in the nineteenth century. But Canada's early federal–provincial relations were also influenced by Québec nationalism, strong provincial identities and localism.

Four issues have dominated Canada's development since Confederation in 1867: its relationship with Britain and the Commonwealth (Empire), its relationship with the United States of America, the settlement of the country, and the search for Canadian state unity through various refinements of this inherited federal system. In this chapter we are primarily concerned with the question of state unity and the role of Québec in North America.

The evolution of the Canadian state is conventionally interpreted as a function of the dualistic interplay of its history and geography. The post-conquest history was a powerful fillip to state-building, for it invoked the pivotal role of two founding European peoples, the French and the British in coming to terms with the huge task of taming nature and constructing a political and communication system which would link the Atlantic with the Pacific, the Old World with the New. The resultant geographical pattern of settlement is displayed in Figure 2:1 which records the ecumene for the whole of the country and the cultural transition zone straddling the historical French and British core regions. It is in this zone that federal attempts at creating a bilingual society in a bicultural landscape have been most intensive. However, as we shall see, they have not yet been fully successful in establishing a legitimate base for the construction of a bicultural Canadian identity. It has been argued that national unity has not been created, precisely because of the adoption of a federal system. Far from solving ethnic and core–periphery differences, it is charged that federation itself renews these schisms periodically because it insitutionalises the very features of geography and history which divided Canada in 1867.

However, others would argue that this history and geography no longer determine the contemporary state structure and identity. The two founding peoples have been demoted and replaced by 'Charter Canadians', that is by native peoples, the ethnic minorities and New Canadians from the Pacific Rim. The only feature these 'Charter Canadian' shared was their systematic marginalization from the process of making and writing about Canadian history. It is unfortunate that women need to be added to the list of Charter Canadians as a category, for it implies a sexist narrative, but as Folch-Serra (1993) has demonstrated so much of what passes as universal narrative is in fact a thinly-veiled Western, white, male and heterosexual perspective. Now these people are encouraged to believe that their time has come, because their charter status has

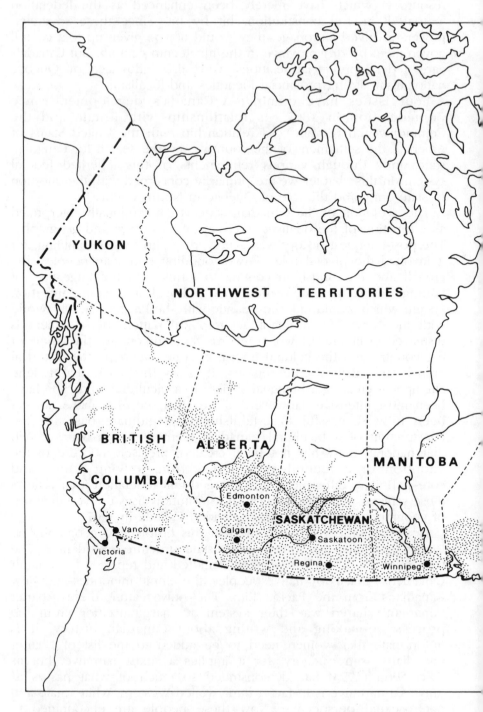

FIGURE 2.1: SCHEMATIC RENDITION OF "THE CULTURAL ZONE" OF
SETTLEMENT

been constitutionally guaranteed. In consequence multiculturalism has replaced biculturalism as the most pervasive, and perhaps also the most popular public paradigm upon which to base state-unity. However, one must be cautious about multiculturalism. For two decades it was assumed to be popular because it had no legal effect in terms of language policy, preferential hiring or national symbols (Noel, 1994), But multiculturalism *in practice* has never been widely supported in either French or English Canada. However, before the Charter groups can realise their rights in full, the question of what is the most appropriate role for Québec within North America has to be addressed yet again.

THE FEDERAL DESIGN: AN EXPERIMENT IN THE NEW NATIONALITY

'In large measure, the federation of British North America was a response to the revision of the Old Colonial System and the outbreak of the American Civil War; and like these two movements for national reorganization, it was essentially an experiment in the new nationality' (Creighton, 1957:304).

Looking back on mid-nineteenth century North America, it is easy to underestimate the scale of difficulties faced by the political leaders and to overestimate the inevitability that both America and Canada would fulfil their national destinies of building states from coast to coast. American continentalism, as Meinig (1993:113) has shown in his magisterial survey, was the official assertion of the 'national necessity of lands never occupied by its citizens'. By contrast, much of Canada's early history was preoccupied with fending off predatory attempts by the expansionist US to acquire British territory. Canada has been named 'the great hostage' in this dispute between Britain and the United States (Meinig, 1993:125). This is particularly true of the prairies where, for example, the economic dependence of the Red River settlement on the supply-centre of St Paul had encouraged a strong annexation movement in Minnesota. In addition the purchase of Alaska had opened up a new geostrategic front in the Pacific north-west which the United States coveted. Constant friction between the US and the Crown characterised the period up until 1871.

Secretary of State Fish echoed a genuine American demand for compensation resulting from British breaches of neutrality during the Civil War, known as the Alabama claims, when he argued that Great Britain should 'withdraw entirely from Canada'. In the event the 1871 Treaty of Washington settled most of the outstanding disagreements between the United States, Great Britain and Canada, although there was still the Alaska Panhandle boundary. At the time of Confederation itself the US remained indifferent to the construction of Canada as 'a nation projected rather than a nation formed' (Morton, 1961:46, quoted in Meinig, 1993:544), due to a 'complacent assumption that it would not make much difference in the long run' (p. 544). It was anticipated that the whole continent would gradually succumb to the attractions of a resurgent Union whose 'manifest destiny' was so powerful that it would brook no obstacles. Seen from this continental perspective internal Canadian issues were paltry affairs. Americans could not have forseen that 'the creation of the Dominion of Canada would eventually be regarded as one of the great exhibits of the British genius' (Meinig, 1993:546). The contrast in attitude and perception of each other's relative importance has characterised US–Canadian relations ever since. Two sovereign systems were born in mid-1860s North America. 'One was a callow, shaky, experimental stucture, as yet uncertain in extent or character, but drawing upon several of the oldest European systems and implantations in North America. The other was a fully restored Union, powerful and expansive, certain to fill out its existing continental framework, and destined – so many of its leaders and people said – to include a great deal more' (Meinig, 1993:546).

A new nation had been born and the search for national unity begun. Donald Creighton's judgement reflects the orthodox Anglo-Canadian view that 'at a time when Great Britain was anxious to reduce her American commitments and when the United States was just emerging from a great civil war, the Fathers of Confederation had risked a complete reorganisation of British North America. In 1871 their new Dominion extended to the Pacific. And the Treaty of Washington ended all important differences between the English-speaking peoples without seriously affecting the new nation which had been founded among them' (Creighton, 1957:320).

The real issue was whether only one new nation had been born following Confederation or whether two pre-existent nations had cooperated to establish a new political system to govern half a continent. Whether Canada is one nation or two is still an ongoing debate, reflecting historical concepts which have become clichés. The most famous is Lord Durham's remark of 1837 that 'I found two nations warring in the bosom of a single state. I found a struggle not of principles but of races.' (Durham, 1922). Others are the replacement of French Canadian identification by 'the Québec nation', and English Canadian interests have now become 'the Rest of Canada.' The implication is clear: Québécois self-identity is historical, clearly defined and 'organic'. The ROC ('Rest of Canada') is a residual category, based upon Anglophone and 'third force ethnic' interests within a rather loose territorial frame.

At the turn of the twentieth century this problem was conceptualised as a lack of congruence between the regional-economic realities of the vast country under liberal capitalism and the ideal conception of how a modern state should function. It was assumed that in time the French Canadian element would dwindle and that the rest of Canada would mould itself into a unique mutation recognisably derived from a transplanted British political culture. Federalism versus regionalism was thus the dominant issue in nation-building for English-speaking Canada, which has witnessed successive periods of centralisation and decentralisation. In the 1920s there was a strong move toward provincial autonomy which resulted in the 'compact theory' of Confederation advanced by Ontario and Québec (Lawton, 1992). This reaffirmation of French-English consociationalism had its roots in the sharing of power and patronage in the pre-Confederation Union of the Canadas (Noel, 1990). Although this initiative to have more federal power delegated to the provinces failed, it did signal the manner in which future federal-provincial relations would be structured. Canadian federalism was to be an ongoing experiment in the art of the possible, ever reforming itself so as to take account of the exigencies of a new situation, but never so bereft of ideas that it knew not what mission it was destined to fulfil.

The Québécois challenge to this position asserts that the original 'two-nations' compact of state-formation negotiated by the French Canadian and British Canadian élites at Confederation had been overthrown after the First World War in favour of an Anglo-conformist state-building project. Because successive attempts at re-negotiating Québec's 'distinct society' status within the federal system had failed, it is argued that the only way for the Québécois to realise their national self-interest was to push for independence within a North American community of free and equal states: a position currently advanced by both the provincial Parti Québécois and the Federal Bloc Québécois.

The consistent federalist response has been to argue that the fundamental rights and opportunities of Québécois citizens are best guaranteed within the Confederation. This vision was most forcibly articulated under Pierre Elliott Trudeau and given real purchase in the late 1960s and the 1970s when Canada underwent a federally inspired and financed conversion to bilingualism and biculturalism. However, the policy provoked a severe backlash against official bilingualism, particularly in Québec where it was emphatically rejected by both the provincial Liberal Party and the PQ. Québec's French-only laws provoked a predictable reaction against bilingualism in English-Canada which, is as discussed below, the Reform Party exploited with notable success in the 1993 federal election (Noel, 1994).

Within ten years the bicultural perspective had given way to a multicultural perspective on Canada's present constituent peoples, which argued that no group should be accorded a superior or preferential place in the country's ethnic hierarchy. The formal initiation of this policy stems from 8 October 1971 when Prime Minister Trudeau announced that multiculturalism was to become the official government policy. After two decades of relative success, multiculturalism has now come under intense criticism because it promises what it cannot deliver, namely group equality in a system which gives value to each group without simultaneously defining what the nature of the common Canadian identity should be. The renewed federalism debate during the past decade has produced another, perhaps more pervasive question which asks whether Canada should be committed to the two-nation model of state-building of earlier generations or to a multiculturally based federalism which has yet to be fully instituted. 'Is our goal the achievement of unity-within-diversity, or of asymmetrical federalism between unequal sectors?' (Fleras and Elliott, 1992:168).

EQUAL PARTNERSHIP

Following Québec's Quiet Revolution, initiated under the Lesage premiership, the Federal Government was accused of having under-represented Francophone interests, and the Québécois were encouraged to search for economic and socio-political solutions within their own provincial/national state framework, by seceding from the federation if necessary. The Federal government's response was to initiate a wide-ranging search for a uniting state ideology which, among other things, led to the establishment of the Royal Commission on Bilingualism and Biculturalism (the B & B Commission) in 1963. Its Preliminary Report appeared in 1965 and its main recommendations, outlined in Book 1 (of the multi-volume B & B Commission Report), advocated the passing of the Official Languages Act, which was published in October 1967. These recommendations have a determining influence on the shape of Canadian federalism and have structured the political context for the next generation (see Oliver, 1993). The cornerstone of the Official Languages Act was that the state was obliged to provide federal public services in either 'official' language at the point of consumer contact. This obligation not only changed the relationship between citizen and state, but altered profoundly the character and operation of the federal bureaucracy.

In effect it transformed an overwhelmingly English-language federal civil service into a sustainable bilingual operation. It also introduced a legal sanction to regulate bilingual behaviour through the establishment of a Commissioner of Official Languages who became pro-active in implementing the mandate suggested by the B & B Commission. The net effects of this initiative were to raise the profile of French, to encourage a vast language training programme, to boost the psychological, instrumental and social status of French immersion programmes, and by such means to further differentiate the public face of Canada from both its British and American sources of influence.

However, such reforms were not entirely successful. For example, they have not satisfied Québécois demands, though they went a long way to redressing the previous century's increased marginalisation of Francophone interests. Bilingual programmes have encouraged a reactive backlash among some English Canadians who are uncomfortable with the development of bilingual practices outside Québec. Renegotiations of the fundamental character of society have allowed Canada's 'third force' (the so-called 'Ethnic Canadians') to articulate their aspirations and demands for a truly plural Canadian identity. The backlash is especially strong in the Western provinces. Cumulatively it is argued that having attempted to appease the Québécois demands by instituting coast to coast bilingualism, the government had in fact re-opened the very question it had sought to solve, namely what is the essential distinctive nature of Canadian society?

The search for a lasting, binding basis of state-nation identity was to occupy the foreground of constitutional politics and public debate for most of the 1970s and early 1980s and is significant today. Trudeau's prescriptive solution for Canada's identity-crisis had been to proclaim a vision of increased 'multiculturalism within a bilingual framework.' The Official Languages Act of 1969, together with the transformed federal infrastructure had made bilingualism a societal norm in many parts of Canada, guaranteed by law and realised by public subvention. It was hoped that, in time, individual orientations and social practice would accommodate the new reality, and that the future of Québec would thereby be sealed within a federal system which not only honoured its national distinctiveness but institutionalised its language and heritage as state policy. The sting of the Québécois grievance would thus be drawn and the politics of confrontation which had been renewed under Québec's Quiet Revolution of the 1960s would be transformed into the politics of accommodation and management-resolution.

The statist, protectionist, anti-liberal conception of Canadian distinctiveness in the 1950s and 1960s gave way to a virulent 'Liberal Nationalism' which Bliss (1992) has critiqued in a provocative attack on Canadian particularism. He suggests that under Trudeau a new state nationalism was created. It was expressed institutionally through such agencies and initiatives as the Canada Development Corporation, the Foreign Investment Review Agency, the National Energy Program, Canadian content regulations and government subsidies for 'Made in Canada' culture. Although initially attractive, this nationalism like all nationalisms was a child of its time, and in its effects it soon became negative and exclusionary. 'It was anti: anti-American, anti-foreign investment, anti-regional, in some ways anti-Québec. It identified Canada and things Canadian with certain trends in one limited period of history – with the age of big government, universal welfare programs, and subsidised culture' (Bliss, 1992:12).

Within this Liberal Nationalism, the federal strategy determined to place a greater emphasis upon multiculturalism and pluralism. However, these were not neutral concepts, there was a particular political and behavioural meaning implied by the terms. Lawton (1992) has argued that the federal definition of multiculturalism was based upon a concept of group rights which was an abstraction. In his view 'this seems to reduce multiculturalism to a synonym for libertarianism: minimising the obstructions for individuals to "do their own thing." Outside of Ottawa and the common system of law, cultural diversity and regional identity had become the reality, while bilingualism (which Trudeau saw as a "quality of individuals and institutions") was a piece of legislation not made real simply by virtue of its Royal Assent. There was little substance to the characterisation of the whole country as a bilingual society. What one had were pockets of bilingualism outside of Québec, and a few historical French language islands. Trudeau's national ideal is better characterised as a nation composed of bilingual individuals whose allegiances were to be with a single, national culture. It is a square peg in a round hole vision; means and ends at the same time.' (Lawton, 1992:137).

Trudeau's mandate was to create a post-compact theory of state-nation formation. It was to forge 'a sense of national identity which would lead Canadians to believe that . . . there is some national will which is more than the sum total of provincial wills' (Johnston, 1990:43). His principal instruments were the Official Language Act (1969), the Department of Regional Economic Expansion (DREE) (1969), and the general encouragement of all things Canadian. This cultural nationalist call to arms was meant to counter the American outpourings, which were threatening to blind Trudeau's Liberal Nationalist vision at its most acute point, namely Canadian consumer choice which shared American cultural tastes and purchasing patterns.

Of these three instruments, the Official Language Act was a qualified success in English Canada, but acted as a spur to independentist action in Québec (Williams, 1994). The DREE has had little impact on Québec alienation, and has failed to achieve its goal of regional development. In fact it may have exacerbated the very tendencies its interventionist policies were meant to placate. This relates to the core–periphery dualism so characteristic of Canadian economic geography. Conventionally centralist experts interpret every dollar spent by the Federal Government in Ontario as an investment in a dynamic burgeoning region while 'regional development programmes directed at the Atlantic Provinces have the attendant negative welfare connotation; they are often viewed as charity' (Lawton, 1992:139). As for the third initiative, that of forging a national culture, the old Conservative preoccupation with articulating a vision of Canada different from, and superior to, that of the United States looked even more appealing during a period in which American society was dominated by the Vietnam War abroad, and poverty-inspired, urban-racial conflict at home. Television commentary and daily newspaper editorials reinforced the cross-border differences more than at any other time in modern history. They admonished Canadians to be thankful for a governmental system which protected them from the evils of an unjust war in the harsh world beyond.

In an attempt to draw out the talent of a multicultural people, the government reconstructed a modern national culture which celebrated 'unity out of ethnic diversity'. This top-down forging of a new identity was based upon federal patronage and public subsidy, wherein any writer, poet, musician, painter or photographer worth their salt could be in receipt of a Canada Council grant to tour the country and explore the outer edges of the intellectual renaissance mediated through state-regulated and state-subsidised national culture. It was Eastern European in scope and 'Express Americain' in style, if not in substance. But what else would one expect a proud government to do except to invest in its own human resources? The problem was that in the light of its mainly British and French past, and overwhelmingly American present, to many critics the new, distinctive face of Canada *was* its government programmes and institutions, its multicultural presses and ethnic interest groups, its forced cultural invention and federalist elite interventionism. If you attacked those you attacked Canada.

The ideology of multiculturalism therefore has been used by central government as a means of uniting the country and giving it a renewed sense of purpose. Multiculturalism, the new national myth, has sought to challenge the compact theory of state-formation as the basis for social unity and inter-group cooperation. Though unlikely to replace the compact theory so long as Québec remains within the federation, multilculturalism continues to be far more than a symbolic gesture to Canadian progress and evolution. It is also a means by which central government can advance specific long term goals and political strategies. Consider the country's predicament. It has a constitutional history which reflects the dominant interests of the French and the English. It has an economic order founded on Montreal and Toronto, whose economic dynamism and political authority based in Québec and Ontario lead these two cities to determine the penetration of the country. In a very real sense power and control still rest with these historic groups located in Eastern Canada. And yet an attempt to mould the rest of the country into this double-core vision has faltered of late; regionalism, separatism and other *isms* have grown to resist this historical core hegemony. Multiculturalism thus serves as a popular official ideology whereby ethnic and regional variation comes to be managed. And yet, unlike earlier ideologies, multiculturalism has no implicit economic mandate, it is an expression of good will and democratic intent, devoid of fiscal or regional development implications. As Fleras and Elliott suggest, 'with few exceptions, multiculturalism is widely endorsed as indispensable for redefining, mediating, and advancing government-minority relations along acceptable channels. This popularity has simplified the task of legitimising multiculturalism as an ideological construct for managing diversity' (1992:108).

Since the mid-1960s several dominant theories in political science and political geography have characterised federal arrangement as the best means by which state unity could be achieved from such regional and ethnic diversity. These theories assumed that in comparison with European style state-nations, multi-ethnic federations would prove to be more flexible political systems and minimise the potential for spatial conflict. However, the exact opposite may also be argued in that a 'federal system exacerbates political antagonisms' (Lawton, 1992). This is because of the in-built separation of powers between centre and province and because of the dialectic nature of state management which is increasingly obliged to respond to external, international currents of behaviour and initiate federal policies which influence the traditional spheres of competence so long associated with provincial state management. The key question becomes whether the Canadian political system can either accommodate or survive the autonomist ambitions of one or more of its constituent provinces.

FEDERAL FAULTLINES

Québec's position within Canadian federalism has always been a matter of debate and as such represents a central faultline which periodically expresses the tensions inherent in any dynamic political system. The conventional compact view of the French as a co-equal founding nation is being challenged both in general by multiculturalism and more specifically by certain significant events in recent Canadian history.

Multiculturalism itself threatens to re-interpret and thereby demote Francophone culture and identity as but one among many identities. This is an attractive perspective for spokespeople of so-called Ethnic Canadians, those of Ukranian, German, Italian and Asian origin especially in Western Canada. Recognising that they are citizens of a North American state whose working language may be English, but whose orientation is pluralistic, their interests are best served by the opening up of trade and communication throughout Canada and the continent. Should they wish to preserve or celebrate their former culture, or share in the activities of fellow ethnics, there are opportunities and incentives so to do. But when it comes to learning French in addition to English, or instead of their own mother tongue or local regional dominant language, many balk at the notion of coast-to-coast bilingualism arguing that because Francophones are disproportionately concentrated within Québec and its borderlands, their political rights should be honoured essentially only where they are place-specific. The rest of Canada should enjoy a broadly multicultural society within a unilingual English system, with an occasional dispensation for third-force ethnic components in such cities as Toronto, Vancouver and Calgary.

Such views are often endorsed by English Canadians because they conform to their own views of what Canada should be like and also because they can 'hide' their prejudices behind the multiculturalism argument. They hope that multiculturalism will never be more than a sop, a one generation knee-jerk reaction to the search for an identity which can no longer be based on either an exclusively English or French identity and heritage. So long as it remains an essentially cultural, individualistic matter it strengthens society and adds a genuinely universal dimension to Canadian civil society.

They would hope that multiculturalism does not eventually directly challenge the traditional hegemony. And yet there is a profound disturbance among English Canadians as to both the logic and the direction of multiculturalism, which in essence amounts to an undermining of their national ideal. Much of the support for the Reform Party in the October 1993 Federal Election was an attempt to re-establish 'the national ideal', based upon adopting a hard line on Québec, a re-assertion of fiscal and moral probity and a return to basics.

FEDERAL INITIATIVES

In the post-war period the politics of federalism has been largely concerned with the question of a working balance. This is effectively a balance between unity and diversity, and in Canada the point of balance has varied greatly over time. Noel (1994) queries 'whether it can shift far enough or quickly enough, to accommodate the strains imposed by Québec nationalism, Western populism, closer integration with the United States and Mexico, and global economic forces is very much in question. The evidence of Meech Lake and Charlottetown is not encouraging. Compounding the difficulty is the emergence of two seemingly irreconcilable notions of democracy, which Meech Lake and Charlottetown put starkly on display and probably intensified.'

However, this balance and all the necessary stages of the policy-making process are designed to give the federal system an internal balance and self-checking mechanism, which critics argue is a conservative force by fiat. Gagnon (1989), for example, cites Richard Simeon's (1976) observation that the policy-making process has to operate within a system which restricts alternatives and innovations. Thus federal initiatives have their own contextual meaning and impact which must be interpreted correctly, else it will seem like unabashed Ottawa centralism, the bane of provincial premiers. 'Effective action can only result by limiting discussion to alternatives which have a realistic chance of achieving favourable consensus from the federal government and from all ten provinces. This is a distinguishing feature of the Canadian polity; the absence of jurisdictional independence requires consensus through competition to succeed.' (Gagnon, 1989:166).

Since the B & B Commission there have been a number of federal initiatives designed to renew the relationship between Ottawa and the Provinces and thereby reduce the probability of regional schisms or separatist victories. Three in particular are important.

THE PEPIN-ROBARTS TASK FORCE ON CANADIAN UNITY

The Task Force was established by Prime Minister Trudeau in the week of the October 1976 election of the Parti Québécois, in order to solicit the public's views on national unity and to reassure anxious citizens that the threat from Québec was being taken seriously. It was significant that the joint chairs of this body represented both 'solitudes'. Far from being merely a conduit for airing national views on whether Canada should support the status quo or recognise the legitimacy of the 'sovereignty-association' option of Québec, the Task Force declared its early intention of searching for a third option. It argued that 'the Members of the Task Force do not feel bound by existing legislation or practices nor are they committed to views of any federal or provincial party . . . [we are] aware that our autonomy is essential to our credibility and usefulness' (quoted in Cameron, 1993:335).

This was crucial because the Task Force's determination to go beyond public consultation and develop a strategic policy focus 'was antithetic to the direction in which the federal government appeared to wish to move' (Cameron, 1993:335). The Final Report was made public in January 1979, two weeks before the critical Vancouver Constitutional Conference, and it contained some far reaching recommendations which have influenced the nature of the subsequent debate. In contrast to Trudeau's strong centralist interpretation of federalism and his emphasis on individual as opposed to communatarian rights, the Final Report recognised that unless Canada reconciled regionalism and duality it was doomed to rehearse the national agonising over unity every decade or so.

Trudeau took exception to much that was in the Report, namely its emphasis on duality and regionalism, its support for decentralist measures to strengthen the provinces in Confederation, and, in particular, its position on federal language policy, all of which David Cameron argues should have been acted upon to save the country from greater risk. His judgement is that 'the Pepins-Robarts Report recognised, accepted and sought to accommodate the very forces in Canadian life and politics that Trudeau was combating. . . . The Task Force was explicit in acknowledging that, politically, regions were best understood as provinces and that, with respect to duality, the key issue was the status of Québec in Confederation. There is no doubt that the Task Force was correct in designating these as the two central forces in the country which required mutual accommodation' (Cameron, 1993:344).

The subsequent failure of both Meech Lake (1987) and the Charlottetown Agreement (1992) to endorse fully the role of regionalism (interpreted as the equality of the provinces) and duality (the need to recognise Québec as a distinct society) within Confederation does not deny the centrality of these forces in shaping Canadian public life. It does, however, demonstrate the inherent difficulty in reaching mutual accommodation in a system which periodically gives the impression that it would rather not gamble on a 'once and for all decision' regarding the future of Québec, for fear that it might be the right one!

In the event, the Trudeau government ignored the Report's recommendations, was itself defeated in June 1979, endured the nine month reign of the Clark Conservative Government with impatience, was re-elected in February 1980 and heaved a collective sigh of relief at the defeat of the Québec referendum in May 1980. Having rejected earlier means of dealing with Québec's distinctivness the government sought to provide a new basis of legitimacy to Canadian political life by patriating the Constitution from its historic, subordinate position under the British Crown and Parliamentary sovereignty.

THE REPATRIATION OF THE CONSTITUTION

The federal response to the Parti Québécois challenge was to overhaul the constitution. McRae suggests that Trudeau's first instrument for reform was the repatriation to Canada of the Canadian written constitution, the British North America Act of 1867 and its subsequent amendments. The second was the incorporation into this constiution of a series of fundamental rights and freedoms, among which were the guarantee of French and English as co-equal official languages and the obligations to uphold certain rights to the use of both official languages throughout the state. The package also included several federal–provincial agreements which were long overdue. Only Premier Levesque refused to accept it, but McRae adds that 'it is doubtful if a Québec government openly committed to sovereignty could have been induced at this time to support any conceivable package designed to renew federalism and to increase legitimacy for the Canadian constitution.' (McRae, 1991:207).

McRae (1991a) has also argued that those who favour a more integrated model of Canadian society face a more difficult task since the implementation of the Charter of Rights in the repatriated and amended 1982 Constitution. This is because the previous balance between the obligations and rights of citizens has been altered due to a flood of litigation 'to determine the nature and limits of the rights defined by the 1982 Charter'. (p. 20).

MEECH LAKE AND CANADIAN UNITY

The Meech Lake Accord was an attempt at restoring 'normal relations' between Québec and the rest of Canada after the difficulties surrounding the Canada Act of 1982. On 30 April 1987, the Mulroney administration and the ten provincial premiers agreed on a constitutional revision which would bring Québec back into the fold with 'honour and enthusiasm' and this was ratified by constitutional accord on 3 June 1987. The price of Québec's signature on the Canada Act had earlier been outlined by Premier

Robert Bourassa, at Mount Gabriel in May 1986. Five of his six original negotiating conditions were subsequently met at Meech Lake, namely:

'i) the recognition that Québec constitutes within Canada "a distinct society";

ii) a formal voice in Supreme Court appointments: three of the nine judges are to be nominated by the Québec Government;

iii) immigration policy: recognition that Québec has a particular interest in this and that it will negotiate an agreement with the Federal Government which will be constitutionally entrenched.

iv) limits to federal spending powers in areas of provincial jurisdiction but provincial bargaining rights strengthened by stipulating that they should be compensated if they chose not to participate in national shared-cost programmes and decide instead to establish similar provincial programmes. This will *not* apply to existing national social programmes, such as Medicare, but only to new programmes established after the new provision comes into effect.

v) the provincial veto on constitutional amendments affecting the province: the principle of unanimity of operation is operative for changes to federal institutions – the Senate, House of Commons, Supreme Court – and for the establishment of new provinces or their extension into the territories'

(Burgess, 1988:18).

The Meech Lake Accord engendered very different reactions in English Canada and Québec. This was because the Québec government agreed to the modification of a number of the conditions but had to present a case that it had gained everything it wanted when it defended the accord to its own constituents. By contrast opponents of Meech Lake within English Canada argued that Québec had been given concessions which were intolerable to most Canadians and had weakened the dualistic nature of federalism. For the first time since Confederation in 1867 Québec's distinct nature had been formally recognised within the Constitution. However, critics argued that 'by creating the illusion that it could lead to increased powers for Québec, the distinct society provision concealed the main shortcomings of the accord, which was precisely that it established no new divisions of power' (Fournier, 1991:22). Such ambiguity was compounded because there was general disagreement about what exactly had been negotiated in relation to such sensitive issues as immigration, federal spending power, the right to veto, the distinct society and the whole question as to whether Canada itself constituted a 'national' society in need of strong central, i.e. federal, government and direction.

Clouded in secrecy, but confident of public acceptance, the provincial premiers assumed that their collective deliberations would be endorsed in each of the ten provincial legislatures long before the official deadline of 23 June 1990. Difficulties emerged in three of the provinces and a crisis First Ministers' meeting was held in Ottawa on 3–9 June 1990. However, the Meech Lake Accord collapsed when on 22 June 1990 the Manitoba and Newfoundland legislatures adjourned without endorsing the constitutional amendment (Williams, 1994:211). The Manitoba case is itself of interest because it represents a good example of the multicultural opposition to the special status of Québec within Confederation and the insistence that Canada evolve toward a more pluralistic basis for statehood.

The fundamental debate, reflected throughout the Meech Lake discussions, was about the consistency of federal policy since the early 1960s. McRae (1992:147) has argued that it was an exercise in symbolic recognition. It was an opportunity to re-affirm Québec's role in Canadian duality, a completion of the 1982 constitutional reform and a fulfillment of the 'equal partnership' first promoted by the B & B Commission in 1963. Secondly, McRae suggests that as it was a two-way process the Accord signalled Québec's commitment to Canada, as well as the recognition by the rest of Canada of its 'distinct society' status. 'This means that those who oppose Meech Lake for its decentralist tendencies may well be working against their own expressed goals of centralization' (p. 147). Thirdly, the most pernicious aspect of the control model of federalism is the assumption that English Canadians, through the federal government, ought to be monitors of Charter rights within Québec and the defenders of Québec's Anglophones. By recognising its status as a 'distinct society' McRae avers that the Accord should have 'put a stop to this fundamentally insulting notion' (p. 147).

Raymond Breton (1992) expresses a more deep-seated reservation about using the constitutional process to resolve contradictions in the socio-political structure. His recent essay is a plea for constitutional stability, for if the Constitution 'becomes an object of regular political bargaining, it will lose its nation building potential and fall into the politics of interests' (p. xiv). This is an important corrective to the centralist, managerial perspective which has dominated the public debate on reform. The Constitution, he reminds us, is a framework within which 'specific arrangements and policies can be negotiated while accommodating the contradictions built into particular situations' (p. xiv). It is not an instrument for normal political bargaining, neither should it be the context wherein symbolic conflict, political mobilization and regional polarization are played out.

Because of this failure to recognize that the Constitution has become 'a statement charged with symbolism' (p. ix) the breakdown of the Meech Lake Accord has given a new edge to the independence versus federalism debate and in its wake spawned a new party, the Bloc Québécois which, following the 25 October 1993 General Election, forms Her Majesty's Official Opposition in Parliament. Its mandate is to negotiate a means by which Québec could separate from the Canadian state to form its own sovereign entity, while maintaining full economic association with both Canada and other partners in NAFTA. The call to liberty and independence has often been a virulent element in post-war Québécois life, but it has not always been a consistent, well understood or an articulated option.

THE INDEPENDENCE OPTION: THE ESSENTIAL *ONE* AMONG MANY

Maurice Pinard (1992) has argued that the Québec sovereigntist movement has passed through three phases: an initial long phase of slow growth up until 1980 after the failure of the referendum, a second phase of 'demobilization' from 1980 to 1988, and a third phase of spectacular growth or 'reemergence' since 1988. These phases are defined, in part, by reference to public opinion polls on the mobilization and demobilization of popular support for the independence of Québec. The record suggests a high degree of popular sympathy for the cause of independence, but much less agreement on the implications of following such a course. Since 1962 broadly similar questions on the support for independence have been asked. Summary trend data based on 99 polls taken between 1962 and October 1993 are interesting and are presented in Table 2.1.

It is evident that during the Quiet Revolution of the early 1960s less than 10 per cent favoured independence, while about 75 per cent were opposed to it. Support grew to reach a peak of 24 per cent favouring independence on the eve of the referendum held by the PQ in 1980. However, the sovereignty-association referendum was defeated by a No vote of 59.6 per cent to a Yes vote of 40.4 per cent. Thereafter public support for independence declined throughout the 1980s to only 10 per cent by 1988.

The resurgence in Québécois support for independence occurred around the late autumn of 1988, and peaked during the late autumn of 1990, when a clear majority favoured independence (56 per cent), falling back to a more usual 37 per cent by October 1993. Pinard (1992:5) suggests that if one concentrated only on the Francophones who constitute 83 per cent of the Québec population, the

Table 2.1 Support for independence in Québec* 1962–1993

Average level of support in:			For %	Against %	Undecided %
1962–1965	(2 polls)		8	76	17
1968–1972	(6 polls)		11	73	17
1973–1974	(2 polls)		16	69	15
1976	(1 poll)		18	58	24
1977	(10 polls)		19	69	13
1978	(3 polls)		14	75	10
1979	(6 polls)		19	71	10
1980	(9 polls)		24	64	12
1981	(2 polls)		23	65	12
1982	(2 polls)		22	68	10
1983	(2 polls)		20	74	7
1984	(1 poll)		16	76	7
1985	(1 poll)		15	74	11
1988	(1 poll)		28	47	25
1989	(3 polls)		34	53	13
1990	(9 polls)		46	45	9
1991	(8 polls)		45	44	11
1992	(6 polls)		36	51	13
1993	(2 polls)		37	52	11
1990	(Feb–April)	(4 polls)	44	46	11
1990	(May–June)	(3 polls)	43	49	8
1990	(Nov–Dec)	(2 polls)	56	36	9
1991	(Feb–June)	(5 polls)	46	43	11
1991	(Sept–Oct)	(3 polls)	43	47	10
1992	(Apr–Sept)	(3 polls)	39	50	11
1992	(Oct–Nov)	(3 polls)	32	52	16

* Questions varied from poll to poll, but referred to either the 'separation' or the 'independence' of Québec, with respondents being asked whether they were favourable to it or not, or whether or not they would vote for it in a referendum. The averages are unweighed.

Source: Pinard (1992) and interview with the author 26 November 1993.

proportions favourable to independence would have been 4 per cent higher in 1985 and about 7 per cent higher since, confirming an earlier suggestion that ethnic nationalism, rather than territorial nationalism, was the driving force of the Québécois movement.

SUPPORT FOR SOVEREIGNTY-ASSOCIATION

A more muted alternative to independence is the option of sovereignty-association. 'By including an economic association with the rest of Canada together with political independence, this option reassures many voters who would otherwise be afraid of the presumed economic costs of complete independence. Indeed, polls have often indicated that people expect lower economic costs from sovereignty-association than from independence (Pinard, 1992:5). It also assumes that the rest of Canada would passively acquiese. However, sovereignty-association is a less clear notion than independence for many of the electorate. Pinard argues that the level of support for sovereignty-association is often higher than for independence because voters are often confused. In 1980 for instance, many thought that under sovereignty-association Québec would retain deputies at Ottawa. This confusion is also reflected in greater variability in levels of support over time. Thus while in 1970 about one in every three citizens in Québec were in favour of sovereignty-association, by 1977 about 40 per cent were in favour. From 1977 to 1985 the rates did not vary significantly, and opposition remained constant at around 45–50 per cent. By Autumn 1990 as many as 65 per cent supported sovereignty-association with only 20 per cent opposing it. It would appear to be the most popular option, and yet a year-by-year comparison of Tables 2.1 and 2.2 would indicate that the proportionate difference between the two radical options is declining, which leads Pinard (1992:8) to suggest that 'at least some of those who now say they favour independence mean in fact that they favour an independent Québec associated economically with the rest of Canada – that is, that they favour only sovereignty-association'.

When faced with the third option of sovereignty without economic association, the trends show increased levels of support peaking at 59 per cent between June and December 1990, just after the Meech Lake Accord foundered on 24 June (see Table 2:3).

Table 2.2 Support for sovereignty* 1988–1992

Average level of support in:		For %	Against %	Undecided %
1988 (1 poll)		27	58	15
1989 (3 polls)		41	46	13
1990 (7 polls)		58	30	12
1991 (12 polls)		52	34	14
1992 (13 polls)		48	37	14
1990 (Feb–June)†	(3 polls)	57	33	11
1990 (June–Dec)	(4 polls)	59	28	14
1991 (Feb–June)	(6 polls)	53	34	14
1991 (Aug–Dec)	(6 polls)	52	35	13
1992 (Feb–June)	(9 polls)	48	37	15
1992 (July–Oct)	(4 polls)	49	39	13

* Questions varied from poll to poll, and referred to 'sovereignty' or to a 'sovereign country', with respondents being asked whether they were favourable to it or not, or whether or not they would vote for it in a referendum. The averages are unweighted.

† June, before Meech's official demise on 24 June.

Source: Pinard (1992).

Table 2.3 Support for sovereignty- association* 1970–1992

Average level of support in:		Favourable %	Unfavourable %	Not stated %
1970	(2 polls)	32	51	18
1977	(2 polls)	40	48	12
1978	(2 polls)	37	49	14
1979	(5 polls)	34	48	19
1980	(8 polls)	42	44	14
1981	(2 polls)	36	47	18
1982	(2 polls)	38	52	11
1985	(1 poll)	34	51	14
1989	(1 poll)	40	44	16
1990	(6 polls)	60	29	12
1991	(7 polls)	58	33	10
1992	(3 polls)	56	36	8
1990 (March–April)	(2 polls)	53	33	15
1990 (May)	(2 polls)	61	27	13
1990 (Nov–Dec)	(2 polls)	65	28	8
1991 (Feb–June)	(4 polls)	60	32	8
1991 (Sept–Dec)	(3 polls)	55	34	12
1992 (Feb–Sept)	(3 polls)	56	36	8

* Only *opinions* – not *vote intentions* – regarding this option are considered in this table. Vote intentions on that option (in hypothetical referenda) tend to be about 5 percentage points lower than simple opinions expressing whether or not one is favourable to the option. The averages are unweighted.

Source: Pinard (1992).

Again some confusion is evident as to what is meant by sovereignty. Blais and Gidengil (1993) reported that in 1993 they asked half their sample if they were favourable or opposed to Québécois sovereignty and the other half if they were favourable or opposed to Québécois sovereignty with the rider *that is, Québec is no longer part of Canada*. Table 2.4 reveals a sharp drop in the proportion favouring sovereignty once the implication is spelled out.

The real difficulty for political prognosis is that Québecers are reported as being favourable to *both* radical challenges to the status quo (as represented by each of the three options discussed above), as well as a renegotiated federalism. However, when confronted by the stark choice between renewed federalism and sovereignty-association, Québecers have consistently chosen the federalist option. During 1990–1991 it was shown that despite the revival, 54 per cent preferred federalism while 43 per cent preferred sovereignty (with an economic association 30 per cent, or without it 13 per cent) (Pinard, 1992:8). More recent surveys in April 1993 and in September 1993 confirm this trend with 55 per cent in favour of a renewed federalism (Table 2.5).

Presumably this renewed federalism would strengthen the character of asymmetrical federalism, with Québec and only Québec

Table 2.4 Opinions on Québec sovereignty

Results	Option 1		Option 2	
Very favourable	18%		14%	
Somewhat favourable	29%	} 47%	25%	} 39%
Somewhat opposed	19%		21%	
Very opposed	19%	} 38%	34%	} 55%
No opinion	15%		6%	

Option 1: half the sample were asked if they were favourable . . . very opposed to Québec sovereignty.

Option 2: half the sample were asked if they were very favourable . . . very opposed to Québec sovereignty, that is, Québec to be no longer a part of Canada.

Source: Blais and Gidengil (1993). I am grateful to M. Pinard for bringing this table to my attention.

being given additional powers through a series of constitutional amendments, following the precedence of a section 94A solution. Russell (1992:178) advises that under section 94A old age pensions and supplementary benefits were made cocurrent fields of jurisdiction. Where there was conflict in these areas, Russell adds

Table 2.5 Surveys on support for independence 1993

Statement 1. % Voting on 'Québec becoming an independent country'
    For = 37%. Against = 50%. Undecided = 13%.

Those who voted *for* were asked to reconsider their options in the light of statement 2. If the rest of Canada refused an economic association with an independent Québec, how would you vote?
    Sustain the choice recorded mentioned in option 1 = 83%
    Reject independence = 13%
    Undecided = 4%

adjustment to statement 1 response in the light of statement 2: For = 31%.
    Against = 55%.   Undecided = 14%.

Source: SOM, *Le Soleil*, 23 April 1993.

A choice of four constitutional options		
A totally independent Québec	8%	
Sovereignty-association	30%	} 38%
More powers for Québec	38%	
Status quo	22%	} 60%
No response	2%	2%
		100%

Source: CROP, *La Presse*, 27th September, 1993.

that the normal rule of federal paramountcy was reversed, and hence provincial law took precedence over federal law. Only Québec took advantage of this ruling and developed its own pension scheme, but this drift toward soft asymmetery could be accelerated so as to distinguish Québec further from the rest of Canada. Such a trend would conform to Québec's self-identification as a separate society whereas the Canadian identity has declined absolutely over the past twenty years, and a Québécois affiliation has replaced the traditional French Canadian self-identification.

The key question is why did 1988 prove to be such a turning point in the reemergence of the Québec separatist cause? If the structural preconditions of resurgent nationalism had been the failure of the Federal and Provincial leaders to renegotiate Québec's position within federation, the mobilizing factors within Québec were the resignation of the moderate PQ leader, Pierre Marc Johnson in 1987, and his replacement in March 1988 by the acerbic Jacques Parizeau. Under his blunt and bombastic leadership the previous 'national affirmation' platform was overturned in favour of a muscular assertion of the independentist option. Parizeau is credited with bringing the party back to life, reenergising many of the older Lévesque party workers who had quit, and distancing his party from the Liberals so as to form a distinct alternative once again. This renewal was accompanied by an unexpectedly vociferous and massive street demonstration in defence of the French language held in Montreal in April 1988. Parizeau and the new PQ leadership were thus far more prepared to take on Ottawa and move the independence cause forward to a higher level of nationalist mobilisation and political struggle.

Undoubtedly the major triggering factor was the failure of the Meech Lake Accord. Prior to 23 June 1990 it had been Québec which had experienced a history of rejecting proposed constitutional revisions: Premier Lesage in his rejection of Fulton-Favreau Premier Bourassa in rejecting the Victoria Charter, and Premier Lévesque in the patriation of the Constitution. Now it was the relatively small provinces of Manitoba and Newfoundland that were in effect rejecting Québec's 'distinct society' status. This was but the latest rebuff Québec had experienced in the post-war period, and led some to suggest that the most profitable way to mobilise independence support was to provoke further Ottawa and English Canada into an exacerbated rejection of Québécois grievances. Separatism would feed once again on rejection and denial, and triumph through such adversity. Idealism and nationalist rhetoric would inspire the people to claim their liberty, some argued, but economic realities had in the past always tempered idealist visions of a free Québec. 'When the chips were down', the electorate opted for economic caution and stayed within the federation. Now it was being demonstrated that Canadian federalism was no longer able to guarantee relative economic advantage, and in stark contrast to earlier generations of voters a significant proportion of the Québécois electorate had come to believe that they would be better off without the economic burden of Canadian unity.

Disparities within the federal system are skilfully manipulated both by the Québécois challenge and by the Ottawa government which seeks to demonstrate the advantages to all of an accommodating system. The most innovative literature on the management of territorial politics in Canada derives from the dominant political economy perspective. A central concern has been the manner in which regional disparities within federation may be handled, but in the absence of a national consensus surrounding their cause and mitigation it becomes a particularly vexed question in any federal system. Mertin (1993:12) reminds us that addressing regional disparity is essentially an equity function most effectively carried out by the unit of government above the level where the disparity occurs. This, of course, is a classic utilitarian stance which legitimises 'centralisation' in any political system. This would suggest a strong federal interventionist role to offset the historical discrepancies between provincial economic performances. It would also account for the great care taken to maintain Québec's relative position within Confederation as one of the three or four leading provincial economies.

However, the history of federal policy on redressing regional disparities has always been subject to fierce criticism by the provinces. When it was narrowly focused on the most dependent regions (e.g. the Atlantic Provinces), it was heavily criticised by the wealthier provinces (e.g. Ontario, Québec and BC). When the policy was decentralised to the provinces it proved unmanageable because the more prosperous regions used the finances to boost their relative advantage *vis-à-vis* the poorer regions, thus confounding the rationale of the policy. At root there is a paradox deeply embedded in the federal–provincial relationship which bedevils a simple solution. 'If economic disparity is ultimately a unity issue, as the Rowell-Sirois Commission, Pierre-Elliot Trudeau, Brian Mulroney and others seem to be convinced it is, then we are in a constitutional-economic vicious circle: national unity requires reductions of regional economic disparities, which requires greater economic centralisation, which, in turn, requires greater national unity' (Mertin 1993:13).

The most recent attempt at achieving national unity was to reintegrate Québec into the constitutional fold and seek to harness its separatist energies along more integrationist lines.

THE CONSTITUTIONAL REFERENDUM, 1992 AND THE CHARLOTTETOWN AGREEMENT

Stung into painful reaction by the failure of the Meech Lake Accord, Québec declared that it would not take part in further constitutional discussions and appointed a Commission on Québec's future (the Belanger-Campeau Commission). Legislation was passed by the National Assembly authorising a referendum on 'sovereignty' to be held on 26 October 1992, unless acceptable federal reforms were received. Federal–provincial negotiations became intense, conscious of the Québécois deadline, and focused on senate reform, aboriginal rights and economic union. Initial agreement was found and the first ministers gathered in Charlottetown in August 1992 to finalise their strategy. Although it incorporated the 'distinct society' clause of Meech Lake, the Charlottetown Accord was very different from previous accords. It advocated a new elected Senate with limited powers in which all provinces would be equally represented.

Québec would have a guaranteed minimum of 25 per cent representation in the House of Commons and three of nine justices on the Supreme Court. In LeDuc's (1993) opinion it promised better arrangements for aboriginal self-government and set out new divisions of federal and provincial powers in domains such as labour, culture, resource allocation and extraction which would be applicable to all provinces, thereby avoiding the conventional contentious issue of special powers for Québec.

The first ministers thought it prudent to test their resolve by advocating a federal referendum which would coincide with that held in Québec on 26 October. 'The decision taken at Charlottetown thus neatly solved several potential problems. It would provide the kind of legitimacy by a vote of "all Canadians" which the constitutional process in Canada sorely lacked, and it would prevent the unravelling of the agreement that had doomed Meech Lake by wrapping the matter up quickly. Little thought was given to matters of organisation, strategy, or even the wording of the question. The vote would be a simple "YES" or "NO" on "the agreement of August 28th" ' (LeDuc 1993:259).

The most important intervention in the subsequent debate was a single speech made by the master of political confrontation, Pierre Trudeau, in September 1992 in Montreal. He ridiculed the agreement, urging people never to appease Québécois separatists whom he caricatured as those 'master blackmailers', whose blackmail would end only when 'Canada refused to dance to their tune' (Macleans, 1992, quoted in LeDuc, 1993:260). His statement was brilliantly timed from the opposition viewpoint, and as ever, his proved to be a decisive, if controversial, voice.

The results produced the 'great big NO' that Trudeau had

anticipated. Across Canada, 54.5 per cent voted 'No' compared with 44.6 per cent 'Yes'. (Table 2.6) Six of the ten provinces rejected the accord, with large majorities against the agreement in all the western provinces. In Ontario there was a tie with 49.8 per cent in favour and 49.6 per cent against. In Québec, 55.4 per cent voted against, as did 51.1 per cent of Nova Scotia's voters. All other Atlantic provinces endorsed the accord with PEI being particularly satisfied with its own role, echoing an earlier prominence when Charlottetown was the site of Canada's first constitutional conference in 1864.

Table 2.6 1992 Referendum vote by province, from east to west

	%	Yes	%	No
Newfoundland	62.9	134 193	36.5	77 881
New Brunswick	61.3	234 010	38.0	145 096
Prince Edward Island	73.6	48 687	25.9	17 124
Nova Scotia	48.5	218 618	51.1	230 182
Québec	42.4	1 710 117	55.4	2 232 280
Ontario	49.8	2 410 119	49.6	2 397 665
Manitoba	37.8	198 230	61.6	322 971
Saskatchewan	44.5	203 361	55.2	252 459
Alberta	39.7	483 275	60.1	731 975
British Columbia	31.7	525 188	68.0	1 126 761
Northwest Territories	60.6	14 750	38.7	9 416
Yukon	43.4	5 354	56.1	6 922
Canada	44.6	6 185 902	54.4	7 550 732

Premier Robert Bourassa's reaction was to remind his audience that the referendum had been held in accordance with a Québec law and on 'constitutional offers that we deemed acceptable. The people of Québec decided not to accept the proposed offers. In the coming months, we will make the economy and public finances our priority. We will work to establish greater political stability' (*Québec Update*, 1992). Press opinion within Québec was divided as to the significance of the result as is evidenced by the following four extracts circulated in the 28 October 1992 edition of *Québec Update*. 'Monday's referendum sounded the death knell for political simpering. A majority of provinces and voters refused to approve an elitist consensus that the political class offered by way of solution to the constitutional crisis . . . after a time-out to heal the wounds, the dialogue will have to resume. And politicians will have to be judged' (Raymond Giroux, editorial writer for *Le Soleil*).

'Never has Canada come so close to a deal that could have been acceptable. It would be surprising if such an opportunity arose for a long, long time. This missed opportunity which is, above all, a failure of Canada in its ability to renew itself, to adapt, and to resolve its tension, threatens to shake up English Canada a lot more than Québec' (Alain Dubuc, head editorial writer of *La Presse*).

'Canada is in better shape this morning that it would have been if Bourassa had lost a referendum of sovereignty. Sometimes what looks like a loss can turn out to be a win after all' (Don MacPherson, a columnist of the *Montreal Gazette*).

'In our view, the principal cause of defeat of the YES option is that Mr Bourassa promoted Québec nationalism, going so far as to hide the Maple Leaf under the Fleur-de-Lis. But he defended federalism poorly. To those who wanted to seal the issue of this campaign, the Premier gave them no reason to display their faith in the new Canadian federation and, as such, manifested a conditional support for the Charlottetown accord' (Jean-V. Dufresne, the veteran political columnist of *Le Journal de Montreal*).

LIBERALS 177, PROGRESSIVE CONSERVATIVES 2

After the constitutional failure, impatience with the ruling Conservative administration was reflected on three fronts. Economically, business interests were increasingly worried about the implications of the NAFTA agreement, arguing that Canada would be 'swamped' by American corporations, and damaged by the transfer of some manufacturing processess to the cheaper labour market of Mexico. Politically the growth of the Bloc Québécois and the Reform Party foreshadowed a breakdown of whatever consensus the Conservatives had managed to construct between East and West, French and English. The Liberals and the NDP were active in their campaigning against Government mismanagement of the economy, accusations of rampant patronage in business and public life and a general unease that the Conservatives had been in power for so long due to their commanding Parliamentary position that public accountability was a forgotten concept in Ottawa. Thirdly, the change in the international climate after the end of the Cold War, to advanced globalisation heralding a presumed New World Order, and the emergence of a slew of new nations such as Estonia, Latvia, Lithuania, Slovenia, Slovakia and the Ukraine reminded Canadians that polical systems and states were merely contingent, not permanent human constructs (Williams, 1993). The unthinkable could happen, and a new Francophone nation-state could emerge on the North American continent. Under the umbrella of a much changed NAFTA agreement the functional consequences of Québec separating might not be all bad, indeed some good might come out of the process for all concerned. The political landscape was thus primed for change: what nobody could dare anticipate in mid-autumn 1993 was the scale of such change.

On Monday 25 October 1993, Canada elected a Liberal government with a landslide victory and decimated the former Progressive Conservative Party which returned only two Members of Parliament. The PC is now described as a perfectly balanced party with equal representation of males and females, Francophones and Anglophones. The NDP also lost considerable ground. The net gainers were the Bloc Québécois, under Lucien Bouchard, which gained 54 seats and the Reform Party, under Preston Manning, which gained 52 seats (Table 2.7). The fact that neither of these opposition parties was in existence a few years ago is ample testimony to the volatile nature of contemporary party politics and the fragmentation of the country into its respective regional camps. (Figure 2.2). But it also bears testimony to the inability of the federal core under Mulroney and Campbell to accommodate sensitive provincial issues. Charles Whebell (1993) has argued that the centre had, by massive control over the newer sources of revenue such as reformed income tax, corporate taxes and trade imposts, been able to *buy off* recalcitrant provincial governments. But this is no longer the case. He argues that 'the budget crunch (which most Canadians are *not* encouraged to understand as part of the globalisation phenomenon) may be the starkly brilliant light that illumines the cracks and "faults" in the federation so that they can no longer be finessed' (Whebell, 1993).

Table 2.7 The Canadian Federal Election Results 1993

Province	Liberal	Prog Cons	New Dems	Reform	Bloc Qué
British Columbia	6	0	2	24	0
Alberta	4	0	0	22	0
Saskatchewan	5	0	5	4	0
Manitoba	12	0	1	1	0
Ontario	98	0	0	1	0
Québec	19	1	0	0	54
New Brunswick	9	1	0	0	0
Nova Scotia	11	0	0	0	0
Prince Edward Island	4	0	0	0	0
Newfoundland	7	0	0	0	0
Northwest Territories	2	0	0	0	0
Yukon	0	0	1	0	0

Party	No. of Votes	% Share	Membs Parl
Liberal	5 449 595	41	177
Bloc Qué	1 823 190	14	54
Reform	2 431 049	18	52
NDP	889 206	7	9
PC	2 133 454	16	2
Other	476 753	4	1

The scale of the Conservatives' loss was a reflection more of the unpopularity of the Mulroney years than of the specific mistakes of the Campbell campaign. However, by overplaying the central role of her personality and underplaying the structure of the package of deals any future Conservative administration would undertake, the Conservative strategists lost any opportunity they might have had of bringing good cheer to the electorate. By contrast Jean Chretien's politics of hope, of renewal and of employment-creation through government intervention was convincing enough to sweep the Liberals to power. And yet, as Table 2.7 and Figure 2.2 demonstrate, it was an uneven conviction, strongest in Ontario and weakest in Québec and in the west. In Ontario all 46 Tory seats and nine NDP seats were lost. In the Maritimes, a sole PC member in New Brunswick stopped the election being a complete rout.

The dominance of the BQ in Québec when allied with the provincial strength of the PQ suggests a formidable platform for the exercise of 'independentist' power. Depending upon how well Her Majesty's Official Opposition performs in Parliament, the strategy of maximising the gains were Québec to secede could be a very delicate tightrope to walk. Conventionally the separatist strategy prescribes that to polarise a polity, the weaker (challenger) side should make large charges/allegations about its opponents, so as to provoke reactionary rhetoric and political action from the incumbent parties, thus legitimising the inciters' claims to be truly discriminated against and threatened. By such means, of course, they consolidate their following and extend the penumbra of sympathisers.

Whebell (1993) argues that this is just what the separatist-sovereigntist side has succeeded in doing *vis-à-vis* Western Canada. The Reformers are definitely anti-Francophone, and some would doubtless welcome Québec's departure. But much of their backlash is directed at all forms of government. They espouse fundamentalist rhetoric and insist on far more accountability from politicians, at whatever level in the hierarchy. They are also conscious that Canada is shifting its focus from the Atlantic to the Pacific Rim and this will project BC and Alberta to greater prominence 'nationally' and within NAFTA, as north–south relations intensify.

However, this relative growth does not diminish the over-concentration of population in Ontario and eastern Québec. A major fact of the new increment of Canadian growth in the period 1981–91 is that over half of it was in Ontario. Even within the core of the St Lawrence lowland the shift of population is towards Ontario, particularly its southern and western parts. Ontario is still the crucial player in Canadian federalism and there are current indications that Premier Bob Rae is willing to demonstrate to Québec and others that those who opt out of federation will lose heavily. The softly-softly approach of Robarts and Davis, including official bilingualism in

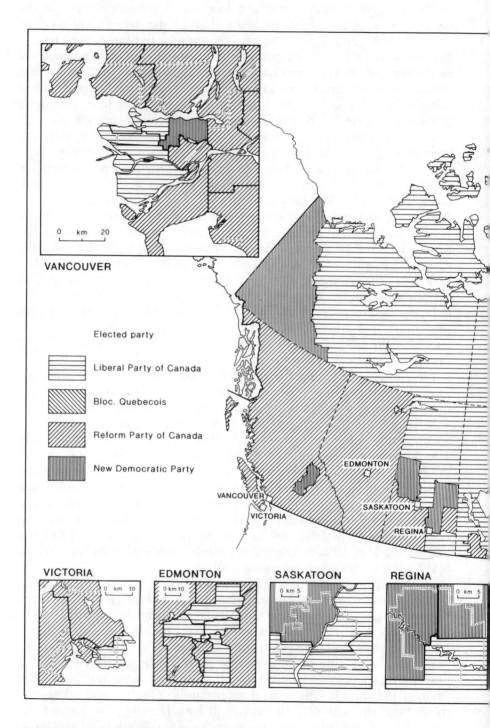

FIGURE 2.2: CANADIAN FEDERAL ELECTION RESULTS, 1993

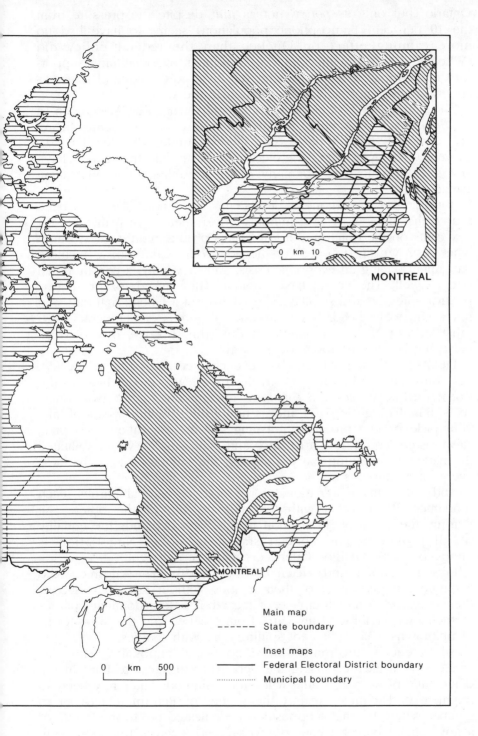

MONTREAL

MONTREAL

Main map

------ State boundary

Inset maps

——— Federal Electoral District boundary

··············· Municipal boundary

0   km   500

0 km 10

Ontario (but only as *policy*, not as *law*, despite the pressure from the 10 per cent Francophone population) seems to have had no more calming effect on Québec than the federal policy did (Whebell, 1993). But the Ontario electorate's overwhelming support for Chretien may reflect its greater sensitivity to the issue of Canada's survival than is normally demonstrated in the west.

The immediate post-election commentary from Ken MacQueen (a *Southham News* columnist) reveals the scale of the difficulties facing any centralist, federal party. The Liberals under Chretien have to overcome the cynicism of the electorate that politicians actually have any long-term answers to many of the troubling questions facing Canadians.

'Canada has undergone a democratic revolution. We have been spared the uncertainty of a minority government, which may save a few cents on the dollar and a few points on the interest rates. But at what cost? We are trapped for the next four years with a fractured Parliament, facing an economic crisis, and inevitably, a constitutional one as well. The voters have spoken. They asked for prosperity, political integrity and stability. They delivered a Liberal majority, and put a gun to its head. If you accept the genius of democracy, you must accept that somewhere within this bizarre Bloc–Reform balancing act are the tools for renewal.

DEVASTATION. Let's see. We've decimated the party of the left, punishing the NDP for its irrelevance. We've devastated the Conservatives, reducing a two-term government to just two lonely seats, humiliating the party and its new leader for nine years of take your pick; broken promises, grasping self-interest, callous economic stewardship, corruption, arrogance and cynicism. We've rehabilitated the national governing party, forgiving the Liberals a past that was every bit as dubious.

And we've made a national force of two regional parties, each fundamentally at odds with the ultimate aim of the other. The Reform, the voice of disaffection in the West demands the equality of all provinces and special status for none. Negotiation is impossible says the Bloc Québécois. Québec must go.

Preston Manning and Lucien Bouchard are brilliant salesmen who captured the discontent of their regions without having to subject their message to the discipline of the whole. Both dominate parties of their own creation. They carry from Québec and the West teams of unknowns to a Parliament spilling over with rookies.

All Chretien's government need do is the impossible. He must create jobs while decreasing the debt. He must restore faith in the democratic process at a time when the Commons has rarely been so fragmented. He must, against the wishes of Reform, reach out to Québec where his major opposition is dedicated not to the failure of a government but of a country. To succeed, even in the short term, he must make appointments based on merit rather than patronage. He must civilise Question Period and delegate to all-party committees a role in writing, not merely refining legislation. He must begin, with the provinces, a study of unemployment insurance and the role of over-extended social programs. He must open the budget process as never before. As for the public, we must cut him some slack. In our frustration, we have given him the mandate to govern a nation, but denied him the tools to succeed'. (MacQueen, as reported in the *London Free Press*, 27 October 1993).

CANADA AND QUÉBEC: OVERLAPPING COMMUNITIES IN SEARCH OF SEPARATE HOMES

The Implications for Québec and Canada

If recent events are projected in an evolutionary manner, the Bloc Québécois should consolidate its opposition in Ottawa and articulate a moderate, but effective, sovereigntist position. Should it perform that task well it will further strengthen the case for a referendum in Québec following the PQ victory in the Provincial election of 12 September 1994. Jacques Parizeau's party won 77 of the 125 seats while the Liberals retained 47 and the PAD won a single seat. Both major parties had the same number of votes overall, with the PQ winning most of the rural, French-speaking ridings, and the Liberals dominating the metropolitan core of Montreal and its environs where English-speakers and allophones are concentrated. The PQ must now decide whether it will go for a referendum based upon a straight sovereignty option, or a sovereignty-association option. This would incorporate a fall back position of ensuring good economic links with Canada within a renegotiated NAFTA. Should this scenario fail, and the electorate decide that the PQ had overplayed its hand, one could speculate upon two further developments. Either Jaques Parizeau and his closest allies would be replaced by figures such as Lucien Bouchard or an acolyte, as being more statesmanlike and trustworthy to deliver an honourable settlement, or a Third Force would emerge, centred around a 'sovereignty within renewed confederation' platform, which would appeal to a wider cross-section of the electorate. Allaire's recent announcement of the formation of Action Québec heralds the sorts of wider development one might see in the near future. Presumably such a force would comprise disenchanted Liberals and moderate Pequistes, especially from among the youth section (Pinard, 1993). Initially such a force would have a minority share of the votes, but were it able to attract to its ranks leading Liberal Ministers or PQ activists it could become a major force at the provincial level, just as the Bloc Québécois emerged at the Federal level.

In reaction one strand of 'centralising federalism' would argue that as economics is at the heart of the Québécois struggle the problem is essentially one of demonstrating the fiscal, tax and business advantages of remaining within Canada. Some would go further and argue that Canada could not afford to let Québec go. However, to reduce this complex socio-psychological relationship to a matter of market exchange is to underestimate the power of identity affiliation on both sides of the argument. Federalists are increasingly likely to target Liberal and Third Force strongholds in the hope of persuading others through them that the *divide et impera* politics of contemporary Canada should not be pushed to its logical limit.

English Canada's Reaction: 'Does My Canada Include Québec?

It is evident that the status quo, which includes Québec within the Confederation, is the preferred option for most Canadians. And yet within English Canada, of late, there has been a double backlash, both against multiculturalism and against the 'special pleading' of a dissenting Québec. It is facile to suggest that the rise of the Reform Party is English Canada's answer to Québec's claim to having a distinct society role within Confederation. And yet there is much force in the argument which suggests that the farther away one is from the border with Québec the less active support there may be for maintaining Québec within Canada at any price. There are good grounds for predicting the eclipse of the myth of the two founding European peoples.

Increased regional polarisation suggests that Québec and Western Canada will be even more averse to some form of reconciliation. It may be assumed that most people in English Canada would accept the result if the majority of Québécois citizens were to opt for independence outside Canada, for then the die would be cast. What they appear not to be able to accept is 'special status and treatment' for Québec inside Canada.

PUBLIC OR PRIVATE HISTORIES AND GEOGRAPHIES?

In the Creighton Centennial Lecture, delivered as part of the University of Toronto History Department's 100th anniversary celebrations on 18 October 1991, Michael Bliss reminded his audience of fellow historians that they had neglected the broad perspective when interpreting Canadian history. His charge was that by succumbing to the 'privatisation' of the historical mind, historians had abandoned the trail blazed by an earlier generation of scholars such as Donald Creighton, A. R. M. Lower, Frank Underhill and Chester Martin. True, these 'grand old men of Canadian history' were often more concerned with 'the public history of the making of Canada than in the private lives of Canadian people'. True, 'there seemed to be a fundamental conflict between the idea of the historian as national sage, as keeper of the Canadian conscience, and the historian as professional scholar. One of these roles would have to go, and it was obvious which one' (p. 7). But at least the older generation were occupied, perhaps preoccupied, with the grand question of an all-Canadian identity, and with interpreting the evolution of the public life of the country for their own and successive generations. It is argued that they communicated to fellow Canadians regardless of rank, discipline, ethnic origin or length of residence, a credible myth which traced the story of first settlement, nation-building, Confederation, evolving English–French relations, the taming of the west and the harnessing of natural resources in the service of society. Since the late 1960s such historians have lost their primacy. More systematic, private history is now being written. Was it historiography which was changing, or had the myth lost its persuasive power in the light of contemporary reality?

Neglecting the grand design, historians were now engaged in problem-oriented specialisation, in documenting the fragmentation of society, and were engaged in a particularism so minute that one could be forgiven for characterising it as an unnatural concern with 'fourth-rate nineteenth-century philosophers, parish politics, and, as J. L. Granatstein recently put it, the "history of housemaid's knee in Belleville in the 1890s" ' (Bliss, 1992:11). Though Canada was faced with the possible secession of Québec, many historians kept their focus firmly on transport history, trade union matters and gender relations. Québec's problems thus became largely the responsibility of Québécois scholars, even while the general public and politicians alike needed a context within which the most recent demands could be set. 'The privatisation of Canadian history occurred at a time in our country's evolution when it was vitally important for citizens to be well-versed in public, political history' (Bliss, 1992:11).

These views need to be taken in context. Far from speaking to all Canadians regardless of ethnic origin, such 'national' historians were accused of being the 'intellectual heirs of Lord Durham' (Noel, 1994). They had little to say to the Québécois masses and were justifiably reviled in Québec, for their perpetuation of an English Canadian national myth. Much of what Bliss says about 'the old school of Toronto-centric "national" historians invites reading as unintentional satire' (Noel, 1994). If so, can there be a truly pan-Canadian 'national' history which appeals to French and English sensibilities? Or is the nature of Canadian dualism such that the 'two solitudes' must perforce seek interpretations from within their own ranks rather than across the cultural divide?

Was geography faring any better in dealing with the evolution of Canadian society, in interpreting the rise of regionalism and the gnawing over of the bones of Confederation post-Meech Lake? Given the academic strength of Canadian geography it is all the more surprising that there are relatively few volumes dedicated to the question of Canadian national unity. The most sustained literature has been that produced at Laval University, offering several Québécois perspectives on such issues (a representative example is Louder and Waddell, 1983). One of the more intriguing conceptualisations has been Cartwright's (1992) demonstration of the spatial exposure of Québec to anglicisation. He argues that because most of Québec is essentially a borderland society the intrusion of English into the region around the CMA of Montreal strikes at the very core of Québécois ethno-linguistic solidarity. When his borderland, cultural zone of transition is represented graphically in an isodemographic map 'the imbalance of the penetration into Québec should be obvious. The perception of a salient of the English language into Québec becomes closer to reality' (Cartwright, 1993:7). His corpus of work is an important attempt to provide policy outlines whereby accommodation and bridges between English and French Canadians may be constructed, but there is surely a need for many other geographers to be involved in this analysis of state unity and group conciliation.

CONCLUSION

The economy, fear over unemployment, and Canada's provision of domestic educational and social services dominate day to day political life. Multiculturalism is coming under increased attack as questions of identity, direction and destiny are re-assessed. Underlying all these uncertainties is the question of state unity. It may be premature to compose a requiem for Canada, but the seeds and inspiration for such a composition are in place. Francophone grievances will continue to be reflected in the strength of Québécois nationalism, but as we have seen, that is an epiphenomenal feature which can be mobilised and rejected relatively easily. Ethnic nationalism in Canada is also highly sensitive to how events in the world unfold, '*and how they are perceived in Québec*' (Noel, 1994). The critical element will be the collective skill of federal and provincial managers in constructing the conditions of possibility whereby Québécois autonomy may be expressed within a plural, tolerant Canadian frame.

Peter Russell, in exacerbated tone, has warned that 'no other country in the world today has been engaged so intensively, so passionately, or for so long in searching for the constitutional conditions of its continuing unity. This inward navel-gazing has drained the creative energy of the leaders. It has frustrated, demoralized and, yes, even bored the people. It has undermined Canada's ability to deal with pressing practical problems within and to respond to global opportunities without. Canadians simply cannot afford to let the great constitutional debate drag on interminably. It is time to bring it to an end' (Russell, 1992:193).

Once again Canadians are engaged in that perennial search to constitute themselves as a sovereign people. Once again a new set of political leaders face the challenge of maximising accommodative federalism without yielding the centre's leadership role. The Canadian federal heritage, 'that great exhibit of British genius', like so many other British endowments worldwide, must be calibrated once again to suit the exigencies of a new age. The resources which Canadians possess to cope with, rather than control their own destiny, are sufficient and abundant. There is nothing lacking other than, of course, a political answer which will command the loyalty of all Canadian citizens. In that ironic sense, everything is lacking. If we allow ourselves to see Canadian federalism as a failure, given the peace, prosperity and quality of life which Canadians have earned together, it does not bode well for political arrangements elsewhere in this troubled world. However, this is to underplay the dynamism of the federal context itself. Noel (1994) has cautioned that 'one of the advantages of federalism is that it provides some useful safety valves and warning signals before anything drastic happens. The success of the Bloc Québécois in the 1993 federal election is a good example of this. A PQ victory in the Québec election, followed by a clear *Oui* majority in a Québec referendum on sovereignty are further steps that have to take place before even serious negotiations begin. If at the same time, English Canada begins to see merit, after all, in a form of assymetrical federalism, a "New Canada" (to borrow Preston Manning's slogan) might be the result – and if it also moves a bit to the right, and keeps the defecit under control, it might even find grudging acceptance in the West.' The constant revision of the federal process is an acute reminder that accommodation and bargaining are the watchwords of any multicultural society. Despite all Canada's domestic turmoil, it is in international comparative terms endowed with a responsive federal political system. Over time this has created a good, safe place to raise a family and earn a daily crust, the ultimate test of the state's obligation to serve its citizens.

ACKNOWLEDGEMENTS

I wish to thank Prof. C. F. J. Whebell, Department of Geography, and Prof. S. Noel, Department of Political Science, University of Western Ontario for their constructive criticism of this chapter. I also wish to thank Professor Maurice Pinard, McGill University, and Professor Ken McRae, Carleton University for discussing these issues with me. This chapter was researched while I was a Visiting Professor at the Department of Geography, University of Western Ontario during 1993.

REFERENCES

Blais, A. and Gidengil (1993) *The Québec Referendum.* Paper read at the CPSA, Ottawa, 6–8 June.

Bliss, M. (1992), Privatizing the mind: the sundering of Canadian history, the sundering of Canada, *Journal of Canadian Studies*, vol 26, No. 4. pp. 5–17.

Bouchard, L. (1993) *Un Nouveau Parti Pour L'Etape Decisive* (Québec:Fides).

Bothwell, R. (1992) *Canada and the United States: the Politics of Partnership* (Toronto:Twayne).

Breton, R. (1992) *Why Meech Failed* (Ottawa:C. D. Howe Institute).

Brodie, J. (1989) The Political Economy of Regionalism. In Wallace Clement and Glen Williams (eds), *The New Canadian Political Economy* (Kingston and Montreal:McGill–Queens University Press).

Burgess, M. (1988) Meech Lake: Whirlpool of uncertainty or ripples on a millpond. *British Journal of Canadian Studies*, vol 3, No. 1, pp. 15–29.

Burgess, M. and A-G Gagnon, (eds), (1993), *Comparative Federalism and Federation* (Hemel Hempstead:Harvester Wheatsheaf).

Cameron, D. R. (1993), Not Spicer and not the B & B: reflections of an insider on the workings of the Pepins-Robarts task force On Canadian unity, *International Journal of Canadian Studies*, vol 7–8, pp. 333–45.

Cartwright, D. G. (1992), A Geographical Aspect of Québec as a Distinct Society, *Paper presented at the 27th International Geographical Congress*, Washington, DC 13 April.

Creighton, D. G. (1957) *Dominion of the North*, (Toronto:Macmillan).

Creighton, D. G. (1986) *The Forked Road: Canada 1939–1957* (Toronto:McClelland and Stewart).

Durham, J. H. L. (1922) *The Report of the Earl of Durham* (London, House of Commons).

Fleras, A. and Elliott, J. L. (1992) *Multiculturalism in Canada* (Scarborough:Nelson).

Folch-Serra, M. (1993) David Harvey and his critics: the clash with disenchanted women and 'postmodern discontents', *The Canadian Geographer*, vol 37, no. 2, pp. 176–84.

Forbes, E. R. and Muise, D. A. (eds) (1993) *The Atlantic Provinces in Confederation* (Toronto:The University of Toronto Press).

Forsyth, M. (1989) *Federalism and Nationalism* (London:Leicester University Press).

Fournier, P. (1991) *A Meech Lake Post-Mortem: Is Québec Sovereignty Inevitable?* (Montreal and Kingston:McGill–Queen's University Press).

Gagnon, A. (1989) Canadian Federalism: A Working Balance. In M. Forsyth (ed), *Federalism and Nationalism* (London:Leicester University Press), pp. 147–68.

Gentilcore, R. L. (1993) *Historical Atlas of Canada: Vol. II, The Land Transformed, 1800–1891* (Toronto:The University of Toronto Press).

Griffiths, N. E. S. (1992) *The Contexts of Acadian History, 1686–1784* (Montreal and Kingston:McGill–Queen's University Press).

Johnston, D. (ed) (1990) *Pierre Trudeau Speaks Out on Meech Lake* (Toronto:Knopf).

Joy, R. J. (1992) *Canada's Official Languages* (Toronto:The University of Toronto Press).

Lawton, W. (1992) The crisis of the nation-state: a post-modernist Canada? *Acadiensis*, vol XXII, no. I, pp. 130–45.

LeDuc, L. (1993) Canada's constitutional referendum of 1992: a 'great big no'. *Electoral Studies*, vol 12, no. 3, pp. 257–63.

Louder, D. R. and Waddell, E. (eds) (1993) *Du Continent Perdu A L'Archipel Retrouvé* (Québec:Les Presses de l'Université Laval).

McAll, C. (1990) *Class, Ethnicity and Social Inequality* (Montreal and Kingston:McGill–Queen's University Press).

Macleans, 18 September 1992.

McRae, K. D. (1991a) The many-sided search for cultural identities in Canada, *Info 21*, no. 15, pp. 18–21.

McRae, K. D. (1991b) Canada: Reflections on Two Conflicts. In J. V. Montville (ed) *Conflict and Peacemaking in Multiethnic Societies* (Lexington:D. C. Heath).

McRae, K. D. (1992) The Meech Lake Impasse in Theoretical Perspective. In *Democracy with Justice:Essays in Honour of Khayyam Zev Paltiel* (Ottawa:Carleton University Press).

MacQueen, K. (1993) Electoral comment, *The London Free Press* 27 October.

Meinig, D. (1986) *The Shaping of America, Vol. 1, Atlantic America, 1492–1800* (New Haven and London:Yale University Press).

Meinig, D. (1993) *The Shaping of America, Vol. 2, Continental America, 1800–1867* (New Haven and London:Yale University Press).

Mertin, M. (1993), Provincial and Federal Economic Development Policy: Pulling The Same Rope, But From Which End? Paper prepared for the 65th Annual Meeting of the Canadian Political Science Association, Ottawa, 6–8 June.

Milne, D. (1993) Whither Canadian Federalism? Alternative Constitutional Futures. In M. Burgess and A.-G. Gagnon (eds), *Comparative Federalism and Federation* (Hemel Hempstead:Harvester Wheatsheaf).

Morton, W. L. (1961) *The Canadian Identity* (Madison:The University of Wisconsin Press).

Noel, S. (1990) *Patrons, Clients, Brokers, 1791–1896* (Toronto:The University of Toronto Press).

Noel, S. (1993) Canadian Responses to Ethnic Conflict, in J. McGarry and B. O'Leary (eds), *The Politics of Ethnic Conflict Regulation* (London:Routledge).

Noel, S. (1994) Private correspondence, February.

Oliver, M. (1993), The impact of the Royal Commission on Bilingualism and Biculturalism on constitutional thought and practice in Canada, *International Journal of Canadian Studies*, vol 7–8, pp. 315–32.

Pinard, M. (1992), The Québec Independence Movement: A Dramatic Reemergence, *McGill University: Working Papers in Social Behaviour.* 1992-06.

Québec Update, 28 October 1992 (London:Québec Consulate General).

Ross, S. and Deveau, A. (1992) *The Acadians of Nova Scotia* (Halifax:Nimbus).

Russell, P. (1992) *Constitutional Odyssey. Can Canadians Be A Sovereign People?* (Toronto:The University of Toronto Press).

Simeon, R. (1976), Studying public policy. *Canadian Journal of Political Science*, vol IX, no. 4.

Simeon, R. (1977), *Must Canada Fail?* (Montreal and Kingston:McGill–Queen's University Press).

Tupper, A. (1993) English-Canadian scholars and the Meech Lake Accord. *International Journal of Canadian Studies*, vol 7–8, pp. 347–57.

Walker, M. (1993) Nice knowing you, Canada. *The Guardian*, 27 October.

Whebell, C. F. J. (1983) The Geography and Politics of Canada. In J. Redekop (ed), *Approaches to Canadian Politics* (Scarborough: Prentice-Hall).

Whebell, C. F. J. (1993) Private correspondence, December.

Williams, C. H. (ed) (1993), *The Political Geography of the New World Order* (London:Belhaven).

Williams, C. H. (1994) *Called Unto Liberty* (Clevedon:Multilingual Matters).

CHAPTER THREE

Belgium's Regional Divergence: Along the Road to Federation

Alexander Murphy

With the publication of the May 1993 revisions to the Belgian Constitution, one of the more centralized states of nineteenth-century Europe became a self-proclaimed federation. The federalist road has been long and winding. It began with the demands of a small group of Flemish intellectuals in the cities of northern Belgium for the right to use their native tongue in public life. Along the way it saw the development of a widespread movement for language rights among speakers of Dutch and related Flemish dialects in the North, the rise of a reactive movement among the speakers of French and related Walloon dialects in the South, and the emergence and subsequent entrenchment of the idea that the linguistic geography of Belgium should be the foundation on which the country's internal political structure should be built. The administrative units that emerged out of this idea did not have significant power until quite recently, however, and something approaching a federal state is only now coming into being.

The emergence of federalism in Belgium has been accompanied by an array of institutional structures that are among the most complex found anywhere in the world. They reflect the long history of intricate maneuvering and elaborate compromise that has characterised Belgium's 'language problem.' The intricacies of Belgium's political responses to ethnolinguistic tensions have attracted considerable attention; discussions of the historical and functional attributes of the Belgian system can be found in many studies of conflict and compromise in multiethnic societies. As a result, we know much about the social circumstances that led to the adoption of particular institutional strategies in Belgium, the nature of power-sharing within the governmental structure, and the role of elites. In keeping with the norms of political analysis, however, commentators on the Belgian political scene have tended to focus much more on institutional than on territorial issues. Consequently, little attention has been devoted to the particular geographical structure of Belgian federalism. Certain important questions are rarely even raised. What has it meant for Belgium to adopt a federal structure in which the territories of the most important administrative units are close reflections of underlying language patterns? Were there alternative territorial configurations on which the federal system could have been built? Do such alternatives still exist?

These questions are at the heart of the discussion that follows. Their pertinence is suggested by the seeming intractability of Belgium's language problem, despite its nonviolent history. During the mid-1980s, a time when the country was already committed to a linguistically-based system of internal governance, Belgians from across the political and economic spectrum were arguing that tensions between the language communities had been essentially diffused; the real problems were economic and social, it was said, and these had little to do with the language problem. Yet the early 1990s saw mounting calls for Flemish autonomy, volatile disputes among the representatives of the language regions over the allocation of resources, and the collapse of the national government over an intense disagreement concerning the differential regional impacts of a telecommunications contract. Any serious analysis of these developments cannot ignore the structural features of political life that may be contributing to polarization along language lines. One of the most important of these features is the concrete political geography of Belgian federalism.

To question the role of Belgium's internal territorial structure in the expression of ethnolinguistic differences is not to argue against federalism, nor is it to suggest that the country had other good options at certain crucial junctures in its historical development. Rather, it is to focus attention on a critical issue both for Belgium and for our understanding of federalism. In the Belgian case, the political-territorial structure of federalism has had a profound effect on ethnolinguistic relations. In a more theoretical vein, the tendency to overlook the concrete territorial dimensions of federalism has arguably impoverished our efforts to understand the nature and character of federal systems. Since the latter issue is at the heart of the discussion that follows, I turn to it first.

THE TERRITORIAL DIMENSION OF FEDERALISM

Federal systems are characterized by the division of power between national governmental institutions and the governments of the distinct political-territorial entities (provinces, cantons, regions, etc.) that collectively constitute the federal state (Elazar, 1987). As such, federalism is 'the most geographically expressive of all political systems. It is based on the existence of regional differences and recognizes the claims of the component areas to perpetuate their individual characters' (Robinson, 1961:2). Despite widespread recognition of the importance of territory in federal systems, theoretical and empirical analyses of federalism have been long dominated by institutionalist concerns (Sharpe, 1987). The focus of attention has been on the sharing of power among different governmental institutions, not on underlying territorial characteristics or identities.

The institutionalist preoccupation with governmental structures, while offering interesting insights into the nature and character of power-sharing arrangements, has not directly concerned itself with the underlying dynamics of regionalist or ethnonationalist movements (Connor, 1978). As such movements grew in importance and visibility in the 1960s and 1970s, commentators began to focus more attention on what was sometimes called 'territorial politics' (Rokkan, 1982; Duchacek, 1986). Followers of this approach have been more sensitive to the impacts of institutional arrangements on substate populations, but they have continued to emphasise the political structure of power-sharing (see Bulpitt, 1983:1).

Despite the central focus on intergovernmental arrangements, commentators in the territorial politics tradition have gone well beyond traditional institutionalist concerns. They have focused attention on the importance of socioeconomic distinctions between centre and periphery, the institutionalisation of territorially based interests, the relationship between government action and client group reaction, and the distributional consequences of particular policy decisions (Rhodes and Wright 1987:5). Since each of these lines of inquiry directs attention to historical questions, some have argued that the body of literature on territorial politics has brought history back into the study of federalism (Urwin, 1985). Historical sensitivity, however, has generally not been matched by geographical sensitivity. Instead, in an important article on the territorial dimension of politics, L. J. Sharpe (1987:148) argues that mainstream political theory treats societies as if they existed 'in a kind of non-spatial limbo'.

Sharpe's comment, which is echoed frequently in the geographical literature (see Knight, 1982; Johnston, 1986; Agnew, 1987), is inspired by the tendency among social scientists to ignore the nature and impact of territoriality. By territoriality I mean the strategies used to exert control over discrete geographical areas and the political and social results of those strategies (see Sack 1986). Sharpe (1987:152–157) goes on to argue that political analyses need to take into consideration the role of boundary demarcation in the determination of majorities and minorities, the unique economic and social characteristics of territories, the ways in which territories shape collective identity, and the relationship between the size of territories and political structures. Although Sharpe's discussion is framed in general terms and is certainly not exhaustive, it points to fundamental territorial considerations that have been missing from most analyses of federalism, even from studies in the territorial politics tradition.

The general lack of concern with the nature and significance of territoriality derives in part from the tendency to treat political regions simply as place-names (Murphy, 1991). An explanation of this tendency is beyond the scope of this chapter, but it is tied to the normative, historicist underpinnings of late-twentieth-century social science (see Agnew, 1989; Soja, 1989). In practice, it has meant that the political-territorial structure of the world is usually presented as a benign framework within which social processes are played out, not as an integral part of those processes. Challenges to this view of territory have been growing for more than a decade as new questions have been raised about the role of space and place in our theories of society (see Gregory, 1978; Giddens, 1985; Harvey, 1989). Although increasingly forceful arguments have been made about the implications of spatial structures for social, political, cultural, and economic processes (see Agnew, 1987; Johnston, 1991), such arguments have received little attention in the theoretical literature on federalism.

A number of factors help account for this state of affairs. One is the relative lack of cross-fertilization of ideas between political geographers and political scientists. Political geographers have written much on the significance of territory (see Gottmann, 1973; Sack, 1986; Johnston, 1991), but their commentaries on federalism have been few and largely empirical. Political scientists, by contrast, have generated most of the theoretical literature on federalism (see Burgess, 1986; Elazar, 1987), but they have generally treated territorial arrangements as if they were a priori 'givens'. Complicating the matter is the relatively undeveloped state of the literature on territoriality and its social consequences; there is still only a small body of empirically grounded studies that seek to develop and expand our understanding of this issue. Finally, the comparative stability of the political-territorial units within many prominent federal states (the United States, Canada, Australia) directs attention away from the processes by which these units came into being and their territorial-cum-social significance.

The small group of commentators seeking to bring territorial issues into the study of federalism (see Sharpe, 1987; Laponce, 1987; Duchacek, 1987; Williams, 1988) are clearly motivated by the recognition that territorial arrangements reflect and influence social processes in ways that are not often recognised. Their writings have helped to focus attention on the relationship between the geographical characteristics of territories and political governance. Yet we are only beginning to understand the complex links between territory and society, and some key issues are rarely even raised. One such issue is the way in which the particular spatial configuration of federal territories affects group identity and intergroup conflict.

There are a number of commentaries that focus on the internal political geography of states, of course, but the questions they raise generally take the geographical parameters of the existing territorial units for granted. Attention is given to the role of Québec in Canadian national politics, the characteristics of the Armenian-Azerbaijani border in the former Soviet Union, the social consequences of ethnic heterogeneity within Indian states, and the problems that unequal resource bases pose for political-territorial stability in Nigeria. It is much rarer that questions are raised about the historical development and spatial configuration of substate territories. The importance of inquiries of this sort becomes immediately apparent if we pose a series of counterfactual questions. Would ethnolinguistic identity and intergroup conflict in Canada be different if Québec had developed as three separate provinces instead of one? Would Armenian-Azerbaijani relations be any different if Stalin had not created an Armenian enclave within Azerbaijan? Would ethnic relations in Nigeria be different if the state had been divided into thirty instead of nineteen constituent units? The obvious 'yes' that each of these questions commands indicates the importance of going beyond questions that take the territorial status quo for granted.

That we have not made much progress in this direction is revealed by the literature on politics and the language problem in Belgium. For all the attention given to the institutional complexities of the Belgian political system, the different socioeconomic characteristics of the different regions, and the problems of dividing resources along ethnoregional lines, there has been little consideration of the ways in which the political geography of Belgian federalism plays a role in identity and conflict. Yet the importance of this issue is clearly revealed in the controversies that have been taking place over such issues as funding for scientific research and surface water management. Although these matters are not inherently ethnic in character, they have invoked considerable tensions along language lines because the regions that control them are self-conscious territorial manifestations of the language groups of Belgium. Hence, every issue that is dealt with at the regional level has the potential of being interpreted as an ethnolinguistic issue as well. To understand the complex relationship between territorial structure and ethnolinguistic tension, we must turn to the particularities of the Belgian case. The goal in so doing is to shed light on the social implications of the internal political geography of Belgian federalism and, more generally, to highlight the importance of incorporating a concern with the spatial and developmental dimensions of territory into our thinking about federalism.

THE RISE OF ETHNOREGIONALISM IN BELGIUM

The modern state of Belgium dates only from 1830. During the preceding three centuries the territory we now call Belgium was ruled first by the Spanish Hapsburgs, then by the Austrian Hapsburgs, then by the French under Napoleon, and finally by the Dutch under William I (Van der Essen, 1915). The Belgian Revolution of 1830 was a nationalist reaction to foreign rule (Logie, 1980). With the partial exception of the area around Liège, Belgium had been ruled as a unit since 1581, the year when the Dutch successfully extricated themselves from Spanish Hapsburg control. Belgian nationalism was born out of the sense of distinctiveness that this common political history engendered.

The nationalism of early nineteenth century Belgium was focused on a territory that was linguistically complex. Since at least the tenth century, the line separating the Romance and Germanic tongues of Europe had stabilized in a position that ran directly through the middle of what was to become Belgium (Kurth, 1898). A variety of Germanic dialects akin to Dutch were spoken to the north of the line, and a variety of Romance dialects related to French were spoken to the south. Over the centuries, standardized French made significant inroads in southern Belgium, and by 1830 a significant proportion of the population of southern Belgium used French. In the north, variants of Dutch became widely used, but by 1830 standardized Dutch had made less progress in northern Belgium than had French in southern Belgium.

Further complicating the linguistic picture in the north was the presence of a numerically small, but socially significant coterie of French speakers in a few of the larger Flemish cities, particularly Ghent, Antwerp, and Brussels. These were generally people of Flemish ancestry who had started using the French language during the eighteenth century when French was the language of education, culture, and government throughout much of Europe (Deneckere, 1954). The use of French was further encouraged during the period of French domination (1794–1815), but at the time of the Belgian Revolution the number of French speakers in northern Belgium remained small. Their economic and political power, however, was far greater than their numbers.

The Belgian Revolution thus took place in a country that was decidedly heterogeneous from the standpoint of language. Language was one of many issues at stake in the movement for Belgian independence – the Francophone elite objected to William I's insistence on the use of Dutch in northern Belgium – but the Revolution was not perpetrated in the name of linguistic nationalism. At its heart was a desire to be free from outside control (De Schryver, 1981).

Newly independent Belgium was established as a parliamentary democracy with a constitutional monarch. There was no widespread sense at the time that Belgium was made up of two ethnolinguistic regions; dialectical differences precluded the development of any indigenous sense of linguistic homogeneity in either northern or southern Belgium and almost no one thought of the Romance or Germanic parts of Belgium as social or political unities (Murphy, 1988). Indeed, the terms Flanders and Wallonia were not even used to refer to northern and southern Belgium, respectively. Hence, the language regions in Belgium were accorded no institutional expression in the government of the new state. Instead, a highly centralised government structure was put into place along with a constitution that called for freedom of choice in language use.

Despite this constitutional guarantee, French was the language of public affairs in nineteenth-century Belgium. Political and economic life was dominated by French speakers who came from the South – the economic heartland of the country at the time – or who were members of the Francophone elite in Ghent, Antwerp, and Brussels. Ironically, there were more speakers of Dutch and Flemish dialects living in Belgium at the time than of French and Walloon dialects; figures from the 1846 census show that 57% of the population used Dutch/Flemish most frequently, whereas only 42.1% used French/Walloon most of the time (McRae, 1986:37). Continued Francophone dominance was ensured, however, by a system that limited the right to vote to large property owners (Polasky, 1981). Moreover, the Francophones in power saw little problem in the use of their language in all official publications and in most other public arenas. Indeed, there was an assumption among many that Belgium would gradually evolve into a French-speaking state (Becquet, 1963:104–106).

A reactionary movement to this state of affairs developed among a small group of Flemish intellectuals who were influenced by romantic nationalist ideas sweeping Europe at the time and who objected to the privileged position of French in public life (see Elias, 1963–1965). The so-called Flemish movement had its roots in efforts to promote the Dutch language and Flemish culture in the late eighteenth century, but it was not until after the birth of the Belgian state that the movement came into its own. Throughout the nineteenth century, Flemish movement leaders were fundamentally concerned with the unequal position of the major languages in Belgium; they promoted the right of the Flemish people to use Dutch in government, education, commerce, and the military. Their efforts were largely frustrated, however, by an entrenched Francophone élite who resisted any changes in the linguistic status quo.

Despite the failure of the Flemish movement to bring about serious reforms in the structure of language use in public life, the movement succeeded in attracting considerable attention to the disadvantaged position of Dutch/Flemish speakers in Belgium. In so doing, it fuelled the development of the idea that the country was composed of two distinct language groups. This idea had little meaning for the many Belgians who lived outside of the major cities, spoke distinct dialects, and thought primarily in local terms. Moreover, it did not translate immediately into widespread calls for regional autonomy along language lines. The nineteenth-century Flemish movement was an urban-based phenomenon generally concerned with individual language rights (De Schryver, 1981:27).

Frustrated by the intransigence of the Francophone elite and galvanised by the increasingly obvious inequities in the structure of language use in Belgium, the Flemish movement began to adopt a more radical stance by the turn of the twentieth century. Flemish radicalism in turn helped to fuel the growth of a Walloon movement that had started in the 1880s to promote Walloon culture and oppose 'excessive' Flemish demands (see Jennissen, 1913). In the middle of everything was the city of Brussels, the capital of the country and historically a Flemish city. Even though the city was situated just to the north of the language line, the city's French-speaking population grew rapidly during the nineteenth century because of the concentration of public functions in the Belgian capital. By 1910 the French speakers were in the majority (McRae, 1986:295). Some of these were Walloons who had migrated to Brussels, but many were of Flemish ancestry. Hence, Brussels was neither a Walloon city from the standpoint of ancestry nor a Flemish city from the standpoint of language. Not surprisingly, the linguistic status of the capital became a matter of contention for both the Flemish and Walloon movements. The former saw the decline of Dutch and local Germanic dialects as an indication of a Francophone attempt to rid Belgium of its Flemish heritage. The latter saw the Flemish effort to maintain the use of Dutch in the capital as an attempt to curtail the basic freedom of language choice.

In the years leading up to World War I, a number of prominent Flemish leaders abandoned an emphasis on individual language rights in favor of a territorial approach to the language problem (Murphy, 1988:92–95). The rapid growth of French in Brussels and a string of legislative defeats in the language arena led them to conclude that the cultural rights of the Flemish people could only be protected by defining a Flemish territory and insisting on the exclusive use of Dutch or Flemish dialects therein (Zolberg, 1974). Nevertheless, no one seriously called into question the political unity of the Belgian state. Flemish leaders were simply searching for a means of guaranteeing cultural and linguistic equality in Belgium.

A significant change occurred during and after World War I that set Belgium firmly on the road to federalism. A growing number of Belgians began to think of their country as an entity composed not just of two peoples but of two distinct ethnolinguistic regions as well. A variety of factors encouraged this development, including: (1) growing recognition of the disadvantaged position of non-French speakers in Belgium resulting from the sociolinguistic structure of the Belgian army; (2) associations that developed among soldiers from all parts of northern Belgium who shared a common experience of discrimination because of their language; (3) an administrative partition along language lines imposed by the occupying Germans during the war, which was designed to curry the favour of Flemish activists; and (4) the acceptance of universal male suffrage after the war, which gradually translated into greater political power for the numerically superior Flemish population (see de Schaepdrijver and Charpentier 1918; Solansky, 1928; Willemsen, 1969). These developments culminated in the acceptance of the first territorially based language law in 1921, a law calling for the use of Dutch in state, provincial, and administrative affairs in the Flemish provinces and districts of northern Belgium, except Brussels (Maroy, 1966). The 1921 law lacked any sanctions for violation and it was not always observed, but it set in motion a series of events that culminated in the adoption of more sweeping language legislation in 1932 (see Sonntag, 1991). The latter called for the use of Dutch in most aspects of public life in northern Belgium. With its adoption 'Belgium accepted in language an analogue to what the Peace of Augsburg had given the Germanies in religion in 1555. The principle was that of territorial, rather than personal, choice.' (Lorwin, 1970:13).

At the heart of the language legislation of the 1920s and 1930s was a territorial vision of Belgium as a state divided into two main language regions, Flanders and Wallonia, and a capital city combining elements of both. This was the vision that eventually became the basis for the political structure of the Belgian state (see Figure 3.1). The language regions were not part of the political structure of Belgium at the time, however, and their territorial extent was subject to change if the decennial census showed a changed majority in any commune. Moreover, violations of the laws were frequent and many institutions in Flanders, including the famous Catholic University of Louvain, did not abandon the use of French.

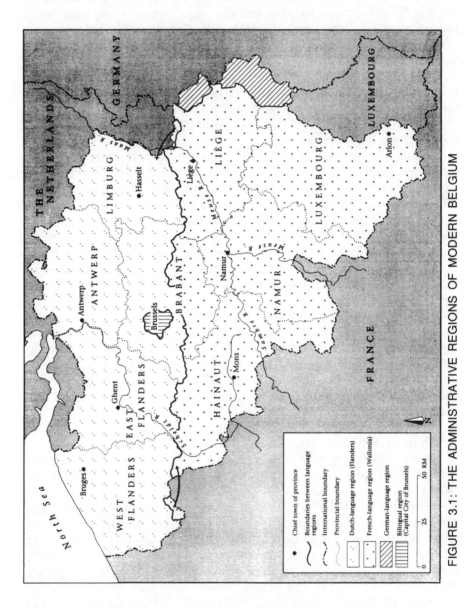

FIGURE 3.1: THE ADMINISTRATIVE REGIONS OF MODERN BELGIUM

The adoption of the 1932 language laws, however, both signalled and helped to further the view of Belgium as a country made up of two distinct ethnic regions.

In light of the significance of this view for the later turn towards federalism, it is worth pausing for a moment to consider other views that might have developed. If there had been true equality for the Dutch language from the beginning, or if the Francophone elite had been more responsive to the Flemish call for individual language rights, Flanders and Wallonia might not have taken on such perceptual significance. Under these circumstances, northern and southern Belgium might not have been seen as discrete historical unities. Alternatively, a territorial approach to cultural rights might have developed that was focused on provinces, the most important administrative subdivisions in Belgium prior to the 1970s (see Figure 3.1). Such an approach might have grown out of a desire to acknowledge local differences, including linguistic differences within Flanders and Wallonia. Under this scenario, some adjustment might have been required in the provincial boundaries to render them more linguistically homogeneous, but the adjustment would have been radical only in the case of Brabant. This approach would have had the added advantage of opening up the possibility for territorial coalitions to develop across language regions. History, however, cannot be undone, and the fact that the two major standardized languages of Belgium emerged as focal points for feelings of discrimination and conflict meant that northern and southern Belgium came to be seen as increasingly oppositional unities.

Ethnoregional opposition intensified through the 1930s as violations of the language laws became more apparent. Capitalising on this state of affairs, the Germans once again divided the country along language lines during World War II. The subsequent rejection of all things associated with the German occupation muted calls for administrative separation for a while, but the already ingrained tendency to frame issues in regional terms meant that such post-war issues as state funding for Catholic schools and the king's alleged collaboration with the Germans became ethnoregional issues as well (Claes, 1963–1964:45). Moreover, concerns over the spread of French into traditionally Flemish territory, both along the language border and around Brussels, led to controversies over the post-war censuses. The eventual refusal of many Flemish mayors even to distribute the 1960 census forms because of concerns over their political-territorial implications led ultimately to a demand that the boundaries of the language regions be permanently fixed (Levy, 1960).

Two bills were passed in the early 1960s that fixed the language boundary in the position shown in Figure 3.1. The bills called for strict unilingualism in Flanders and Wallonia, and established the nineteen communes of Brussels as a bilingual area. In addition, special Dutch-language facilities and rights were guaranteed in four communes just to the south of the language line, and special French-language facilities and rights were guaranteed in twelve communes, six just to the north of the language line and six others immediately adjacent to Brussels. Stabilizing the language boundary did not lead to a relaxation in ethnoregional tensions, however. The exact positioning of the language boundary had come about through a political compromise, not through field investigation (Verdoodt, 1978:14–15), and controversies over its location, particularly in the Fourons in eastern Belgium, fuelled interregional tensions (Hermans and Verjans, 1983). Moreover, efforts to retain French language programmes and facilities at the Catholic University of Louvain in Flanders sparked a national debate over language and regionalism that ended in the transfer of the French-speaking part of the university to a new campus south of the language line (Goffert, 1969). With both Flemings and Walloons feeling victimised and with so many issues being cast in ethnoregional terms, it is not surprising that, by the late 1960s, pressure was mounting for a change in Belgium's unitary state structure.

THE INSTITUTIONALISATION OF FEDERALISM

Given the territorial polarisations described above, it is not surprising that Flanders, Wallonia, and Brussels were seen as the basic building blocks on which a decentralised state would have to be built. The construction of a decentralised system was complicated by the special character of Brussels. Speakers of both the major language groups lived in the capital, but by the late 1960s Francophones outnumbered Dutch speakers by approximately four to one (Centre de Recherche, 1970). Most of the Francophones did not consider themselves to be Walloons, however, and many Dutch-speaking Flemings thought of the city as a part of Flanders. This meant that there was an inexact correspondence between language regions and language communities, and that different segments of the Belgian population had different views on what the status of Brussels should be.

As the centrifugal tendencies of regionalism deepened, some modification in the unitary structure of the state became necessary. The first major step was taken in 1970 with the adoption of amendments to the Constitution that started Belgium down the road to federation. At the core of the 1970 constitutional revisions was the official recognition of (1) four linguistic regions – a Walloon region, a Flemish region, a bilingual Brussels region, and a German region, the last encompassing a small area in southeastern Belgium that had been acquired from Germany after World War I, and (2) three cultural communities – French-speaking, Dutch-speaking, and German-speaking (see Wigny, 1972). In the aftermath of these revisions, councils were established for the French, Dutch, and German cultural communities, as well as for the Walloon and Flemish regions. In each case, the councils were made up of members of the national Parliament with the appropriate linguistic or regional affiliations. No agreement could be reached on forming a Brussels regional council, however; the Flemings thought Brussels should not have the same regional status as Flanders, whereas the Walloons and the French-speaking inhabitants of Brussels wanted the capital to be a third official region in Belgium (De Ridder and Fraga, 1986).

The particularities of the institutional structures that emerged out of the 1970 constitutional revisions and associated legislative enactments are extraordinarily complex, but a brief overview of their character and subsequent evolution is necessary if the nature of the Belgian federal system is to be understood. Under the terms of the 1970 Constitution as revised and fleshed out by additional legislation, competence over a some aspects of cultural and educational affairs was vested in the French- and Dutch-speaking cultural councils (the German cultural council had more limited powers), whereas the regional councils were given control over specified social and economic matters. The powers of the cultural and regional councils were narrowly circumscribed, however, and fiscal allocations from the national government were small.

Despite the limitations of the 1970 constitutional revisions, they initiated the process of governmental decentralisation, which has since gradually widened and deepened. During the 1970s the cultural councils were established, as were the Flemish and Walloon regional councils. In addition, each of the established councils was endowed with its own executive. The autonomy of the latter was often in question, however, since the chief executive could be a national government minister as well. Getting this cumbersome administrative structure off the ground proved to be difficult and time-consuming, but by the late 1970s it was more or less in place, paving the way for the next round of constitutional revisions in 1980.

The 1980 revisions grew out of the need to deal with problems that had emerged with the institutionalization of the 1970 revisions, as well as with continued centrifugal tendencies along ethnolinguistic and ethnoregional lines. The new constitutional provisions, together with associated legislative enactments, converted the cultural councils into 'community' councils and expanded their competence over such matters as broadcasting, tourism, health care, social welfare, and scientific research. The authority of the Walloon and Flanders regional councils was also enlarged to encompass such issues as urban planning, environmental affairs, housing, water use, regional economic development, energy, and employment (see Senelle, 1980). In addition, Parliament approved the merging of the Flanders regional council and the Dutch community council into the 'Flemish Council' to reflect the commonality of interest between region and language community in northern Belgium. The delegates from Brussels, however, were given only advisory powers when the merged council met to consider regional issues. A Court of Arbitration was also set up to deal with conflicts between the various governmental institutions. Finally, the executives of the Walloon regional council, the French community council, and the Flemish council were separated from the central government ministry (McRae, 1986:167–168). Absent from the 1980 revisions, however, was a determination of the status of Brussels, since the impasse over the capital city's status still had not been resolved.

The most recent, and most definitive, steps toward federation have taken place during a three-phase revision of the Constitution between 1988 and 1993. The first two phases, completed in 1988 and 1989, widened the competencies of the regional and community institutions still further, established regional institutions for Brussels, and significantly expanded the budgets of the regional and community institutions. The resulting structure of the Belgian government is shown in Figure 3.2. Important new powers over education were transferred to the community level, and the regions acquired complete responsibility over infrastructure, public transportation, employment, and the use and conservation of natural resources (Senelle, 1990). Budget allocations to the five subnational governments grew from 8.4 per cent of the total national budget to 33 per cent (41 per cent excluding payments on the public debt) (Hooghe, 1991). The Brussels problem was resolved by establishing a council and an executive for the capital region with somewhat more limited powers than their Flemish and Walloon counterparts; the national government retained significant control over regional issues that have national and international ramifications.

The institutions of the region of Brussels reflect a commitment to the dual representation of Flemish and Francophone inhabitants. The Brussels executive has two Dutch-speaking and two French-speaking ministers elected by the regional council, plus a president similarly elected. Members of the council itself are divided into two language groups in proportion to the percentage of votes cast for Dutch- and French-speaking 'lists', and special protection mechanisms can be invoked when minority interests are threatened. In addition, there are French and Dutch community commissions for Brussels with competence over a variety of personal, cultural, and educational

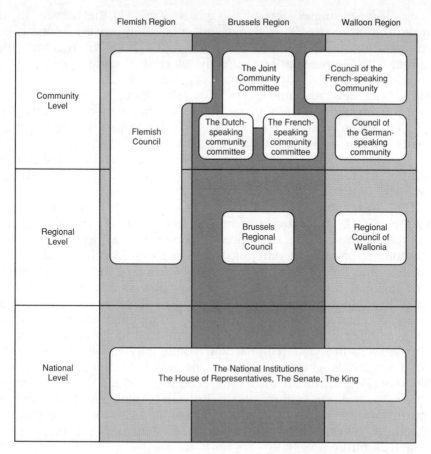

FIGURE 3.2: THE INSTITUTIONAL STRUCTURE OF THE BELGIAN
GOVERNMENT

matters. They are composed of the French- and Dutch-speaking
members of the regional council plus two members of the
appropriate language group within the regional executive (Senelle,
1990:162–163). They meet both separately and jointly. When meeting
separately, they make decisions on matters affecting 'uni-community'
educational institutions, rest homes, cultural programmes, and the
like. When meeting jointly, they make decisions about 'bi-
community' institutions and affairs. Brussels community commissions
are necessary because control over such matters by the French and
Flemish community councils would be difficult and divisive in a city
in which there is no easy means of identifying which inhabitants
belong to which language group (Group Coudenberg, 1989:32).

In the third phase of the most recent round of state reforms
(1992–1993), the final steps were taken towards the establishment of
what Article 1 of the Belgian Constitution now describes as a federal

state. The key ingredients of this phase were (1) the transfer of all residual powers to the regional and community governments, (2) a restructuring of the Senate to make it the body of regional and community representation (directly elected Senators became the regional/community representatives), and (3) the devolution of substantial new responsibilities over agriculture, scientific research, and foreign trade to the regions (Reuter Library Report, February 7th, 1993). In addition, the substate governments were given treaty-making rights with foreign governments for matters within their competencies. The federal government retained substantial control in the fiscal arena, however, as it did in the realms of defence, diplomacy, and social security.

By almost any reckoning, then, Belgium is now a federal state (Witte, 1992). Its particular form of federalism is unique and not entirely territorial; the existence of community as well as regional institutions provides a different twist on the classical federal model. At the same time, the regions are the bedrock of the federal system. The regional councils possess significant powers and, in the Flemish case, the regional and community councils have merged. Moreover, many community issues are debated in regional terms and have regional effects; the existence of separate community commissions in Brussels ensures that regional and community initiatives frequently have similar geographical foundations and implications. Hence, the map of Belgium that shows the country divided into a Flemish region, a Walloon region, and a Brussels capital region is the one that undergirds much of Belgian political life. And the social changes that have accompanied the evolution of that map are shaping the country's future.

FEDERAL FORM AND SOCIAL CONSEQUENCE

As we have already seen, the ideological roots of linguistic regionalism were established well before the 1970 constitutional reforms. Consequently, issues ranging from the status of Brussels to funding for Catholic schools were already being understood and debated in ethnoregional terms. The tendency to view issues in these terms intensified as the move toward a linguistically based federal system gained momentum in the 1960s. With the institutionalization of that system over the past twenty-five years, an array of political and social interests have been cast in the mould of Belgium's tripartite regional structure. In the process, interaction patterns have come increasingly to mirror regional patterns, identities have been crystallised along regional lines, and cross-cutting cleavages have been weakened.

Before focusing on these developments, it is important to note that, despite the dramatic headlines that have appeared in a number of foreign papers over the past year (e.g., LaFranchi, 1992), Belgium is probably not on the brink of a Czechoslovak-style breakup. Most surveys show a substantial majority of the Belgian population opposed to a complete parting of the ways between Flanders and Wallonia, and the peculiar status of Brussels precludes any neat partitioning of the country. Moreover, much of the financial and political elite in Brussels is concerned about the negative economic and political ramifications of separatist tendencies. At the same time, regionalism has strengthened over the past several decades, and it is not inconceivable that it could strengthen still further. It is thus important to understand the ways in which the structure of the system itself may be implicated in these developments.

At the heart of the matter is the particular territorial structure of Belgian federalism itself. The theoretical literature on multiethnic states tells us that those dominated by two distinct ethnic groups – so-called bicommunal polities – are the most likely to fail (Duchacek, 1988). The potential instability of bicommunal polities derives from the lack of opportunity for the communities to alter their relationship through shifting alliances or coalitions; in particular, the inability of a minority group to strengthen its position by sharing power with a third group can lead to serious resentment. Although Belgium is not a classic bicommunal polity because of the Brussels situation, the regionalization process has brought the country closer to this model by structuring so many interests in terms of the opposition between French-speaking Wallonia and Dutch-speaking Flanders. This, in turn, has produced polarities that, typical of bicommunal systems, have both taken on a life of their own and overridden other potential polarities.

The territorial structure of Belgian federalism has promoted social polarisation along ethnoregional lines in at least two mutually reinforcing ways: (1) it has led to a restructuring of key social and economic arrangements to reflect underlying ethnoregional divisions, and (2) it has bestowed ethnoregional significance on a variety of issues, including many that have nothing to do with language or culture. A brief examination of each of these developments shows how they have promoted identification at the regional level while rendering regional differences a fundamental source of tension.

Social and economic restructuring

The imposition of a limited regime of regional unilingualism in the 1930s initiated a process of linguistic segmentation that made it increasingly difficult for Francophones to live and work in Flanders and for Dutch speakers to do the same in Wallonia. Hence, with the exception of a few communes around Brussels and along the language border where minority language rights were eventually guaranteed, Flanders and Wallonia have become more linguistically homogenous (De Vriendt and Van de Craen, 1990). The trend towards linguistic homogeneity can be attributed in part to language shift, but migration has played a role as well. Whatever the cause, daily life in Flanders and Wallonia is increasingly carried out in an essentially unilingual context.

Accelerated movement toward a linguistically based federal system not only furthered regional unilingualism; it precipitated the division of a host of social and economic institutions along language lines as well. An early example of the latter was the division of the Belgian broadcasting services into Dutch- and French-language wings, which eventually were completely separated. With this split, news and entertainment programs were generated by distinct entities that had 'no explicit mandate . . . to promote integrative values, or even mutual understanding, across linguistic lines' (McRae, 1986:249). Although the division was linguistic rather than regional, it inevitably had ethno-regional implications; the Flemings of Flanders and the Walloons of Wallonia were confronted with different programming that often stressed the regional concerns and issues pertinent to the target audience.

Other institutional divisions followed that helped to focus attention at the regional level. Once again, these were prompted in significant part by the evolving structure of Belgian federalism. One of the most important was the division of the major political parties (Christian, Socialist, and Liberal) along language lines. Regionalist political parties sprang up in Flanders, Brussels, and Wallonia in the 1950s and early 1960s in response to demands for greater regional autonomy. As these demands intensified in the late 1960s, the regionalist parties gained considerable ground. Moreover, the major parties had to take stands on regional issues. The pressure eventually became too great, forcing the parties to split into separate Dutch- and French-language wings (Fitzmaurice, 1983). Although the newly divided parties managed to recapture some of the votes they had lost to the regionalist parties, the division of the political parties blunted one of the major cross-cutting cleavages that had existed in Belgian society (Claeys, 1980).

Prior to the split of the major parties it was well known that the Socialist party was strongest in the old industrial areas of the Sambre-Meuse Valley in Wallonia, whereas the Christian party was dominant in the North. At the same time, each of these two parties enjoyed significant support in both regions, and the positions they assumed on key social and economic issues often united people from north and south. After their division, however, the wings of the old parties began to diverge on a growing number of issues. Moreover, since the Socialists assumed a position of dominance in Walloon regional institutions and the Christian Democrats in their Flemish counterparts, the Socialist-Christian cleavage increasingly came to be seen as one that corresponded to, rather than cut across, ethnoregional lines.

The broadcasting services and the political parties are but two of a host of institutions that have been divided along linguistic and regional lines. Organisations ranging from trade unions to the Belgian Bar Association to the national water regulatory board have been so divided. Even the Roman Catholic Church has adjusted the boundaries of its dioceses so that they will correspond to the division between language regions (Beaufays, 1988:69). Many of these divisions were necessitated by the structure of a system in which political power was organised along language community and language region lines. At the same time, their net effect has been to reinforce regional structures and identities. They have done so by diminishing opportunities for interregional interaction and communication, by weakening cross-cutting cleavages, and by providing regionally grounded institutional frameworks within which interests can be articulated and goals can be pursued. Moreover, as the process of federalism deepens, regional social and economic institutions are likely to become even more powerful (Hooghe, 1991:66), thereby reinforcing these tendencies.

Political polarization along ethnoregional lines

Polarisation over language issues is nothing new in Belgium, and continued controversies surrounding such issues as the right of French speakers to use their language in the communes surrounding Brussels is hardly surprising. More remarkable, however, is the extent to which issues surficially unrelated to language and culture have become points of contention between Flemings and Walloons. This too is a product of the particular territorial form of Belgian federalism. Because primary powers are vested in territorial units that correspond closely to language divisions, almost every issue with differential regional impact has the potential of sparking ethnoregional polarisation.

This tendency is particularly evident in the economic sphere. Throughout the nineteenth and early twentieth centuries, Belgium's economic centre of gravity lay in the heavily industrialised Sambre-Meuse Valley (Riley, 1976). After World War II, however, the older industrial areas fell into decline and the centre of gravity moved to the Brussels–Antwerp corridor. This transformation accompanied the growing perceptual significance of the language regions in Belgium, and it consequently was understood in ethnoregional terms: Wallonia was losing out to Flanders. The fact that there were (and still are) economically depressed parts of northern Belgium and economically vital areas in the south became less important than what this development suggested about the relative standing of the two major language regions.

With the institutionalisation of a linguistically based federal structure, the comparative economic status of Flanders and Wallonia has taken on new significance. Now practically every issue of economic aid to a particular industry, neighbourhood, commune, or province carries with it larger questions of interregional equity. In addition, many national programmes that benefit one region more than another are questioned. Consequently, debates over regional fiscal issues have been one of the greatest sources of instability over the past several years (see Couttenier, 1992).

A recurrent theme in interregional fiscal debates is the Flemish concern that national fiscal policies effectively put the inhabitants of Flanders in the position of subsidising Wallonia. They point particularly to social security, a matter that has remained under national government control. The disproportionate share of national benefits that Walloons receive under the social security programme has become something of a rallying point for Flemish nationalists. In 1992, for example, Wim Van Deyck, a member of the Flemish Nationalist Student Union, was widely quoted for claiming that every Flemish family could buy a new automobile every four years if it were not for annual revenue transfers from Flanders to Wallonia (LaFranchi, 1992:6). Although his figures are suspect, his argument does reflect an undercurrent of concern that has fuelled Flemish separatism (Hill, 1993).

From the Walloon perspective, fiscal allocations that are made in proportion to regional wealth have created unacceptable imbalances in, for example, funding for schools (Dawance, 1990). In 1990 Walloon teachers went on strike for some weeks to protest their salary and benefit packages. Their woes were a direct consequence of a French-speaking community budgetary allocation that was insufficient to provide support packages equivalent to those being received by Flemish teachers (Kellaway, 1990). Much was made of the interregional imbalances, and lack of sympathy from many Flemings helped to fuel Walloon regionalism.

The tendency to interpret most issues in regional terms extends beyond the fiscal arena to such issues as the routing of the high speed train through Belgium and funding for research and development (Abbott, 1992). When it was revealed that more than three-quarters of the Belgian budget of the European Space Agency was spent on contracts with firms in Brussels and Wallonia, for example, loud protests were lodged about the unfair treatment of

Flanders. A more dramatic controversy unfolded in 1991 when a decision was made by the national government to permit two financially ailing arms makers in Wallonia to sell weapons to the Middle East (see Fitzmaurice, 1992:179–180; Couttenier, 1992:349–350). The Flemish parties objected, ostensibly on moral and geopolitical grounds. In response, the French-language parties sought to block the approval of a large telecommunications contract that would have benefited Flemish firms disproportionately. Flemish leaders responded by opposing an agreement that would have allowed the proceeds from television licences to be used to help pay the salaries of French-language teachers. The ensuing controversy eventually prompted the collapse of the governing coalition and new elections had to be called.

In each of these instances issues that would not necessarily pit north against south were interpreted in that way because of the particular configuration of Belgian federalism. Under other circumstances one could imagine debates over fiscal policy focused on competition between the industrial heartland of central Belgium and the agricultural periphery of the northeast and the far south. One could image controversies over school funding between richer cities and poorer towns. One could imagine high-profile competitions between communes or districts within Flanders and Wallonia for telecommunication contracts. Or one could imagine disputes over arms sales between pacifist university communities and industrial centres where jobs were dependent on continued arms production. But the structure of federalism imposes a different geographical logic on these matters – a logic in which linguistic identity, institutional politics, and social interest are largely spatially coincident and mutually reinforcing.

ASSESSMENT AND CONCLUSION

One of the basic features of a federal system is that it provides 'incentives for structuring group/class conflicts along territorial lines' (Bakvis and Chandler, 1987:4). When the territories in question are spatial surrogates of large-scale, potentially self-conscious cultural communities, most territorial conflicts become community conflicts as well. In the process, feelings of ethnicity are strengthened and new issues take on ethnoterritorial significance. This is the Belgian experience in brief, and it is at the heart of the challenges facing the country in the years ahead.

Belgium has been greatly changed by the social, political, and institutional divisions that have followed in the wake of federalization. These have grown out of linguistic differences, but they have promoted even greater differentiation. It is difficult to document this process with any precision, but there can be little doubt that a sense of Flemish distinctiveness has heightened over the past several decades. A public opinion poll taken by the Dutch-language newspaper *De Standaard* in September 1992 showed 30.9 per cent of Flemings in favour of outright independence for Flanders. This was far from a majority, but it was a much stronger statement of regionalist thinking than was evident in surveys taken a decade earlier (see Delruelle and Frognier, 1980–1982). Moreover, the increasing willingness of Flemish political leaders to speak openly over the past several years about regional autonomy and even independence provides evidence of the growth of ethnoregionalist sentiment.

Ethnoregional identity is weaker in Wallonia than it is in Flanders, but it is developing among Walloons as well. To quote Liesbet Hooghe (1991:98):

> The Walloon nationalist movement is having a unifying effect. It is transforming the Walloon region into a distinct society, something Wallonia had never really been before. It spoke diverse dialects, and it was culturally and socially predominantly attuned to Brussels' Francophone middle class culture. At best, Wallonia consisted of several subregional cultures. But that may be changing now. More and more Walloon nationalists explicitly distance themselves from Brussels and from the *Communauté française*, and define themselves as *wallon*.

Even in Brussels a certain degree of regional-cum-social distinctiveness has emerged (Murphy, 1989). Fed by functional discontinuities between Brussels and the other language regions, French- and Dutch-speaking residents of the capital are increasingly framing their interests in national and international terms, rather than in ethnolinguistic terms.

None of this is meant to suggest that many Belgians do not maintain a strong commitment to the integrity of the state. As evidence to the contrary, in April 1993 some 30,000 people participated in a demonstration against separatism in Brussels (Lannin, 1993). Moreover, there is some truth to the frequently heard comment that politicians are often responsible for promoting ethnoregional discord. Yet Belgian politicians operate within an institutional framework that has developed out of an underlying social issue, and their decisions in turn shape the context within which Belgians necessarily lead their lives. And the particular political-territorial character of that context has promoted ethnoregional polarisation despite the best efforts of those seeking greater harmony and unity.

Against this backdrop, it is doubtful that settlement of the remaining ambiguities in Belgium's institutional structure will resolve the language problem once and for all. Instead, divisiveness is likely to continue both because the system encourages interregional comparison and because there are limited possibilities for the development of cross-cutting cleavages. If Belgians are to move beyond the polarities of the present system, some rethinking of the territorial structure of federalism will be required. Most obviously, consideration must be given to the possibility of devolving greater powers to the provinces. With the exception of Brabant, the provinces are unilingual and would thus be in a position to guarantee the linguistic status quo. At the same time, with greater say in economic and social matters, the provinces could enter into shifting coalitions that would help to disentangle language community issues from many economic and social issues. Thus, Limbourg and Luxembourg could find themselves on the same side of certain agricultural and social issues, just as East Flanders could be aligned with Hainaut on certain industrial and labour issues.

The possible advantages to such an arrangement are suggested by reference to the Swiss case. Switzerland is a federal system made up of twenty-six cantons. There also four major language groups found in the country. The cantons of Switzerland are, for the most part, homogeneous from a linguistic standpoint (McRae, 1983:77–78). At the same time, each major linguistic region comprises multiple cantons. Since primary powers are vested in the cantons, the territorial structure of Swiss federalism discourages the development of ethnonationalism across language community lines (Steiner, 1983:166). Political parties do not correspond to language regions and the press rarely refers to language regions when discussing economic and political affairs. Moreover, crosscutting cleavages are easily expressed in the cantonal system. Language regions stand out only occasionally in maps of post-World War II voting patterns in Switzerland (Sanguin, 1983:181–217), and the voting behaviour of cantons on constitutional issues is associated far more with sociopolitical patterns than with language (Eschet-Schwarz, 1989).

There are, of course, issues in Switzerland that break down along language lines, most notably the recent vote on participation in the developing European Economic Area (Widmer and Buri, 1992). The division between Protestants and Catholics also functions as a strong cross-cutting cleavage in Switzerland. In addition, there is some indication that language divisions are beginning to express themselves more forcefully in the Swiss political arena (Gilg, 1987). The likelihood of the development of Belgian-style linguistic polarisation is small, however, since the territorial structure of Swiss federalism ensures that cross-cutting cleavages will remain strong.

The Swiss case highlights the potential advantages of a system in which federal territories are not derivatives of the spatial structure of large-scale cultural divisions. For Belgium, it suggests a possible avenue for mitigating ethnoregional polarisation. It is not difficult to understand why this avenue has not yet been followed; social and political developments with their roots in the nineteenth and early twentieth centuries gave the Belgians little alternative but to pursue a federal system structured along language region lines (Senelle, 1989:72). As the need to ease the centrifugal tendencies of the present system intensifies, however, the questions that are surfacing about the potential role of the provinces in Belgium's political future (see Group Coudenberg, 1987) are likely to take on more significance.

The larger lesson of the Belgian and Swiss cases is that the actual geographical configuration of federalism matters. We simply cannot afford to discuss the nature and tendencies of federalism without reference to the underlying spatial configuration of federal territories themselves. If Belgium had sought to retain a unitary state structure in the face of the pressures of the past few decades, conflict would arguably be worse than it is today. At the same time, the particular political geography of Belgian federalism has generated its own set of conflicts. Recognition of this point highlights a critically important qualification to the common generalisation that federalism reduces conflict.

ACKNOWLEDGEMENTS

Research for this chapter was supported by the National Science Foundation of the United States under grant number SES-9157667. I am grateful for research assistance provided by Dominique Saillard, Steven Huter, and Nancy Leeper. Nancy Leeper also drafted the figures.

REFERENCES

Abbott, A. (1992) Bifurcated Belgium shows the strain from collaboration between cultures. *Nature*, 358, 6 August, p. 445.

Agnew, J. A. (1987) *Place and Politics: The Geographical Mediation of State and Society*. Boston: Allen and Unwin.

Agnew, J. A. (1989) The Devaluation of Place in Social Science. In J. A. Agnew and J. S. Duncan, eds., *The Power of Place: Bringing Together Geographical and Sociological Imaginations*. Boston: Unwin Hyman, pp. 9–29.

Bakvis, H. and Chandler, W. H. (1987) Federalism and Comparative Analysis. In Herman Bakvis and William H. Chandler, eds., *Federalism and the Role of the State*. Toronto: University of Toronto Press, pp. 3–11.

Beaufays, J. (1988) Belgium: A Dualist Political System? *Publius: The Journal of Federalism*, 18 (2), pp. 63–73.

Becquet, C. (1963) 'Interaction des Ethnies dans la Belgique Contemporaine.' *Journal de la Société de Statistique de Paris*, 104 (4–6), pp. 104–131.

Bulpitt, J. G. (1983) *Territory and Power in the United Kingdom.* Manchester: Manchester University Press.

Burgess, M. (1986) *Federalism and Federation in Western Europe.* London: Croom Helm.

Centre de Recherche et d'Information Socio-Politique (1970) L'Evolution Linguistique et Politique du Brabant (1), *Courrier Hebdomadaire du CRISP*, 466/467, 16 January.

Claes, L. (1963–1964) The Process of Federalization in Belgium. *Delta*, 6 (4), pp. 43–52.

Claeys, P. H. (1980) Political Pluralism and Linguistic Cleavage: The Belgian Case. In S. Ehrlich and G. Wootton, eds., *Three Faces of Pluralism: Political, Ethnic, and Religious.* Westmead: Gower, pp. 169–189.

Connor, W. (1978) A Nation is a Nation, is a State, is an Ethnic Group, is a . . . *Ethnic and Racial Studies*, 1 (4), pp. 377–400.

Couttenier, I. (1992) Belgian Politics in 1991. *Res Publica*, 34 (3–4), pp. 347–370.

Dawance, J.-P. (1990) Les Politiques Budgétaires de la Région Wallonne et de la Communauté Française. *Res Publica*, 32 (2–3), pp. 279–298.

Delruelle, N. and Frognier, A. P. (1980–1982) L'Opinion Publique et les Problèmes Communautaires. *Courrier Hebdomadaire du CRISP*, 880 (9 May 1980), 927/928 (3 July 1981), 966 (11 June 1982).

Deneckere, M. (1954) *Histoire de la Langue Française dans les Flandres, 1770–1823, parts II–III.* Ghent: Romanica Gandensia.

De Ridder, M. and Fraga, L. R. (1986) The Brussels Issue in Belgian Politics. *West European Politics*, 9 (3), pp. 376–392.

De Schryver, R. (1981) The Belgian Revolution and the Emergence of Belgium's Biculturalism. In A. Lijphart, ed., *Conflict and Compromise in Belgium: The Dynamics of a Culturally Divided Society.* Berkeley: Institute for International Studies, University of California, Berkeley, pp. 13–33.

De Vriendt, S. and Van de Craen, P. (1990) *Bilingualism and Belgium: A History and an Appraisal.* Occasional Paper no. 23. Dublin: Centre for Language and Communication Studies, Trinity College.

Duchacek, I. D. (1986) *The Territorial Dimension of Politics Within, Among, and Across Nations.* Boulder: Westview Press.

Duchacek, I. D. (1987) *Comparative Federalism: The Territorial Dimension of Politics.* Lanham, MD: University Press of America.

Duchacek, I. D. (1988) Dyadic Federations and Confederations. *Publius: The Journal of Federalism*, 18, pp. 5–31.

Elazar, D. J. (1987) *Exploring Federalism.* Tuscaloosa, AL: University of Alabama Press.

Elias, H. J. (1963–1965) *Geschiedenis der Vlaamsche Gedachte, 1780–1914*, 4 vols. Antwerp: De Nederlandsche Boekhandel.

Eschet-Schwarz, A. (1989) The Role of Semi-Direct Democracy in Shaping Swiss Federalism: The Behavior of Cantons Regarding Revision of the Constitution, 1866–1981. *Publius: The Journal of Federalism*, 19, pp. 79–105.

Fitzmaurice, J. (1983) *The Politics of Belgium: Crisis and Compromise in a Plural Society.* London: C. Hurst & Company.

Fitzmaurice, J. (1992) Belgian Paradoxes: The November 1991 Election. *West European Politics*, 15 (4), pp. 178–182.

Giddens, A. (1985) *The Constitution of Society.* Berkeley: University of California Press.

Gilg, P. (1987) Stabilität und Wandel im Spiegel des Regionalen Abstimmungsverhaltens. *Schweizerisches Jahrbuch für Politische Wissenschaft*, 27, pp. 121–158.

Goffert, V. (1969) La Crise de Louvain, du 1er Janvier au 31 Mars 1968. *Res Publica*, 11, pp. 31–76.

Gottmann, J. (1973) *The Significance of Territory.* Charlottesville, VA: University of Virginia Press.

Gregory, D. (1978) *Ideology, Science, and Human Geography.* London: Hutchinson.

Group Coudenberg (1987) *Quelle Belgique pour Demain?* Rapport Coudenberg. Paris: Duclot Perspectives. (Also published in Dutch under the title *Naar een Nieuw België?* Tielt: Lannoo.)

Group Coudenberg (1989) The New Belgian Institutional Framework. Pamphlet of the Group Coudenberg, Brussels, April.

Harvey, D. (1989) *The Condition of Postmodernity.* Oxford: Basil Blackwell.

Hermans, M. and Verjans, P. (1983) Les Origines de la Querelle Fouronaise. *Courrier Hebdomadaire du CRISP*, 1019, 2 November.

Hill, A. (1993) Survey of Flanders. *The Financial Times*, 4 May, p. 1.

Hooghe, L. (1991) *A Leap in the Dark: Nationalist Conflict and Federal Reform in Belgium.* Occasional Paper no. 27. Ithaca, NY: Western Societies Program, Cornell University.

Jennissen, E. (1913) *Le Mouvement Wallon.* Liège: La Meuse.

Johnston, R. J. (1986) Placing Politics. *Political Geography Quarterly*, 5 (supplement), pp. S63–S78.

Johnston, R. (1991) *A Question of Place: Exploring the Practice of Human Geography.* Oxford: Blackwell.

Kellaway, L. (1990) Belgian Teaching Strike Highlights Reform Failure. *The Financial Times*, 16 October, p. 2.

Knight, D. B. (1982) Identity and Territory: Geographical Perspectives on Nationalism and Regionalism. *Annals of the Association of American Geographers*, 72 (4), pp. 512–531.

Kurth, G. (1898) *La Frontière Linguistique en Belgique et Dans le Nord de la France*, 2 vols. Brussels: Académie Royale des Sciences, des Lettres et des Beaux-Arts de Belgique.

LaFranchi, H. (1992) Belgium Ponders Flemish Split. *The Christian Science Monitor*, 30 September, p. 6.

Lannin, P. (1993) Thousands Demonstrate for United Belgium as Federalism Looms. *The Reuter Library Report*, 25 April.

Laponce, J. A. (1987) *Languages and Their Territories*. Translated from the French by Anthony Martin-Sperry. Toronto: University of Toronto Press.

Levy, P. M. G. (1960) *La Querelle du Recensement*. Brussels: Institut Belge de Science Politique.

Logie, J. (1980) *1830: De la Régionalization à l'Indépendence*. Gemgloux: Duculot.

Lorwin, V. R. (1970) Linguistic Pluralism and Political Tension in Modern Belgium. *Canadian Review of History*, 5 (1), pp. 1–22.

McRae, K. D. (1983) *Conflict and Compromise in Multilingual Societies: Switzerland*. Waterloo: Wilfrid Laurier University Press.

McRae, K. D. (1986) *Conflict and Compromise in Multilingual Societies: Belgium*. Waterloo, Ontario: Wilfrid Laurier University Press.

Maroy, P. (1969) L'Evolution de la Législation Linguistique Belge. *Revue du Droit Public et de la Science Politique en France*, 82, pp. 449–501.

Murphy, A. B. (1988) *The Regional Dynamics of Language Differentiation in Belgium: A Study in Cultural- Political Geography*. Chicago: University of Chicago, Geography Research Paper No. 227.

Murphy, A. B. (1989) The Territorial Dimension of Sociolinguistic Patterns and Processes in Brussels. *Taal en Sociale Integratie*, special issue on 'Het Probleem Brussel sinds Hertoginnedal (1963): Linguïstische Aspecten,' Piet Van de Craen, ed., 13, pp. 117–128.

Murphy, A. B. (1991) Regions as Social Constructs: The Gap Between Theory and Practice. *Progress in Human Geography*, 15 (1), pp. 22–35.

Polasky, J. (1981) Liberalism and Biculturalism. In Arend Lijphart, ed., *Conflict and Compromise in Belgium: The Dynamics of a Culturally Divided Society*. Berkeley: Institute for International Studies, University of California, Berkeley, pp. 34–45.

Rhodes, R. A. W. and Wright, V. (1987) Introduction. *West European Politics*, special issue on 'Tensions in the Territorial Politics of Western Europe,' edited by R. A. W. Rhodes and V. Wright, 10 (4), pp. 1–20.

Riley, R. 1976. *Belgium*. Studies in Industrial Geography. Boulder: Westview Press.

Robinson, K. (1961) Sixty Years of Federation in Australia. *Geographical Review*, 51 (1), pp. 1–20.

Rokkan, S. and Urwin, D. W., eds. 1982. *The Politics of Territorial Identity: Studies in European Regionalism*. London: Sage.

Sack, R. D. (1986) *Human Territoriality: Its Theory and History*. Cambridge Studies in Historical Geography. Cambridge: Cambridge University Press.

Sanguin, A.-L. (1983) *La Suisse, Essai de Géographie Politique*. Gap: Editions Ophrys.

de Schaepdrijver, K. and Charpentier, J. (1918) *Ontwikkelingsgang der Vlaamsche Frontbeweging*. Brussels: De Raymaeker en Peremans.

Senelle, R. (1980) *The Reform of the Belgian State*, vol. III. Memo from Belgium no. 326. Brussels: Ministry of Foreign Affairs, External Trade and Cooperation in Development.

Senelle, R. (1989) 'Constitutional Reform in Belgium: From Unitarism Towards Federalism.' In M. Forsyth, ed., *Federalism and Nationalism.* New York: St. Martin's Press, pp. 51–95.

Senelle, R. (1990) *The Reform of the Belgian State*, vol. V. Memo from Belgium, 'Views and Surveys', no. 198. Brussels: Ministry of Foreign Affairs, External Trade and Cooperation in Development.

Sharpe, L. J. (1987) The West European State: the Territorial Dimension. *West European Politics*, special issue on 'Tensions in the Territorial Politics of Western Europe', edited by R. A. W. Rhodes and V. Wright, 10 (4), pp. 148–167.

Soja, E. W. (1989) *Postmodern Geographies: the Reassertion of Space in Critical Social Theory.* London: Verso.

Solansky, A. (1928) *German Administration in Belgium.* New York: Columbia Studies.

Sonntag, S. K. (1991) *Competition and Compromise Amongst Elites in Belgian Language Politics.* Plurilingua XII. Brussels: Research Centre on Multilingualism and Bonn: Dümmler.

Steiner, J. (1983) Conclusion: Reflections on the Consociational Theme. In H. R. Penniman, ed., *Switzerland at the Polls: the National Elections of 1979.* Washington, DC: American Enterprise Institute for Public Policy Research, pp. 161–177.

Urwin, D. (1985) The Price of a Kingdom: Territory, Identity and the Centre-Periphery Dimension in Western Europe. In Y. Mény and V. Wright, eds, *Centre–Periphery Relations in Western Europe.* London: Allen & Unwin, 1985, pp. 151–170.

Van der Essen, L. (1915) *A Short History of Belgium.* Chicago: University of Chicago Press.

Verdoodt, A. (1978) 'Introduction.' *International Journal of the Sociology of Language*, special issue on Belgium, A. Verdoodt, ed., 15, pp. 5–18.

Widmer, T. and Buri, C. (1992) Brüssel oder Bern: Schlägt das Herz der 'Romands' eher für Europa? Ein Vergleich der Einstellungen von Deutsch- und Westschweizerinnen zur Europa-Frage. *Schweizerisches Jahrbuch für Politische Wissenschaft*, 32, pp. 363–387.

Wigny, P. (1972) *La Troisième Révision de la Constitution.* Brussels: E. Bruylant.

Willemsen, A. W. (1969) *Het Vlaams-Nationalisme: De Geschiedenis van de Jaren 1914–1940.* Utrecht: Ambo.

Williams, C. H., ed. (1988) *Language in Geographic Context.* Clevedon: Multilingual Matters.

Witte, E. (1992) Belgian Federalism: Towards Complexity and Asymmetry. *West European Politics*, 15 (4), pp. 95–117.

Zolberg, A. R. (1974) The Making of Flemings and Walloons: Belgium, 1830–1914. *Journal of Interdisciplinary History*, 5, pp. 179–235.

CHAPTER FOUR

Federalism, Hindu Nationalism and Mythologies of Governance in Modern India

Stuart Corbridge

'India regularly confounds its critics by its resilience, its survival in spite of everything. I don't believe in the Balkanization of India . . . It's my guess that the old functioning anarchy will, somehow or other, keep on functioning, for another forty years, and no doubt another forty after that. But don't ask me how.'
Salman Rushdie, 1987 (in Rushdie, 1991, p. 33)

INTRODUCTION

Social scientists are in the business of asking the question 'how', even if the answers they provide are often inconclusive and necessarily provisional. In this chapter I want to address the question of the future shape of India with reference to the challenges that are being mounted against the country's four founding mythologies: democracy, socialism, secularism and federalism. The second part of the chapter returns to the problems of nation-building and economic development that faced India at Independence in August 1947, and were widely debated by the Constituent Assembly which sat until the promulgation of the Constitution of the Republic of India in 1950. Particular attention is paid to the ways in which a secular conception of Indian identity was promoted in the 1950s, and the means by which various language and ethnic groups were accommodated to the idea of India as a nation-state by virtue of the federal principles mapped out between 1950 and 1956. This period coincided with a period of Congress political dominance at both Centre and State levels of government. This was an era of 'command politics' (Rudolph and Rudolph, 1987), when a strong central state, personified by Prime Minister Nehru, largely imposed its will on Indian civil society and secured the consent of most State governments for the policies of

New Delhi (Kochanek, 1968).

The third part of the chapter considers the erosion of the institutional arrangements that sustained this period of command politics and the associated founding mythologies of secularism and federalism. Because the erosion of a 'strong state' in India has been the subject of intense debate, this part of the chapter also outlines the views of several noted commentators on the changing face of India, including those of Atul Kohli, Lloyd and Susanne Hoeber Rudolph, Achin Vanaik, Paul Brass, Sudipta Kaviraj and V. S. Naipaul. All these authors agree that an emerging challenge to India's federal structures is intimately bound up with a wider reinvention of the political vocabularies of modern India (associated in part with the rise of Hindu nationalism), but they differ significantly in the factors they single out as being of particular importance. For Kohli and Brass the key to India's 'growing crisis of governability' is to be found in the emergence of a genuinely pluralist politics in India post-1964, and in the deinstitutionalisation of the Congress Party. For Vanaik and Naipaul, in very different ways, and also for Kaviraj, the 'painful transition' in India is more directly bound up with the uneven economic development of the country, with the emergence of regional bourgeoisies keen to prosecute a politics of sub-nationalism, and with the rise of a Hindu nationalism that is reawakening a language of belonging that was only surficially erased from the political discourse of the state in the Nehruvian period, and which was never far from the lips of ordinary people.

The fourth part of the chapter focuses on the secessionist struggles in Punjab and Kashmir, and on the mushrooming demands for a redrawing of the federal map of India. The chapter concludes with some remarks on the prospects for the territorial integrity of India in the light of a continuing economic liberalisation and an apparent drift towards communal and caste-based politics in parts of the country. I join with Vanaik in arguing that a burgeoning Hindu nationalism is not 'essentially uncontrollable in impact and internal dynamic' (Vanaik, 1990, p. 149), and is partly offset, for many of its petty bourgeois supporters, by the integrating forces associated with economic liberalization and a telecommunications revolution. Although it is clear that India's much-vaunted 'unity in diversity' is under threat, and is sometimes being held together only by state coercion and a mounting disregard for minority groups, it is far from clear that India is a Yugoslavia in the making. There are good reasons for believing that Western accounts of the relationships between nationalism, federalism and secularism cannot easily or effectively be applied to accounts of these 'same' relationships in a South Asian context.

1947–1964: BUILDING A FEDERAL INDIA AFTER PART(UR)ITION

When India and Pakistan emerged from British India in August 1947 they did so amid terrible scenes of carnage and mass-migration. Millions of people were killed at partition/parturition, with Muslims being killed as they headed to West Punjab and East Pakistan, and Hindus being slaughtered as they escaped a new country that many feared would be run by and for Muslims. In January 1948 Mahatma Gandhi was assassinated in Delhi by a member of a militant Hindu organisation, the Rashtriya Swayamsevak Sangh (RSS). Gandhi was blamed by many Hindu nationalists for consenting to the partition of a country which supposedly was Hindu from the Indus to the Bay of Bengal.

Against this background it is not surprising that the first Prime Minister of India, Pandit Jawaharlal Nehru (the father of Indira Gandhi and the grandfather of Rajiv Gandhi) tried to forge a new India in which the modern religions of secularism and economic development would take the place of the divisive and 'backward-looking' ideologies associated with Hinduism, Islam and Sikhism. Nehru was not able to impose his will on India without challenge, but the period of his premiership did coincide with a remarkable degree of official agreement on the raison(s) d'être of modern India. Although occasional references were made to a Gandhian conception of India as Bharat (the Hindi word for India), the discourse of the state in the 1950s and 1960s was mainly addressed to questions of secular nation-building and economic modernisation, and had little need of a political vocabulary invoking more 'primordial' conceptions of identity and belonging. In this period of command politics the Congress Party in New Delhi, and in many State Assemblies, committed itself to producing a new India and a new Indian 'body' to reside within it. In place of the backward-looking markers associated with caste and untouchability (the latter of which was made 'illegal' in 1950), the body of India (and Indians) was to be refashioned by 'modern' forms of education and health-care, and by occupations that would demand new skills of a workforce liberated from superstition and tradition.

This modernising project is still present in much of the iconography of official India. It is present in the flag of the Republic, for example, which marries a neutral white to the green and orange of Islam and Hinduism in a 'secular' whole that does not so much disavow religious truths as demand their impartial treatment by a modernised state and a modernising civil society. Likewise, the one hundred rupee banknote is adorned on the front by the scripts of each of the fourteen official languages used in the Republic of India, and on the back by women transplanting rice and picking tea, by a farmer driving his tractor, and by a modern dam which is linked to the production of electricity. In this official India there is no place for the temple or the mosque or the Gurdwara, nor is there any hint of communal or caste tensions. The India that Nehru and the Congress Party set out to build in the 1950s was based on an official disregard for these aspects of India's cultures or pasts. In their place the state provided its own mythologies of governance, with mythology being understood here in the sense intended by Roland Barthes (Barthes, 1972) – as a set of conventional but unstated beliefs about how people should lead their daily lives. Most of these mythologies have already been alluded to. Possibly the most tenacious, because least examined, was/is the mythology of democracy. This suggests that India post-1947 was/is a democratic country, wherein a parliamentary system based on five-yearly elections on a first-past-the-post constituency basis is allied to a system of universal suffrage. The three remaining mythologies of governance were, and have been until recently: (1) 'socialism', or a commitment to the building up of a mixed economy in which the state is largely responsible for infrastructural provision and the development of heavy industries; (2) secularism, or an equal regard for all religions *and* an insistence that the languages of religion be kept out of the affairs of the state and nation-building; and (3) federalism, or the consensual management of India's many ethnic groups and subnationalities according to an agreed set of legislative and financial principles, with particular regard being paid to the linguistic bases of India's fabled 'unity in diversity'.

In this chapter it is the federal mythology that most obviously concerns us, although I will argue that it must always be understood in relation to the three other mythologies of governance. The Constitution of India provides for the Republic to be governed as a federation that reserves certain powers, duties and moneys for the Central Government in New Delhi, certain others for the States and Union Territories that make up the Republic (Figure 4.1), and still others for a Concurrent List (Dandekar, 1987). Crudely stated, the States are entrusted with the so-called nation-building activities of health and education, and with a continuing responsibility for agricultural development. State Plans have to be submitted to New Delhi for approval, and State policies and programmes are mainly supported by revenues raised from State sales taxes, agricultural taxes and grants-in-aid from Central Government. The Chief Minister of a State Legislative Assembly will usually belong to the political party that secures a majority in the five-yearly elections. New Delhi is represented, by a Governor who can in certain circumstances recommend the dissolution of a State government. Central Government, meanwhile, takes responsibility for the country's major industrial and infrastructural projects and for defence and foreign

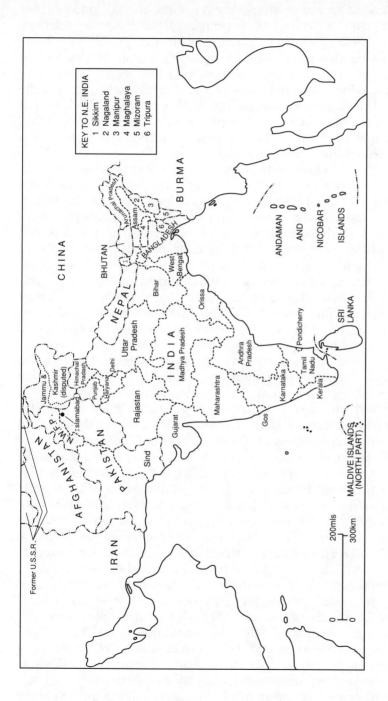

FIGURE 4.1: THE STATES OF INDIA

relations. Its revenues tend to come from more elastic sources of incomes and its revenue buoyancy *vis-à-vis* that of most States provides it with a source of leverage in Centre–State relations (Chatterjee, 1994). This fact, together with the possibility of the Centre imposing Governor's Rule or declaring a state of Emergency, has encouraged some observers to conclude that federal democracy in India is somehow less federal – or more centralised – than is the case in the United States or Switzerland. This may well be true, but India's federal democracy was carved out of a complicated political structure bequeathed by the British, and not forged out of a process of frontier colonisation and territorial accretion.

The division of Centre–State responsibilities and revenues in India was largely settled by 1950. This left the question of what constituted a State, and whether India was best served by the system of Provinces and Presidencies that the British had relied upon. Most representatives in the Constituent Assembly argued that it was not. Moreover, a revised system of federal units promised new bases of power for politicans and others inside and outside the Congress Party. Following agitations in the Andhra region of the old Madras Province, New Delhi moved in the early 1950s to appoint a States Reorganization Commission (SRC). The Commission duly published its Report in 1955 and the Government of India acted on most of its recommendations in its States Reorganization Act of 1956.

The key to the reorganisation of the map of India lay with the principle of a linguistic reorganisation of States. The SRC urged that new States should be created in India only on the basis of conformity with 'traditional' and 'major' linguistic regions. On this basis the old province of Madras could reasonably be divided into the more manageable States of Tamil Nadu (for Tamil speakers) and Kerala (for Malayalam speakers), with a Kannada-speaking Karnataka emerging from parts of Bombay, Coorg, Mysore and Madras. In 1960 Bombay was divided again to create Maharashtra (for Marathi speakers) and Gujarat (for Gujerati speakers). Even the division of 'greater Punjab' in 1966 – into Punjab, Haryana and Himachal Pradesh (the last in 1971) – was ostensibly effected on linguistic grounds. New Delhi maintained that Punjab was not being created as a Sikh-majority State (which it became, just), but as a State for Punjabi speakers. In this manner an important principle was reaffirmed: religious appeals were to be kept out of the official politics and languages of the state. Three other principles were also affirmed in these rounds of States reorganization (after Brass, 1994, pp. 172–73): (1) there would be no recognition of secessionist demands (as in Nagaland); (2) there would be no concessions to politicians seeking to demonstrate language differences to further 'capricious' divisions of existing administrative units; and (3) there would be no agreements to reorganisation where 'the demand was

made by only one of the important language groups concerned'
(Brass, 1994, p. 173).

Such were, and are, the formal political arrangements which
underpin a federal Republic of India. But what gave these
arrangements substance in the Nehru years was something more
intangible, which has to do with political style as well as the
presence or absence of competition between political parties. Paul
Brass has several times drawn attention to the differences in
approach to Centre–State relations that characterised the
premierships of Nehru and his daughter, Indira Gandhi. The contrast
puts Nehru in a favourable light. Whereas Indira was minded to
intervene in Centre–State relations in a negative way, to undermine
the power-base of State party bosses, Nehru supposedly backed off
such personal confrontations and allowed regional Congress chiefs
to take decisions in line with local sentiments. In similar fashion,
where Indira was minded to gather power resources close about her
in a 'kitchen cabinet', and by means of a narcissistic populism
('Indira is India, India is Indira'), Nehru is portrayed as a confident
leader who was able to rise above such petty intrigues.

There might be some truth in this contrast, but there are times
when Brass comes close to imposing a form of psychological
stereotyping on the wider political canvas he is seeking to describe.
What surely mattered more, as Brass also recognises, is that Nehru
could afford to be confident and expansive in the 1950s, in large
part because the main opposition to the Congress Party came from
within the ranks of the party itself (Nandy, 1980). (When pushed,
Nehru was not averse to dissolving Communist – and Congress –
governments in a State like Kerala.) By contrast, Mrs Gandhi took
over a Congress Party in which she faced considerable opposition
and which had to compete seriously with other parties at a national,
and more especially a State, level. It was against this background
that Mrs Gandhi began to 'pervert' the high politics that many have
associated with her father, and to act in a manner that would call
into question the federal compromise mapped out between 1950 and
1956. Under Mrs Gandhi and later Prime Ministers, the mythologies
of governance that seemed to hold India together well enough in
the 1950s began to be unpicked, and a good deal of this unpicking
came from government actors anxious to find new ways of appealing
to an electorate faced with a choice of political representatives.

A GROWING CRISIS OF GOVERNABILITY?

Paul Brass is not the only noted observer of India who has focused
on the deinstitutionalisation of the Congress Party as a key moment

in India's 'growing crisis of governability'. This last phrase is more often associated with Atul Kohli, an Indian scholar resident in the US who has made a number of telling interventions in debates about democracy, discontent and development in modern India (Kohli, 1990a; see also Kohli, 1987, 1988, 1990b). Like Brass, Kohli is a political scientist, and he generally looks for and finds political causes for political failures and successes. In his major study of *Democracy and Discontent: India's Growing Crisis of Governability* (Kohli, 1990a), Kohli sets out to provide chapter and verse on the increasing violence and banality that supposedly characterise politics and civil society in India, and on the wider political climate that has called forth these unhelpful pathologies.

The gist of a well-documented and often subtle argument is as follows. Kohli joins with other commentators in presenting the mid-1960s as a watershed in the history of post-Independence India. In 1962 China invaded India more or less with impunity and two years later a much weakened Nehru was dead. In 1965 a second war with Pakistan over the Kashmir question healed some opening wounds, but the years 1965–67 also saw a devastating failure of the monsoons, famine in Bihar, and the suspension of planning – or Planning (as godhead) – between the end of the Third Five Year Plan period in 1966 and the beginning of a Fourth in 1969. This period also coincided with the emergence of Naxalite (or Maoist) forces in eastern India (Dasgupta, 1975), bloody battles between Communist factions in the streets of Calcutta, and the capture of the Uttar Pradesh Legislative Assembly by Chief Minister Charan Singh and his supporters and coalition partners. Charan Singh championed the cause of rural India – and Jat farmers especially – against a 'colonial' urban India (Byres, 1988). Congress suddenly found itself out of power in India's most populous State; a State that is key to the Hindi heartland that must be won by any political party hoping to rule India as a whole. The Congress Party then added internal insult to external injury by splitting in two in 1969. Mrs Gandhi forged a Congress-R party in opposition to a Congress-O run by ageing party bosses from the South of the country, the so-called Kamaraj Syndicate.

As things turned out the bifurcation of the Congress Party worked to, Mrs Gandhi's advantage in the short run, thanks largely to another Indo-Pak war in 1971 when Mrs Gandhi posed as the liberator of Bangladesh from the vicious imperialism of (West) Pakistan. But in the longer run new pressures were mounting on the Congress-R, or the Congress-I as it is now formally known. Kohli joins with Brass and the Rudolphs (Rudolph and Rudolph, 1987) in painting a picture of a 'new' Congress machine in the 1970s that is increasingly at odds with the expansive aspirations voiced by Nehru, and fostered, more or less confidently, by a Congress Party apparatus that reached down to every small town and to many Panchayats and villages (Figure 4.2). Perhaps fearful of a fresh challenge to her powers from within the Congress-R, Mrs Gandhi now began to display the populistic, narcissistic, and centralising qualities that Salman Rushdie ascribes to the Black Widow who stands at the dark heart of his allegorical account *Midnight's Children* (Rushdie, 1982). All the above-mentioned critics read the Emergency as a sign of the growing weakness of Mrs Gandhi's Congress machine, and not as a sign of its ability to command (or command by consent). It was the inability of Mrs Gandhi to control events in States like Gujarat and Bihar (Wood, 1975) that prompted her to suspend democratic federal rule in India in the dark years of 1975–77 (Selbourne, 1977).

Where Kohli adds colour to this picture is in his accounts of the paradoxes of democracy in a poor economy dominated economically and politically by a weak but highly interventionist state. Kohli is closer to the Rudolphs than to Brass in his account of

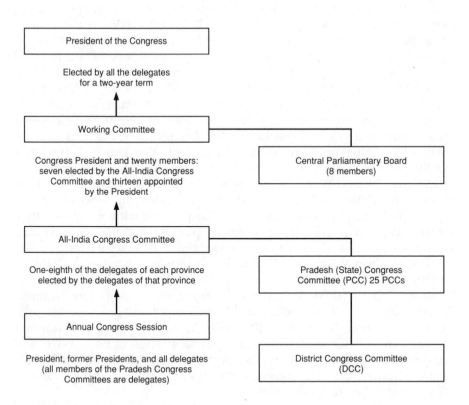

FIGURE 4.2: THE ORGANISATION OF THE INDIAN NATIONAL CONGRESS

a weak-strong state in India through the 1970s and beyond. Precisely as a new postcolonial ideology of egalitarianism took hold in the country as a whole – and with previously disenfranchised groups like the Dalits untouchables/Scheduled Castes in particular – so also did 'new' political parties, movements and leaders emerge to court these voters. Instead of a strong central government dictating to the people in their name and for some supposed common or 'national' good, Central and State governments in the years after Nehru began to respond to the demands of sundry interest groups and political constituencies.

Some of the consequences of this were predictable enough: a fiscal crisis of the state emerged as government spending outstripped the willingness of governments to raise new revenues (Bhagwati, 1993). Some consequences were less predictable, but are well enough documented by political scientists like Kohli, Brass and the Rudolphs. In terms of Centre–State relations, first, a general fiscal crisis of the state was transferred to local and regional levels, as States run by Congress and non-Congress Governments alike made bids for scarce Central funds (as they did also during the ill-fated years of the Janata Government, 1977–80). New possibilities emerged for regional political parties to make their mark *in opposition to New Delhi*, and the growing complexity of the political map of India in the 1970s has since become more complex still. In mid-1994 a minority Congress government is in power in New Delhi and the Congress Party holds sway in Punjab (largely by default, given the reluctance of many Sikhs to vote in the 1992 Lok Sabha (national) and Vidhan Sabha (State Assembly) elections) and in States like Himachel Pradesh and Karnataka. The Union Territory of Delhi is firmly under the control of the Hindu nationalist party, the Bharatiya Janata Party (BJP), which is also the largest party in Rajasthan. Bihar and Uttar Pradesh are under the control of the Janata Dal and the Bahujan Samaj Party–Samajwadi Party combine respectively, two (or three) political parties that like to proclaim their socialist and pro-poor credentials, but which are more obviously the vehicles for rural India and for an unstable coalition of Other Backward Castes/Classes (OBCs), Muslims and Scheduled Castes (Yadav, 1993). In the South, Legislative Assemblies continue to be directed, if not dominated, by regionalist parties like the Telugu Deman in Andhra Pradesh and the Dravida Munnetra Kazagham (DMK) in Tamil Nadu. These parties often survive and rule in tandem with the Congress Party, which remains the only truly national party, but the Congress Party cannot rely on the support of these and other regional parties.

The wider point, of course, at least for Kohli and many political scientists, is that democratic federal governance in India has been weakened over the past fifteen years or more by a political system that lacks strong ideological (or secular ideological) moorings, and which has encouraged voters and politicians alike to see the government of India, at all spatial scales, as a source of income and personal power, and not as a dispassionate and efficient sponsor of justice and development. Banality and corruption are two words that are often mentioned in this rather bleak account of an India threatened by growing anarchy. Even the secessionist struggles of Punjab and Kashmir can be worked into this weak-strong state, command-demand politics thesis (or theses), as we will see in the next part of the chapter. Politics is said to be about style and not substance, and the possible break-up of modern India is being presaged by a descent into a banal politics of personal and group advancement (Patel, 1985), and/or a politics that is more than ever ready to mobilise votes and voters on the basis of the very primordial identities of caste and religious community that the founders of the Republic of India sought to banish from the vocabularies of the state and ultimately, from the mindsets of newly modern Indians (Sudarshan, 1994).

There is much to be said in favour of this account of India's growing crises of governability; deaths from communal and caste-related violence have risen alarmingly from the levels common in the 1950s and mid-1960s (Weiner, 1989), and India demonstrably lacks a single unifying political party of the type that marked the Nehru years. But herein lies another type of paradox, as the reader will be aware. Violence has been growing in most countries since the 1960s, as individuals and groups of people have become less willing to accept the words and deeds of those who would rule in their name. Put another way, an apparent and growing crisis of governability isn't only, or mainly, a sign of the weakness or banality of democracy and democratic politics in a poor country like India; rather the reverse, as Kohli acknowledges. More generally still, the growth of democratic politics in India has extended well beyond the traditional political parties that stand centre-stage in the accounts of Kohli and Brass. If the commentator's eye is allowed to wander away from the Congress Party and its travails – and its deinstitutionalisation was surely always on the cards given its emergence as a broad-based nationalist movement that united otherwise diverse interests under a common banner (Amin, 1984) – then it begins to take in the political activities of groups as diverse as the Chipko movements (Guha, 1989), women campaigning for stronger liquor laws (Kumar, 1993), or farmers' movements like Shetkari Sanghatana and the Bharatiya Kisan Union (both challenging 'urban bias' in the development process: Bentall and Corbridge, 1995; Nadkarni, 1987; Omvedt, 1991). It would also notice the efforts of initially lone battlers against corruption and injustice, like J. P. Narayan in the 1970s and G. R. Khairnar more recently. Significantly, many of these movements and individuals are seeking to mobilise 'authentically Gandhian' conceptions of politics as empowerment through selfless participation, and nation-building by sacrifice and non-violence. All of these movements affirm the vitality of the democracy that has taken root in India since Independence, even if they are employing political tactics and grammars that are sometimes at odds with the normalising and modernising ambitions of the Nehru years and India's major political parties (Corbridge, 1993).

Sudipta Kaviraj is more attuned to this shift in political grammars than many other commentators (see also Kothari, 1994). In a penetrating essay on 'State, society and discourse in India', Kaviraj argues that: 'The independent Indian state followed a programme of modernity which was not sought to be grounded in the political vocabulary of the nation, or at least of its major part. As a result, precisely those ideals – of a modern nationalism, industrial modernity, secular state, democracy and minority rights – came in the long run to appear not as institutions won by a common national movement, but as ideals intelligible to and pursued by the modern elite which inherited power from the British. More than that: subtle and interesting things began to happen to this logic of "modernisation" which have gone unnoticed in the works of its supporters or opponents. Precisely because the state continued to expand, precisely because it went in a frenetic search of alibis to control ever larger areas of social life, it had to find its personnel, especially at lower levels, from groups who did not inhabit the modernist discourse . . . Since major government policies have their final point of implementation very low down in the bureaucracy, they are reinterpreted beyond recognition' (Kaviraj, 1991, p. 91).

This is an arresting observation, although it is possible that Kaviraj pushes it too far. An oil and water analogy for a modernising Indian state and a reluctant (timeless?) civil society is not entirely convincing. But Kaviraj is able to point up the paradoxes of Indian democracy in a way that partly eludes Brass and Kohli. For Kaviraj: 'The paradox . . . is that if Indian politics becomes genuinely democratic in the sense of coming into line with what the majority of ordinary Indians would consider reasonable, it will become less democratic in the sense of conforming to the principles of a secular, democratic state acceptable to the early nationalist elite. What seems to have begun in Indian politics is a conflict over intelligibility, a writing of the political world that is more fundamental than traditional ideological disputes' (ibid., pp. 93–94).

What Kaviraj has in mind here, most obviously, is the rise of the BJP. After a thirty year period when the human body was written out of élite Indian politics in favour of abstractions like development, employment growth, social justice and the like, some

BJP politicians are now anxious to ally a politics of economic liberalization to a body politics that draws on one or more versions of Hinduism. In some cases, this body politics makes use of the Hindu concept of *brahmacharya* (celibacy), such that a sense of national weakness and openness to foreign idols and icons is traced back to a loss of self-control over the (male) body and its constitutive physical substances. In a startling recent essay in the *Journal of Asian Studies*, Joseph Alter has elaborated on the connections between celibacy, sexuality and nationalism in north India (Alter, 1994). Alter concludes his essay with a stirring injunction from Shivananda, an ideologue whose writings are often called upon by BJP politicians: 'Brothers! Liberate our dear Mother India from poverty and resurrect her true power and glory! India's freedom is dependent on each and everyone's freedom, and everyone's freedom is achieved once the yoke of poisonous slavery has been caste [*sic*] off. We, like our forefathers, must achieve this end by controlling our semen' (Shivananda, 1984; quoted in Alter, 1994, p. 156).

But the politics of the body and the rise of the BJP are not the only objects of Kaviraj's gaze. When Kaviraj writes of a new threat to the 'elite ideals' of secular democracy and minority rights, he clearly also has in mind a threat to the federal structures and territorial integrity of modern India. His close attention to the fragmenting rhetorics of postcolonial (and post-Nehruvian) politics in India points up a possible new challenge to the unity of India made in the name of the very diversity that once gave that unity its precarious logic. To this extent, at least, if not in many others, the work of Kaviraj reminds one of V. S. Naipaul's most recent book on South Asian politics and culture, *India: a Million Mutinies Now* (Naipaul, 1991).

Naipaul is not a popular figure with most Indian politicians and intellectuals, and his books on India from the 1960s and 1970s – *An Area of Darkness* (Naipaul, 1964) and *India: a Wounded Civilization* (Naipaul, 1977) – have been roundly, if often carelessly, condemned as unsympathetic and ethnocentric. But Naipaul has always been an acute observer of 'Other' societies, and *Mutinies* is by no means the glib and grim book that its title suggests. If I understand him correctly, Naipaul too, rather like Kaviraj, is sensitive to the Janus-faced nature of democracy and discontent in a country that has survived almost fifty years of nation-building and which is now described by the World Bank as an industrial economy in transition (World Bank, 1989). Towards the end of his book Naipaul admits that: 'What I hadn't understood in 1962, or had taken too much for granted, was the extent to which the country had been remade; and even the extent to which India had been restored to itself, after its own equivalent of the Dark Ages – after the Muslim invasions and the detailed, repeated vandalising of the North, the shifting empires, the wars, the 18th-century anarchy' (Naipaul, 1991, p. 517). More directly, Naipaul concludes that while 'Independence was worked for by people more or less at the top; the freedom it brought has worked its way down. People everywhere have ideas now of who they are and what they owe themselves. . . . The liberation of spirit that has come to India could not come as release alone. In India, with its layer below layer of distress and cruelty, it had to come as disturbance. It had to come as rage and revolt. India was [is] now a country of a million little mutinities' (Naipaul, 1991, p. 517).

Taken out of context these last three sentences might confirm a critic of Naipaul in his or her worst estimations of the novelist's too easy powers of declamation. But while Naipaul is wary of mutinities supported 'by twenty kinds of group excess' (ibid.), including sectarian excess, religious excess and regional excess, he also notes that there is 'in India now what didn't exist 200 years before: a central will, a central intellect, a national idea' (ibid., p. 518). 'The Indian Union', Naipaul concludes, is 'greater than the sum of its parts; and many of these movements of excess [have] strengthened the Indian state, defining it as the source of law and civility and reasonableness. The Indian Union [has given] people a second chance, calling them back from the excesses with which, in another century, or in other circumstances (as neighbouring countries showed) they might have had to live: the destructive chauvinism of the Shiv Sena [Hindu neo-fascists in Bombay], the tyranny of many kinds of religious fundamentalism (people always ready in India to let religion carry the burden of their pain), the film-star corruption and racial politics of the South, the pious Marxist idleness and nullity of Bengal' (ibid.).

There is much to value in this perspective, even if Naipaul sometimes weakens his thesis by the literary conceit of exaggeration. Naipaul, like Kaviraj and Vanaik (to whom I will come shortly), has a sense of the countervailing forces that pull India back from the apparently enveloping forces of Hindu nationalism, lawlessness and possible disintegration. Some political scientists have always been keen to warn that India is about to break up. In 1960, Selig Harrison suggested that the genie of lingustic and regional chauvinism had been unleashed by the States Reorganisation Commission and would pave the way for 'a future of anarchy and fascism, wherein totalitarian small nationalities would rise up to torture the body politic' (Harrison, 1960, p. 3). In the 1960s and 1970s India would face its 'most dangerous decades' (the subtitle of Harrison's book). Paul Brass, too, finds it hard to escape from a linear narrative of descent (and dissent) in his accounts of the politics of India since Independence. In the Preface to the second edition of his book in the New Cambridge History of India series, Brass speaks of an 'old political order . . . in decay' (Brass, 1994, p. xiii), of parties that 'lack effective or popular leadership, compelling ideals, and local organization' (ibid.), and of 'the BJP, the political party spokesman for militant Hindu nationalism, [appearing] to be ascendant, heading relentlessly toward the achievement of its goal of attaining national power' (ibid., p. xiv). For Brass, in 1993–94, it is the tearing down of the mosque at Ayodhya, Uttar Pradesh, in December 1992 by Hindu militants that *defines* the trajectory of modern India. Thus defined, India is more or less bound to self-destruct, more or less bound to tear apart at the seams, possibly in Punjab or Kashmir. But this is surely not the whole story. What is just as remarkable as Ayodhya and the (mainly urban) communal rioting that immediately ensued is the counter-movement in favour of secularism that followed not much later, and that was noisily promoted by the daily press, the major weekly or fortnightly magazines, many student bodies, and a majority of politicians and business people. For whatever reasons, the founding myths of democracy and secularism have struck deeper into India than Brass, or even Kaviraj, seems prepared to acknowledge.

But what of the myth of federation? In my view, the political commentator who has most advanced our understanding of the complex and paradoxical interweavings of India's four mythologies of governance is the Marxist journalist, Achin Vanaik. Chapters 3 and 4 of Vanaik's book *The Painful Transition: Bourgeois Democracy in India* (Vanaik, 1990) offer a subtle and largely convincing account of communalism, Hindu nationalism, nationalism and Centre–State relations, notwithstanding the unhelpful doctrinal Marxism that bookends each chapter. Vanaik shares with Kaviraj and Naipaul a deep regard for the nuances of modern Indian politics and for the contradictions of Hindu nationalism. Writing of the latter, he notes that: 'Nationalism as a political movement, national identity, and nationalist ideology did not develop in the wake of religious decline [in India]. A Hindu religious "renaissance" was central to the emergence of all three' (Vanaik, 1990, pp. 140–41). This alone puts the history of nationalism in India at odds with (accounts of) the history of nationalism in Europe. Nationalism in India has never called to mind an 'imagined community' that substitutes for the imagined communities of religion, as was the case in parts of north-west Europe (Anderson, 1983). By the same token, Vanaik suggests that Hindu nationalism in modern India is less threatening than some would maintain, and should not be described as Hindu fundamentalism (see also Graham, 1990). Like Naipaul and Kaviraj, Vanaik contends that the diverse languages of religion and community/caste have continued to dominate at the level of civil society in India since Independence, notwithstanding the early efforts of the state to promote secularism in their place. It follows, perhaps, that the 'emergence' of the BJP is neither exceptional nor as alarming as its rhetorics and recent election results might suggest. What really matters is the politics of the BJP once it is in power; whether or not it will impose a 'Hindu' education system in schools, or attack the *sharia* laws that govern some aspects of Muslim family life. It is one thing to mobilise votes on the basis of community rivalries and communal divisions, and another to prosecute policies that straightforwardly seek to put into practice the rhetorical claims and promises made in election campaigns. It is also important to understand that the BJP is an uneasy coalition of what Varshney calls centre-right and right-wing politicians (Varshney, 1993), with the former group subscribing to a more inclusive view of Hinduism than the latter (which includes the RSS and the Vishwa Hindu Parishad (VHP)).

Vanaik recognises that this is a thin line to tread and as a Marxist himself he is not well disposed to the 'reactionary' claims of the BJP, let alone those of Hindu assimilationists who maintain that: 'A Hindu means a person who regards this land . . . from the Indus to the Seas as his fatherland (*pitribhumi*) as well as his holy land (*punyabhumi*)' Savarkar, 1989, quoted in Varshney, 1993, p. 31). But the argument Vanaik wants to make is a serious one. Vanaik contends that: 'Classical Hinduism spanned the spectrum from atheism to the crudest forms of animism. Such a tradition can be conducive to the formation of a secular state, but it is far less able than Christianity to accommodate itself to the secularization of society itself' (ibid., p. 148). More importantly, he maintains that: 'Hindu nationalism is the outcome of a process wherein this classical legacy has undergone historicization, territorialization and dogmatization. As long as the Indian secular state does not seek to seriously challenge the expansion of religious influence outside its domain, the two are capable of comfortable coexistence. Though civil society in India is weak, its institutions are expanding and developing. It is an area of contestation in which secular forces are most definitely not backed by the state. The struggle lies between an expanding and self-confident Hinduism as well as an orthodox Islam engaged in a powerful operation of retrenchment within an inward-looking Muslim community, on the one hand, and, on the other, the secular mechanisms of expanding market relations, modern technology and science, corporate and non-corporate bureaucratization, urbanization, and class divisions and struggles in industry and agriculture' (ibid., pp. 148–49).

This is very well put and it is a prognosis for India that more exactly fits the events of the first half of the 1990s than the rather apocalyptic visions of Brass and Kohli. Vanaik has a proper sense of the fluidity of Hinduism and the unwillingness of many of its followers to be tied down to 'fundamentals'. The cult of Rama, the seventh incarnation of Vishnu, might be strong in parts of north India, but it does not play well in the South (where ethnic anti-Brahmin movements have long been strong: Manor, 1992), or even in some areas of Rajasthan where Rama is sometimes accounted a buffoon rather than a hero. So also with the BJP: despite its best efforts, the BJP has yet to make much headway beyond the Hindi heartland, and even there it is painted by opposing politicians as a party of and for high-caste Indians, and of the town rather than the countryside (Malik and Singh, 1992). The rise to power of the BJP does give cause for concern, but it would be unwise to assume that its ascent is relentless or preordained. The Hindu constituency that the BJP seeks to mobilise is not undivided, and the party has suffered electoral setbacks in Uttar Pradesh post-Ayodhya (see also van der Veer, 1994).

This insight is further developed in Vanaik's remarks on market relations and telecommunications, each of which bear directly on the federal structures and futures of the Republic of India. Once again, Vanaik's approach to Centre–State relations is dialectical in the best sense. Just as communalism is presented as a pre-modern *and* modern phenomenon which stands in relation to (and in competition with) the secularising forces of the Indian state, so also is the increasing decentralisation of some aspects of Indian life read as '[implying] new forms of integration and reorganisation of the structures of power within India's bourgeois democratic set-up' (Vanaik, 1990, p. 128). Vanaik argues that: 'Just as greater regional-ism can be the consequence of greater capitalist economic integration of India, greater overall integration can be the result of greater decentralisation of powers, all of which reinforces that special paradox of political instability within a larger bourgeois democratic durability' (ibid.).

It is not difficult to put flesh on the bones of this argument. The great virtue of Vanaik's approach is that it seeks to understand the changing federal structures of India in relation to the changing mythologies of governance in India more widely, *and* in relation to the quickening, but uneven, economic transformation of the country. This last point is underdeveloped by many other commentators. Most challenges to the federal map, or structure, of India are not driven wholly by economic forces or demands, but it is important to take these imperatives seriously. Vanaik suggests that the cultural and lingusitic diversity of India offers a set of political opportunities for regional and national bourgeoisies seeking power over given territories and a greater share of the public purse.

There is a lot to be said for this contention. The movement to create a separate Jharkhand State in southern Bihar and contiguous Districts of West Bengal, Orissa and Madhya Pradesh highlights the continuing vitality of ethnic markers in regionalist politics – to the extent that the Jharkhand could ever be a 'tribal'-dominated State: see Corbridge, 1988 – but in many more cases, 'centre–state conflicts and inter-state tensions are now primarily focused on economic and political not cultural issues' (Vanaik, 1990, p. 124). In regions as diverse as Bombay (with Shiv Sena) and Assam, so called 'sons of the soil' movements have emerged to seek to protect the employment prospects of 'local people' (or ethnic groups) against the claims of a swelling tide of migrant labourers (see also Breman, 1985). In the Punjab, too, not a little of the distrust of New Delhi has been prompted by local concerns that the food procurement policies of Central Government are working against the economic interests of farmers in India's bread-bowl. Meanwhile, in terms of day to day politics, the rise to power of regionalist parties like the Telugu Desam in Andhra Pradesh speaks in part to the possibility of economic and political resources being captured by and for members of local proprietary groups or 'regional bourgeoisies'. Just as the BJP draws its support mainly from high-caste north Indians, and the Janata Dal from the OBCs, so many sub-nationalist movements or parties are powered by students seeking privileged access to state education facilities, or members of local rural and urban petty bourgeois groupings wanting well-paid state employment (see also Kochanek, 1987). Vanaik reminds us that: 'At the end of 1977, state governments employed 5.2 million people compared to 3.1 million employed by the central government and 6.2 million by large-scale industry. State and local employment accounted for 50 per cent of total public employment in India and the rate of growth of employment was fastest in the state government sector. State-based linguistic exclusivity obviously favours the middle-classes in each state' (Vanaik, 1990, p. 124).

The fact that Centre–State tensions are often sharper outside the Hindi heartland confirms that the federal strains now affecting India cannot be reduced to economic factors alone (Hardgrave, 1983), but Vanaik would accept this with caution. The conclusion that we might reasonably develop here is that fears for India's territorial integrity can be overdone. In most cases, sub-national movements in India are pressing Central Government for a greater share of public power and the public purse, and deals can often be struck to accede to some of these demands. To this extent, Nehruvian models of Centre–State bargaining have not been abandoned (Dua, 1985). More generally, the rise of regional parties in parts of India can again be read as proof of the vitality of India's democracy; it is not just (or even) a harbinger of the imminent demise of an 'artificial empire' or 'nation-state'.

The politics of regionalism in India cuts two ways at once. On most occasions the emergence of 'regionalist' politics serves as a safety-valve in a country where the forces of centralisation are otherwise very strong. This safety-valve has its own safety-valve in that most regionalist movements are not undivided, but are championing the claims of particular ethnic, caste and class groupings whose loyalties can sometimes be affirmed or weakened by central government actions that play upon these multiple social and political identities. That said, an emboldened BJP might conceivably pose a threat in the future, if it is not checked by the more liberal instincts of the middle-class that lends it support, and more tangible threats have come recently from secessionist movements in Punjab and Kashmir (Akbar, 1985). In Punjab and Kashmir a set of economic grievances stoked up by the uneven and state-sponsored capitalist development of the country as a whole have reinforced a more elemental crisis of identity and belonging that some would attribute straightforwardly to communal tensions and religious differences. In the fourth part of this chapter, I want to suggest that even in these two regions a presumed threat to the integrity of India can be overstated. Proponents of a Balkanization thesis need to have greater regard to the coercive capabilities of the Indian state (Mathur, 1992), and to the integrative forces that bind even the Punjab (if not Kashmir) into the fabric of a nation-state that has remained more or less unchanged, in territorial terms, since its founding at midnight on 15 August 1947.

FEDERAL CHALLENGES: PUNJAB AND KASHMIR

The territorial integrity of India has been strongly challenged since 1980 in Punjab and Kashmir, as well as in north-eastern frontier States like Nagaland and Mizoram. In all these regions or States there have been well-articulated demands for national independence that have enjoyed a measure of local support, and have been prosecuted by force of arms by some political activists. New Delhi has been faced here by secessionist movements which cannot easily be dealt with by means of the pork-barrel politics that it often resorts to as a means of dealing with oppositional State governments, or demands for the formation of new States, Union Territories or Hill Councils within the federal Republic of India. In the north-west and north-east of India at least some of the unifying forces that can be found elsewhere in the Republic are absent or undeveloped. Kashmir and the north-eastern States are remote from the emerging boom-towns of central and western India (Bangalore–Bombay–Ahmedabad–Delhi), and have legitimate reasons to complain about a lack of inward investment by New Delhi (Lamb, 1991). In these two regions, too, as in Punjab, the majority population is not Hindu, and the rise of Hindu nationalism is understandably not welcomed by majority

119

populations which are by turns Islamic, Christian and Sikh. There are also good reasons for believing that the 'insurgencies' apparent in all these regions have been funded in part by hostile foreign governments to the west and east of India.

But none of these reasons alone, or in combination, suggest that India is bound to break up. There are countervailing forces at work. In the north-east these forces are usually coercive, but they are effective none the less (Singh, 1987). Movements for a separate Naga country have been ruthlessly repressed by Indian 'police operations' since the 1950s. Given the strength of the Indian army in this part of India, and the region's geopolitical significance to New Delhi, it is inconceivable that a population numbering less than two million can pose a serious threat to the unity of India. But what of Punjab and Kashmir? Once again, there are centrifugal as well as centripetal forces at work, and it is misleading to assume that these two cases or regions pose an equal or similar threat to the current boundaries of India.

The Punjab crisis, and the associated demand for a separate State of Khalistan, has a long and complicated history which cannot be given here (see Jeffery, 1994). The relative quiescence of the Punjab in the 1990s, as compared to the mid–late 1980s, cannot only be attributed to the coercive capabilities of an occupying Indian army. The decline of the Punjab crisis as a *secessionist crisis* lends credence to the writings of those who have portrayed the Khalistan movement as a front for the economic demands of Jat Sikh farmers (Bhushan, 1984), as a movement captured and driven forward by students and disenchanted youths (Grewal, 1990), and as a monstrous by-product of an extraordinary period of mismanagement of Centre–State relations by Mrs Gandhi (Brass, 1988; Wallace, 1990). The economic demands of Jat farmers became particularly acute when the first wave of the Green revolution in the Punjab stalled in the mid–late 1970s. Farmers who had planted their fields with high-yielding varieties of wheat needed assured supplies of irrigation water to support the use of chemical fertilisers; they also desired some control over the industries that provided inputs to a newly mechanised farming system, and over the prices set for their grains by the Food Corporation of India. A pervasive feeling that Punjab was serving as an 'internal colony' for the rest of India was heightened by changes in army recruitment policies in the 1970s, which served to reduce the number of jobs in the forces for the sons of Sikh families. Sikhs in the Punjab were also alienated from New Delhi by the latter's refusal to transfer Chandigarh to the State, and by New Delhi's apparent willingness to drain water from the Punjab for use in Haryana, Rajastahan and Delhi itself.

Paul Brass is not alone in arguing that the building crisis in Punjab in the early 1980s could have been bought off by a quick and fair settlement of these grievances (such as Nehru might have fostered). Negotiations could have been entered into with the moderates running the Akali Dal, the main organisation representing the interests of Sikhs in the Punjab. In the early 1980s, however, Mrs Gandhi accepted the most inflamed rhetoric of the Akali Dal at face value, and sought to combat the Akalis by promoting a still more extreme proponent of Sikh nationalism, Sant Jarnail Singh Bhindranwale. In this manner, the Government of India fought 'fire' with fire, in the process stoking up a politics dominated by religious appeals for a holy land instead of reaffirming Central Government's attachment to the myth of secularism.

We know now that this approach to the Punjab crisis was suicidal, both for the region as a whole and for Mrs Gandhi herself. When it became known that Bhindranwale and his supporters in Amritsar were engaged in the 'assassinations of innocent Hindus in the Punjab' (Brass, 1994, p. 195), Mrs Gandhi was compelled to turn on the monster she had helped to fashion and finance. In June 1984 Mrs Gandhi gave permission for an army assault on the Golden Temple in Amritsar. Operation Bluestar was a success of sorts, militarily, but it fanned the flames of the Khalistan movement in an entirely predictable manner and led, on 31 October 1984, to the assassination of Mrs Gandhi in New Delhi by two Sikh bodyguards. Several days of organised anti-Sikh rioting followed (Tambiah, 1990), before a brief period when Rajiv Gandhi and moderate elements in the Akali Dal tried to restore peace in the Punjab by means of a negotiated settlement. In May 1987 Punjab was again placed under President's rule and it has been heavily policed by government forces since that time. But peace of a sort has also returned to the region because most Punjabis do not share the secessionist sentiments of the militant pro-Khalistanis. The prosaic truth about the region is that economic prosperity is at least as important to most Sikhs as a possible Sikh State. Sikhism as an ideology or faith has never made much of a territorial conception of identity (Pettigrew, 1984), and most Sikh farmers know their future prosperity depends on selling grain to the rest of India, or remittance of monies from cities like Delhi where they are an affluent minority group. What remains of the Khalistan movement is an armed rump, albeit one capable of creating problems for the security forces from time to time. Significantly, some of the main supporters and financiers of the Khalistan movement are reputed to live or work abroad, in cities like London, Toronto and Vancouver. Although most Sikh families in the Punjab are deeply suspicious of New Delhi, their daily lives are so interwoven with 'Hindu' north India (though trade, travel and telecommunications) that the possibility of leaving India is not often entertained, and in any case would not be permitted by the Government of India. It is also worth noting that many Hindus in the Punjab, as elsewhere, draw few distinctions between themselves and Sikh families, even if the level of inter-marriage between the two communities has dropped markedly since the early 1980s.

All of which leaves Kashmir. The crisis in Kashmir is undoubtedly a more serious crisis for the Republic of India than the crises in Punjab or Nagaland. This is so for four reasons: (1) the Kashmir valley is overwhelmingly Muslim and predominantly Kashmiri speaking; (2) the movement for an independent Kashmir State is openly supported by Pakistan; (3) the people of Kashmir have not been given an opportunity to vote on the territorial affiliation of Kashmir – as part of India, as part of Pakistan, or as an independent country – despite promises to this effect by several Prime Ministers of India; and (4) Kashmir has not been integrated into the fabric of modern India in the same way as most of northern and peninsular India, or even Punjab and Jammu.

Set against this, it bears repeating that there is nothing inevitable or pre-ordained about the present struggle in the Kashmir Valley. It is still not clear how Kashmiris will vote if they are offered the choice of leaving India, and much of the 'credit' for stoking up the grievances of Kashmiris must be laid at the door of successive Indian governments which have tried to destabilise only moderately antipathetic State Governments in Srinagar, and have failed to provide the region with funds to diversify its economic base. Whether a Government of India acting in good faith can now resolve the Kashmir crisis is a moot point; the politicisation of Kashmiri politics by Hindu and Islamic militants makes this unlikely. But it is even more unlikely that Kashmir will be allowed to leave the federal Republic of India. The Kashmir question is bound up with the geopolitical strategies of India and its tense relations with Pakistan. It is also bound up with one of India's founding myths: the myth of unity in diversity through federation. Were Kashmir to leave India this myth would be brought into question and India's borders would be tested elsewhere. It is for this reason, as much as any other, that the Indian army will not allow this to happen. Kashmir will be kept as part of India by force, and the myth of democracy, in this part of India at least, will be subordinated to the myth of federalism.

CONCLUSIONS

If the broad argument of this chapter is correct, India is not about to face a period of territorial fragmentation akin to that faced by Yugoslavia or the ex-Soviet Union; Salman Rushdie's 'guess' about the continuation of India's 'old functioning anarchy' is surely right in this respect. The myth of federalism in India may no longer be phrased in the accommodationist tones of Nehru and a hegemonic Congress Party, but it remains a mythology that is strongly adhered to and prosecuted by the Indian state and the pan-Indian media. The myth of a federal India is also continually reinforced from without, with reference to Pakistan, and is sufficiently flexible within to accommodate many of the demands made on any prevailing map of federation. This process of accommodation in turn is backed up by the government of India's near-monopoly of the means of violence within the Republic, by the enduring nature of India's myth of democracy (even when it is suspended in 'crisis-affected' areas), and by the enduring, if eroding, appeal of the myth of secularism. A new India is also being welded together by the forces of economic liberaliastion. A pan-Indian middle-class of some two hundred million people is already in evidence, and while this class lends support to various regionalist or sub-nationalist movements, it is also being encouraged to look 'outwards' by new export opportunities and foreign competitors. Significant amounts of money are also being returned to India by a large population of non-resident Indians working in countries like the UK and Canada, and the Gulf States. Rather unexpectedly, the myth of socialism has been abandoned in the India of the 1990s, and has been ditched without significant challenge from the major political parties or oppositional social movements. This fact alone confirms that a new sense of Indian identity, and of India's future, is emerging, even if one likely effect of economic liberalization is a widening of the regional income inequalities that already divide west and east India.

None of this means that India's federal structures are efficient or uncontested. This chapter has highlighted many challenges to the federal arrangements that currently obtain in India, and it is not unlikely that the Government of India will have to accommodate the more pressing claims of the Jharkhand movement in east India, or even the demand for a State of Uttarakhand in the north-west corner of Uttar Pradesh. Whether this process of accommodation will continue to be effected on a case by case basis remains to be seen. (Goa is the latest addition to India's list of 'full' States: Rubinoff, 1992). In theory, all of the major political parties in India are now committed to the idea of a second 'States Reorganization Commission', and to the creation of up to ten new federal units (see also Khan, 1992). In the long run, this may serve India very well. The population of Uttar Pradesh alone in 1991 had reached close to 150 million, and it is difficult to see how a State of this size can be effectively represented and governed by one Legislative Assembly. Politically, too, New Delhi might find it convenient to challenge strong regional governments by assenting to demands for the break-up of existing States (as in Bihar, where a Janata Dal government is being pressed by Jharkhandi activists). For good reasons and 'bad', therefore, there are reasons to suppose that the internal map of India will be redrawn before too long, even as its external boundaries will be jealously policed against possible challenges. The best hope for India is not just that the old functioning anarchy survives, but that it functions rather better than it has done since the mid-1960s.

REFERENCES

Akbar, M. (1985) *India: The Siege Within* (Harmondsworth: Penguin)

Alter, J. (1994) Celibacy, sexuality, and the transformation of gender into nationalism in north India *Journal of Asian Studies* 53: 45–66

Amin, S. (1984) 'Gandhi as Mahatma: Gorakhpur Disrict, Eastern UP, 1921–2'. In R. Guha (ed.) *Subaltern Studies III* (Delhi: Oxford University Press), pp. 1–61

Anderson, B. (1983) *Imagined Communities: Reflections on the Origin and Spread of Nationalism* (London: Verso)

Barthes, R. (1972) *Mythologies* (London: Jonathan Cape)

Bentall J. and Corbridge S. (1995) Urban–rural relations, demand politics and the 'new agrarianism' in north-west India: The Bharatiya Kisan Union *Transactions of the Institute of British Geographers* 20

Bhagwati, J. (1993) *India in Transition: Freeing the Economy* (Oxford: Clarendon)

Bhushan, B. (1984) The origins of the rebellion in Punjab *Capital and Class* 24: 5–13

Brass, P. (1988) The Punjab crisis and the unity of India. In A. Kohli (ed.) *India's Democracy: An Analysis of Changing State–Society Relations* (Princeton: Princeton University Press), pp. 169–213

Brass, P. (1994) *The Politics of India Since Independence* (2nd Edn) (Cambridge: Cambridge University Press)

Breman, J. (1985) *Of Peasants, Migrants and Paupers: Rural Labour Circulation and Capitalist Production in West India* (Delhi: Oxford University Press)

Byres, T. (1988) Charan Singh, 1902–1987: an assessment *Journal of Peasant Studies* 15: 139–189

Chatterjee. P. (1994) Development planning and the Indian state. In T. Byres (ed.) *The State and Development Planning in India* (Delhi: Oxford University Press), pp. 51–72

Corbridge, S. (1988) The ideology of tribal economy and society: politics in the Jharkhand, 1950–1980 *Modern Asian Studies* 22: 1–41

Corbridge, S. (1993) Colonialism, post-colonialism and the political geography of the Third World. In P. Taylor (ed.) *Political Geography of the Twentieth Century: a Global Analysis* (London: Belhaven), pp. 171–205

Dandekar, V. (1987) Unitary elements in a federal constitution *Economic and Political Weekly* XXII: 1865–70

Dasgupta, B. (1975) *The Naxalite Movement* (Delhi: Allied)

Dua, B. (1985) Federalism or patrimonialism: the making and unmaking of Chief Ministers in India *Asian Survey* XXV: 793–804

Graham, B. (1990) *Hindu Nationalism and Indian Politics: the Origins and Development of the Bharatiya Jana Sangh* (Cambridge: Cambridge University Press)

Grewal, J. (1990) *The Sikhs of Punjab* (Cambridge: Cambridge University Press)

Guha, R. (1989) *The Unquiet Woods: Ecological Change and Peasant Resistance in the Himalaya* (Delhi: Oxford University Press)

Hardgrave, R. (1983) The North-east, the Punjab, and the regionalisation of Indian politics *Asian Survey* 23: 1171–81

Harrison, S. (1960) *India: the Most Dangerous Decades* (Princeton: Princeton University Press)

Jeffery, R. (1994) *What's Happening to India?* (2nd Edn) (London: Macmillan)

Kaviraj, S. (1991) On state, society and discourse in India. In J. Manor (ed.) *Rethinking Third World Politics* (Harlow: Longman), pp. 72–99

Khan, R. (1992) *Federal India: a Design For Change* (Delhi: Vikas)

Kochanek, S. (1968) *The Congress Party of India: the Dynamics of One-Party Democracy* (Princeton: Princeton University Press)

Kochanek, S. (1987) Briefcase politics in India: the Congress Party and the business elite *Asian Survey* XXVII: 1278–1301

Kohli, A. (1987) *The State and Poverty in India: the Politics of Reform* (Cambridge: Cambridge University Press)

Kohli, A. (ed.) (1988) *India's Democracy: an Analysis of Changing State-Society Relations* (Princeton: Princeton University Press)

Kohli, A. (1990a) *Democracy and Discontent: India's Growing Crisis of Governability* (Cambridge: Cambridge University Press)

Kohli, A. (1990b) 'From majority to minority rule: making sense of the 'new' Indian politics. In M. Bouton and P. Oldenburg (eds) *India Briefing, 1990* (Boulder: Westview), pp. 1–23

Kothari, R. (1994) Fragments of a discourse: towards conceptualization. In T. Sathyamurthy (ed.) *State and Nation in the Context of Social Change, Volume 1* (Delhi: Oxford University Press), pp. 38–54

Kumar, R. (1993) *A History of Doing: an Illustrated Account of Movements for Women's Rights and Feminism in India, 1800–1990* (London: Verso)

Lamb, A. (1991) *Kashmir: a Disputed Legacy, 1841–1990* (Hertingfordbury: Roxford Books)

Malik, Y. and Singh, V. (1992) Bharatiya Janata Party: an alternative to the Congress (I)? *Asian Survey* XXXII: 318–36

Manor, J. (1992) BJP in South India: 1991 General Election *Economic and Political Weekly* XXVII: 1268–77

Mathur, K. (1992) The state and the use of coercive power in India *Asian Survey* XXXII: 337–49

Nadkarni, M. (1987) *Farmers Movements in India* (Delhi: Allied)

Naipaul, V. S. (1964) *An Area of Darkness* (London: Andre Deutsch)

Naipaul, V. S. (1977) *India: a Wounded Civilization* (London: Andre Deutsch)

Naipaul, V. S. (1991) *India: a Million Mutinies Now* (London: Minerva)

Nandy, A. (1980) *At the Edge of Psychology: Essays in Politics and Culture* (Delhi: Oxford University Press)

Nandy, A. (1988) The politics of secularism and the recovery of religious tolerance *Alternatives* XIII: 177–94

Omvedt, G. (1991) Shetkari Sanghatana's new direction *Economic and Political Weekly* XXVI: 2287–90

Patel, S. (1985) The debacle of populist politics *Economic and Political Weekly* XX: 681–2

Pettigrew, J. (1984) Take not arms against thy sovereign *South Asia Research* IX: 102–23

Rubinoff, A. (1992) Goa's attainment of statehood *Asian Survey* XXXII: 471–87

Rudolph, L. and Rudolph, S. H. (1987) *In Pursuit of Lakshmi: the Political Economy of the Indian State* (Chicago: Chicago University Press)

Rushdie, S. (1982) *Midnight's Children* (London: Jonathan Cape)

Rushdie, S. (1991) *Imaginary Homelands* (London: Granta)

Savarkar, V. (1989) *Hindutva* (Bombay: Veer Savarkar Prakashan)

Selbourne, D. (1977) *An Eye to India* (Harmondsworth: Penguin)

Shivananda, S. (1984) *Brahmacharya Hi Jiwan Hai* (Allahabad: Adhunik Prakashan Graha)

Singh, B. (1987) *The Problem of Change: A Study of North-East India* (Delhi: Vikas)

Sudarshan, R. (1994) The political consequences of constitutional discourse. In T. Sathyamurthy (ed.) *State and Nation in the Context of Social Change, Volume 1* (Delhi: Oxford University Press), pp. 55–86

Tambiah, S. (1990) Reflections on communal violence in South Asia *Journal of Asian Studies* 49: 741–60

Vanaik, A. (1990) *The Painful Transition: Bourgeois Democracy in India* (London: Verso)

van der Veer, P. (1994) *Religious Nationalism: Hindus and Muslims in India* (Cambridge: Cambridge University Press)

Varshney, A. (1993) Battling the past, forging a future? Ayodhya and beyond. In P. Oldenburg (ed.) *India Briefing, 1993* (Boulder: Westview), pp. 9–42

Wallace, P. (1990) Religious and ethnic politics: political mobilization in Punjab. In F. Frankel and M. Rao (eds) *Dominance and State Power in India, Volume II* (Delhi: Oxford University Press), pp. 416–81

Weiner, M. (1989) *The Indian Paradox: Essays in Indian Politics* (New Delhi: Sage)

Wood, J. (1975) Extra-parliamentary opposition in India: an analysis of populist agitations in Gujarat and Bihar *Pacific Affairs* XLVIII: 313–34

World Bank (1989) *India: an Industrializing Economy in Transition* (Washington DC: World Bank)

Yadav, Y. (1993) Political change in north India: interpreting Assembly election results *Economic and Political Weekly* XXVIII: 2767–72

Ethnicity and Territorial Politics in Nigeria

Martin Dent

Nigeria, as the only well-established federation in Africa, has attracted an abundance of academic study. Its historical development has been traced in many works, such as Mackintosh (1966) and Panter-Brick (1978). The late K. Ezera (1961) wrote a classic study of colonial and independence developments and J. S. Coleman (1958) is the acknowledged authority for the pre-independence period. E. O. Awa (1964) also produced an authoritative study of the operation of Nigerian Federal Government, while legal aspects of Nigeria's federal balance have been exhaustively analysed by B. O. Nwabueze (1983). The financial aspects have been dealt with by Adedeji (1969) and more recently by S. E. Oyovbaire (1985). It is the purpose of this chapter to develop at a deeper level the themes introduced in an earlier work by this author (Dent, 1989) in order to show the unique characteristics of Nigerian federalism and the place it occupies in the global pattern of federal systems. This chapter takes up four themes: the problem of partitioning; the effects of the doctrine of federal character; cooperative federalism; and the attempt to create an autonomous third arm of federalism in elected local government councils and directly elected local government chairmen.

All federal political systems involve some element of autonomous decision-making at a state or other subordinate level, combined with central decision-making by the national or federal government. In the ten or so political systems which are generally classified as federal both in their formal constitution and in their practice, there is a mechanism for the division of power usually through exclusive or concurrent lists of subjects together with a concept of residual power (see chapter one). This similarity in basic structure co-exists with wide difference of operation arising from the different political cultures and regional diversity of the states concerned. Where, as in the case of Nigeria, ethnicity is of prime importance, the dynamics of the political system involve dispute and adjustment over territory between different groups.

The Nigerian federal system exhibits some features common to all such divisions of power between the centre and the periphery. But it also has very important elements which are peculiar to Nigeria. The most important of these are the tendency towards the partitioning sub-division of units and the attempt to impose fair shares upon the states in the allocation of jobs and benefits through a doctrine of federal character. From this practice there springs the attempt to create a Nigeria of states of equal population size.

HISTORICAL BACKGROUND

The first element that strikes any observer of Nigerian political history and present-day political demands is a vigorous and continuous campaign for sub-division of units. Nigeria could almost be compared to a biological cell which sub-divides and sub-divides again, creating more and more replicas of itself. Nigeria was first formed in 1914 by the amalgamation of North and South. The rivalry between the British administrations in these two regions was so great that a humorist remarked that it was only the presence of the Nigerians that prevented the British in the North from going to war with those in the South. This polarity of ethos was in time absorbed by Nigerians themselves and still constitutes the greatest single division in the nation.

Twenty-five years later the Southern Region was divided into the Eastern and the Western Regions. During the 1950s Nigeria's political awakening and movement towards independence was characterised by great regional rivalry and by dispute as to whether or not the three large regions should be sub-divided into a greater number of states. Rejecting the strongly expressed wishes of Nigeria's minorities in North, West and East to have their own separate regions, the British colonial government left Nigeria at independence in 1960 with a federation of three units. Today Nigeria is sub-divided into thirty states (Table 5.1). If this tenfold increase were repeated in the next thirty-three years Nigeria would have far more units than any other federation in the world. General Babangida, when announcing the latest increase from twenty-one to thirty states in 1991, said this should neutralise 'if not completely eliminate' further agitation for states in the future (*West Africa*, 2–8 September 1991, p. 46). This prohibition, however, is difficult to enforce, since there has developed in Nigeria a culture of localism within the one Nigerian nation. Nigeria could almost be described as a 'son of the soil nation', in which each geographical sub-group fights untiringly for the recognition of its own local group as a separate state, or if that is not possible, at least as a separate local government area.

Table 5.1 The States of Nigeria

Former regions			
Northern	*Western*	*Mid-Western*	*Eastern*
Sokoto	Lagos	Edo	Awka
Kebbi	Ogun	Delta	Enugu
Niger	Oyo		Owerri
Kwara	Oshun		Abia
Katsina	Ondo		Akwaibom
Kano			Cross River
Jigawa			Rivers
Kaduna			
Plateau			
Benue			
Yobe			
Borno			
Adamawa			
Taraba			
Kogi			
Bauchi			

This is in marked contrast with other federal states. In the United States for instance, only one state (West Virginia), has ever been created out of another state; almost all the other states have been constituted from territory that has first been administered by the federal government or, in the case of the original thirteen, by the colonial government. In Canada, in the British North America Act, Quebec and Ontario were created as separate provinces out of the 'United Canada Province' in 1867, but there has in general been stability in provincial boundaries. The same applies to Australia. The German *Länder* have not been subject to sub-division, nor have the Swiss cantons, with the single exception of the creation of Jura canton after a violent campaign. Malaysia has lost Singapore through secession, but otherwise its state structure has remained intact. Only India has experienced the same extreme pressure as Nigeria for the creation of new states. Indeed in India the proponents of the creation of new linguistic states have been willing even to sacrifice their lives for this cause (as in the case of Potti Sririmula, who starved himself to death in a successful campaign for the creation of a Telegu-speaking state of Andhra in 1952). Nigerians have never gone to this extent, but have involved themselves in frenetic peaceful agitation for the creation of more states, each state creation cause attracting its own political organisation. In the Indian case the central all-India government had the strength to allow only a fairly small number of new states to be created, while refusing further demands and keeping the number of states to twenty-five and seven union territories.

The three regions in which Nigeria was divided at independence were each dominated by a majority tribe or ethnic group constituting about two-thirds of the regional population: the Hausa Fulani in the North, the Yoruba in the West and the Ibo in the Eastern Region. The remainder of the population in each region consisted of a number of minority tribes with their own separate cultures and languages. The most important of these were the Edo people, the Ijaw, the Ibo, the Itchekiri and the Ishan peoples in the Mid-Western part of the Western Region, the Ogoja, Calabar, Ibibio, and Rivers peoples in the Eastern Region and the Kanuri, Tiv, Idoma, Jukun, Nupe, Bachama, Birom, Angas and other Middle-Belt peoples in the Northern Region. The Northern Region had a special ethos all its own and a pride in its identity. Its political centre of gravity rested in the old Muslim Fulani-Hausa kingdom established by Shehu dan Fodio in the nineteenth century, and in the old Islamic Kanuri kingdom of Bornu, which was bound together with its old rival, the Fulani empire, in the new ruling party, the Northern People's Congress. The North's population constituted around 55% of the total population of Nigeria and was in fact greater than that of any other state in Africa with the exception of Nigeria itself. (The North had 56 per cent of the population in the 1952 census, and 54 per cent in the 1963 census.) It was inevitable that such an over-mighty region would overshadow the federal government and provoke fear of domination among the Southerners.

It is noteworthy that only one of the new states in Nigeria, the Mid-West, was created by constitutional process after a plebiscite during the civilian rule under the First Republic in 1963. All the other twenty-six new states were created under military government. In 1966 the civilian government was overthrown by a military coup, largely engineered by officers at the rank of captain or major, most of whom were Ibos. The Ibo people had an interest in unitary government in Nigeria, since they had more academically qualified people seeking jobs outside their own ethnic area. In May 1966, after the first military coup of 14 January, pressure from the Ibo young Turks in the army and civilian sectors induced the head of state, General Ironsi, who was himself an Ibo, to introduce his ill-fated decree number 34, which swept away Nigeria's federal structure of four regions, replacing it with a system of unitary government, formally declared by decree and to be implemented bit by bit. This was extremely unpopular in the North since it seemed to remove from Northern people the right to manage their own affairs through Northern native authorities and district officers responsible to a Northern Regional government. The resultant coup by the Northerners in July inflicted considerable loss of life on Ibo officers and men, killed General Ironsi and brought Yakubu Gowon to power. Gowon is himself a Middle Belt man of Plateau origin from

131

the Angas tribe. He was brought up in the small Christian village of Wusasa in the large Muslim town of Zaria, thus he was both a Christian and a Northerner with a sympathy both for the cause of the minority peoples and for the North. In this, his ethnic origin was the same as that of the Middle Belt soldiers, who constituted the majority of the riflemen of the Nigerian army and who held effective power after the July coup in 1966, which had to some extent the nature of a mutiny.

The whole unity of Nigeria was in danger. Gowon quickly reversed decree number 34 and re-established federalism. Nigeria's brief and disastrous experience with unitary government convinced all future leaders that only through federalism could so large and disparate a state be held together as one nation. The Nigerian federal government has grown progressively stronger in subsequent years, but always by the gradual accretion of power within the federal system.

The July coup, which brought Gowon to power, did not occur in the Eastern Region where the military Governor, Colonel Ojukwu, responded to ardent Ibo pressure for secession by a series of actions rejecting the authority of the federal government. Since that government could no longer ensure the safety of Ibos in Nigeria and since the Eastern Region contained most of Nigeria's oil reserves, it was natural for the Ibo people to think in terms of creating their own independent state which they called Biafra, which would be invigorated by their tumultuous and modernising energies.

Faced with the knowledge that Ojukwu was about to declare independence, Gowon made his own constitutional coup and divided the four Nigerian regions into twelve states: six in the North; three in the East; Lagos; the Mid-West, which had already been created; and the Western State. This act of state creation was of crucial importance in Nigeria's history. It broke the old mould and replaced it with the new Nigerian pattern, where the major tribes lost their dominance and the minorities for the first time came into their own and had a profound effect upon Nigerian government.

Gowon's act of state creation had been prefaced by a good deal of drawing up of maps of possible new states by influential people and pressure groups. The old monolithic unity of the North had been undermined by the death of its first Premier, the Sardauna of Sokoto in the first coup on 14–15 January 1966, and by the quarrel between Sokoto, the capital of the old Fulani empire and Kano, the greatest commercial city of the North, which had resulted in the growth of a Kano state movement in 1964. Furthermore the balance of military power was in the hands of the men of the Middle Belt. When the Ad Hoc Constitutional Conference had met in September 1966, officers and private soldiers of minority Middle-Belt origin, especially from the Tiv, had agitated for the creation of their own state. I remember a Tiv soldier coming up to me at this time in Lagos, when I was on an academic visit to Nigeria and asking me 'D. O. (I was formerly District Officer, Tiv Division), do you think that our dream will now be fulfilled?' When I asked him what dream he was referring to he replied 'Our own state, of course.' I said that I hoped it would be. This shows the enormous emotion and expectation with which a large number of ordinary Nigerians desire to see their own area made into a separate state.

Gowon wanted also to weaken the position of Ojukwu in the coming civil war, by winning the allegiance of the minority peoples in the Eastern Region. Plans for state creation were prepared in great secrecy by the federal government. Gowon told me subsequently that even when they went to the lavatory, members of the supreme military council would take their copies of the plan with them so that they could not fall into unauthorised hands (informal interview, London, 1979). The announcement of the state creation was accompanied by the declaration of a state of emergency and the appointment of a military or police Governor for each state. Biafran secession followed within three days and civil war six weeks later, but the foundation of Nigerian Federalism had been laid.

By the simple law of competition and size it is clear that the federation consisting of a larger number of smaller states will tend to have a stronger central government than one with a smaller number of larger states. Prior to the state creation under Yakubu Gowon, political parties had sought to resist the sub-division of their areas of support: after this state creation they came to welcome further sub-division, since it gave increased representation for their supporters in the senate and also a larger share of revenue allocated from the federal government, partly on a basis of population, but partly on a basis of equality between states. Gowon's action in creating twelve states in May, 1967 was announced at the time as an interim measure. We are bound to wonder, however, whether it would have been possible to make this into the final act, creating a stable twelve-state system. When Gowon was overthrown and succeeded by the regime of General Murtala Mohammed, a further planned action of state creation was initiated, first sounding out opinion through a commission and then taking a decision in the Supreme Military Council and implementing it through a decree. This resulted in the creation of seven more states, bringing the number to nineteen, ten in the North and nine in the South.

The pressure for the creation of new states continued unabated, even though military government would not allow any open campaign for state creation during its periods of rule. All the way through the Shagari civilian regime, which came to power by election in 1979, the various pressure groups working for the creation of separate states for their particular areas collected money

FIGURE 5.1: THE STATES OF NIGERIA 1993

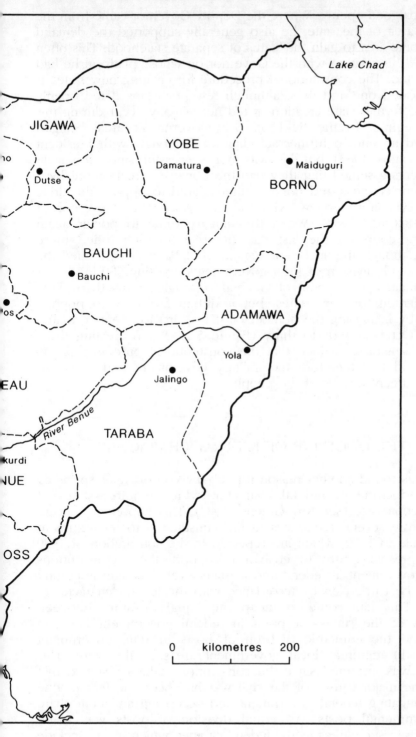

and campaigned openly. Where the Deputy Governor came from the minority area of the state, he also generally supported the demand for his home area to gain the status of separate statehood. This often embittered his relation with the Governor on whose platform he had been elected. The constitutional procedure for creating new states is a complicated one and thus, although few politicians dared openly to oppose further state creation, it did not actually occur during this civilian regime. In the field of local government areas Shagari counselled an end to further sub-division (interview with President Shagari, Lagos 1983) but he was not successful since the state governments assumed that they had the power to create more local government councils and none of them dared to oppose the drive for sub-division (interview with the late Aper Aku, Governor of Benue, Makurdi, 1982). When the military came to power again through a coup on the last day of 1983 they rescinded these creations, though the successor regime of Babangida continued the process of sub-division of local governments, creating 500 in all.

The military government of General Babangida refused to allow open agitation for new states, but it did in fact bow to popular pressure by increasing the number of states, first to twenty-one and then, in October 1991, to thirty (Figure 5.1). When creating these states Babangida explained that the constitutional process was too difficult and that therefore the military government had to act to meet the urgent desires of the people.

THE DOCTRINE OF FEDERAL CHARACTER

Nigeria has found another reason for sub-division of states springing from its doctrine of federal character, which requires states of roughly equal size (see Kirk-Greene, 1983). This important concept springs from several references in the constitution to the return to civilian rule in 1979, which are repeated in the constitution of 1989 for the present return to civilian rule. Both these constitutions require government at federal and at state level in certain important areas, to be carried on in accordance with the federal character of Nigeria. This has come to mean the equal division, between indigenes of the states, of posts in federal government between states, and the equitable division of posts in state government between the different local government areas in the state. This principle was instituted since the constitution makers assumed that one of the major causes of the civil war had been the fear of one tribe dominating federal government and occupying an unfair share of governmental posts. An equal division of posts was made mandatory in such areas as the federal cabinet, which has to include at least one Minister from each state. The doctrine has also come to represent a principle of fair shares between the various political and geographic areas, even where it has not been declared mandatory under the constitution. As might be expected, this principle has been welcomed by the less educationally developed states, especially in the North, and attacked by those states and local government areas which have a higher than average number of qualified people. The balance between equal competition and fair shares is always a hard one to strike and can result in considerable political tensions, as were encountered for instance in the allocation of university places through the Nigerian federally operated Joint Admission and Matriculation Board (JAMB).

The most important consequence of this doctrine, and of Nigeria's federal structure of division into thirty states and into 500 local government areas, is the spread of centres of development over the whole country as opposed to their concentration in a smaller number of places. Clearly in many fields of activity concentration produces external economies. Positive action is needed to ensure a fair share for every area. The creation of new states and new local government areas has been regarded by their inhabitants not just as an administrative measure or a convenience, but as an enhancement of their local collective identity. There are, however, considerable disadvantages to this policy of federal character in the spread of facilities. As one cuts the cake into ever smaller slices the temptation remains to regard the resulting entities as in every respect equal to the former large regions or states. The Governors wish to surround themselves with the same pomp and extravagance. When I complained to a friend of mine, a Commissioner in Benue-Plateau state, about the excess of motorcycle escort of the Governor and his over-large offices, my friend replied 'Come off it, this is not England but Nigeria; unless the Governor goes around with this sort of pomp and panoply, people will not respect him' (informal interview with Isaac Shaku, Jos, 1968). The same attempt to maintain a style which the state cannot afford applies to the state legislature and the state civil service heads and commissioners. The proportion of government expenditure under the Second Republic (1979–83) needed to maintain the state legislatures was far higher than in the United States, whose constitution was in many ways the model for the Nigerian constitution of 1979. This cost was much inflated by the enormous allowances of some 80,000 naira each (about £40,000) which the legislators at federal and state level voted for themselves.

It has come to be accepted in Nigeria that each state must have a university, a newspaper of its own run by the state government, a state broadcasting service and a number of state-run commercial enterprises, most of which make a loss. It is also probably the case that corruption at state level has even more disastrous consequences than it has in the operation of the federal government. There is no provision for the federal audit service to monitor state finance, and the state audit commission, though protected from interference by the letter of the constitution, is in fact in no position to challenge the extravagance of a powerful Governor. Nigeria has no equivalent of the British district auditor who has independent authority to hold local officials responsible for misdirections of expenditure. Under the Second Republic some states, such as Benue, managed their finances so badly that they were unable to pay their teachers and other staff for several months.

Nigeria faces a very difficult problem in that large governmental bodies have a strong tendency to fail to cope with their task. There is therefore a considerable advantage in the kind of decentralisation to states and local government areas involved in a federal structure. On the other hand, without proper monitoring, these units may develop the faults which are often associated with irresponsible local units of political power. There is a need to develop a means for the federal government to be able to exercise a check on corruption and exceptional incompetence, while not interfering in the normal exercise of state or local government authority, nor imposing the requirement for authorisation of action by a central body.

In matters of policy, however, the federal government has had no difficulty in inducing state governments to resonate to its major tunes. Such major federal initiatives as the Universal Primary Education scheme launched by Gowon, or the Abandoned Properties Administration, which he set up to welcome the Ibos back into the premises from which they had been driven in the ethnic cleansing of the 1966 riots in the North, were faithfully executed by the states, who set up their own units to implement federal policy and cooperate with federal bodies. In the case of the Universal Primary Education scheme this was made palatable by a generous federal grant per student. The drastic disciplinary actions of Mohammed Murtala, which involved the dismissal of some 9,000 government and parastatal staff, who were considered corrupt or 'dead wood', were started by the federal government but adopted with great vigour by the states. The Governor of Benue-Plateau told me that the popular desire to purge the civil service in the state had become so strong that his problem was to keep it within reasonable bounds. It was in danger of becoming a witch hunt (interview with Governor, Makurdi, 1975).

Nigeria, like many other developing countries, places great emphasis on development planning. A humorist has remarked that most developing countries would like to erect a small temple in their capital, on the altar of which they would put the current five year plan. Nigerian capital expenditure has been controlled by the provisions of five year plans, even from colonial times. The apogee of the planning process was probably the third National Development Plan adopted under the Gowon regime for the years 1975–1980. The plan was produced by 140 professionals of the Central Planning Office of the Federal Ministry of Economic Development and Reconstruction, and incorporates both federal and state capital expenditure (National Development Plan, p. 9, para 3). Unfortunately the optimistic provisions of this plan, which envisaged a total expenditure of 32 billion naira (about £20 billion at the then rate of exchange), were rendered ineffective by the dramatic fall in oil revenue and the wastefulness of government expenditure.

Once a doctrine has been incorporated in the constitution and has captured popular imagination it tends to extend its area of operation beyond that which is constitutionally mandatory. The doctrine of federal character has also come to be applied to the distribution of government institutions and facilities. Those who decide where to put them guard themselves against accusations of tribalism or preference for their own local area by opting for even distribution among states in the federation, or among local government areas in the state.

Nigeria's state structure is unusual for its tendency to sub-divide and also for the equality of population size among the states and among the local government areas. This has resulted in a situation unique among federations where the population of the largest state is only just over twice as great as that of the smallest. This is in great contrast to the enormous difference in population between Quebec or Ontario in Canada and Prince Edward Island, or of California or New York and Alaska or Vermont in the United States. In the Indian federation Uttar Pradesh has a population of 111 million, whereas the states of Sikkim, Mizoram and Aunachal Pradesh each have populations of under a million. Australia has a marked contrast in population size, having a twelvefold difference between the populations of New South Wales and Tasmania. Malaysia has a marked difference between the populations of the states of Johore and Perlis. The effect of the Nigerian structure is to give legitimacy to territory over ethnicity. It is noteworthy that hardly any of the Nigerian states exactly correspond with the area inhabited by a particular tribe. Some states are areas inhabited by a number of different ethnic groups such as Benue, which contains both Tiv and Idoma tribes or Cross River, which is inhabited by a large number of small different ethnic groups in former Ogoja province and by the Efik and other peoples in the former Calabar province or Plateau, which contains the relatively large ethnic groups of the Birom and the Angas, the Yergam, the Mahavul, together with many smaller tribes. Other states are dominated by the Hausa, the Yoruba or the Ibo, but each is only one of several states in which these tribes predominate. Nigeria has thus used territory as a surrogate for ethnicity, which has a beneficial effect. No ethnic group feels that it is in danger of total domination by another; on the other hand, ethnicity is not given specific recognition in the constitutional arrangements in the same way as it was in former Yugoslavia with its ethnic names for republics, or in Canada where Quebec province exactly corresponds with the area of majority French-speaking population and openly puts forward the claims of that language group and culture. The late Chief Awolowo was an ardent advocate of the idea of ethnic states, a position perhaps influenced by his desire to bring the Ilorin Yoruba back into the Western Region to join their fellow Yoruba, rather than remaining in the Northern Region, where they had been since the beginning of the colonial period. Chief Awolowo's concept of ethnic states has, however, never been implemented.

The forces making for breakdown into localism have indeed been strong. Furthermore the shift from large regions to smaller states has removed some of the major tensions from Nigerian politics. The civil war marked a great change in the status of the federal government. No state is now strong enough to seek to be a political force on its own in the way that old pre-civil war regions were.

LOCALISM AND FRAGMENTATION

The emphasis has been on a vigorous localism. This has enhanced the sense of identity of local territorial and clan loyalties and added an exuberance and self-confidence to local communities. This local loyalty has been just as strong in the constituent local government areas of Kano states, where there is no concept of separate clans, as it has been in Tiv areas of Benue state, where the territorial divisions correspond to a traditional family tree involving the whole of the Tiv people and tracing their origin to the assumed first ancestor named Tiv. In Kano the former prestigious Kano Native authority, which existed until some fifteen years after the end of colonial rule, has been replaced with over forty separate local government units, while the former Tiv Native Authority has been replaced by about ten separate elected local governments directly under the state government of Benue. This has, however, been at the cost of a narrowing of the field in which administrators, politicians and petty contractors can operate. Nigeria is characterised by an ardent sense of the rights of the 'son of the soil' as opposed to the stranger. Nearly 100 per cent of civil servants in state service or of legislators in state assemblies are indigenes of the state where they are serving. This is a far higher percentage than in almost any other federation. At the time of the break-up of the Northern Region in 1967 there was a saying among Northern civil servants, 'Don't be a peace corps'. This meant 'Go home to your state of origin and enter its civil service rather than serving abroad outside it like a member of the US peace corps!'. Local contractors also had enormous preference over those from elsewhere in the allocation of state government contracts. This has created a vested interest in the retention of the smaller state units, which ensures that the process of sub-division is irreversible.

In local government areas also 'son of the soilism' is rampant. One can illustrate this from the case of the Tiv people who, during colonial rule and after independence until 1968, were united in one Tiv division with one local government institution originally known as the Tiv Native Authority. This Authority was presided over by the Tor Tiv, the paramount Chief, whose office remains as a traditional focus for the unity of the Tiv people. The *Jir Tamen* or 'Great Judgement' comprising the clan and kindred Heads from each of the fifty-eight clans met three times a year under the Presidency of the paramount chief Tor Tiv, with the District Officer Tiv present in order to discuss and give judgement upon the major policy issues facing the Tiv people and upon individual legal cases brought before it. Today, however, there is no more Tiv division, nor Tiv Native Authority. Only the office of the Tor Tiv remains as a symbolic and traditional centre for the Tiv people. Local government offices nearly all serve in their own areas and they find it increasingly difficult to operate as they used to in other parts of Tiv. They would tend to be regarded as strangers from another part of the genealogical tree of Tiv, rather than as 'sons and daughters of Tiv', members of a common Tiv tribal family.

Despite this intense localism some of the old tensions remain from regional, tribal and religious identities, which operate on a larger scale. The sense of the unity of the North did not entirely disappear with the break-up of the region in 1967. It was bound together both by the linguistic chieftainly and religious ties of the old Hausa-Fulani, to which about 60 per cent of the North had belonged before colonial rule, and by the ethos of good and sensible government respecting local custom, which had been fostered under the indirect rule regime of the colonial period. I have a vivid picture in my mind of a sergeant in the military police, whom I met in the National Heritage Hut of the Nigerian Museum in Lagos in 1978. He stood before the picture of Sir Frederick Lugard, first Colonial Governor of the North, and said to me, 'Great man Lugard; he made us Northerners'. Even after the sub-division of the North in 1967, a good deal of the political sense of Northern unity remained. This was instanced in 1978, when the newly formed National Party of Nigeria, which went on to win the 1979 elections and provide the government for the civilian regime of the second republic, deliberately zoned its major offices. It was declared that the Presidential Candidate must come from the North, the Vice-President from the South, and the Party Chairman from whichever of the two major Southern tribes failed to get the Vice-Presidency. The positions of President of the Senate and Leader of the House were zoned to the minority tribes. There was a tacit expectation that, at the end of the two-term rule of Shehu Shagari, the First President of the Second Republic, the presidency would rotate to a Southerner. Each major regional and tribal group would need to have their share of the most senior officers, so that no one would feel left out and aggrieved. The units of this rotation were the old regions of North and South and the four ethnic groups of Hausa-Fulani, Yoruba, Ibo and the minority tribes in North and South. In the primary elections to choose Presidential candidates for the return to civilian rule in 1993 this zoning principle seems to have disappeared as regards the choice of the Presidential candidate, though once he is chosen other major offices are allocated by parties so as to give regional balance. It is noteworthy that in the election of 12 June 1993, which was cancelled by the federal government, a Southerner, Alhaji Abiola seems to have won a majority in several Northern states including Kano.

Where the ethnic, religious and tribal cleavages failed to coincide one found 'hinge groups', whose divided loyalties were of crucial importance in the balances of political power. The Tiv people, for instance, and the other Christian people of the Northern Region, sometimes sided with the North, as in the large vote for the National Party of Nigeria and President Shagari in the 1979 election. On other occasions, as in the sharp dispute between Christians and Muslims over the part to be played by Muslim personal law in the constitution, the people of the Middle Belt headed the campaign against the Muslim 'Sharia' proposals for the creation of a special body at federal level to hear Muslim personal law cases on appeal.

It is of the utmost importance in Nigeria that the sharp conflicts at national level which arise from time to time should not degenerate into inter-tribal, inter-religious or interregional battles. Nigerians realise the danger of this and treat such issues with the extreme care. The federal constitution and system of government has been of great assistance to Nigerians in enabling them to weather the various shocks to which the political system has been subject.

ENSURING UNITY: NIGERIANISM AND BALANCED DEVELOPMENT

It now remains to examine the structure and operation of the federal system of government and also to examine the Nigerian ethos and philosophy of federalism which helps to keep the country together. As Awa states (1976), federalism is not 'a mere structural device for linking units of the government to the inclusive whole' (p. vii), it has a function to assure balanced development, and it has to have fundamental objectives and directive principles of state policy. These are described in Chapter 2 of Nigeria's present constitution (1992 Constitution, sections 12–14). Their purpose is both to ensure national integration and to 'preserve and promote the Nigerian cultures which enhance human dignity and are consistent with the fundamental objectives which are provided in this chapter'. In Nigeria as in several other federations there is an ideal of *e pluribus unum* (one from many). To obtain this unity, however, Nigerians realise that they need some distinctive ideology or political culture – something which they can call 'Nigerianism'. The task of describing this national ideology presented great difficulties to the Sub-Committee of the Constitutional Drafting Committee, which considered the matter in 1967. The minority of left-wing intellectuals wished to define it in terms of socialism, but the majority of more pragmatic Nigerians won the day and substituted a number of general principles of good government and of welfare politics to achieve economic, social and cultural objectives. During the debate in the committee on fundamental objectives in the Constitutional Drafting Committee in 1976, the Nigerian economic philosophy was said to be 'mixed economy'. A vigorous Nigerian ethos has grown up in all parts of the federation, which demands freedom of expression and the ability at all levels to engage in trade.

The problem of ensuring even development has been a difficult one. The South of Nigeria experienced more rapid educational development than the North, since in the earlier colonial period education was largely provided by missionaries, and the missionaries were forbidden to operate in most of the Muslim parts of the North, which constitute the majority of that region. In the years before and after independence therefore, Nigeria faced a situation where the South, though slightly smaller than the North in population, had some ten times as many educationally qualified people at all levels from first school attendance to university graduates. This gave to the North, which considered that its own traditional ethos was just as valuable for government as Western educational qualification, a fear of Southern domination, which would take the bulk of jobs and business opportunities in the Northern Region, unless Northerners were able to protect themselves through their regional government. The maintenance of the federal pattern of government was therefore of the utmost importance to Northerners.

Nigeria is a political system where numerous cross-cutting tensions are held together by balance in a common culture and a rather complicated political system. The constitution was originally drawn up in a series of conferences under civilian rule before independence. Its federal provisions embody an exclusive list of subjects reserved for the federal government in which to legislate and take executive action, and a concurrent list where both federal and state governments can operate according to the precise provisions of the constitution.

The federal exclusive list contained 66 items including defence; currency; foreign affairs; banking; federal trunk roads; mining and minerals including oil; income tax and company tax; regulation of political parties; census; elections at both federal and state level and certain functions to do with regulation of trade and commerce. The federal government has, however, been given the power to make laws for the federation to promote and enforce the observance of the fundamental objectives and objective principles of state policy contained in the state constitution. This power, under Section 58(a), has not been used extensively, but remains as a potential source of federal involvement in state affairs in the future for the eradication of corruption.

The concurrent list includes detailed provisions for educational responsibility. The federal National Assembly has the power to make laws for educational and professional education, but a state can also set up a university. The state is in general responsible for primary and secondary education. In the field of education, however, as in many other spheres, there is an intermingling of federal and state initiative. The federal government has posted two or three members of its own federal education inspectorate to each state, to help the state inspectors with the task of monitoring primary and secondary schools. The federal government has drawn up a broad National Curriculum prescribing the subjects to be taught in primary and secondary schools, though it does not say much about the content. The federal government has itself set up two federal high schools in each state which it finances and manages. These schools are more liberally provided with resources than their state counterparts. They have competitive entry and high prestige. The subsequent revisions of the 1979 constitution in 1989 for the second return to civilian rule have not altered the lists of exclusive and concurrent subjects significantly.

The constitution assumes that residual powers rest with the states though it does not say so specifically. The report of the Sub-Committee on Division of Powers, set up by the Constitutional Drafting Committee, recommended that residual powers should be declared as resting with the states, and that the states also had responsibility for law and order, except on occasions when they had to call in the federal government because the situation was beyond their control, or in situations of proclaimed emergency (Reports of Constitution Drafting Committee, vol 2, section 25, p. 163).

In the operation of the constitution the federal government has realised the enormous importance of cooperation between the federal, state and local government levels and has recently created a special committee for inter-state relations, in which Dr Yakubu Gowon, the former Head of State, is to play a prominent role. Each of the states has established a special office in Lagos with a civil servant of permanent secretary rank at its head, to help in the liaison with the federal government and to make sure that the state receives all the money due to it. During the second republic President Shagari appointed a Presidential Liaison Officer to each state, for the coordination of the activities of the federal agencies in the state and for relations with the state government. Unfortunately the people appointed to this office were mostly failed politicians of the President's own National Party of Nigeria (NPN) and they were much resented by Governors belonging to other parties. The spirit of party played a much larger part in the politics of the second republic than it does in the United States. The Governors of the twelve out of nineteen states ruled by parties other than the NPN took to meeting as a kind of front bench of the opposition. They called themselves the 'Radical Governors' and regarded the chief purpose of their meeting as opposition to the President. This was a dysfunctional practice, since it is not appropriate for the role of leadership of the opposition to be undertaken by the State Governors who control a level of administration whose task it is to mesh in with the federal government in day to day business. In the present crisis, arising from the annulment of the 12 June election of Alhaji Abiola as President, the federal government would have liked to obtain a consensus among all thirty of the State Governors, but unfortunately the Governors of the four Yoruba-speaking states of Ondo, Ogun, Oyo and Oshun refused to attend, since they upheld the claim of their fellow tribesman, Chief Abiola (*West Africa*, 27 Sept.–3 Oct. 1993, p. 1724). The unity of the Governors in support of the maintenance of the position of the federal interim government under Chief Shonekan has been further split by the meeting of all but three of the SDP Governors, which has come out in open opposition to the federal government's plan to hold new elections for the Presidency.

Nigeria, unlike the United States, but in common with Canada and Germany, gives an important role to Executive Federalism. This is a practice in which the heads of the state, province or land governments consult regularly with the President in an advisory role in the formulation of federal policy. In the United States, in contrast, the State Governors have all met together with the President on only three occasions since the inauguration of Washington in 1789. In Nigeria the constitution expressly provides for a National Economic Council, where the Governors of each state meet together with the

Governor of the central bank, the chairman of the National Revenue and Fiscal Commission and the Federal Minister for Economic Development, under the chairmanship of the Vice-President, to advise the President on economic affairs and to coordinate economic planning. The Governors of the states are also members of the prestigious Council of State, together with one Chief from each state, all former Presidents and Chief Justices of Nigeria, the Vice-President, the Attorney General, the President of the Senate and the Speaker of the House of Representatives. The President presides over this council, whose task it is to advise him on the prerogative of mercy, the award of honours, the appointment of members of the National Electoral Commission, the Federal Judicial Service Commission and the National Population Commission which conducts the census. It can also advise, if asked by the President, on any other matter including the maintenance of law and order. Although the role of these councils is advisory, their advice carries weight. President Shagari used to cultivate good relations with Governors of all states and to consult them on Nigerian affairs. We may expect a similar practice under civilian rule in future, for the Nigerian political culture is one in which 'big men' expect to consult with one another, whatever political differences they may have. The consequences of a failure to maintain this liaison can be disastrous, as was made clear in the lack of cooperation between the Federal Authorities and Abubakar Rimi, the radical Governor of Kano, in the handling of the violent Maitatsine cult, the suppression of whose rebellion cost 5,000 lives.

The constitution contains a mechanism for the control of the police unique to Nigeria. The Nigeria police are a federal body controlled by a Nigeria Police Council and by an Inspector General, who is a federal official. The Governors of states, however, as the chairmen of the State Security Committees, may give directions to the Commissioner of Police in charge of the police force in that state with respect to the maintenance of public order. The Commissioner of Police must then either obey these instructions or request that the matter be referred to the President or to the relevant Federal Minister. Normally one would expect the relationship between the Governor and the Commissioner of Police in his state to be a close one, so that this provision which protects the integrity of the police force is now unlikely to have to be used except on rare occasions.

It is common in federal systems in less developed parts of the world for the federal government to have emergency powers to take over the entire government of a state when it judges that an emergency and a threat to law and order exists. The Indian provision for Presidential Rule, which has been used extensively in recent years, is an example of this power. In the Nigerian independence constitution this power was not very clearly expressed, but it was used by Abubakar Tafawa Balewa to take over the government of the Western Region for several months following a fight in the regional legislature. This power was not used at all by President Shagari during the period of civilian rule under the second republic from 1979 to 1983. Provision is, however, made for declarations of emergency in Section 12 of the 1989 constitution, under certain specified conditions. During the long periods of military rule in Nigeria, however, from 1966 to 1979, and from 1983 to 1993, the federal government has continued to exercise emergency powers to legislate for any part of the federation on any subject which it deems necessary and to take executive action in areas outside the exclusive and concurrent lists. This power was taken by the first military government under General Ironsi in its first decree immediately after taking power. No military government has reversed this decree. The military hierarchy is a unitary one, characterised by obedience to orders, and nearly all the Nigerian states, with one exception, were under military or police Governors appointed from the centre. One might therefore have expected military federalism in Nigeria to be a contradiction in terms, with no effect upon the process of government. In fact, however, the existence of state governments, with their executive councils consisting of people from the state, appointed by the Governor to control state ministries, and to make state law under his chairmanship, has ensured that there is a real sphere of participation in legislation and administration reserved for the state. This provides a focus for vigorous state loyalty and creates a powerful vested interest in the state for those employed by it or enjoying its patronage in contracts and other benefits. The violent Northern reaction to the unitary government provisions of Ironsi's decree Number 34 in May 1966 showed how powerful state loyalty is in Nigeria, even under military government. It is also a remarkable fact of Nigerian political culture that the new states created by the central government by decree have very soon attracted the same sort of intense loyalty as did the previous larger units. It is as though one can give Nigerians a particular football jersey, allocate them to a particular team at one's discretion, yet find that they identify vigorously with that team. In this sense there is a teachability in Nigerian culture.

The only part of Nigeria removed from ethnic and local state loyalty is the new capital of Abuja, which is specifically declared to be federal territory where the ownership of all the land shall vest in the government of the federal republic and where all legislative and executive power shall be vested in the National Assembly of Nigeria and the President of the federation (*1992 Constitution*, Chapter 9, Sections 311–316). The site for the capital was chosen by a special committee of Nigerian geographers, economists and anthropologists,

set up under the Murtala regime. After visiting several of the new
specially created capitals of states such as Brasilia, Islamabad and
Canberra, the committee chose a site very near the middle of
Nigeria, in an area which was not inhabited by any of the major
tribes. A spacious and extremely expensive capital has been in
process of creation for the past fifteen years and most of the
institutions of federal government have been transferred there from
Lagos.

The institutions of government at federal and regional level,
before independence and up to the military coup, were based upon
the Westminster model of parliamentary government, where the
Prime Minister exercises effective power and the Head of State has
only a formal and titular position as a focus for national unity. In
1979, however, Nigeria, after very intense debate in the
constitutional drafting committee and in the subsequent constituent
assembly, opted for a model with a directly elected executive
President. There was no apparent direct influence from United States
advisers, but none the less Nigeria's constitution in 1979 and in 1989
has followed the United States model very closely. This would
appear to be because a country needing a democratic, Presidential
and federal constitution with a strong element of the rule of law and
judicial review has no other model on which to draw. The Nigerian
constitution, however, is far longer and more explicit than that of
the United States. Government at federal and state level is checked,
advised and monitored by a considerable number of specialised
commissions, councils and tribunals. In theory most of these bodies
are independent from the political control at federal and state level.
In practice, however, there is a polarity of power around the federal
President and the State Governors which is not easily contained in
these constitutional bounds.

As in all federations the financial provisions are of paramount
importance. Nigeria has a greater percentage of transferred revenue
than any other federation, since nearly 90 per cent of government
revenue is collected by the federal government from the oil
companies and from the profits of the Nigerian National Petroleum
Corporation. About half of this revenue is retained by the federal
government. Ten per cent is allocated directly to the local government, by-passing the states, which in the past when they had the
power were apt to raid the local government allocation to find funds
to spend on state government projects. The remainder is divided
among states according to a mandatory revenue allocation formula,
which has been subject to periodic review after the most vigorous
debate and dispute between the federal government and the states.
It is unfortunate that a disproportionate amount of time and energy
has been spent by the federal legislature on this dispute. The 1992
constitution sets up a new body at federal level called the Revenue,

Mobilisation Allocation and Fiscal Commission, among whose duties is: 'To review from time to time the revenue allocation formulae and principles in operation to ensure conformity with changing realities' (*1992 Constitution*, Section 26, Second Schedule).

The President is intended to have a special role as the representative of the whole Nigerian people. His election provides an opportunity to demonstrate the federal character of Nigeria. He has to obtain not only a majority of the votes cast, but also not less than one-third of the votes cast in each of at least two-thirds of all the states of the federation under Section 132(i). A candidate requires this special majority to demonstrate that he has overall and not just regional support. If no candidate achieves this support in the popular vote the election is repeated and the winning candidate is required to get a majority of the votes cast and also not less than one-third of the votes in each of a majority of all the states of the federation. In the very unlikely eventuality of neither candidate achieving this, the election is decided by the vote of the members of all of the legislatures, federal and state. The people of Nigeria look to the President for leadership. They overload his office with tasks and expectations, which he often lacks the formal powers to fulfil. He operates under the same sort of limitations as a US President in that he lacks powers of compulsion, both over the two houses of the federal legislature and over the State Governors. Even the two bodies responsible for the elimination of corruption, the Code of Conduct Bureau and the Code of Conduct Tribunal, which he is given the power to appoint, were unable to operate effectively under the Second Republic. Two years after the inauguration of the republic only three people in government service had made the declaration of assets required in the Code of Conduct, whereas over a million should have done. The chairman of the Code of Conduct Bureau, Alhaji Isa Keita, declared sorrowfully that all efforts to improve the moral quality of Nigerian public life had failed utterly and that only God could save Nigeria. His ineffectiveness came under considerable criticism, but the political will to eradicate corruption seemed to be absent and as so often happens in Nigerian political life, senior people caught out in corruption were also lynchpins in the chains of coalition on which the President relied for his political effectiveness. President Shehu Shagari, though personally honest, was surrounded by many rogues and lacked the disciplinary style and political power to get rid of them. He did, however, attempt to show a moral lead by establishing a committee of Chiefs, elder statesmen and religious leaders, both Muslim and Christian to work for 'ethical revolution'. The initiative was well founded, but in the absence of effective political action it failed to gain credibility. Shagari had always to contend with the powerful pressure groups in his party at both state and federal level, whose main interest was the obtaining of jobs contracts and privileges from the federal government and who were always seeking to dictate whom he should appoint to the cabinet. After his re-election, Shagari was able to exclude from his cabinet all except seven of the former members and to appoint a number of highly respected technocrats, such as Chief Emeka Anyaoku, the present Secretary General of the Commonwealth. By this time, however, it was too late. Umaru Dikko, his relative by marriage and campaign manager, was one of those reappointed, despite allegations of corruption, and the military had already begun to make plans for the coup which eventually occurred on 31 December 1983. We may conclude that the Nigerian federal system, like that of the United States, requires a strong President, but that the incumbent must use his personality and popular support, together with the respect which Nigerians ascribe to the office, in order to achieve results in fields where he can not give executive orders. Nigeria faces the same dilemma as that described by President Lincoln at the time of the US civil war: 'Is there in all republics this inherent and fatal weakness? Must a government of necessity be too strong for the liberties of its own people or too weak to maintain its own existence?'

Only two parties are allowed under the Nigerian constitution and the military government of General Babangida decided that none of the political associations which had formed were fit to be allowed to constitute one of these two parties. The military government therefore set up two parties by decree, one 'slightly to the left of centre' called the Social Democratic Party and one 'slightly to the right of centre' called the National Republican Convention. Both these parties are required by the constitution to have a governing body which reflects the federal character of Nigeria by having members belonging to not less than two-thirds of all the states comprising the federation. The parties are forbidden to have any tribal, sectional or religious element in their name or emblem and have to uphold the fundamental objectives of Nigeria, especially as regards Nigerian unity (*1992 Constitution*, Sections 219–227). Parties and candidates are monitored by the National Electoral Commission, a federal body which has interfered considerably in party matters, dissolving the governing bodies of both parties on one occasion and also cancelling the entire primary election of Presidential candidates and ordering a re-run. Whatever government is in power in Nigeria will be extremely conscious of the dangers of religious polarisation between Muslim and non-Muslim and of regional feeling between North and South. One may expect the government and the National Electoral Commission to continue to monitor the electoral process to prevent the emergence of extreme wings of parties advocating religious intolerance or regional or tribal bias.

Federalism is not only a system providing for the relations

between the central government and the states, it is a whole philosophy and practice of the sharing of power at various levels. In the Nigerian case a great deal of emphasis has recently been placed on the autonomy of elected local government within its special sphere of operation. The constitution itself lays down in Section 7 that: 'the system of local government by elected local government councils is under this constitution guaranteed'. Chapter 8 of the constitution goes on to lay down exact detail for the direct election of local government chairmen, who appoint supervisory councillors for each department. In this sphere Nigeria has copied the United States model of the elected mayor with executive power. The local government councils are also elected but have no power to remove the chairman except by way of a resolution declaring him incapable of discharging the function of his office, involving medical examination. The chairman can also be removed by impeachment or by a recall motion approved by half the voters. The power of state governments over local governments has in the past been used, on a large scale, to interfere and to remove local government chairmen and councils of whom the State Governors disapprove. Such action is now, however, expressly forbidden and the state governments have been instructed to disband their own ministries of local government, since they no longer have any power in this sphere. The finances of local governments are strengthened by a mandatory provision for the allocation of 10% of Nigeria's revenue direct to them. The local government structure in Nigeria has been described as the 'Third arm of federalism'.

CONCLUSIONS

Nigeria contains about a quarter of the inhabitants of black Africa. It is far more populous than any other African state. It has therefore a continual problem in accommodating the diversity of peoples and holding the country together. Its political system has left room for a great deal of bargaining and inter-governmental relations between state and federal governments. Without this activity, the various groups in Nigeria would not be able to remain together. There has also been a considerable level of activity by the federal government and by the state governments at its request, to inculcate national unity in the thinking of Nigerians. MAMSER, the directorate for social mobilisation, has been extremely active during the Babangida administration, seeking to indoctrinate Nigerians to a love of their common country through seminars, publications and propaganda. It is hard to measure the success of this direct socialisation. When the conditions of acute enmity between groups exist and one group feels dominated or cheated, this kind of propaganda is not strong enough to prevent polarity. Thus during the Ironsi regime in 1966, a programme of propaganda for unitary government failed to placate the Northerners whose leaders and senior soldiers had been murdered in the coup that brought an Ibo, General Ironsi, to power. Similarly, after the May, July and September massacres of Ibos in 1966, the ardent popular pressure for secession from Nigeria by the Eastern Region proved irresistible. It was only slowly and through the most careful inculcation of the need to bind up the nation's wounds and recreate unity that General Yakubu Gowon, the Head of the Federal Military Government, was able to bring back those formerly in secession into willing acceptance of loyalty to Nigeria after the civil war.

The present crisis over the cancellation of the election of Alhaji Abiola as President has made Nigerians conscious of the danger of polarisation along regional lines, though fortunately in this case the dispute between Abiola and Babangida has not raised issues of religion. The caution with which Nigerians have approached these issues and the continual emphasis on the need to preserve the unity of the nation indicates that Nigeria's experience of nation building under federal government has not been in vain. Nigeria will, however, need to adopt some formal political understanding between all parties in a conference to place a moratorium on the creation of new states and new local government areas, and will need to concentrate on measures to make government at federal, state and local government levels more efficient in order to recover from the present paralysis of development.

REFERENCES

Adedeji, A. (1969), *Nigerian Federal Finance* (London: Hutchinson)

Awa, E. O. (1964), *Federal Government in Nigeria* (California: University of California Press)

Awa, E. O. (1976), *Issues in Federalism* (Ethiope Publishing House,)

Coleman, J. S. (1958), *Nigeria: Background to Nationalism* (Berkeley: University of California Press)

1992 Constitution of Nigeria (Reproduced for mass distribution by the Directorate for Social Mobilisation, PMB 27, Abuja)

Dent, M. J. (1989), Federalism in Africa with special reference to Nigeria. In M. Forsyth (ed.) *Federalism and Nationalism* (Leicester: Leicester University Press)

Ezera, K. (1961), *Constitutional Developments in Nigeria* (Cambridge: Cambridge University Press)

Kirk-Greene, A. H. M. (1983) Federal Character: Boon of Contentment or Bone of Contention? *Ethnic and Social Studies*, Volume 6, Number 9, October, pp. 457–476

Mackintosh, J. P. (1966), *Nigerian Government and Politics* (London: Allen & Unwin)

Nwabueze, B. O. (1983), *Federalism in Nigeria under the Presidential Constitution* (London: Sweet and Maxwell)

Oyovbaire, A. E. (1985), *Federalism in Nigeria: a Study of the Development of the Nigerian State* (Macmillan)

Panter-Brick, K. (ed.) (1978), *Soldiers and Oil: the Political Transformation of Nigeria* (London: Frank Cass)

Reports of Constitution Drafting Committee (1972) (Lagos: Federal Ministry of Information)

Third National Development Plan (Lagos: Central Planning Office, Ministry of Economic Development, 1975–80)

West Africa, 2–8 September, 1991

West Africa, 27 September–3 October, 1993, p. 1724

PART II

The Break-up of Socialist Federations

Federation, Defederation and Refederation: from the Soviet Union to Russian Statehood

Graham Smith

Russia, as the world's newest multiethnic federation, is unique among federations in having been born out of the collapse of a federation, the Soviet Union. This raises questions not only about why one form of federation collapsed only to be replaced in the one-time metropole of the Soviet empire by another, but about whether a post-Soviet Russia can succeed in keeping together what was the USSR's 'inner multiethnic empire' through a federal arrangement when Moscow was eventually unable to secure the territorial integrity of its one-time 'outer empire'. The chapter is divided into three parts. Firstly, it explores why the Soviet federation disintegrated. What in particular are teased out here are the complex federal institutional structures of territorial control which although facilitating the maintenance of ethno-regional stability for over seventy years, proved ultimately incapable of adjusting to the resurgent aspirations of sub-state nationalisms of the late 1980s. Secondly, we consider the emergence of defederation on to the political agenda during the last few years of the Soviet Union's existence, examining the tensions between the centre and the union republics over the question of ethno-regional sovereignty. Finally, the chapter explores how the new Russian state has attempted to refederate its own multiethnic society following the defederation of the Soviet Union in 1991. Here it is argued that the federal project, although more democratic than its Soviet predecessor, none the less faces similar obstacles in its associational relationships with its ethno-regions, most notably the lack of a federal culture of associative democracy to generate a sense of coexistence and well-being.

FEDERATION AS FEDERAL COLONIALISM

What in part made the Soviet Union 'an odd empire' (Suny, 1991) was the nature of its federal arrangement. Based on an 'historic compromise' between a Russian-dominated Communist Party and its urban-based non-Russian allies, federalism's main architect, Lenin, in effect provided for a degree of cultural and administrative autonomy to the major ethno-regions (or union republics) in return for their giving up their national sovereignty and becoming members of a highly centralised federal polity. What was therefore born into existence in 1922 was a federation that was to become increasingly centralised in form throughout the Stalinist years and which employed totalitarian techniques in order to ensure the continuing imposition of centralised communist party rule over the nationality-based union republics. Although the elimination of mass terror as a means of centralised territorial control by Stalin's successors heralded a greater degree of flexibility in relations between the centre and the union republics, post-Stalinist regimes preserved many features of Stalinism, notably the centralised one-party state federal system. Federalism in effect functioned as a means of managing a multi-ethnic empire, but it was not a form of rule analogous to 'internal colonialism' or, as was officially claimed, based on 'a federation of sovereign states'. Rather, the relation between Moscow and its ethno-regions can be more appropriately considered as one of federal colonialism (Smith, 1989, 1990, 1991). It contained four essential features.

1. The Soviet federation denied the ethno-regions the right to national self-determination but allowed its union republic leaderships some, albeit highly circumscribed, autonomy in running their republics. So, despite the claim of article 72 that 'each (union) republic shall retain the right freely to secede from the USSR', this was emasculated by article 73, notably clauses 2 and 4, which affirmed that the highest bodies of the USSR state authority had the right both to 'determination of the state boundaries of the USSR' and 'settlement of other matters of All-Union importance'. In essence, article 72 was merely a front to create an appearance that union republics were sovereign states (Bruchis, 1988: 123). By retaining control over the appointments, promotions and dismissals of local party and state officials in the ethno-regions, the centre was able to ensure the loyalty of the local political leadership, while the established practice of appointing 'outsiders' (usually Russians) to certain key local positions, notably to that of Second Party Secretary whose primary function was analogous to that of a proconsul, further reinforced centralised control and the expedition of the centre's policies. Provided however that their leaders confined themselves to 'safe issues' (e.g. questions of resource allocation and distribution), the union republics did enjoy some autonomy in the running of local affairs. It was however a highly asymmetrical arrangement both in terms of the

theoretical right of ethno-regions to secede from the Union and in their ability to practice autonomy, with the fifteen union republics enjoying more rights and greater protection for their national cultures than the other more minor nationality-based autonomous republics, most of which were located within the Russian union republic.

2. As part of central policy, Moscow remained committed to a redistributive philosophy of federal resource allocation which, although far from meeting the official goal of eradicating differences in economic and social well-being between the ethno-regions, none the less ensured a flow of capital from the metropole (Russian) republic and the other more developed republics (e.g. Estonia, Latvia, Ukraine) to the less developed republics, notably the Central Asian republics and amongst the ethno-regions of 'the inner Russian empire'.

3. The upward mobility of natives within the ethno-republics was aided by affirmative action policies through preferential access to higher education and to party membership which contributed to the nativisation of a local political leadership and to the growth of an indigenous intelligentsia. The Soviet federal structure thus had an impact on local social formations, facilitating the growth of an indigenous national élite with a vested interest in the continuation of federal-type institutions. Its impact was however uneven, more a feature of the union republics than the autonomous republics where natives held far fewer positions of authority and where the appointment of Russians to key positions within the republic political apparatus was much more evident.

4. Each of the non-Russian ethno-republics possessed a native culture and language aided by a variety of institutional supports – such as a native-language-based education system – provided as a consequence of its federal territorial status. Thus federation in effect acted as a form of protection against pressures to linguistically and culturally assimilate into the state-dominant Russian language and culture. Institutional protection for national cultures was again least developed among the administratively more minor ethno-regions. Such peoples had fewer publications per head of population in their local vernaculars than the non-Russian union republic-based nationalities.

Until the late 1980s, the Soviet federation seemed to function as a perfect system of ethno-regional control. This was supplemented throughout the Brezhnev years (1964–82) with a series of policies that were largely conciliatory in tone towards the ethno-regions and which, in essence, prioritised considerations of social stability over economic or political reform. The Brezhnev regime, in effect, presided over a federal polity in which the centre preferred the pragmatic preservation of the status quo to any more radical programme for social and economic transformation. And yet the stresses and strains of this federal compromise were evident before late 1980s reform communism gained the upper hand.

Firstly, throughout the middle to late Brezhnev years relations between Moscow and the non-Russian union republic leadership had never been so good (Bialer, 1986). Moscow required of its ethno-regional leaders political loyalty and only a moderate overall commitment to realistic economic growth targets. A policy of putting greater trust in native and local cadres had made political life in the republics less volatile and more comfortable. In return, the native political leadership could be relied upon to ensure social stability within their union republics. Events which threatened to undermine regional stability, as for instance when the echoes of unrest resulting from the activities of Solidarity in Poland in 1980–81 reverberated in the Baltic republics and Ukraine, were quickly and effectively dealt with by the provincial federal leadership. Republic leaders therefore closely identified themselves with the centre's conservatism. Yet the centre's 'trust in cadres', combined with its increasing benign neglect of the day to day running of life in the republics, had furnished the native leadership with a degree of power and patronage over their territories probably far more than at any time in Soviet history (Shlapentokh, 1988). Local empire-building also made those in positions of authority susceptible to large-scale corruption. By the late 1970s, racketeering, report padding, nepotism and organised crime were rife in a number of republics, notably in the Central Asian republics. What such practices illustrated was that Moscow had in effect lost control over vital spheres of social and political life within some of its borderland union republics.

Secondly, a purposeful centrally-formulated regional policy had set itself the goals of ensuring not only that a considerable redistribution of resources occurred through the federal budget to the less developed republics but that employment continued to be created for peoples within their own ethno-regions, even where there was an over-abundance and over-concentration of particular skills or types of labour. Yet it was becoming increasingly apparent as the Brezhnev years unfolded that with the centre's unwillingness to take on board structural economic reform, a stagnating economy could no longer afford to meet the growing material and employment expectations of the republics. Central Asia's continuing 'demographic explosion' meant that the state was finding it increasingly difficult to meet the welfare needs of its growing population and to find the resources necessary to reverse the increasing trend towards underemployment in the countryside. So although considerable strides had been made during the Brezhnev years in improving the material lot of the less developed republics, in terms of real per caput consumption, republic differences were increasing, with the most developed federal units, Russia and the

Baltic republics, gaining ground (Schroeder, 1986). Moreover, by the late 1970s a number of republics, notably Ukraine, Belarus, Moldova, Kyrgyzstan and Lithuania, saw their levels of total investment decline (Bahry, 1987). There were, therefore, signs that as a consequence primarily of economic stasis, the unprecedented high standards of living enjoyed throughout the republics in the 1970s could no longer be sustained in the 1980s.

Finally, within the arena of nationalities policy, Moscow preferred to nurture the idea of consolidating what it claimed was the emergence of 'a new historic community, that of the Soviet people (*Sovetskii narod*)' that purportedly transcended the continuing existence of ethno-regional identities and which at least within the public arena no longer talked of implementing *sliyanie* (eradicating ethnic divisions) as the basis for creating the ideal communist society. Any discussion of abolishing the nationality-based union republics had also been removed from Moscow's agenda, quashed in 1977 during revisions to the federal constitution on the grounds that any such moves would have been 'premature and dangerous' (*Pravda*, 5 October 1977). Reaffirmation of the federal structure, therefore, continued to ensure an important support for native institutions, while preservation of affirmative action policies, although not without its critics, continued to facilitate native upward mobility within the union republics. The preservation, then, of native-based republic institutions continued to establish niches for incumbents drawn from the indigenous cultures. This enabled ethnic divisions to remain an integral part and reference point of native public life and an organisational basis for reinforcing ethno-regional identities.

During the Brezhnev years, then, a national intelligentsia was able to flourish. Indeed, during this period it constituted the fastest growing social group within the union republics. Such representation was particularly notable in the culturally-related professions like teaching, the national media and the arts, which reflected employment opportunities available as a result of union republic status and of the monopoly that the native intelligentsia enjoyed over access to the language and culture of their ethno-regional communities (Russian migrants were notorious for their unwillingness to learn the local language). The increasing nativisation of the upper echelons of republic life was not just restricted to the cultural professions; natives had also come to play a far more prominent role within the local political, administrative and economic machine. Moreover, this native social stratum contrasted with previous generations who had gained position more by their political credentials than by educational qualifications. Such changes reflected what Lewin (1992) has more generally referred to as Soviet society's urban revolution of the Brezhnev years, a process characterised by the growing strength in all spheres of public life of a new urban intelligentsia of diploma-holders who increasingly came to displace and challenge the hegemony of the previous social formation.

For this stratum in particular, the privileges of federation were in a tense relationship with the frustrations and discordances characteristic of the Brezhnev years: a system which largely confined native mobility opportunities to the namesake nationality-republic; an overly centralised production system which inhibited local technical and professional initiative; a centrally-imposed migration policy which increasingly brought Russian migrants into competition with natives for urban jobs, based on Moscow's lack of understanding of local labour markets and insensitivity towards the poor state of regional urban service provision and housing needs; a culturally standardising centre which by the late 1970s had reactivated a policy which insisted upon fluency in the Russian language as a precondition for professional employment and to expanding opportunities for the teaching of Russian in republic schools and universities; and centrally managed ministerial-industrial interests riding roughshod over the local environment. It was this new social stratum that came to form the natural constituency of support for Gorbachev and reform communism. But it was also this stratum which was to take advantage of the unfolding liberalising climate, and was to prove pivotal in demanding more of federation than reform communism was prepared or able to deliver.

THE GEOPOLITICS OF DEFEDERATION

It was therefore not until the late 1980s that the whole federal project was opened up to public scrutiny. What provided the necessary conditions for federalism to emerge on to the political agenda was the centre's eventual acknowledgement that socio-economic reform could not be effectively implemented without civil society's participation as catalyst in facilitating 'reform from above'. Having disabled the state-censored society through the twin policies of glasnost and democratisation, the centre in effect purposely invited a multiethnic society to engage in the making of perestroika, without considering the likely implications of its actions. Consequently, the federal question became quickly bound up with 'a revolution from below' in which the ethno-regions came to shape the nature of the federal agenda.

Despite far-reaching proposals for taking on board economic reform, and later for social democratisation, the new reform-minded Gorbachev leadership continued in the crucial first three years of its existence to treat the nationalities question as of tangential concern. Thus in the leadership's programme for economic modernisation, extended at the 1986 Party Congress to include proposals to devolve economic powers to the union republics through regional self-economic management (*khozraschet*), no attempt was made to link such policy shifts to the nationalities question. Instead Gorbachev chose to reiterate Brezhnev's faith in the idea of *Sovetskii narod* and of the continuing flourishing and rapprochement of inter-ethnic relations (Gorbachev, 1986). This insensitivity to the fact that federal politics were inextricably bound up with an ethnic content capable of disrupting the rolling agenda of centrally-initiated reform began towards the end of 1986 to have serious consequences throughout the federation. Thus in December 1986, as part of reform communism's attempt to stamp out the abuse of power (*razlozhenie*) in the ethno-regions associated with many local political élites, the First Party Secretary of Kazakhtsan, a Kazakh, was replaced by a Russian from outside the republic, thus departing from what had become accepted practice throughout the non-Russian union republics of appointing natives to such key positions. Riots followed in Kazakhstan. Throughout 1986 and 1987, a series of ethnic demonstrations followed as the ethno-regions responded to the consequences of and limits to the centre's reform programme. But rather than incorporating the nationalities question into the reformist agenda, Moscow simply dealt with each crisis as it arose on a case by case basis in an attempt to contain events in the ethno-republics. This was also evident in its handling of the Nagorno-Karabakh episode in which, in response to the demands of the Armenians of Nagorno-Karabakh to transfer their enclave from Azerbaijan to neighbouring Armenia, Moscow took the view that resolution to the problem lay in an economic development package to the region; when this proved ineffective in halting the escalation of the conflict, the enclave was transferred to direct control from Moscow, in January 1989, only to cede control back to Azerbaijan ten months later, further fuelling conflict over the disputed territory. The idea that the renegotiation of federal boundaries should take place was not on the centre's agenda (Smith, 1995).

The 'revolution from above' quickly became 'a revolution from below' in which the ethno-republics seized the initiative, setting the pace in putting the issue of federation on to the reform agenda. This ethno-regional challenge to Soviet federation contained a variety of powerful resources to draw upon. Firstly, the union republics were already 'statelets in embryo', with complete governmental institutions, national symbols, continuous traditions of cultural production in their own literary vernaculars and even the (theoretical) right to secession written into the federal constitution. Through federalism, the union republics were in effect furnished with the institutions, organisation, and access to resources to make ethno-regional group mobilisation more likely. Secondly, the union republics had amassed a series of grievances against the centre that could easily be translatable into ethno-regional mobilisation. This was greatly facilitated by glasnost, as the ethno-regions were permitted for the first time in Soviet history to publicly re-examine their past and current relationship with Moscow. Relations were further undermined by the inability of perestroika to redress economic stagnation and falling living standards. And finally the union republics required a local leadership not only willing to challenge the federal status quo but also capable of mobilising their national constituents behind the cause of greater home rule, if not independent statehood. Within the arena of federal politics, a number of republics saw by 1990 new federal leaders either replace those who had supported the federal status quo or change their preferences in taking an increasingly radical stance on regional autonomy. At the forefront were the Baltic republics which, in setting up grassroots-based social movements in support of perestroika in 1988, quickly became autonomist in their demands, eventually replacing the old guard local communist party leadership as the focus of local federal power (Smith, 1994). By 1990, all the union republics, including Russia, had followed the lead of the Baltic republic political leadership in declaring their right to some form of national sovereignty.

For its part, Moscow had come round to recognising that the whole reform programme depended upon a resolution to the federal question. As Gorbachev had noted in a 1989 summer address to the country, 'inter-ethnic conflict threatens to determine, not only the fate of perestroika, but also the integrity of the Soviet state' (*Soviet News*, 5 July 1989). Despite however its belated willingness to rethink the federal question, Moscow remained consistent in its opposition to any proposals emanating from the ethno-republics that challenged the Soviet Union's territorial integrity. Thus by 1990, three main positions on federation were detectable: those of the decentralist federalisers (reform communists), the centralist re-federalisers (conservatives), and the secessionists. What became Gorbachev's belated federal programme can in part be seen as an attempt to strike a compromise between those within Moscow (and their largely communist party-based supporters in the ethno-republics) who wanted to resecure the hegemony of central-party rule and those more radically-minded ethno-republics, notably the Baltic republics and Georgia, which by 1990 were rejecting any federal compromise and were calling for secession.

For the reform communists, rethinking the federal question followed a similar logic to many other aspects of Gorbachev-initiated reform in which 'the Stalinist command administrative system' provided the framework for critique of past failings, and the return to Leninist principles as the basis for preserving the unity of a federal polity. To do otherwise would have undermined the very legitimacy of the Soviet state. It was not the original conception of Leninist federation that was deemed to be faulty, but rather the 'command-administrative system' that followed it. As a leading article in *Kommunist* put it, as Lenin's notion of national self-determination and social justice for the nationalities had never been effectively implemented, it was the Stalinist and Neo-Stalinist command-administrative system which was responsible for deviating from the path of preserving the right of nations to self-determination which had caused current nationality unrest (*Kommunist*, No. 9, 1989). As Gorbachev noted, the sources underlying present-day ethnic tensions emanate from a variety of distortions and past acts of lawlessness, the result of which was a nationalities policy that displayed 'indifference towards ethnic interests, the failure to resolve many of the socioeconomic problems of the republics and autonomous territories, deformations in the development of the languages and cultures of the country's people, the deterioration in the demographic situation, and many other negative consequences' (*Pravda*, 6 July 1989). There was thus an urgent need, as Gorbachev saw it, 'to draft a new federal treaty that is in keeping with present day realities and with the demands of the development of our federation and of each of its peoples' (*Izvestiya*, 16 March 1990).

The Leninist ideal of federation was eventually proposed in a New Federal Treaty, which although in its earlier drafts was dictated by the centre and imposed strict limits on the permissible, in its final formulation involved the participation of those republics willing to enter into a voluntary federal arrangement and which offered considerable scope for providing a basis for a more decentralised federation (*Pravda*, 24 November 1990, p.1; *Izvestiya*, 22 February 1991). It envisaged a federal system in which the republics would be able to choose voluntarily what powers to delegate to the centre and decide what republic laws have priority over federal laws, and vice versa. Membership of the federation could only be entered into voluntarily: this in effect recognised what had been constitutionally enshrined in the original, centrally-imposed federal treaty of Lenin, but which had remained nothing but a theoretical possibility. Thus in striking a new federal compromise between Yeltsin's Russia and the political leadership of the other nine pro-union republics, Gorbachev had in effect rejected imposing through force a federal arrangement from above. The so called 9 plus 1 federal Treaty agreement, eventually approved on 15 August 1991, signalled not only Gorbachev's recognition of the sovereignty of the ethno-republics but also the right of those that wished to opt out of the federal union. However, the right-wing Moscow coup four days later, rather than leading either to a re-centralised federation as its supporters wanted or, when the coup failed, to ratification of a more decentralised Soviet federation along the lines proposed by the Federal Treaty, instead issued the Soviet Union's final death warrant. Ethno-nationalism had triumphed over federation.

Ultimately a federation, albeit one more decentralised, but none the less one which still clung to its legitimation based on seventy years of state socialism, could no longer be justified for a number of reasons. Firstly, the official ideology which underpinned Gorbachev's conception of federation was bankrupt. As Gellner puts it, 'The . . . secular ideology was strong enough to suppress . . . nationalism, as long as it retained faith in itself and the determination to use all means to retain control.' (1991:132). In having renounced repression, in part in order to retain Western goodwill, other than in selected and provoked incidences, Gorbachev resisted using coercion in order to keep the federation together. This was to help ensure that compared to the disintegration of Yugoslavia, the end of the Soviet federation was a remarkably peaceful affair. Second, the idea of federation is often used by federalisers as a powerful weapon for uniting peoples against a common enemy, as Lenin had so skilfully done in the early 1920s. With the end of the Cold War, what justification could be made for a federation grounded in the need for common regional security had gone. For the nationalistically-minded republics, new geographical fault lines were opening up that exploded the myth of a federal society based on multiethnic co-existence. Finally, the idea that federal unity was crucial to national economic well-being also floundered. Gorbachev had made a great play about 'a common economic space' and said that because of republics' inter-dependency, fragmentation would be a cost that would spell economic disaster for even the richer republics. It was an argument that had only limited appeal not least because of the failure of the federation's reformers to revitalise the national economy and to reverse falling living standards. In the world of the 1990s, economic sovereignty was no longer conceived by many of the republics as a condition of nation-statehood. Indeed the secessionist-minded republics played up the idea that their future well-being lay in going simultaneously national and global, of attaining their political sovereignty but securing their material prosperity through membership of new regional markets and trading blocs. For the least developed and less separatist minded Central Asian republics, however, with their higher degree of federal dependency, the economic argument against defederation had greater attraction. It was the Central Asian republics in particular that 'seemed to recognise that "sovereignty" had limitations mindful of those Lenin had recognised in 1922 when the union was formed' (Hazard, 1991:136).

THE REFEDERATION OF RUSSIA

In finding a way of managing its multiethnic polity, Russia is unique among the post-Soviet States in opting for the retention of a federal structure. Of the eighty-eight territories that make up the new federal map, thirty-two are based on ethnic criteria, namely twenty-one republics and eleven autonomous territories (Figure 6.1). In so doing, the new Russian state has set itself the task of convincing the peoples of its own non-Russian ethnic republics and territories that through federal recognition, their rights to determine their political, economic and cultural affairs will be safeguarded, and that the benefits of such an arrangement outweigh the costs of pursuing any alternative strategy, including nation-statehood. However, within these ethno-regions the notion of federation retains a pejorative meaning associated with a highly centralised system of Soviet rule, reinforced by concerns about a centre which while initially sympathetic to local sovereignty, has put in place political structures that resemble at best a highly centralised federal system, thus bringing into question Moscow's commitment to establishing a more decentralised federation. The central task now confronting a federal Russia is therefore between refederating along more decentralist lines or moving towards a highly centralised system of federation which may come to resemble the previous federal structure. Either way, the risks of defederation and geopolitical fragmentation are great.

For the architects of the New Russia, a more democratised federal arrangement was held up as a new beginning in relations between the centre and its ethno-regions. For Russia's first President, Boris Yeltsin, such a redesignated federal arrangement held a number of attractions. Firstly, in the transition to securing Russian statehood (1990–91), Yeltsin saw in supporting the autonomist demands of Russia's ethno-regions a way of strengthening his own power base and of undermining Gorbachev's position as President of the Soviet Union. Thus Yeltsin openly encouraged Russia's own ethnic regions to declare themselves as sovereign entities with greater political powers. And in return, several of the ethno-regions boycotted Gorbachev's last-minute referendum in 1991 to keep the Soviet Union together. By so doing the ethnic regions signalled their support for Yeltsin and for the establishment of an independent Russia. Secondly, federalism offered a way of speeding up Moscow's commitment to the country's democratisation. By 1990, Yeltsin argued that the only way that Russia could be effectively democratised was by restructuring the country 'from below' in which the various ethnic regions should have whatever powers they wished (*Literaturnaya gazeta*, 15 August 1990). Finally, federalism was envisaged as a territorial strategy to prevent the break-up of

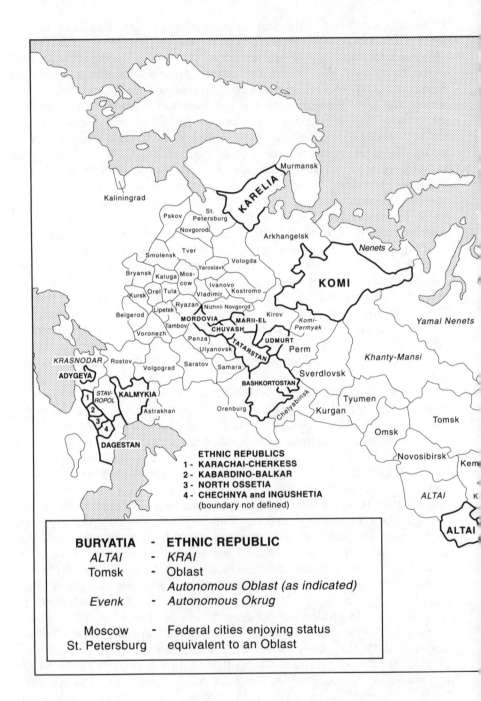

FIGURE 6.1: THE RUSSIAN FEDERATION

Russia. By arguing that the ethnic regions should be granted substantive powers over the running of their own regional affairs, Yeltsin was in effect attempting to prevent the centre from becoming the focus of increasing frustration and animosity. Through adopting an accommodationalist line, Yeltsin was in effect trying to deflect support for secession and so ensure the territorial preservation of the new Russia.

The new federal idea was encapsulated in the Federal Treaty of 31 March 1992. Two of the twenty-one republics, Tatarstan and Chechnya, refused to sign. Following a series of constitutional wrangles and revisions, the new federal treaty became the basis in December 1993 of Russia's new constitution (*Rossiiskaya gazeta*, 25 December 1993), declared into existence by the centre following a referendum with only twelve of the twenty one republics voting in favour[1]. It in effect fell short of the scale of sovereignty that many of the ethnic regions had originally envisaged. Although the new federal constitution accepts the principle of self-determination for nations, this is in effect nullified by article 4 which ensures the integrity and inviolability of the Russian federation, thus preempting secession. Thus striking at the heart of this tension between the centre and the ethno-regions is the omission from the federal constitution of the right of the ethno-republics to secede, if they so wish, from the Federation, a right which was built in to the original 1992 Federal Treaty (*Rossiiskaya gazeta*, 18 March 1992, p. 2). This, as the republics see it, is the abrogation of the basic right of nations to practice, if they so want, the right of national self-determination, a right that, in theory at least, was available even during Soviet rule to the union republics. Compared with federations in late modern democracies, the federal constitution also contravenes a basic 'given', that central authorities may not unilaterally redefine the powers of regional governments (see chapter one). In the Soviet constitution, the President has been given powers both of judicial review (i.e. to suspend acts issued by the executive bodies in Russia's provinces) and of arbitration between federal and local bodies or between constituent members of the federation. Yet, some republics, notably Bashkortostan, Tatarstan, Sakha and Tuva, have adopted their own local constitutions and in the process have proclaimed the supremacy of their own republic laws over Russian federal laws, thus violating the new constitution which forbids republics and regions within the federation to pass legislation that contradicts the country's basic law.

Russia's transition from initially signalling a decentralised federation to one in which power has become more centralised but largely ineffective over the republics, threatens to undermine federal stability, leading possibly to defederation. Three arenas of tension have emerged as central: the relationship between the new federation and democracy, centre–local economic relations, and issues of cultural rights and autonomy.

While the New Russia has declared its commitment to democracy through a federal system of government, the republics criticise Moscow for continuing to practice the 'dictate of the centre'. The fear is that Russia, given its historically centralising impulse, is again sliding back towards a centralised-authoritarianism (*Rossiiskaya gazeta*, 26 May 1993). According to Tarlton's seminal essay on federalism, in polities where each locality differs in terms of a range of criteria from the national state in general (e.g. ethnicity, language, economic development), 'relieving the tensions and discord . . . requires not further recognition of diversity and their protection in the complicated processes of ever increasing federalisation, but rather increased coordination and coercion from the centralising authorities in the system' (1965:874). Tarlton was clearly concerned, as indeed Moscow is, that 'when diversity predominates, the "secessionist potential" of the system is high and unity would require control to overcome disruptive, centrifugal tendencies and forces' (p. 875). Many centralists in Moscow have called for a 'harsh federation', with greater dependence of the regions on the centre, insisting that without strong power it would be impossible to effect Russia's successful transition towards the market and economic prosperity (Sakwa, 1993). Indeed within certain spheres of federal politics, centre-building strategies to 'contain ethno-regionalism' are already apparent. These have involved reemphasising the need for bilingualism within the ethno-republics, through playing up the importance of the Russian language as a factor in inter-regional communication, to using force to re-secure federal control over wayward republics (e.g. Chechnya) and arming local Russian-based pro-federal organisations against nationalist-secessionist movements in the North Caucasus. Yeltsin's dismissal of the Russian Parliament in October 1993 and its replacement with rule for three months by Presidential decree was also interpreted in the ethno-regions as symptomatic of the fragility of the centre's commitment to refederation and to decentralising political power, even although Yeltsin did live up to his promise that it was a temporary measure. Moreover there is concern over such constitutional claims that in the New Russia what should take precedence 'is the individual and his [*sic*] inalienable rights' and that collective rights, such as ethnic rights, are of secondary concern. (*Rossiiskaya gazeta*, 13 June, 1993). The ethno-regions therefore remain suspicious of Moscow's commitment to a federal Russia in which both their participation in decision-making and their rights as regional citizens are guaranteed.

Yet the centre is particularly sensitive to allowing the ethnic republics more leeway in managing their own affairs than in the other regions, oblasts and krays. This is especially evident with regard to central appointments at the regional level. In contrast to the other provincial units, the ethnic republics have been exempted from the centre imposing the appointment of key administrative officials, and are allowed to determine their own systems of government and to elect their leading officials, including their heads of state. Consequently, Moscow appears willing to practice a form of asymmetrical federalism in which the potentially ethnically most problematic are allowed more flexibility than the non-ethnic regions. However, such differentiated practices have not been without their critics. The Russian provinces argue that they are being discriminated against, their resentment being targeted at what they see as both centralist-authoritarian practices and privileged ethnic minorities (*Literaturnaya gazeta*, No. 16, 1994, p. 11).

It would however be mistaken to assume that within their own localities, democracy is necessarily high on the agenda of the ethnic republics. It is a mistake, as experiences elsewhere show, to claim that the desire for local accountability automatically leads to greater local democracy. There is no basis in political theory for claiming that smaller territorial units would be more hospitable to democratic politics. In Russia and its regions, where local civil society is weak and where there is no tradition of pluralist democracy, this is likely to be especially problematic. In some republics, notably Mordovia and Kalmykia, where Moscow has in effect lost control over local affairs and where the regions are pursuing their own economic and political policies, authoritarian trends are already detectable. In these *de facto* sovereign states, conservative-minded leaders, many of whom were in power during the late Soviet period, justify semi-authoritarian rule by claiming that it provides both social stability and economic direction in times of political uncertainty. These political leaders are also willing to play the nationalist card to justify their actions, based on the logic that it is only through a strong and united state that local interests will be safeguarded against encroachment by the centre.

The nature of economic relations between the centre and the ethnic republics has also emerged as a major issue, shaped by the status of the ethno-republics being amongst some of the least developed of Russia's regions and of having to readjust to far-reaching economic restructuring. Most of the ethnic republics want to pursue their own local paths to development, free of central interference, but while retaining the material benefits that accrue from membership of a federal union. Adjusting from being a centrally planned economy in which each region was told what to produce and where product markets were guaranteed as part of central planning has been extremely painful. With little guidance or effective coordination from the centre, the ethnic republics have had to find their own market niches for their products as well as to secure their own product deliveries. The chaos of this transition to market exchange between the regions has meant that the centre has been singled out for failing to provide effective economic policies in order to minimise disruption in the supply and demand for commodities between the regions.

In taking greater control over their local economies, the republics therefore see a way of using their own resources to revitalise their local economies. Although such policies have gone hand in hand with a commitment to achieving a successful transition to market economies, local political élites in many of the ethno-republics, aware of having to strike a balance between engaging in structural adjustment and continuing to secure the support of their constituents, have been reluctant to move too fast for fear that too radical a policy would undermine their authority within the locality. Consequently many local leaders continue to seek maximum subsidies from the federal government for their public sector heavy industry, so postponing decisions that would lead to factory closures and large-scale local unemployment (Hanson, 1994).

Other ethno-republics have pursued a more radical set of economic policies, combined with local initiatives tailored towards going simultaneously more global and local. One republic at the forefront is the south-western republic of Kalmykia. In order to escape from being one of the poorest and least economically viable of the Russia's republics, Kalmykia has introduced a far-reaching programme of market liberalisation designed to restructure its economy from its specialist export dependency on agriculture and other primary products to one based on greater economic diversification through establishing a range of competitive manufacturing-based industries. It is a programme for economic renewal which plans to rely on outside capital investment through tax-free incentives and which is designed to end the republic's dependency on economic subsidies from Moscow (Tolz, 1993). It is however also a developmental strategy which combines a commitment to rapid economic growth with the idea of the strong local state, one in which securing economic growth takes precedence over promoting a pluralist democracy.

The ability of the ethno-republics to follow their own paths to development is however constrained by fiscal budgetary policies. The centre is seen as demanding too much in terms of fiscal revenue from impoverished regions while in return for the increased burden of fiscal responsibilities, the republics feel that they are not receiving their fair dues from the federal budget. Moneys allocated to the federal budget, it is argued, mean that the regions have had to cut back on much-needed local public spending, be it on economic investment or on social welfare. What benefits accrue to the republics from such redistributive policies, however, have little

173

relevance to considerations of regional equity. Thus those republics that under the federation treaty are allowed to retain a large proportion of their locally collected taxes are also receiving large subsidies from the centre. Overall, only 10 per cent of federal transfers in 1992–93 were being directed to the poorer ethno-republics and regions, while the remaining 90 per cent were being allocated to the richer and more geopolitically problematic republics. Thus Sakha received well over five times the national average, Bashkortoskin double the national average, and Tatarstan a third more than the national average (*Moskovskii novosti*, No 28, 9 July 1993, p. 2).

Finally, relations between the centre and the ethno-republics are being shaped by issues of cultural rights in which the question of Russian hegemony is of widespread concern. The ethnic regions want to reclaim their local identities through promoting their own national languages, national cultures and religions. Yet the ethno-regions fear that instituting their right to be culturally different is at odds with a federal structure in which a strong and regionally-insensitive centre may be keen to re-establish its own cultural dominance through promoting Russification. This is especially pertinent given the sizeable Russian presence in the ethno-republics and the fear that local Russians may again be used as agents of centrally-initiated policies of Russification. In promoting their own national cultures, however, many ethno-regions have also been accused by the centre of initiating an overly nationalistic form of cultural dominance. This has fuelled tensions between local Russians and natives and as a consequence many Russians, fearful of their future, have left in large numbers (*Izvestiya*, 4 July 1992, p. 3). It is a fear not without substance. A handful of republics have even gone so far as to propose a definition of local citizenship in which the right to participate in republic elections would be open only to those who are of the local nationality (*Literaturnaya gazeta*, 21 May 1992). In some republics, where the dominant local culture is Islamic, the fear of the establishment of a fundamentalist state is also causing concern among local Russians, notably in Muslim Tatarstan.

THE LIMITS TO DEFEDERATION

Such centralising strategies of coping with an ethnoregionally diverse federal union have added fuel to the separatist cause. Yet we should not assume that such practices will necessarily lead to defederation and the replacement of federation by new nation-states. Given their strategic location within the structure of federal politics, the role of native political élites is crucial to mobilisation behind the separatist cause. As a consequence of perestroika, these élites became more indigenous in composition in the mid to late 1980s, but the personnel installed during the Gorbachev period has remained largely unchanged despite the Soviet Union's disintegration (*Rossiiskaya gazeta*, 4 March 1992, p. 2). These political élites have had to limit their career ambitions to provincial politics, in part due to a lack of opportunity to progress beyond the horizons of their own ethnic republics. If Russia is to take on more the features of Western-style federations this may change but, as Hanson notes, for the present 'because there are still no effective structures of political parties linking the careers of local politicians to positions at the national level, most local politicians . . . are not subject to any party discipline that would make them conform to Moscow's policies (1994:23). Such élites therefore tend to look back on the republic, to engage in a rhetoric of federal politics which uses highly charged calls for 'sovereignty' and 'national self-determination' in order to maximise benefits from the federation but which so far, with the exception of Chechnya, has fallen short of calling for outright independent statehood.

But even if such a political élite were willing to engage in separatist politics, there are a number of factors which militate against their constituents engaging in mass political mobilisation behind independent statehood. Firstly, there is the lack of a shared conception of national self-determination within many ethno-republics where any understanding of an ethnic right to national self-determination does not necessarily coincide with a territorial meaning of the term. Russians constitute a majority of the population in nine republics (Adygeya, Buryatia, Gornyi-Altai, Karelia, Khakassia, Mordovia, Udmurtia, Komi, and Sakha), and a sizeable minority in all the others (Table 6.1). In some other republics, notably in Dagestan and Kabardino-Balkaria there exists a variety of ethnic groups, with differing conceptions of the relationship between their understanding of national and territorial self-determination. Indeed, in many respects, the existence of tensions at the local level between such ethnic groups vying for local political hegemony not only weakens mobilisation behind the separatist cause but has the potential to be used by an unscrupulous centre as part of a policy of divide and rule.

Although many Russians in the ethnorepublics have supported local autonomy, they are more likely to continue to identify with their territorial homeland, Russia, and support the preservation of a Russian federation. Not to do so would, in the case of a number of republics, transform their status from being part of the majority nation to that of a minority whose ethnic rights and status are more likely to be challenged. Thus given the sizeable if not majoritative status of Russians in a number of these republics, any local

Table 6.1 Composition of the Russian Federation's Ethno-Republics

	Population ('000s)	% Titular		% Russian
Central Russia				
Bashkortostan	3.9	22		39
Chuvashia	1.3	68		27
Karelia	0.8	10		74
Komi	1.3	23		58
Marii-El	0.8	43		47
Mordovia	0.6	32		61
Tatarstan	3.6	49		43
Udmurtia	1.6	31		59
North Caucasus				
Adygeya	0.4	22		68
Chechnya ⎫				
Ingushetia ⎭	1.3	58		23
Dagestan	1.8	80		9
Kabardino-Balkaria	0.8	53		39
Kalmykia	0.3	45		38
Karachi-Cherkesia	0.4	31	(Karachis)	42
		10	(Cherkess)	
North Ossetia	0.6	53		30
Siberia				
Buryatia	1.0	24		70
Gorny-Attai	0.2	31		60
Khakassia	0.6	11		79
Sakha	1.1	33		50
Tuva	0.3	64		32

Source: Based on data from the 1989 All-Union Soviet Census. *Natsional'nyi sostav naseleniya SSSR (Moscow: Finansy i statistika, 1991)*

referendum on secession is likely to result in support for remaining part of the Russian federation.

Secondly, there are the economic costs of defederation. Despite the resource-endowed richness of many of these republics, such as Sakha which accounts for most of Russia's gold and diamond output and of oil-rich Tatarstan and Bashkortostan, their territories are unlikely to be transformed into 'Kuwaits of Northern Eurasia' overnight. As a consequence of Soviet rule, their economies remain inextricably dependent on that of Russia and in some cases, notably Tatarstan, this is reinforced by their landlocked status. At the other end of the economic spectrum are poor republics like Kalmykia and Tuva which still depend on large economic subsidies from Moscow. The nature of this economic dependence and the tangible benefits of remaining part of a larger and integrated trading community are likely to outweigh the greater economic uncertainty of independent statehood.

Finally, it is important not to underestimate the centuries-long impact on ethnoregional identities of being part of Russia. The weakness of federal institutional supports during the Soviet period in combination with both a more limited economic development and the effective integration into the Russian culture and language has meant that a large cultural intelligentsia willing and able to act as bearers of the separatist cause is poorly developed. Moreover, for the majority of non-Russians who retain a strong sense of national identity, the sense of national self – be it of Bashkir, Buryat or Chuvash – does not necessarily conflict with remaining part of a muticultural Russia.

CONCLUSION

There is nothing inevitable about federation facilitating the development of democratic practices. Indeed, there are growing doubts as to whether Russia can legitimately claim to be on trajectory to constructing a democratic-based federation (Roeder, 1994). The increasing powers that the executive has secured since September 1993 from the Federal Assembly and of the President's capability and willingness to use coercion to resecure hegemonic control over a wayward republic like Chechnya in December 1994, signals a very different project to that of federative democracy. For their part, the ethno-regions, while generally reluctant to engage in the identity politics of secession, have also displayed a weak commitment to building a democratic federation. As experiences elsewhere show, for a federation as a particular organisational form of democratic rule to work successfully, it not only requires appropriate institutional structures, procedures and conventions, but must also be matched by a set of socially-held beliefs that value both unity and respect difference. Without such a commitment both from the centre and the localities, the federal project will be unable to manage Russia's multiethnicity other than through coercive means.

NOTE

1. The Chechen republic decided not to participate in the December 1993 referendum, while in the other eight ethnic republics the draft constitution either was rejected or, following agreed electoral procedures, was invalid (at least 50 per cent of the electorate had to go to the polls for the referendum to be valid).

REFERENCES

Arutyunyan, Yo. V. *et al.*, (1992) *Russkie. Etno-sotsiologischeskie ocherki* (Moscow: Nauka)

Bahry, D. (1987) *Outside Moscow. Power, politics and budgetary policy in the Soviet republics* (New York: Columbia University Press)

Bialer, S. (1986) *The Soviet paradox:. External Expansion, Internal Decline* (London: Tauras).

Broxup, M. (1995) Tatarstan and the Tatars. In G. Smith (ed.) *The Nationalities Question in the Post-Soviet States* (Longman, London, 2nd Edition)

Bruchis, M. (1988) The nationality policy of the CPSU and its reflection in Soviet socio-political terminology. In P. Potichnyi (ed.), *The Soviet Union Party and Society* (Cambridge: Cambridge University Press), pp. 121–41

Gellner, E. (1991) Nationalism and politics in Eastern Europe, *New Left Review*, No. 189, 127–36

Gorbachev, M. (1985) *Ibrannye rechi i stat'i* (Moscow)

Gorbachev, M. (1986) *Politicheskii doklad tsentral'nogo komiteta KPSS XXV11 S'ezdu Kommunsiticheskoi Partii Sovetskogo Soyuza* (Moscow)

Gosudarstvenyyi komitet SSSR Po Statistike Soobshchaet (1991), *Natsional'nyi sostav naseleniya* (Moscow), vol. 11

Hanson, P. (1994) The centre versus the periphery in Russian economic policy *RFE/RL Research Report*, 3(17), pp. 23–28

Hazard, J. (1992) Managing nationalism: state, law and the national question in the USSR. In A. Motyl (ed.), *The Post-Soviet Nations. Perspectives on the Demise of the USSR* (New York: Columbia University Press), pp. 96–140

Izvestiya, 16 March 1990

Izvestiya, 22 February 1991

Izvestiya, 13 February 1992

Izvestiya, 4 July 1992

Izvestiya, 17 May 1993

Kommunist, 1989 No. 9

Lewin, M. (1992) *The Gorbachev phenomenon. A Historical Interpretation* (Berkeley: University of California Press)

Literaturnaya gazeta, 15 August 1990

Literaturnaya gazeta, 21 May 1992

Literaturnaya gazeta, No. 16, 1994

Moskovskie novosti, 9 July 1993

Pravda, 5 October 1977

Pravda, 6 July 1989

Pravda, 17 August 1989

Pravda, 24 November 1990

Roeder, P. (1994) Varieties of post-Soviet authoritarian regimes, *Post-Soviet Affairs*, 10(1), pp. 61–101

Rossisskaya gazeta, 4 March 1992

Rossiiskaya gazeta, 18 March 1992

Rossiiskaya gazeta, 19 May 1993

Rossiiskaya gazeta, 26 May 1993

Rossiiskaya gazeta, 13 June 1993

Rossiiskaya gazeta, 25 December 1993

Russiiskie vesti, 15 June 1991

Sakwa, R. (1993) *Russia. Politics and Society* (London: Routledge)

Schroeder, G (1986) Social and economic aspects of the nationality problem. In R. Conquest (ed.), *The Last Empire. Nationality and the Soviet Future* (Stanford: Hoover Institution), pp. 290–313

Sheehy, A (1993) The CIS: a Shaky Edifice *RFL/RL Research Report*, No. 1, pp. 38–43

Shlapentoch, V. (1988) The XXVIIth Congress – a case study of the shaping of a new party ideology *Soviet Studies*, XL(1), 1–20

Smith, G. (1989) *Planned Development In The Socialist World* (Cambridge: Cambridge University Press)

Smith, G. (1990) The Soviet federation. From corporatist to crisis politics. In M. Chisholm and D. Smith (eds), *Spared Space. Divided Space. Essays on Conflict and Territorial Organization* (London: Unwin Hyman), pp. 84–105

Smith, G. (1991) The state, the nationalities question and the union republics. In C. Merridale and C. Ward (eds) *Perestroika. The Historical Perspective* (London: Edward Arnold), pp. 202–16

Smith, G. (1994) *The Baltic States. The National Self-determination of Estonia, Latvia and Lithuania* (London: Macmillan)

Smith, G. (ed.) (1995) *The Nationalities Question in the Post-Soviet States* (London: Longman, 2nd edition)

Suny, R. (1991) Incomplete revolution.; national movements and the collapse of the Soviet empire *New Left Review*, No. 189, pp. 111–26

Tarlton, C. (1965) Symmetry and asymmetry as elements of federalism: a theoretical speculation *The Journal of Politics*, vol 27, pp. 861–74

Tolz, V. (1993) Russia's Kalmyk Republic Follows Its Own Course, *RFE/RL Research Report*, vol. 2(23), pp. 38–43

Yugoslavia: Politics, Federation, Nation

Vesna Popovski

Because of its distinctive and independent socialist route to modernity, Yugoslavia was considered a unique and stable multi-ethnic polity. Primarily because of its uniqueness, analysts were able to argue that '. . . the idea of some form of Yugoslav unity is stronger than the desire for national polarization and exclusiveness' (Vucinich, 1969, p. ix). National problems, it was further contended, were at most likely to be restricted to competition for scarce economic resources (Vucinich, 1969). Even after Tito's death and ethnic disquiet in the Kosovo region, Singleton (1985) was confident that more democratic debate had provided 'a new point of departure for the creation of a more democratic but still socialist Yugoslavia' (p. 285), although he did add the caveat that 'if the present leaders do not recognise this, and if they attempt to silence debate by the imposition of a "firm hand", possibly with the cooperation of the army, this may worsen the situation' (p. 285). Smith (1986b) went even further in suggesting that Yugoslavia could be seen as a 'real hope for the consolidation of the state and its institutions', and as 'a model for more intractable "state-nation" conflicts' (pp. 261–262). Finally, as Binns observed as late as the late 1980s, 'The Socialist Federal Republic of Yugoslavia (SFRJ) has developed in its federal institutions, "consociational" structures of conflict-resolution which have enabled it to survive the death of its founder and economic and political crisis' (1989, 143).

There were others who took a less sanguine view, observing that by the late 1980s a political vacuum existed in Yugoslavia which potentially could lead to total entropy, chaos and anarchy. But who and what was likely to fill that gap? (Sunić, 1987, p. 66). That question remained unanswered. Yet Yugoslav society was not insensitive to the problem: as one popular joke went, 'In ten years there will be ten states in Europe: Eastern Europe, Western Europe and eight Yugoslav states' (Mijanović, 1987, p. 63).

This chapter is primarily concerned with how the Yugoslav

federal structure of government attempted to furnish a means of reconciling the demands of particular ethnic nationalisms with the maintenance of the wider unity of the state but why it ultimately failed to balance national and ethnic group demand-making. It is divided into four parts. Firstly, differing normative conceptions of Yugoslav federalism and post-federalism as put forward in the crucial period of the late 1980s and early 1990s are explored. Next, these conceptions are juxtaposed in relation to a historical analysis of the federation on the basis that each normative model contains its own inherent historical legitimacy. In the third section, consideration is given to the ascendancy of Serbia in federal Yugoslavia and the role that the Serbian and Slovenian leaderships played in redefining relations between Yugoslavia's constituent units. The final section briefly examines the consequences of the federation's fragmentation and of the search in what is now the epicentre of ethnic conflict, Bosnia and Hercegovina, to find a post-federal solution to ethnic crisis (see Figure 7.1).

DIFFERENT PERSPECTIVES AND MODELS OF FEDERALISM

Federalism refers to the balance of political power between central and local governments with the aim of preserving both similarities between them and the identities of different units. This is implicit in King's (1982) definition of federation as 'an institutional arrangement, taking the form of a sovereign state, and distinguished from other such states solely by the fact that its central government incorporates regional units in its decision procedure on some constitutionally entrenched basis.' (pp. 89–93) (see also chapter one). Therefore, federalism can be understood as an organising principle and federation as a form which corresponds to this principle.

If we accept that federalism is an organising principle then we should be aware that federalism approached from a legal point of view is normative and cannot serve as a model, as Neumann (1974) argues. For him, how a particular federation functions can be fully comprehended only by bearing in mind that federation is based upon two diametric principles, insisting simultaneously on keeping unity and preserving difference. These two approaches are inter-connected because the former introduces the essence of federalism, while the latter cannot function without the former because otherwise non-constitutional and conflictual outcomes are likely. This point is important in an analysis of a multinational socialist federation. Such a type of federation insists on the concept of sovereign statehood (but without wishing to apply it) in which federalism is based upon an authoritarian principle and not upon

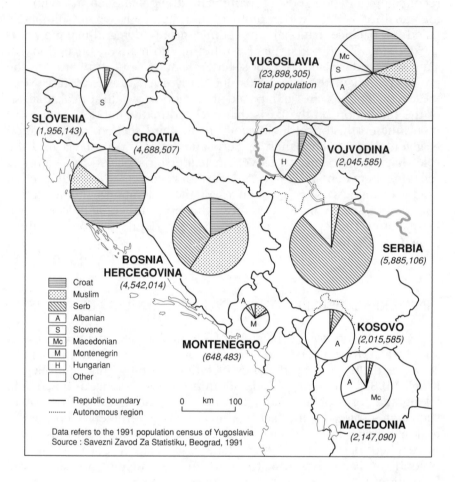

FIGURE 7.1: ETHNIC COMPOSITION OF FEDERAL YUGOSLAVIA, 1991

constitutionalism and compromise. In connection with the problems associated with the Yugoslav federation, four models in particular had been developed by the end of the 1980s and can be listed as follows: (1) national self-management as a basis of federalism, (2) citizens defined by their nation and the question of confederalism, (3) self-management as a political element of federation and (4) democratic federation (Samardžić, 1990, pp. 43–59).

   (1) *National self-management as a basis of federalism.* This model held that the Yugoslav federal idea was a special model which could not be compared to federal ideas in the West. The 1974 Constitution, according to this model, introduced 'dialectical blending of class and nation', self-management and federalism and self-management rights

and 'sovereign rights'. Therefore, self-management within the federal republics and federation as an outcome of the federal republics were the two main principles of this model. Both these principles underpinned the importance of a federal republic. It follows that the 'ruling role of the working class' was an ideological notion which did not play an important part in the functioning of the polity. Power belonged to the federal republics, in effect to their ruling élites. Thus the basis of this model was the idea of national sovereignty. In Slovenia, this model developed into the idea of an asymmetric federation in which 'each republic would negotiate its own terms of power sharing and power distribution with the central government in a federation' (Cohen, 1993, p. 62).

(2) *Citizens defined by their nation and the question of confederalism.* This model was developed as a critical response to the functioning of the Yugoslav federation interpreted by the 1974 Constitution, and as a set of ideas was held most evidently in Slovenia and Croatia (Lerotić, 1989, pp. 185–280). In discussions about Yugoslavia as a possible or already existing confederation, the main issue focused on relations between the Yugoslav nations. A nation was defined as having its own state. Thus it was argued that the only way to organise the Yugoslav state was on the basis of a confederation in which Yugoslavia could only be a sum of its sovereign parts. The problem with this model was not that it insisted on the Yugoslav confederation but that it saw two main principles of the democratic state, the individual and nation. Two different rationales were put forward: for the sovereign state the individual, and for confederation the nation.

Yet the modern idea of democracy is not based on the nation. Therefore, an individual does not get *status politicus* through the nation but by being an autonomous subject *stricto sensu*. This second Yugoslav model was seen as an answer to both the functioning and the non-functioning of the Yugoslav federation guaranteed by the League of Communists of Yugoslavia (SKJ) and the Yugoslav People's Army (JNA). This proposal was accepted by the newly founded political parties in Slovenia (the Slovenian Democratic Union) and Croatia (the Croatian Social Liberal Party) in 1989.

(3) *Self-management as a political element of federation.* This model was constructed largely in response to the 1974 Constitution. Self-management was an underlying principle of the Yugoslav federation. Self-management was seen as a politico-institutional structure and federalism as a way of organising a multinational federation. Therefore, self-management or the 'labour principle' was to be an institutional guarantee of 'social legitimacy and sovereignty of labour' (Mirić, 1984). Because Yugoslavia was a multinational federation, the parliament should have had not only 'a house of

183

working councils' but also 'a house of nations'. It is not clear what the background to the third proposed house, 'a house of citizens' was to be, as the procedure of how to elect members of different houses was not explained. Moreover there was obvious discrimination against those not designated as 'working people'. It is a model which came into existence without criticism in Serbia.

(4) *Democratic federation.* This model drew upon contemporary Western literature on democracy, offering arguably the best way out of Yugoslavia's political and economic crisis. It argued that the only way to organise the Yugoslav federation was to incorporate the citizens, as individuals, as the only constitutional factor, a perspective not taken up by the previous models. Missing from the first model, in the second it applies only to a federal republic while in the third it does not play any important role because the 'labour principle' dominates or organises the other two principles. The main problem with the Yugoslav federation was that it was constituted on the national principle in which the general and individual levels were absent. The only political subject was derived from the political representation of nation. That representation was not democratic in two ways: (1) it was not based on the individual but upon 'consensus and collectivity'; (2) the division of power between the central state and federal units can be deemed democratic only if basic rights are guaranteed by the Constitution and function politically as such. For the Yugoslav federation, as a multinational federation, the concept of federal consensus is of paramount importance. It has constitutional and institutional dimensions. The constitutional dimension covers a collective character of the fundamental decision that Yugoslavia is a multinational state. If Yugoslavia had been a democratic federation and the basic rights had been respected then the consensus, from the point of view of the functioning of the federation, would have legitimated majority decisions. This would have meant that decisions would be made by the majority and be valid only if they suited every individual, for in this model the institutional dimension guarantees rights both to the federal units and individuals. Therefore, it was proposed that the Yugoslav Parliament should have two houses, one which would represent citizens and the other federal units. The first house should be based upon the 'one person, one vote' principle and make decisions according to the majority vote. The second house should use the parity principle and reach decisions through consensus. The next step should be concerned with the division of power: on the one hand between the central state and federal units, and on the other hand between the two houses of the Parliament. This view was held by the Association of Yugoslav Democrative Initiative (Puhovski, 1989). Unfortunately in the former Yugoslavia there was no space to publicly discuss such a model, based as it was on the

precept of developing a democratic culture (not only in form but also in content) and of realising the importance of citizenship as much as ethnicity (Denitch, 1993, pp. 142–156). At the beginning of the 1990s, however, two further models were developed: the Slovenian confederational model and the Serbian federational model. The former view of constitutional reform was advanced in mid-1989 (*Za konfederalno Slovenijo*, 1990). Slovenes introduced this reform using the League of Communists of Slovenia (SKS), being aware that this was still the only platform to initiate debate. Slovenes were pushing the principle of 'one unit, one vote' in federal decision-making, something which was not welcomed in Serbia, where it was argued that the principle would mean that 'one Slovene equals five Serbs'. The Serbian leadership was outraged by the idea of asymmetric federation (the first model) which was in Slovenia seen as a step from federalism towards confederalism (the second model). Slovenian public opinion was fully supportive of the movement towards more independence in republican questions, especially in the economic and military spheres (Mastnak, 1991, pp. 54–57). The concept meant that a 'particular republic might, for example, enjoy wide-ranging autonomy in selected spheres of activity such as economic development, education, linguistic and cultural matters, yet their domains, such as defense and foreign policy would remain the responsibility of a federal government functioning on the basis of interregional agreement' (Cohen, 1993, pp. 62–63). Slovenia openly admitted that it was afraid to be treated in the future like Kosovo, where the state had by 1989 imposed emergency rule.

Slobodan Milošević, who had been elected as Head of the League of Communists of Serbia in 1986, formed two commissions in the late 1980s to outline economic and political reforms. He was the head of the first one, claiming expertise as a former Director of the Belgrade Bank. Presumably because of his Marxist background, his starting point was economic reform. The broader context of his economic reform was still a socialist society and a self-management system with state intervention in the economy. Regarding the existing state role in the economy, he argued that there was too much bureaucratization in the name of the state which prevented market-oriented reforms. Consequently, an 'anti-bureaucratic revolution' was needed. Later, in July 1989, he produced a synopsis for political reform for the Yugoslav federation. It was argued that Yugoslavia should be a 'modern democratic and efficacious federation' which should employ two different mechanisms in its decision-making processes: the principle of inter-regional unanimity which should be limited to discussions about constitutional issues, and the principle of qualified majority which should be applied in all other cases. Such decision-making processes would have a positive impact on generating economic development and through it development of the whole of society, and would not support 'partial interests' of Slovenia and Kosovo. Political pluralism was understood as an umbrella for parties 'created on a democratic and socialist basis'. As the head of the Milošević Commission's committee for political reform explained: 'Logic does not exclude the possibility that tomorrow there would be eight communist parties and socialist parties, but not parties whose programmes advocate the reprivatization of social wealth, a return to capitalism. Here is that barrier' (Cohen, 1993, p. 58).

There is no common ground between the Slovenian and Serbian models. They were in effect constructed for two different countries. In actuality they were different because Slovenia and Serbia perceived the basis of the Yugoslav federation differently. To understand the genesis of these models, we need to analyse the history of the Yugoslav federation (Vodopivec, 1992, pp. 220–241), for these models are legitimate outgrowths of it.

THE HISTORY OF THE YUGOSLAV FEDERATION

There were many ways of interpreting the national question in the first Yugoslavia (1918–1941) (Gross, 1981, pp. 177–180). The importance of the Orthodox Church in Serbia and the perception of a state tradition in Croatia made crucial contributions in shaping their own national ideologies. National ideologies were developed in the 19th century and they could not be fundamentally restructured in the newly established state. The new state was unable to solve the national question because of the way in which centralism and unitaristic Yugoslavism developed before and after the first world war and were bound up with one another. Federalism was opposed by the majority of Serbian politicians and, most importantly, by the monarch, King Aleksandar. They saw centralism as the only way to organise the state. For them, the national question did not exist because Slovenes, Croats and Serbs were three different tribes of the same nation. Croats especially were of the opinion that Serbs, Croats and Slovenes were one people, but they saw the three Yugoslav tribes as equal. Thus, Ante Trumbić and Frano Supilo, Presidents of the Yugoslav Committee, thought in terms of a new state entity, while Nikola Pašić, President of the Radical Party, thought in terms of Piedmontisation. Unitaristic Yugoslavism stressed the former: one nation, one culture, one loyalty. This was acted out by a policy of assimilation. In Serbia that policy was understood as assimilation into a Serb nation. The Yugoslav idea among other nations was understood as a multinational culture but it was soon (in the new state) either sacrificed at the altar of centralism or abandoned (Dugandžija, 1987, pp. 86–100).

On 29 November 1943 during a meeting of the Anti-Fascist Council of National Liberation of Yugoslavia (AVNOJ), the new Yugoslavia (called Democratic Federal Yugoslavia) was founded as a federal state made up of six republics. At that point in time it was not stated whether it would be a republic and socialist, or whether or not it would keep the Karadjordjevic dynasty. Socialism entered the stage as the ideology of the Communist Party of Yugoslavia (KPJ). The Party played the main role during the war as an organisational force behind the liberation struggle. It is important to point out that its main organising principle was federal, for after the November meeting the Councils of each republic met, organising themselves as governing bodies in their own republics. That principle combined with use of nationalism, especially among nations not acknowledged in the Kingdom, was essential for mobilising Croats, in particular, behind the partisan cause (Irvine, 1993, pp. 89–203).

These decisions were sanctioned by the parliament of the new state, called the Federal People's Republic of Yugoslavia, in November 1945. The new constitution was passed in January 1946 and the socialist federation established. It was argued that it had two distinguishing characteristics: the member states voluntarily joined the federation and they were equal. Its socialist characteristics were seen in solidarity among different member states as of real rather than normative equality (Čulinović, 1952, pp. 161–167). Despite being officially referred to as federal, the new state was organised according to a communist party model in which centralization was to be the main principle ruling the country (Bilandžić, 1978, pp. 39–90). The country was ruled by the Politburo of the Central Committee of the Communist Party of Yugoslavia (Carter, 1982; Crnobrnja, 1994, pp. 65–78). After the war political parties took part in the first elections but the KPJ forced them from the political stage (Koštunica and Čavoški, 1985).

There were three reasons why the newly established state was declared federal. Firstly, Tito was aware of both inter-ethnic tensions in the Kingdom and national feeling among different nations, and encouraged mutual respect and equality among nations, introducing more of brotherhood than of unity in political life. Secondly, he was aware of the dominant role Serbs played in the Kingdom and wanted to make them more equal notwithstanding the reality of their majority and their spatial distribution. Thirdly, because of the pre-war experience, it was felt that the new state had to be anti-centralist. Yugoslavia was a federation of equal states but they were treated as administrative units.

The schism with Stalin had paramount consequences when it

came to the ideological character and economic future of the country, if not the political prospects (Carter, 1982). Yugoslavia tried to find its own path to a 'better future'. Tito argued that the schism opened a way for worker self-management instead of administrative-centralist management, social property instead of state property, the party–state difference instead of the party ruling over a state apparatus, and local autonomy instead of centralism. All these changes were implemented in the 1953 Constitution Law. The changes meant that local government was the beneficiary and not the republics themselves. On the other hand, the KPJ, now renamed the League of Yugoslav Communists (SKJ), remained as the ideological vanguard and was in charge of the recruitment of managerial and political personnel.

Thus the ruling élite naïvely hoped that, on the one hand, federalism was an answer to all national tensions and, on the other hand, the national question would be solved because class relations had been solved. Part of that hope was built upon a concept of 'Yugoslavism' introduced by Edvard Kardelj, the most important party ideologue. In official documents this concept was never interpreted as a Yugoslav nationalism but as a Yugoslav socialist patriotism or Yugoslav socialist consciousness understood as the 'strengthening of socialist workers community within all Yugoslav nations. This type of Yugoslavism supports and depends upon the development of national cultures and languages' (*The Seventh Congress of the SKJ*, 1958, p. 1058). This attitude towards a Yugoslav nation is understandable if the history and reality of the Yugoslav idea are taken into account – the Yugoslav idea in its usage was very often misused, especially when it came to unitarism. However, the concept was based upon, on the one hand, reification of a Yugoslav victory in the Second World War and the famous '*Ne*' to Stalin and, on the other hand, on the hope that rapid economic growth, self-management and federalism would quickly eliminate traditional loyalties and conflicts among different nations.

The Yugoslav state had developed a state identity but it did not know how to deal other than through authoritarian methods with inter-ethnic conflicts. It was not until the Eighth Congress of the SKJ in 1964 that the national question came on to the official agenda (Alter, 1989, pp. 132–133). From the beginning of the 1960s the pace of economic growth was slowing down and there were different opinions about it, from the argument that the decentralisation process was leading towards anarchy, to stressing that étatisme still played an important role and not self-management, as it had not had a chance to develop. Only a small minority pointed out that there was no need for the existence of a communist party. These discussions were in the background, not only of the 1963 Constitution but also of the Eighth Congress.

During the Eighth Congress it was argued that a disjuncture had developed between the principle of national equality and economic development, especially with regard to republican GNP. However, at the same time, nationalism started to re-emerge using mostly economic arguments, claiming that the economic structure of the central state should slowly 'wither away' as the SKJ had been suggesting since the 1950s. As a result the Constitutional Amendments were passed in 1967 concerning mostly economic issues. The federation had lost quite a few of its economic functions but enough were preserved to cause a constant crisis on the federal level as each republic pushed its own interests.

In 1968, for the first time, the republican congresses of the SKJ were held before the all-Yugoslav Congress, and with it the process of federalization of the SKJ began. Republican parties decided for the first time about their 'political platform and orientation' and chose their representatives in the federal bodies. This event is very important in understanding the series of events at the beginning of 1970s leading up to the 1974 Constitution. The first crisis, which is usually not discussed in the literature in connection with the constitutional changes, is connected with the student movement in 1968 throughout Europe. Yugoslav students were demanding social and political reforms, more equality, more democracy and more real socialism (*Študensko gibanje*, 1982; *Praxis*, 1968, 1971). The second crisis was connected with an international loan given for building roads in Yugoslavia in which Slovenia openly argued that it felt discriminated against (the so-called 'cestna afera'). However the most important event happened in Croatia in 1971 (the so-called Croatian Spring) when the League of Communists of Croatia (SKH) demanded more economic independence (Irvine, 1993, pp. 258–272). The critical point was reached not with this demand but when Croatian nationalists joined the movements reviving the Croatian question or, in other words, when they put forward a claim for Croatian independence. The last point is connected with the previous one in that the need for economic reforms was discussed among liberal-oriented politicians and economists, especially in Serbia, Slovenia and Croatia. They were arguing that the power of both the Party and federation should be diffused in favour of the economic structures and the republics.

Most of the political power lay with Tito and the Party. By 1966 the conservative forces in the country were defeated and, immediately after, liberal forces (the so-called 'rotten liberals') were defeated also. Tito was afraid of nationalism spreading throughout the country because of the political consequences that might follow. However, he feared that more decentralisation would mean the end of the leading role of the SKJ as many voices were challenging the one-party system, and discussing the rule of law (*Staatsrecht*) and democracy (through, for example, the student movement and a group around *Praxis*). In this connection, two points should be made. Firstly, Tito was fighting the leaderships of Croatia, Serbia and Slovenia and that means that his policies could not be interpreted as evidence of nationalistic agitation. He made sure that he was seen as a defender of socialism against nationalism. Secondly, loyal party members in each republic were fighting their own leadership. The defeat came from within, from their own republics and their own nations (except that in Croatia a number of the leaders were Serbs).

'In fact, the constitution of 1974 was Tito's answer to the intraparty opposition of national and modernizing provenance' (Banac, 1992, p. 173). *De jure* the 1974 Constitution Yugoslavia was defined as a 'self-management federalism'. According to the first paragraph of the Constitution, sovereignty was based upon two principles: the working class and nation. Thus, Yugoslavia was considered a federation because it was a multi-national state pursuing self-management based upon negotiation and agreement. The working class, it was argued, should 'rule' social production, and the nation the federal state. It is therefore important to highlight firstly, the working class and nations can primarily exercise rights in their federal republics and secondly, rights which are of common interest for the whole federation can be negotiated and agreed upon only in a federal context. It seems that the concept of self-management federalism resulted in a multinational federation which ideologically emulates the concept of the working class.

In practice, such events reflected the SKJ's wish to re-establish itself over political, economic and cultural affairs. However, that could have not been done directly. A way out was seen to be to gradually turn Yugoslavia into a federation of self-management socialism and a 'non-party form of pluralism' (Kardelj, 1978). The two most important spheres where self-management was realised were the economy and local communities. The economy was perceived as the most important field and various institutions were introduced, later named 'contractual economics'. The local community and the economy gained more power in a hope that they would be a locus of power where 'self-management pluralism of interests' would transcend ethnic and republican identity (Goati, 1989, pp. 5–15). However, an unintended consequence was republicisation. Republics and autonomous provinces (Kosovo and Vojvodina) gained and continued to ask for more power, even drawing upon the idea of self-management to justify their claims. This in effect was how the national question re-entered the political arena (Schoepflin (1993b, p. 190) argues similarly).

Tito's death had serious consequences for the political, economic and social life of all Yugoslavs. Yugoslavia lost not only a stateman with enormous prestige in the world community, but also a figure who held the country together, despite losing his popularity towards the end of his life. Yugoslavia was faced with what seemed immense problems: a huge foreign debt and a poor record of investment. The disastrous state of the economy had its national and political interpretation, and not only an economic explanation. Everything erupted in Kosovo. The most undeveloped part of Yugoslavia introduced national conflict as the only answer to its own federal problems.

In the 1980s Kosovo was functioning differently from the rest of Yugoslavia, not just because terror raged throughout the province but because of its nature, and the way it was carried out and perceived in the rest of the country (Magaš, 1993, pp. 3–73). It was terror not against an individual or a political group but against the whole nation. The problem seemed difficult to solve – one can abandon political ideals but how does one abandon its own national belonging? The terror was carried out by the Serbian political leadership, only one leadership. The rest of the country watched the terror taking place in front of their eyes. It was only a matter of time before not only the other political leaderships but also the public would respond to the terror.

In the 1980s new social movements were entering the cultural scene. Punk was the first such movement in Yugoslavia, mostly in Slovenia (Mastnak, 1991, pp. 45–64). It is of paramount importance because it was fighting for an independent space, for a new social and political language and for a citizen as against a subject. There is something extremely interesting about the movement. In terms of membership, it is important to note that only two groups were involved, teenagers and young intellectuals. They used the radio station *Radio Študent* and a weekly newspaper of the official youth organisation *Mladina* (from the mid 1980s) to offer an alternative way of thinking about socialism. Here a new political culture developed. There were two objects of its critique: one was Tito, but not directly, and the other was the Yugoslav People's Army (JNA). The Slovenian Youth Organisation refused to take part in the youth rally in 1986, arguing that the whole concept was outdated because Tito was dead. Since the Second World War youth relays had been organised to celebrate Tito's birthday and the 'brotherhood and unity' of the youth of Yugoslavia.

It was much more difficult to criticise the Yugoslav Army. It was still seen as the Army which liberated Slovenia during the Second World War, so their criticism could not be direct. Firstly, their critique did not concentrate on the Army's constitutional position. According to the Constitution the Army was a defender of socialism ('the leading ideological force'). The Army had its own party organisation which was a constitutive member of the Federal Party. The Minister of Defence was an *ex officio* member of the collective

Federal Presidency. Secondly, their critique did not address a Slovenian contribution to the federal budget. However, in 1988 they criticised Army expenses which had mostly to do with generals' caprices (e.g. villas) and arms trade to the Third World countries which was made public through the Ethiopian case. The Army retaliated severely, and the *Mladina* journalists were sentenced to prison by the Military Court. Slovenian public opinion was outraged but it did not help. The Army stepped in as a defender of socialism with the result that both of them (the Army and socialism) lost credibility. Soon after, the Army got involved in defending Serbian nationalistic interests, especially in Kosovo. In response, Janez Janša, a *Mladina* journalist sentenced to prison and a future Minister of Defence, proposed to form a 'parallel army' out of the existing territorial defence units. Two years later these units played a crucial role in defending Slovenian independence.

At the end of 1980s the Army was very much Titoist and Yugoslav. Its political role came from its position within the Party. That position made every action legitimate, as much as party actions were legitimate. The Army was slowly losing its legitimacy because the SKJ was losing it. In the late 1980s Slovenia and Croatia were discussing military budget cuts and 'parallel armies'. By that time only Serbia was welcoming the Army, claiming that it was the only state which would like to preserve a Yugoslav federation and continue a socialist project. Serbian reasoning was purely pragmatic: the leadership needed the Army to fight in Kosovo. Veljko Kadijević, Minister of Defence, not being terribly keen on Milošević, pushed through the depoliticisation of the Army in December 1990. (It must have been a difficult decision, because the Army was formed by the Party in 1941.) The next stage could have been based either on a regimental basis, using the Partisan Army option, or a republican basis. This was never done. Instead, the Army was getting more and more involved on the Serbian side. At this point the national composition of the Army played an important role: sixty per cent of officers were Serbs (Gow, 1992, pp. 139–152). Political delegitimation and economic impoverishment pushed the Army to align with the side which was using a familiar language (Yugoslav federation, socialism, etc.) and which belonged to the same national group (in that order).

New social movements were slowly spreading outside Slovenia. They are important because they influenced the intellectual environment in the rest of Yugoslavia. From the mid-1980s there had been debates about democracy and the distinction between state and civil society. What is interesting is that there was hardly any discussion about the nation, nation-building and nationalism, especially in the western parts of the country. Even events in Kosovo did not put them on the agenda. Yugoslav republics were living their separate lives or treading an increasingly centrifugal path. Forces of control had very different patterns of behaviour: in Kosovo they were crushing (literally) Albanians; in Slovenia they were fighting against a newly independent social space, they were fighting against difference and otherness.

In Slovenia itself two commissions were formed to deliver a stabilisation programme. They tried to use once again a familiar formula, reforms *for* people not *by* people. The second commission did not want even to start a discussion about political reform. It was argued, as before, that only political changes could facilitate economic changes.

The financial support, in the form of loans and aid, was still coming. An informal club ('Friends of Yugoslavia'), on the initiative of the USA, was even formed to help Yugoslav economic reform, which was thought to be progress. The geo-strategic position of Yugoslavia (in relation to Eastern Europe) was still important to the West.

In the end, reform did not take place: only the rhetoric of self-management was employed. There were two possibilities, democratic or nationalistic, i.e. to introduce political organisations based on human rights or on national interests (Dimitrijević, 1991, pp. 77–84). Serbia was definitely moving towards the latter. Its League of Communists (SKS) turned into the League of Nationalists and consequently into the party of Serbian nationalism. Other communist parties were slow to respond. They did not want to follow the Serbian way but they were afraid of introducing pluralism of interests. In a nutshell, their time was running out and they were not aware of it.

Only the Slovenian party leadership realised that a way out was a multi-party system that was slowly entering Slovenian society. The Slovenian Youth Organisation in 1988 declared its 'struggle for power'. The League of Communists responded using two strategies. Milan Kučan, its President, was arguing that the Slovenian society should follow the non-party way. On the other hand, members of the League were pointing out that the time had been reached to 'descend from power'. Two other important points need to be taken into account. The first came from within Slovenia as a response to the Serbian argument for more centralisation, and was called 'asymmetric federalism'. The other was the other side of the same coin, a response to the Serbian leadership's plan to suspend the autonomy of the Kosovo province. (In February 1989 the federal presidency passed a declaration on emergency measures for Kosovo.)

THE DOMINANCE OF NATIONAL MODELS

In 1986, Milošević came to power through an internal party coup using nationalistic rhetoric. He argued that Serbia was discriminated against within Yugoslavia, both politically and economically, and effectively stirred up populistic-nationalistic passions. Slovenian and Croatian politicians and public were critical of such simultaneous élitism and populism, and of the lack of democratic culture. However, a group of Serbian intellectuals, members of the Serbian Academy of Sciences, endorsed the position of national communists and formulated their own position in the so-called *Memorandum*, which laid the platform for Milošević's policies towards Kosovo and the rest of Yugoslavia. The document portrayed the rest of Yugoslavia as an enemy of the Serbian state which had not allowed the Serb nation 'to determine their own national interest'.

Milošević insisted in his *realpolitik* on a show of strength and national unity. He argued that all Serbs should unify behind the Serbs of Kosovo and that the political leaderships of Vojvodina and Kosovo should resign because they showed no sympathy ('have no heart') for them. The aim was to destroy the autonomy of these two provinces and to secure the hegemony of the Serbian nation. The 1974 Constitution gave each republic and province much more power within the federation. Serbs saw it as a 'system error' (Samardžić, 1990, pp. 37–40) and interpreted it as an attack on Serbia. The new Serbian Constitution, adopted in March 1989, finally made Serbia an 'equal' republic in Yugoslavia (Basta-Posavec, 1991, pp. 109–125). It did not matter that the slogan 'Kosovo – Republic' did not only mean secession, it did not matter that hundreds of thousands of Albanians were against curbing their province's autonomy, it did not matter that 1,300 miners were on hunger-strike deep in the pits to protest against the same plan, it did not matter that Azem Vllasi, the leader of the province and only a month earlier removed from the Central Committee of the SKJ, was illegally arrested.

Slovenia reacted against the Serbian position, with the Slovene opposition organising a meeting of solidarity with the miners. The strike went on for a week and the lives of the strikers were seriously endangered. However, both Serbian and federal leaders did not want to talk to the miners, except for Vllasi. Federal leaders hoped that granting further concessions to Serbia would in the future oblige it to obey federal agreements. The meeting in Slovenia was important because for the first time the representatives of the party and oppositional groups gave speeches at the same meeting. The Serbian leadership reacted by encouraging Serbs to rally in the streets against Slovenia and to go to Slovenia and hold a 'rally for truth' concerning Serb treatment in Kosovo. They went but were stopped on the Slovenian border. The immediate effect was that the

League of Communists of Slovenia announced within one month that it would 'strive for the creation of the multiparty system' and the law on political organisations was passed.

Milošević abolished the autonomy of Kosovo and Vojvodina, struck a deal with the leadership in Montenegro, and responded arrogantly demanding that a Federal Party congress meet as soon as possible. He was aware that he had secured the support of both provinces, Montenegro and the Army, and that he had to act quickly to crush Slovenia. In January 1990, the Fourteenth Extraordinary Congress of the SKJ took place, the last such meeting. The Slovenian communists demanded reform of the SKJ, including further decentralisation. Milošević openly admitted that this meant 'a war among Yugoslav nations'. Being outvoted on each single issue, the Slovenians walked out of the congress hall. The SKJ ceased to exist.

During the bitter struggle between Serbia and Slovenia, Croatia remained silent. Croatian politicians still remembered 1971 and the way Tito handled the 'Croatian Spring'. The Communist Party of Croatia was disoriented. The party leadership, under the influence of their leader Stipe Šuvar, believed that Yugoslavia would continue to exist through deals with Serbia and Milošević. They believed that they held two aces in their hands. They did, but they did not know how and when to use them. Firstly, they were supporting Slovenia but a belief that Yugoslavia could be saved through negotiations with Serbia made them only silent supporters. When they openly supported the Slovenian party leadership, it was too late, the SKJ ceased to exist and with it Socialist Yugoslavia also. The wait and watch principle proved to be pointless. Secondly, the party leaders strongly believed that greater autonomy of the Croatian state within Yugoslavia could be obtained in return for greater autonomy for the Serbs in Croatia. It meant that the party leaders, despite their knowledge and opinion about the *Memorandum*, agreed that the question of the Serbs in Croatia should be solved in negotiations with the Serbian leadership, not with the local Serbs only.

In the *Memorandum* it was stated that 'the solution of the national question of the Serbs in Croatia is the most important political question of the day'. At the same time, it was argued that 'the unity of the Serb nation in Yugoslavia is the crucial issue of its existence'. That was the conclusion, and the premises were as follows: Serbia gave on the altar of Yugoslavia its own state and more than 2.5 million victims in the two world wars. In socialist Yugoslavia it was denied statehood or, in other words, it was the only nation without its own state, a state which would include all Serbs. The authors never tried to explain why all Serbs had to live in one state or, even more importantly in the context of later events in Croatia, why the Serbian state is wherever the Serbs live. That was taken for granted.

Croatia and its claim to statehood were viewed, by the Serbian leadership, as nationalistic, which was defined as 'quasi-fascistic' (Banac, 1992, p. 174) or fascistic. These lines were especially highlighted in contacts with the local Serbs. On the other hand, rallies in Serbia had a formative influence on Croatia's own national awakening. The party leadership did not pay any attention to all these events, still hoping that a deal with Serbia was possible. At the same time, in the spring of 1989 the Association for the Yugoslav Democratic Initiative was formed by intellectuals who were publicly arguing the need for multiparty democracy. As a first political organisation opposing the leading role of the SKJ, it was an umbrella for different political opinion and discussion. The core members jealously guarded of the autonomy of intellectual activity from political pressures. However, the pressure was easing down. Political trials took place but not a single sentence was passed. Soon the first political party was formed, the Croatian Social Liberal Party. It was technically illegal but nobody cared. The SKH was silent even in Croatia. Numerous political organisations mushroomed in a short period of time. Lively public and political activity was taking place. However, from the very beginning, the national and nationalistic perspectives were of major importance. Milošević's rhetoric, rallies for truth in Serbia and the 'timber revolution' of local Serbs in the summer of 1990 made some political groups respond in the nationalistic way. This can be understood (not justified) if we compare Slovenia, in which a national perspective was also developed, and Croatia. Croatia had borders with Serbia, the local Serbs and the silent party leadership.

However, nationalism is an important ideology and political movement in the whole of Central Europe. It was a predominant ideology in the last century during national awakening, nation-building and state-building. As Herder pointed out in the last century, nationalism in this region is inward-looking and has either mild or assertive xenophobic characteristics. From a contemporary democratic perspective, nationalism prefers organic to individualistic approaches and it is not entirely incompatible with authoritarianism (Schoepflin and Wood, 1989, pp. 24–28).

THE BREAK-UP OF YUGOSLAVIA

The 'real socialist' system stopped the beginning of the process of modernisation, understood as a synonym for democratic revolution, which was taking place in a number of Eastern European countries. The crisis of the 'real socialist' system clearly pointed out the failure of the socialist modernisation process (Kalanj, 1994, pp. 211–229).

Whatever had been on the margins of society, suppressed and unofficial was now mainstream. The old system entailed romanticism which glorifies the collective as a subject, not individual subjects. That collective is almost always the nation. Therefore, the break-up of 'real socialist' societies introduces the same problems and contradictions which real socialism wanted to sweep under the carpet (Fanuko, 1992, pp. 51–62). In Croatia and Serbia, much more then in Slovenia, national movements are mass movements which are developing ethnocentrism as *the* value system (Hodžić, 1991, pp. 115–128). Uniqueness (of its own nation), apriorism (leading to a genealogical approach) and selectivity (of past events) are its main features. The crisis of the system awakened suppressed layers of consciousness, a hope which builds upon the myths of the past an idea of strength and all the possibilities of its own nation (Supek, 1992, pp. 87–207). It even went one step further: a historical vertical was made and all the past was concentrated in one single moment for *the* final battle which would be led by the ruling élite. This clearly indicates that the main role in developing and fanning ethnocentrism is played by the same élite (Katunarić, 1988, pp. 161–164). That was the situation in the late 1980s and the beginning of the 1990s, when the Slovenian and Croatian multiparty elections took place.

The Slovenian electorate, despite seventeen parties taking part in the elections, had to decide to vote in reform socialism or postsocialism. Slovenes decided in their parliamentary elections to vote for the centre-right party coalition, DEMOS. As in other Eastern European countries it was a vote against communists much more than a vote for the party that came into power. In their presidential elections Slovenes voted in the head of the former League of Communists. That does not come as a surprise if we remember that Kučan was strongly supporting the Slovenian interests on the federal level. This was much more a vote showing respect for his fights on the federal level and a criticism of Serbian politics. The results of the Slovenian elections clearly showed that the most important issue was to demonstrate that one is a Slovene and then reveals one's political affiliations.

A week later the first multiparty elections took place in Croatia. The SKH, analysed now in the perspective of the forthcoming elections, did not have the time and skills to take on a new image. Oppositional parties had established their images already in the second part of 1989 and all of them insisted on the national interests of Croatia and/or the Croats (Đurić *et al.*, 1990). During the election campaign the two models for restructuring the Yugoslav federation appeared. The Croatian Democratic Union (HDZ) from the very beginning argued that Yugoslavia should be a confederation or, preferably, an alliance of states just like the European Community.

The centre would have hardly any power. Two issues were especially discussed, the Army and economic policies. Given the role of the Yugoslav Army in Kosovo, it was argued that Croatia should establish its own Army. The second issue is connected with economic aid to underdeveloped regions of Yugoslavia. That issue was analysed through the Croatian (and Slovenian) point of view of being financially exploited by the rest of Yugoslavia. The decision was easily made; Croatia should not finance these regions any more. It is worth mentioning at this point that Franjo Tudtman, President of the Union, was discussing changing the borders of Bosnia and Hercegovina. Only after the elections would he openly say that these two republics 'constitute a geographical and political unity, and have always formed a joint state in history' (Cohen, 1993, p. 97).

The former communists (SKH-SDP) and the Coalition of National Accord (KNS) were supporting reforms of the existing federation. Especially, communists were keen on the Prime Minister's economic reforms and constitutionals amendments, hoping, once again, that economic changes are the panacea for Yugoslavia. Both parties were opposing changes of the borders between the six republics.

HDZ won the elections. Two issues should be taken into account. Like in Slovenia, the voters were casting their votes *against* the League of Communists. However, Croatia was engulfed by a nationalism far more evident than in Slovenia.

In the rest of the country there were communist governments in power, with the Serbian one, especially not keen on changes. In May 1990, the annual president was inaugurated: a representative from Serbia, Borislav Jović. He, as a supporter of Milošević, strongly attacked multiparty elections, claiming that in 'those difficult times' the country should unite to escape a 'pluralistic chaos'. The new governments of Croatia and Slovenia continued to discuss the reorganisation of the federation. They endorsed the con/federal models that adhered most clearly to the traditional goals of their national movements.

The civil war and then the independence war put the military issue on the agenda. Slovenia was much more vocal, asking for depoliticisation of the Army, military service to be performed in a native republic and in a native language. Croatia was silent on this issue for two reasons. It was unable to deal with the Serbian minority. Tudjman always tried to point out that the Serbs would be given all 'democratic rights'. However, the rhetoric of his party was often nationalistic. The fact is that the Serbs felt threatened. Unfortunately, just a few people in the ruling party or the Government tried to understand the reasons for the perceived threat. Was it really necessary to talk about a 'well-organised conspiracy' and not to do anything (e.g. negotiating)? That obviously meant supporting a group which was pushing for political autonomy. The Serbs of Croatia were throughout their history close to Serbia proper. They were traditionally supporters of Yugoslavism, not always understood as unitarism (Banac, 1984). During the Second World War the genocide against the Serbs took place by ultranationalistic Croats and Moslems (*Ustaše*). It was insensitive to allow their insignia to be freely sold in the streets of Croatian cities or to sing their songs. Without taking into account the whole history of the Serbs in Croatia, the events starting in 1989 clearly indicate that ethnic nationalism was rapidly spreading among the Serbian communities in Croatia and Bosnia and Hercegovina. It was clearly connected with the Serbian nationalistic attitude towards not only the Albanians but, especially, the Croats and then the Muslims. On the other hand, the Croatian government did not want to provoke the intervention of the Yugoslav Army, which was slowly loosing its Titoist and Yugoslav background.

In June 1991, Slovenia and Croatia declared independence, which led to the bloodiest war in this part of the world. Slovenia knew very well that she would like to secede and stood fast. Her military forces were well organised and equipped. The Yugoslav Army originally wanted to secure the borders but it was swiftly defeated. The Slovenian act of independence was illegal, as was the Army intervention. But by this time nobody cared any more.

Slovenia won its independence war in ten days. Croatia was standing aside and watching. It is difficult to say that if it had joined Slovenia the war in Croatia would have been shorter. Croats were studying the reactions of the West, especially of Germany, and of Serbia. They were aware that they were not militarily ready to confront the JNA. They thought that the war in Slovenia could be won by the JNA and did not want to provoke military intervention. Last (but not least), this point is connected with the question of Krajina Serbs (local Serbs), which nobody was ready to tackle.

Fighting started in Croatia with irregular skirmishes at the same time as the war in Slovenia. The JNA was humiliated by the swift defeat in Slovenia and provocations in Croatia (blockading barracks and cutting off communal supplies). It therefore decided to fight back and joined the Serbian irregular forces (Vasić, 1993, pp. 3–28). In six months it captured nearly one-third of Croatia. The UN did not want to intervene in the matters of Yugoslavia because it was a sovereign state. As I argued earlier, Yugoslavia had not existed *de facto* since January. Nationalistic feelings, more precisely hatred, were spreading fast. The mass media played a 'dirty' role in fanning nationalistic feelings. As I pointed out earlier, everybody was getting ready for the final battle. In the summer of 1991, it was clear that the war would be bloody and that it would spread to Bosnia and Hercegovina. Because of that, the UN Blue Helmets should have intervened, and peacemaking did not make sense any more. In the former Yugoslavia nobody was ready to negotiate a peace plan.

How did the West tackle the problem? Croatian (and Slovenian) independence was acknowledged in January 1992. With the independence came the UN peacekeeping forces, occupation of one-third of Croatia's territory, and thousands of dead and hundreds of thousands of refugees. And, of course, all this had taken place as a result of a war which had never been officially declared. In the spring of 1994, the most important political question, the Serbian question, merely started to be tackled (discussing borders), with no agreement how to solve it (Pupovac, 1994, pp. 8–9). Meanwhile, the economy was in tatters, totally preoccupied with the war in Bosnia and Hercegovina.

Bosnia and Hercegovina (BiH) differed from the other Yugoslav republics in that it did not have an ethnic majority. Bosnian Muslims are Islamised Slavs who were acknowledged as a separate nation for the first time in 1971. The first multiparty elections in the autumn of 1990 brought into power a national coalition government. Very soon it was clear that there existed a division along national lines. On 10 January 1991, at the first session of a special round of discussions on the future of Yugoslavia organised by the Federal Presidency, BiH and Macedonia proposed a state organised along a combination of federal and confederal lines yet at the same time stressing their right to secession and to protecting the inviolability of federal borders. It was then for the first time that the Bosnian Serbs allied with Serbia and Montenegro argued that a unilateral secession by republics was not acceptable because it would separate the ethnic minorities from their core-nations. This was fourteen months before the war broke out. Since then, ethnic tensions had been growing mostly because they were fanned from outside, primarily from Serbia (Ali and Lifschultz, 1993). By February 1992, Alija Izetbegović, President of Bosnia and Hercegovina, was sincerely hoping that the war could be prevented. He again argued for 'asymmetric' or 'graded federation' in which Slovenia and Croatia would have confederal attachments to the rest of the country, organised on federal lines. Soon after the fighting started, which turned into a bloodier war than in Croatia. Serbian forces (with the personnel and equipment of the JNA) joined the Bosnian Serb Army. Bosnian Croats were backed by the official Croatian Army and by paramilitary forces of the ultranationalist Party of the Right in Western Hercegovina, which was captured by the Croats and renamed Herceg-Bosna (Letica, 1992, 245–249). The Bosnian Muslims started to receive some assistance (aid and weapons) from the Islamic countries (some of whom have tried to 'export' Islamic fundamentalism too).

The destruction of BiH was not caused only by the Serbian leadership but came also 'in the form of miscomprehension and fatal interference of the leaders of the West' (Malcolm, 1994, p. 251). In March 1992, the EC suggested that BiH should be divided along ethnic lines into the Union of States of Bosnia. This plan was rejected by the Muslims, who still hoped to preserve the old Yugoslav borders of BiH.

An EC-UN conference was organised in Geneva in October 1992 where Vance and Owen introduced a peace proposal which was negotiated over the following three months, and finally offered to the 'three warring sides' in January 1993. Behind the plan was a *fait accompli* 'logic'. And that 'logic' was based on ethnic lines. They tried to hide it, to satisfy Muslims, arguing that BiH should be divided into ten regions. Those ten regions were divided into three groups of three provinces, while Sarajevo was to be designated an open city (Figure 7.2.). Only the Croats accepted the plan, as they were given more territory than they controlled. The Serbs rejected it immediately because they were expected to give up territory that they had already conquered. The Muslims rejected it because it acknowledged the division along ethnic lines (Cohen, 1993, pp. 243–253).

In August 1993, the Owen–Stoltenberg plan was on offer, resembling the previous 1992 EC plan. The Bosnian Serbs would be given 52 per cent of the territory, the Croats 18 per cent and the Muslims 30 per cent. Again the plan was rejected by the Muslims (Crnobrnja, 1994, p. 215).

In March 1994, the Croats and Muslim of Bosnia and Hercegovina entered into a federation drawn up by the Clinton administration. What motivated them to accept were three things: firstly, they wanted to end a bitter ethnic war between Croats and Muslims, secondly, to break the agreement between Croats and Serbs to carve up BiH, and thirdly, to put aside the previous two plans which were based on ethnic criteria. In actuality, this plan divided BiH into two zones, both of which would seek the protection of Croatia and Serbia. (Already a confederation between the Bosnian federation and Croatia had been discussed.) As a result, a ceasefire was achieved but a political solution has still to be found. In effect, this plan acknowledged that only ethnicity counts. On the ground, tensions between Croats and Muslims persist (Puhovski, 1994, pp. 7–8). Muslims and Croats were given 51 per cent of territory, *de facto* they control together 30 per cent. This dispute will be solved with a lot of difficulty, as a new peace plan drawn in July 1994 shows. The new map insists on the same numbers but was redrawn as a result of fighting in the previous four months (*The Economist*, 9 July 1994, p. 37). The Bosnian Serbs were given 14 days to accept this 'make-or-break deal'. Again they said no. For the first time they were not supported by Serbia due to the effect that international sanctions are having on the Milošević regime. Also, Russia, a traditional

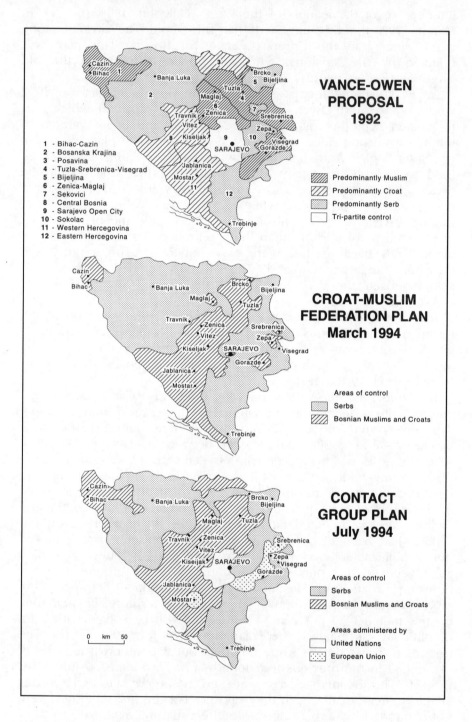

FIGURE 7.2: POST-FEDERAL BOSNIA-HERCEGOVINA

Serbian ally, withdrew its support. Consequently, on 4 August, Serbia decided not to support the Bosnian Serbs if they rejected the plan (*The Guardian*, 5 August 1994, p.22). They were given another two months by the international community (until 15 October) to accept the plan, otherwise the Americans would lift the arms embargo and start selling weapons to the Bosnian Muslims.

CONCLUSION

The Yugoslav federation has ceased to exist, and the reasons for its demise are more internal than international. The political leaders in the 1980s could not agree upon constitutional reform. At the same time, the economy was performing badly in part due to the fact that it had become politically rudderless. To gain support, the national leaders, led by Milošević, turned towards their nations, rediscovering ethnic nationalism as a mobilising ideology.

One type of collective ideology was in effect swopped for another. However, democracy is now slowly developing in Slovenia. In Croatia the war legitimates the party in power. Unfortunately, the political opposition and the rest of the population agree with that, and without having developed a democratic culture, they wait to be given rights and to be allowed to express their opinion. In Serbia a 'new' authoritarian regime is in power which does not leave a lot of space for the political opposition and is ready to use well-established methods to silence them. Kosovo lives a double life. Serbs and Albanians live there without (literally) meeting each other. Albanians are still silent, hoping that the Gandhian method will bring them victory. Macedonians are hoping that economic recovery will help them to continue to exist as an independent state despite the irredentist policies of all their neighbours.

The 'citizens' of the newly independent states have been so deeply affected and even psychologically damaged by the appalling warfare that they will need some time to fight for the space to express different opinions. The public and private spheres no longer exist as separate entities – the public sphere dominates. Civil society was rediscovered in the 1980s but it has to be rediscovered again. It is being sacrificed at the alter of ethnic nationalism. Therefore, the old Hobbesian formula has to work the other way around: people have to be ready to risk a part of their security in order to obtain more freedom.

ACKNOWLEDGEMENT

This chapter is dedicated to my late father who taught me to love people for who they are, not what they are.

REFERENCES

Ali, R. and Lifscultz, L. (eds) (1993) *Why Bosnia? Writings on the Balkan War.* Stony Creek, Connecticut: The Pamphleteer's Press.

Alter, P. (1989) *Nationalism.* London, Edward Arnold.

Banac, I. (1984) *The National Question in Yugoslavia: Origins, History, Politics.* Ithaca and London, Cornell University Press.

Banac, I. (1992a) The Fearful Asymmetry of War: the Causes and Consequences of Yugoslavia's Demise. *Deadalus,* Volume 121, No. 2, pp. 141–174.

Banac, I. (ed.) (1992b) *Eastern Europe in Revolution.* Ithaca and London, Cornell University Press.

Basta-Posavec, L. R. (1991) Ustavna demokratija i (ne)demokratska konstitucija drustva, u: *Raspad Jugoslavije* (zbornik). Beograd, Institut za evropske studije, pp. 109–118.

Bilandžić, D. (peto izdanje 1978) *Društveni razvoj socijalističke Jugoslavije.* Zagreb, CDD.

Binns, Ch. (1989) Federalism, Nationalism and Socialism in Yugoslavia, in: Forsyth, M. (ed.). *Federalism and Nationalism.* Leicester, Leicester University Press, pp. 115–146.

Burgess, M., Gagnon, A.-G. (eds) (1993) *Comparative Federalism and Federation.* London, Harvester Wheatsheaf.

Carter, A. (1982) *Democratic Reform in Yugoslavia: the Changing Role of the Party.* Princeton, Princeton University Press.

Cohen, L. (1993) *Broken Bonds: the Disintegration of Yugoslavia.* Boulder and Oxford, Westview Press.

Crnobrnja, M., (1994) *The Yugoslav Drama.* London, I. B. Taurus Publishers.

Čulinović, F. (1952) *Razvitak jugoslavenskog federalizma.* Zagreb, Školska knjiga.

Cviic, C. (1991) *Remaking the Balkans.* London, Royal Institute of International Affairs and Pinter Publishers.

Denitch, B. (1993) *After the Flood: World Politics and Democracy in the Wake of Communism.* London, Adamantine Press.

Dimitrijević, V. (1991) Upotreba ljudskih prava, u: *Raspad Jugoslavije* (zbornik). Beograd, Institut za evropske studije, pp. 77–84.

Dugandžija, N. (1987) *Jugoslavenstvo.* Beograd, Mladost.

Đurić, D., Munjin, B. and Španović, S. (ur.) (1990) *Stranke u Hrvatskoj.* Zagreb, Radnicke novine.

The Economist (1994), 9 July, p. 37.

Erasmus (1994) Special Issue: Okrugli stol Srbi i Hrvati. Zagreb, No. 5.

Fanuko, N. (1992) Dediferencijacija i rat, in: Čaldarović, O., Mesić, M. and Stulhofer, A. (ur.). *Sociologija i rat.* Zagreb, Biblioteka Revije za sociologiju, pp. 51–62.

Forsyth, M. (1989) Introduction, in: Forsyth, M., (ed.), *Federalism and Nationalism.* Leicester, Leicester University Press, pp. 1–7.

Goati, V. (1989) *Politička* anatomija jugoslavenskog društva. Zagreb, Naprijed.

Gow, J. (1991) *Yugoslav Endgames: Civil Strife and Inter-state Conflict.* London, The Centre for Defence Studies, No. 5.

Gow, J. (1992) *Legitimacy and the Military: the Yugoslav Crisis.* London, Pinter Publishers.

Gross, M. (1981) O integraciji hrvatske nacije, u: Gross, M. (ur.). *Društveni razvoj u Hrvatskoj: od 16. stoljeća do početka* 20. stolječa. Zagreb, Liber, pp. 175–190.

Held, J. (1993) *Democracy and Right-Wing Politics in Eastern Europe in the 1990s.* Eastern European Monographs. New York, Columbia University Press.

Hobsbawn, E. (1992) *Nations and Nationlism Since 1789.* Cambridge, Cambridge University Press.

Hodžić, A. (1991) Etnocentrizan društvenih grupa i nacionalnih zajednica, u: *Položaj naroda i medunacionalni odnosi u Hrvatskoj* (zbornik). Zagreb, Institut za društvena istraživanja, pp. 115–128.

Irvine, J. A. (1993) *The Croat Question: Partisan Politics in the Formation of the Yugoslav Socialist State.* Oxford, Westview Press.

Kalanj, R. (1994) *Modernost i napredak.* Zagreb, Antibarbarus.

Kardelj, E. (1978) *Pravci razvoja političkog sistema socijalističkog samoupravljanja.* Beograd, Komunist.

Katunarić, V. (1988) *Dioba društva.* Zagreb, Sociološko društvo Hrvatske.

King, P. (1982) *Federalism and Federation,* London, Croom Helm.

Koštunica, V., Čavoški, K. (1985) *Party Pluralism and Monisam: Social Movements and the Political System in Yugoslavia, 1944–1949.* Boulder: Eastern European Monographs, Columbia University Press.

Kulturni radnik. Special Section: Federalizam i konfederalizam. Zagreb, Vol. 42. No. 1, pp. 5–117.

Lerotić, Z. (1989) *Jugoslavenska politička klasa i federalism.* Zagreb, Globus.

Letica, S. (1992) *Obećana zemlja: Politički antimemoari.* Zagreb, Globus International.

Lydall, H. (1989) *Yugoslavia in Crisis.* Oxford, Clarendon Press.

Magaš, B. (1993) *The Destruction of Yugoslavia: Tracking the Break-up 1980–92.* London, Verso.

Malcolm, N. (1994) *Bosnia: A Short History.* London, Macmillan.

Mastnak, T. (1991) From the New Social Movements to Political Parties, in:

Yugoslavia in Turmoil: After Self-management, Simmie, J. and Dekleva, J. (eds). London and New York, Pinter Publishers, pp. 45–64.

Mijanović, V. (1987) Round Table Discussion in *Yugoslavia. The Failure of Democratic Communism,* New York, Freedom House.

Mirić, J. (1984) *Sistem i kriza.* Zagreb, CKD.

Mirić, J. (1990) *Iskušenje demokracije: Da li je moguća Jugoslavija kao demokratska zajednica?* Zagreb, Radničke novine.

McFarlane (1988) *Yugoslavia: Politics, Economics, Society.* London, Pinter Publishers.

Neumann, F. (1974) *Demokratska i autoritarna država.* Zagreb, Naprijed.

Pavlowich, S. K. (1971) *Yugoslavia.* London, Ernest Benn.

Pavlowitch, S. K. (1994) Who is 'Balkanizing' Whom? The Misunderstanding Between the Debris of Yugoslavia and Unprepared West. *Daedalus,* Vol. 123, No. 2, pp. 203–223.

Poulton, H. (1993) *Balkans: Minorities and States in Conflict.* London, Minority Rights Publications.

Praxis (1968) Special Issue: Studentsko gibanje. Zagreb.

Praxis (1971) Special Section: Trenutak jugoslavenskogsocijalizma. Zagreb, Vol. 8, No. 3–4.

Praxis International (1994) Special Issue: the Rise and fall of Yugoslavia. Vol. 13, No. 4.

Puhovski, Z. (1989) Aporetika 'real-socijalističkih' reformi. Zagreb, *Naše teme,* No. 1–2.

Puhovski, Z. (1990) *Socijalistička konstrukcija zbilje.* Zagreb, Pitanja.

Puhovski, Z. (1994) A Shot-gun Wedding. London, *War Report,* May 1994, No. 26, pp. 7–8.

Pupovac, M. (1994) Moving Towards Peace in Krajina? London, *War Report,* May 1994, No. 26, pp. 8–9.

Pusić, V. (1992) A Country By Any Other Name. *East European Politics and Societies,* Vol. 6, No. 3, pp. 242–259.

Ramet, P. (1984) *Nationalism and Federalism in Yugoslavia,* 1963–1983. Bloomington: Indiana University Press.

Rizman, R. (1991) *O etnonacionalizmu.* Ljubljana, Krt.

Samardžić, S. (1990) *Jugoslavija pred iskušenjem federalizma.* Beograd, Stručna knjiga.

Samardžić, S. (1991) Dilema of Federalism in Yugoslavia – Problem of Sovereignty in a Multinational Federation. *Praxis International,* Volume 11, No. 3, pp. 377–386.

Schoepflin, G. (1993a) *Politics in Eastern Europe: 1945–1992.* Oxford, Basil Blackwell.

Schoepflin, G. (1993b) The Rise and Fall of Yugoslavia, in: McGarry, J. and O'Leary, B. (eds), *The Politics of Ethnic Conflict Regulation.* London, Routledge, pp. 172–203.

Schoepflin, G., Wood, N. (eds.) (1989) *In Search of Central Europe.* Cambridge, Polity Press.

Sekelj, L. (1990) *Jugoslavija struktura raspadanja.* Beograd, Rad.

R. W. Seton-Watson and Yugoslavs, Correspondence 1906–1941. (1976) London–Zagreb, British Academy–University of Zagreb.

The Seventh Congress of the SKJ. (1958) Beograd, Kultura.

Shoup, P. (1968) *Communism and the Yugoslav National Question.* New York, Columbia University Press.

Singleton, F. (1985) *A Short History of Yugoslav Peoples.* Cambridge, Cambridge University Press.

Smith, A. D. (1986a) *The Ethnic Origins of Nations.* Oxford, Basil Blackwell.

Smith, A. D. (1986b) State-making and Nation-building, in: *States in History,* Hall, J. (ed). Oxford, Basil Blackwell.

Sociologija (1990) Special Section: Kriza federalizma. Beograd, Vol. 32, No. 4, pp. 528–557.

Študensko gibanje (1982) Ljubljana, Krt.

Sunić (1987) Round Table Discussion, in *Yugoslavia: The Failure of Democratic Communism* (1987) New York, Freedom House.

Supek, R. (1992) *Društvene predrasude i nacionalizam.* Zagreb, Globus.

Teorija in praksa (1984) Special section: V središču pozornosti: Federalizem. Ljubljana, Vol. 21, No. 12, pp. 1388–1439.

Tvrtkovic, P. (1993) *Bosnia Hercegovina: Back to the Future.* London, Polprint.

Vasić, M. (guest co-ed.) Who is in Control?. *War Report,* January 1993, No. 17, pp. 3–28.

Vodopivec, P. (1992) Slovenes and Yugoslavia. *East European Politics and Societies,* Vol. 6, No. 3, pp. 220–241.

Vucinich, W. S. (1969) *Contemporary Yugoslavia.* Berkeley: University of California Press.

Za konfederalno Slovenijo (1990) Ljubljana, Znanstveno in publicistično središče.

Czechoslovakia: the Disintegration of a Binational State

Robert J. Kaiser

Ethno-territorial conflict is the essence of the nationalist agenda throughout Eastern Europe and the former USSR, and indeed is a nearly ubiquitous feature of the contemporary ethno-political landscape in much of the rest of the world. It was not so long ago that politicians and scholars in the capitalist west and the socialist east were pronouncing ethnic nationalism dead or dying, yet the so-called 'new nationalisms' have risen to challenge the legitimacy and longevity of multinational, multi-homeland states in both the first and second worlds. Of course, the former colonial South has been engulfed since decolonisation in ethno-territorial conflict, which shows no sign of abatement. We are truly at the height of the Age of Nationalism today, which has survived the setbacks of fascism and world reaction against it, and Marxism-Leninism, to emerge as the dominant political ideology of the late twentieth century.

This nationalism is clearly a geographic strategy, though its geographic dimension is rarely the focus of studies on nationalism. Recent events have certainly substantiated the statement made by Anthony Smith over a decade ago that 'whatever else it may be, nationalism always involves a struggle for land, or an assertion about rights to land' (Smith, 1981, 187). The goal of nationalism is territorial restructuring, the attempt to make state borders congruent with the borders of the national homeland (Williams, 1986; Williams and Smith, 1983), and to make the nation as independent as possible within them (Breuilly, 1982). Nationalism is the essential equivalent of national territoriality, defined as the attempt made by nationalists to gain control over the destiny of the nation by asserting their right to sovereignty in their ancestral homeland (Kaiser, 1991, 1993).

Derived from dozens of programmes of nationalist political organisations, the nationalists' geopolitical image of Utopia is a world of ethnically pure, autarchic nation-states whose borders coincide with the imagined borders of the ancestral homeland in which the nation experienced a mythical Golden Age at some point in the past. This idealised geopolitical image of the way the world should be obviously does not conform to the reality that most polities are multinational, multi-homeland states which are increasingly interdependent. Nationalists typically view this reality as a series of problems to be overcome. Three basic problem sets are identified by nationalists in the current geopolitical structuration of the world:

—The world economic system has not become more autarchic, but has instead become more interconnected and interdependent in a global capitalist economy.

—The world political system has increased to nearly 200 states, but the number of nation-states whose borders include one and only one nation and homeland has not increased dramatically. The vast majority of states in the world today are multinational, multi-homeland states.

—The geographic area proclaimed as the ancestral homeland contains members of other ethnic groups, who may be recent in-migrants but who also may claim to be indigenous to the region.

Of these three problem sets, nationalists appear most flexible on the question of autarchy, and most seem willing to accept a subordinate position in the world economy so long as they are in political control of their homelands. Of course, nationalists do not press equally forcefully at all times for independence, but rather press for as much independence as the times and circumstances will allow (i.e. 'to become as independent as possible'). Federal systems that provide varying degrees of sovereignty to the nation in its homeland are normally perceived as an acceptable compromise by nationalists, although even after they have successfully negotiated greater sovereignty in a more politically decentralised federal restructuring, they often continue to press for greater independence.

In multinational, multi-homeland states, nationalist political élites of subordinate nations press for greater sovereignty in regions claimed as their ancestral homelands. This national separatism is frequently felt not only in the political arena, but also in the sociocultural and economic sectors of society, and if successful results in a process of confederalization over time (Kaiser, 1991). On the other hand, central state authorities (often representing the interests of a politically dominant nation) seek to retain power at the centre. This tension between unitarism and separatism is found in most multinational, multi-homeland states, and was a core ingredient in the Czech–Slovak relationship as it developed during the state's existence.

Federal systems, occupying the middle ground between unitary and confederal states, have often been used as a means of ethno-territorial conflict management. Federation was even viewed by Lenin as a means of solving the national problem (Smith, 1990; Kaiser, 1991). However, as has become obvious since the late 1980s, the structuration of the multinational, multi-homeland socialist states as federations providing nominal sovereignty to nations in their homelands contributed to the rise of national consciousness and territorial nationalism, and ultimately served as a mechanism in the hands of nationalists seeking first to gain greater sovereignty in confederated states, and then to declare their outright independence.

Of the three problem sets listed above, there appears to be least flexibility on the question of ethnic purity of the homeland, and the presence of ethnic "others" has typically served as a catalyst for rising national assertiveness. Ethnic cleansing is neither a new phenomenon nor a geographically isolated response, but is unfortunately an all too common occurrence. Indeed, Connor (1986) appears correct to consider 'that segment of a people living outside the homeland' as a diaspora, which will never truly be made to feel 'at home'.

TERRITORIAL NATIONALISM IN CZECHOSLOVAKIA

The above discussion of nationalism implies that ethno-territorial conflict may occur on at least two distinct levels as nationalists seek to redress the inadequacies of the real world.

Level One: conflicts arising from self-determination movements by indigenes whose members seek to gain greater sovereignty over their national homelands.

Level Two: conflicts among neighbouring groups over the geographic extent of the national homeland, which are exacerbated when the borderlands are also areas of ethnic minority concentration (adding an ethno-demographic dimension to a historic dispute).

Czechoslovakia, from the time of its creation in 1918 to its demise in 1993, faced ethno-territorial conflicts at both levels described above. First, and most significant, the ethno-territorial conflict between Czechs and Slovaks was almost exclusively level one, and the border between the Czech lands and Slovakia was one of the few in the state that was not in dispute. There were not substantial demands for border revisions on the basis of either historical or ethno-demographic claims. It may even be said that Czechoslovakia's disintegration was relatively harmonious (the 'Velvet Divorce') not because of the Czech's quiescent 'national character', as some news analysts have suggested, but because the two levels of ethno-territorial conflict did not overlap in this case.

The interstate borders of Czechoslovakia were clearly not

congruent with either historical or demographic homelands, but had border regions populated by members of groups other than the state 'nations' of Czechs and Slovaks (Figure 8.1). Level two conflicts mainly occurred between Czechs and Slovaks on the one hand and ethnic minorities living in border regions but whose nation and homeland extends to include the majority of the neighbouring state (Germans in Sudetenland before World War II, Magyars in Southern Slovakia, Poles in Northern Czechoslovakia, Ukrainians/Ruthenians in the easternmost part of the state before World War II). Obviously, level one ethno-territorial conflicts are more likely to challenge the legitimacy of the multinational, multi-homeland state, while level two ethno-territorial conflicts challenge the legitimacy of the borders as drawn. At least in the context of Czechoslovakia, these level two conflicts have held the potential to become interstate conflicts (e.g. Sudetenland in the past; Southern Slovakia today).

THE FORMATION OF CZECHOSLOVAKIA

Czechoslovakia was created in 1918 out of the remnants of the disintegrating Austro-Hungarian Empire. However, this outcome was by no means certain even as late as 1917. Czech nationalists, including Tomas Masaryk, were pressing for a looser, more confederated Austria-Hungary, and shifted to a more radical independence movement only after a tilt towards Germany in Austria raised renewed concerns about German dominance over the Czech lands (Obrman, 1993, 46). The United States also favoured the continued existence of Austria-Hungary up to 1917, hoping that this stance would help to drive a wedge between Austria and Germany. According to Kelly (1992, 187), 'Far from being the liberators of the subject peoples of Austria-Hungary, Wilson and his administration were quite willing to sacrifice the nationalities' political aspirations in order to shorten the war.' If Austria had been willing to accept a more confederal structure prior to 1918, the empire might very well have survived World War I. When Austria finally agreed to accept federalism on 6 October 1918 in an effort to preserve the empire, it was 'too little, too late' (Kelly, 1992, 199).

Early non-binding agreements on the political future of Bohemia, Moravia and Slovakia (Cleveland Agreement, 1915; Pittsburgh Agreement, 1918) described the state as a loose confederation of two equal nation-states (the Czech Lands and Slovakia). In 1919, Edvard Benes, future president of the republic, described the state to be created as 'a sort of Switzerland', which also indicated that the state would become a loose confederation (Seton-Watson 1965, 327). This more decentralised confederation was certainly the favoured future

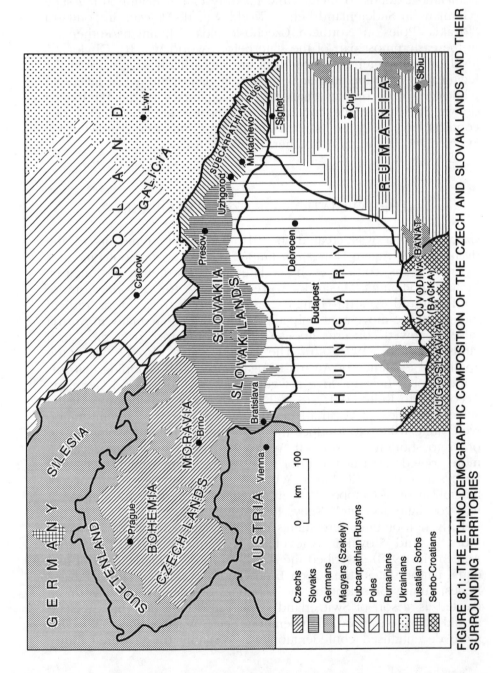

FIGURE 8.1: THE ETHNO-DEMOGRAPHIC COMPOSITION OF THE CZECH AND SLOVAK LANDS AND THEIR SURROUNDING TERRITORIES

as perceived by Slovak and Ruthenian nationalists. However, although the First Republic (1918–38) provided the Slovaks and Ruthenians with much greater cultural and even territorial autonomy than they had had under Magyar rule, Czechoslovakia was constructed primarily by Czech political élites as a much more unitary state controlled by Czechs. This caused a rising reactive national separatism among the Slovak and Ruthenian nationalists, and also encouraged irredentism among the Sudeten Germans and the Magyars of southern Slovakia.

THE INTERWAR PERIOD

Slovak national separatism

The history of Czech–Slovak relations in Czechoslovakia has been marked by a fairly consistent effort on the part of Slovak nationalists to gain greater control over their own lives and the fate of their nation by gaining greater independence in Slovakia (i.e. national territoriality), and Czech resistance to this Slovak national territoriality. For their part, Czech nationalists sought to solve their Slovak 'problem' through the promotion of assimilation of Slovaks to a Czech national identity (i.e., nation-building through Czechisation) under the rubric of 'Czechoslovakism'.

Czechs did not claim Slovakia as a historical part of their ancestral homeland, and so no real *level two* ethno-territorial dispute emerged.[1] In addition, few Czechs lived in Slovakia, and this situation did not change appreciably after independence (Tables 8.1–8.3). The claim to Slovakia was ethnically based on the idea that Czechs and Slovaks were branches of the same nation, which implied that Czech nationalists would seek to reunify this nation through the assimilation of Slovaks after independence. Although the more sensitive Czech political élites proclaimed that Czechs and Slovaks would merge to become a new 'Czechoslovak' nation, the general consensus among Czech political élites was that the Slovaks were a lesser part of the Czech nation. Even as late as 1943, Benes stated that:

> I am of the firm conviction that the Slovaks are Czechs and the Slovak language is only one of the dialects of the Czech language . . . I cannot stop anybody from calling himself a Slovak, but I shall not agree with a declaration that a Slovak nation exists (Steiner, 1973, 53).

Table 8.1 Ethno-national composition of the population, Czechoslovakia 1921–91
(absolute totals and percentages)

Nation	1921	1930	1950	1961	1970	1980	1991
Total (1000s)	13 003	13 998	12 338	13 746	14 345	15 283	15 577
Percentages:							
Czechs*	52.5	53.1	67.9	66.0	65.0	64.1	63.1
Slovaks	15.1	16.3	26.3	27.9	29.3	30.6	31.0
Germans	24.7	23.6	1.3	1.0	0.6	0.4	0.3
Magyars	5.1	4.3	3.0	3.9	4.0	3.8	3.8
Ruthenians†	0.8	0.8	0.6	0.4	0.4	0.4	0.3
Poles	0.8	0.7	0.6	0.5	0.5	0.4	0.4
Other‡	1.0	1.2	0.3	0.3	0.3	0.3	1.1

* Czechs: for 1991, the Czech percentage given above includes self-declared Czechs (8,416,652 or 54.0 per cent of the total population), as well as 'Moravians' (1,368,350 or 8.8 per cent of the total population identified themselves as 'Moravians' in 1991) and 'Silesians' (44,851 or 0.3 per cent of the total population). This was the first time that the published census results included data for self-declared 'Moravians' and 'Silesians'.

† Ruthenians: includes data for Ukrainians and Russians as well as Ruthenians (the last category was seldom included in the censuses, which often provided only one category for a combination of these ethno-national communities). In 1991, Ruthenians were given as a separate category (19,123 or 0.1 per cent of the total population), compared to 21,501 Ukrainians (0.1 per cent of the total) and 6,451 Russians (0.04 per cent). The above figures are for Ruthenians in the postwar Czechoslovak borders only. For Ruthenians in Subcarpathian Rus' and in Ukraine, see Table 8.4.

‡ Other: The increase in 1991 represented the growing ethnic resurgence of Gypsies in the state, who comprised 108,705 or 0.7 per cent of the total population and exceeded the number of Poles, Germans and Ruthenians in the state. According to many analysts, even this higher number vastly understates the number of Gypsies in Czechoslovakia, which has been estimated variously from 240,000 to 550,000 (Pehe, 1993, 18).

Source: 1921–61: Jurecek, 1968; 1970: Czechoslovakia (FSU) 1971; 1980: Czech Republic 1985a; 1991: CSFR 1992, 15–18.

Table 8.2 Ethno-national composition of the population, Czech Republic 1921–91
(absolute totals and percentages)

Nation	1921	1930	1950	1961	1970	1980	1991
Total (1000s)	10 010	10 674	8896	9572	9808	10 292	10 350
Percentages:							
Czechs*	67.5	68.4	93.8	94.3	94.5	94.6	94.8
Germans	30.6	29.5	1.8	1.4	0.8	0.6	0.5
Poles	1.0	0.9	0.8	0.7	0.6	0.6	0.6
Slovaks	0.2	0.4	2.9	2.9	3.3	3.5	3.1
Magyars	0.1	0.1	0.2	0.2	0.2	0.2	0.2
Ruthenians†	0.1	0.2	0.2	0.2	0.2	0.1	0.1
Other‡	0.5	0.5	0.3	0.3	0.4	0.4	0.7

* Czechs, 1991 = Czechs, 8,363,768 (81.2%); Moravians, 1,362,313 (13.2%); and Silesians, 44,446 (0.4%).

† Ruthenians, 1991 = Ruthenians, 1,926 (0.02%); Ukrainians, 8,220 (0.1%); and Russians, 5,062 (0.05%).

‡ Other, 1991 = 32,9.03 Gypsies (0.3% of total).

Source: As in Table 8.1.

Table 8.3 Ethno-national composition of the population, Slovakia 1921–91 (absolute totals and percentages)

Nation	1921	1930	1950	1961	1970	1980	1991
Total (1000s)	2994	3324	3442	4174	4537	4991	5274
Percentages:							
Slovaks	65.1	67.7	86.6	85.3	85.5	86.5	85.7
Magyars	21.7	17.6	10.3	12.4	12.2	11.2	10.8
Czechs*	2.4	3.7	1.2	1.1	1.1	1.1	1.1
Ruthenians†	3.0	2.9	1.4	0.9	0.9	0.8	0.6
Poles	0.2	0.2	0.1	0.0	0.0	0.0	0.1
Other‡	2.8	3.2	0.3	0.2	0.2	0.3	1.6

* Czechs, 1991 = Czechs, 52,884 (1.0%); Moravians, 6,037 (0.1%); and Silesians, 405 (0.01%).

† Ruthenians, 1991 = Ruthenians, 17,197 (0.3 %); Ukrainians, 13,281 (0.3%); Russians, 1,389 (0.03%).

‡ Other, 1991 = Gypsies, 75,802 (1.4%).

Source: As in Table 8.1.

This Czech view of the Slovaks as a lesser part of the Czech nation had a clearly detrimental effect on Czech–Slovak relations in the state after 1918, and proved counterproductive to the ultimate goal of nation-building through assimilation. This Czech attitude and political agenda served as potent catalysts for the rise of Slovak national consciousness and nationalism during the interwar period.

The ethnic justification for merging the Czech lands and Slovakia was not the only rationale given by Czech nationalists. The Czech political élites also wanted to include Slovaks in the new state as a demographic counterweight to the Germans, who were about half the size of the Czech population and about the equal of the Slovaks (Table 8.1). Over the course of time, the Slovaks would be assimilated and the 'Czechoslovak' nation would be able to determine its own future without regard to the wishes and interests of the formerly dominant German minority (Leff, 1988, 35).[2]

This 'Czechoslovakism' was visible in the name selected for the state – Czechoslovakia instead of Czecho-Slovakia, the latter of which was used in earlier documents and was clearly favoured by Slovak nationalists. The name adopted reflected the unitary nature of the state, and the failure to structure it as a federation of two national homelands. In fact, during the interwar years Slovakia was merely one of five historical territories (Bohemia, Moravia, Silesia,

Slovakia and Subcarpathian Rus'). The assimilationist orientation of the Czech political élites was also apparent in the statistics collected, which most often presented ethno-demographic, economic and socio-cultural data about Czechs and Slovaks together in one column for 'Czechoslovaks'.

One could certainly question the degree to which a Slovak national consciousness had become mass-based by 1918. While a nationalistic élite existed and agitated in favour of the rise of a mass national movement in Slovakia beginning in the 1830s, they had a limited impact on the nationalisation of the masses during the remaining decades of the nineteenth century, particularly after 1867 (Hroch, 1985, 98–99). Magyar political dominance and Magyarisation in the socio-cultural sphere placed severe constraints on Slovak nationalist agitators, and the rural Slavic peasants in the region retained a localist mentality that was only beginning to give way to a broader Slovak national consciousness by 1918. In the census of 1919, a question on nationality was asked for the first time, and it was clear that peasants generally, and Slovak peasants in particular, had difficulty answering the question (Johnson, 1985, 80):

> One census-taker related just how difficult it was by listing some of the answers he got – 'Slovak as well as Hungarian'; 'It's all the same'; 'Hungarian-Slovak'.

The same general confusion about national identity was noted by census takers in 1921 (Leff, 1988, 18).[3]

Slovak nationalists shared the Czech desire for independence from a formerly dominant group – in the Slovak case the Magyars. None the less, few Slovak nationalists shared the view that their people were merely an ethnic branch of a greater Czechoslovak nation. Czechoslovakism from the Slovak nationalist perspective appeared as little more than Czechisation of the Slovak people, with the end result of the process not a Czechoslovak but a Czech nation, and the loss of Slovak identity. In this context, the Czechs appeared as little better than the Magyars who had subjected Slovaks to Magyarisation during the nineteenth century. The Slovak nationalist goal of a dual polity composed of two equal nations in a federal or even confederal state was clearly at odds with the Czech 'nation-building' agenda, with its end goal the creation of a unitary Czechoslovak (or Czech) nation-state.

In this historical context, it is not surprising that the Slovak nationalist vision of their proper place in an independent Czecho-Slovakia was that of a co-equal nation in a dual federation. It is also not surprising that the Czech perception of Slovaks as younger (and lesser) brothers who would welcome the chance to 'rejoin' the Czech nation would cause a reaction among the Slovak nationalists, who would view this as little more than Magyarisation with a Czech face. The very nearness of the two national communities in ethno-cultural and linguistic terms added to the Czech misperception, for it 'deluded the majority Czech nation into the imprecisely formulated hope that the two nations had identical interests – that Slovakia could be induced to behave like a lost tribe returned to the fold' (Leff, 1988, 7).

The socio-economic and demographic trends during the interwar period indicated that there was a nationalisation of the Slovak masses into a more cohesive Slovak nation, rather than a Czechisation of the Slovaks. A Slovakisation was clearly evident in the school system, where a 'Slovaks first' hiring policy was put in place, and where the expansion of the system benefited primarily Slovak students who went from a position of serious under-representation before 1918 to relative over-representation by the mid-1930s (Johnson, 1985, 127–128). While these so-called 'Czechoslovak' schools had the goal of political socialisation of the Slovak masses toward a Czechoslovak identity, the local control over education by upwardly mobile Slovaks tended to have the opposite effect of Slovakising the peasantry.[4]

After an initial period of in-migration of Czech public servants during the 1920s, a 'Slovaks first' hiring policy was also apparent throughout the economy, and particularly in the high status occupations. In addition, economic development was occurring prior to the Great Depression of the 1930s, though Slovakia remained under-developed relative to the Czech lands. It has often been assumed that regional economic inequality, coupled with limited economic opportunities for Slovaks, fueled the demands for greater Slovak independence during the 1930s. However, Slovak unemployment was actually below the rate experienced in Bohemia and Moravia during the 1930s. Rather, a growing perception of relative deprivation among a rapidly expanding Slovak intelligentsia, coupled with economic decline in the 1930s and the rising national consciousness among the Slovak masses, created the socio-economic and socio-political impetus for independence by the late 1930s (Johnson, 1985, 307–313):

> The young Slovak 'intelligent' was not unemployed but perceived him-self to be underemployed. The Hungarian experience had led the Slovak to believe that education was the road to success and esteem and influence . . . Problems arose when the members of the Slovak intelli-gentsia did not find themselves in full control of their own destiny, as many had expected they would be . . . The problem was that the Slovak intelligentsia had greater expectations than could be realized.

The Slovakisation that occurred became increasingly pro-independence and anti-Czech in orientation, as indicated by the success of Slovak political parties committed to a more confederal arrangement or outright independence. The failure of Czech political élites to accommodate this desire for a more confederal arrangement, or even to include the Slovak People's Party in the ruling coalition, placed Slovak nationalists in the position of political opposition, and tended to radicalise their demands, leading up to the first division of Czechoslovakia in 1938–39 (Leff, 1988, 85). Slovak separatism may have facilitated the demise of Czechoslovakia and the success of Nazi Germany, but this national territoriality on the part of the Slovaks cannot be separated from Czech nationalism during the interwar period, and the Slovak nationalist reaction to it.

Ruthenian national separatism

Like the Slovaks, the Ruthenians (Rusyns) of Subcarpathia were a subordinate ethnic minority in a relatively under-developed part of Hungary. The Ruthenian intelligentsia was becoming nationalised during the mid-nineteenth century, but was also subjected to Magyarisation between 1867 and 1918. Also like the Slovaks, a Ruthenian national consciousness was not well-defined among the peasant masses of the region, who retained a much more localised sense of identity and homeland prior to 1918. During the interwar period, Subcarpathian Rus' was treated as a separate administrative region, but was not given the territorial autonomy promised in the *Generalni Statut* of 1919. The Ruthenian nationalists were unhappy with both their lack of political autonomy and their borders, which they felt gave Ruthenian land to Slovakia. Socio-cultural and socio-economic trends, and particularly expanding literacy, education and non-agrarian economic activity during this period tended to enhance the national identity of Ruthenians in this area, although the Czech language was promoted here, and skilled Czechs migrated to the region and dominated the higher status occupations that had been vacated by the Magyars (Table 8.4). Consequently relatively less in the way of a 'Rusyn-first' restructuring of the ethnic stratification system was in evidence (Magosci, 1978).

Anti-Czech sentiments rose in Ruthenia during the 1930s, as did Ukrainian irredentism towards the region. Ruthenia declared its independence as the Republic of Carpatho-Ukraine on 15 March 1939, only to be conquered and occupied by Hungary a few days later. After the war, most of this region was attached to Ukraine on the basis of the ethnic justification that Ruthenians were part of the Ukrainian nation. This assumption was certainly questionable. While the Ruthenian political élites were divided as to whether Ruthenians were an independent nation, part of the Ukrainian nation, or part of the Russian nation, the masses – who remained highly rural and localised during this time – did not achieve a national consciousness

Table 8.4 Ethno-national composition of the population, Subcarpathian Rus'
1921–89 (absolute totals and percentages)

Nation	1921	1930	1959	1970	1979	1989
Total (1000s)	607	725	920	1057	1156	1246
Percentages:						
Ruthenians*	61.5	61.6	74.6	76.5	77.8	78.4
Magyars	16.8	15.1	15.9	14.4	13.7	12.5
Jews	13.2	12.6	1.3	1.0	0.3	—
Czechs†	1.6	2.9	—	—	—	—
Slovaks	1.7	1.9	1.3	0.9	0.7	0.6
Russians‡	—	—	3.2	3.3	3.6	4.0
Romanians	2.2	1.7	2.0	2.2	2.3	2.4
Gypsies	0.1	0.2	0.5	0.6	0.5	1.0
Other §	2.9	4.1	1.1	1.1	1.1	1.2

* Ruthenians: from 1959 to 1989, this category was listed as 'Ukrainian' in the Soviet censuses for Subcarpathian Oblast, Ukraine.

† Czechs: From 1959 to 1989, the Soviet censuses for Subcarpathian Oblast, Ukraine Czechs were not listed separately. Most Czechs left for the Czech Republic during the late 1930s.

‡ Russians: included in the Czechoslovak censuses within the category 'Ruthenians'. From 1959 to 1989, Russians were listed separately.

§ Other: for 1989, this figure includes Jews, who were not listed separately.

Source: 1921: Czechoslovakia 1921, Johnson 1985, 81; 1930: Magosci 1978, 13, Johnson 1985, 81; 1959: Tsentral'noye Statisticheskoye Upravleniye pri Sovete Ministrov SSSR (TsSU SSSR) 1963, vol. 2, 176; 1970: TsSU SSSR 1973, vol. 4, 175; 1979: Goskomstat SSSR 1989, vol. 4, part 1, book 2, 35; 1989: Statisticheskiy Komitet Sodruzhestva Nezavisimykh Gosudarstv (SNG) 1992, vol. 7, part 2, 54.

(Magosci 1978).[5] While it is difficult to assess the degree of mass-based Ruthenian national identity or the extent of popular demands for independence in the former Subcarpathian Ruthenia, the recent movements in the region for greater territorial autonomy in a federated Ukraine do indicate that at minimum a degree of ethno-regional distinctiveness continues to be felt among at least some of the population living there (Kolossov, 1992, 42–44).

German and Magyar separatism

If the Slovak nationalists were not satisfied with their status as lesser brothers to the Czechs, the Germans and Magyars remaining in Czechoslovakia must have been even more pessimistic about their chances in the new state. As the formerly dominant ethnic communities in the region, they experienced the greatest loss of status in the new Czechoslovakia that was being restructured around the Czech and Slovak ethno-national communities. The de-Germanisation and Czechisation of socio-cultural, economic and political life in Bohemia and Moravia preceded independence (Cohen, 1981), and this restructuring of the ethnic stratification system in the Czech lands accelerated after 1918. In reaction to this, Germans did attempt to secede from Bohemia and join Austria at the end of World War I, but this was not successful (Seton-Watson, 1965, 325). In Slovakia, Magyar dominance and Magyarisation continued and even increased during the late nineteenth and early twentieth centuries, and were reversed only after independence. Slovak nationalists after 1918 implemented a 're-Slovakisation' program, in principle to reclaim the Magyarised Slovaks and to Slovakise those Slavic peasants who did not yet realise they were Slovaks. However, the re-Slovakisation programme went beyond this reclamation project and also set about assimilating the Magyars in order to restructure Slovakia as an ethnically homogeneous nation-state.

The de-Germanisation and re-Slovakisation processes were apparent in the demographic statistics of the period, as German and Magyar demographic strength in the state – and particularly in the cities – underwent a dramatic decline after 1918. However, the data from the pre-1918 and the post-1918 periods are not comparable, since the pre-1918 ethnic statistics are based on language, while the post-1918 data are based on national self-identity. The linguistic assimilation of Czechs toward German (earlier) and of Slovaks toward Magyar inflated the pre-1918 German and Magyar figures. Linguistic assimilation was the extent to which Germanisation and Magyarisation went for the most part, and did not result in the psychological assimilation of the Czechs and Slovaks to a German or Magyar national consciousness. In fact, both linguistic Germanisation and Magyarisation were catalysts for rising nationalism among the upwardly mobile Czechs and Slovaks during the nineteenth century, and so were counterproductive to their ultimate goal of assimilation.

The reversal of previous acculturation patterns represented in these statistics does indicate a growing Czech and Slovak national assertiveness, and a rather dramatic decline in status for the German and Magyar communities. Both Czechs and Slovaks set about restructuring their internal ethnic stratification systems, which increasingly favoured the indigenous Slavic groups at the expense of the formerly dominant Germans and Magyars. Coupled with the fact that these communities were concentrated geographically on the border with their mother countries, where irredentist nationalism was on the rise, the status decline experienced by the Magyars and Germans in interwar Czechoslovakia – in areas that they perceived as part of their ancestral homelands – is a classic case of level two ethno-territorial conflict that contributed to the disintegration of the state from 1938 to 1945.

POSTWAR TRENDS IN NATIONAL TERRITORIALITY

At the end of World War II, Czechoslovakia was re-created, with two notable changes. First, the state had lost the Subcarpathian Rus' region in the east to the USSR (see above). Second, the re-created state was ethnically cleansed of its national minorities (Tables 8.1–8.3). Of course, the vast majority (86.1 per cent) of Jews in the state were exterminated between 1939 and 1945, and their losses were nearly as high in Slovakia (83 per cent) as in the Czech Lands (89 per cent). Gypsies were also targeted for elimination, though their losses were much higher in the Czech Lands (50 per cent) than in Slovakia (1 per cent) (Pearson, 1983, 200). The overwhelming majority of Germans who survived World War II were expelled from the state, although their land was retained and resettled by Czechs and Slovaks.[6] All told, the German population in Czechoslovakia declined by well over three million people. The number of Magyars and Poles in the state also declined precipitously during and immediately after the war, so that the state approximated to a much greater extent the Czecho-Slovak duality that the name implied. By the 1950 census, Czechs made up nearly 94 per cent of the population of the Czech lands, while Slovaks had become nearly 87 per cent of Slovakia's total population (see Tables 8.2 and 8.3).

The loss of Germans also robbed Czechs of one of their original reasons for wanting to incorporate Slovakia and Slovaks into their independent state in 1918 (see above). It could be said that the failure of Czechoslovakism or Czechisation to achieve much success among the Slovaks during the interwar period had indicated that there was a serious flaw in the second major reason for Slovakia's incorporation (i.e. the reclamation of a lost tribe). During the postwar period, Czechisation was limited primarily to non-Czechs living in the Czech Lands of the state, while a Slovakisation of non-Slovaks was apparent in Slovakia (Kaiser 1988). These ethno-demographic and ethno-cultural trends reinforced the growing divide between the two regions (i.e. a *de facto* federalisation of the state), even as they signalled the successful implementation of programmes to solve the national problems in each increasingly homogeneous 'nation-state'.

Slovak national separatism

The nominally independent Slovak state (1939–1945) has often been viewed as a sham, as a fascist puppet state of Nazi Germany. However, although the degree of independence in Slovakia during this time was limited by the realities of World War II, it is also true that Slovak independence was greater during this period than it had

221

been in interwar Czechoslovakia. According to Leff (1988, 90), 'the Slovak state was a watershed in the consolidation of Slovak national self-affirmation'. Throughout the postwar period, Slovak national élites would continue to press for greater political decentralisation of the state, and the period of nominal independence stood as a constant reminder that Slovaks and Slovakia were developed enough as a nation and homeland to go it on their own.

As was the case prior to the creation of Czechoslovakia in 1918, Czech political élites once again promised that the new state would be structured as a federation based on the principle of two equal nations. Also as in the past, at least from the perspective of Slovak nationalists, the Czechs failed to live up to their promises, although some territorial autonomy was granted in the late 1940s.

The late 1940s was also a period of high Slovak nationalism, even among the Communist Party élites. In fact, the Communist Party had become popular in Slovakia by appealing to the national territoriality of the Slovaks with a programme favouring both greater independence for Slovakia (in a federated Czechoslovakia, in a federated USSR, or as an independent nation-state), and also an anti-Magyar agenda. During this period, the nationalistic goal of an ethnically pure nation-state became a dominant objective, and re-Slovakisation continued apace. This programme was coupled with a planned deportation and population transfer to Hungary that would rid Slovakia of approximately 150,000–200,000 Magyars who could not be re-Slovakised, who were to be exchanged for the approximately 100,000 Slovaks living in Hungary (King, 1973, 54). This would leave approximately 150,000–200,000 'Magyarised Slovaks' to be re-Slovakised (Srb, 1975, 99). This programme of ethnic cleansing in Slovakia had the support of Benes, who stated that 'There is no room for minority problems . . . Members of minorities who refuse to return to their national state . . . will be definitely sacrificed and given up to national assimilation by the other state' (King, 1973, 53).

This population transfer programme was halted in 1947 after about 60,000 Magyars had been expelled or transferred and approximately 40,000 Slovaks had been gathered in (Wynne, 1953, 11). The Slovaks of Hungary who were returning to the homeland were not necessarily greeted with open arms. The fact that they spoke Hungarian and did not act like Slovaks raised concerns that these were not 'real Slovaks,' and that their return would not help to homogenise the population of Slovakia (Janics, 1982, 181). Here was a new population in need of Slovakisation.

The ethnic purification of the Czech Lands and Slovakia was connected in theory at least to the federalisation of the state. As stated by Benes, 'If we have no Germans or Hungarians among us, decentralisation will not only be possible but will be absolutely essential for the whole population' (Leff, 1988, 94). The planned federalisation of the state was curtailed by the communist takeover of the state in 1948, and although territorial autonomy did exist, the state operated under a highly unitary political power structure until 1968.

During the early 1950s, a purge of Slovak nationalists from the Communist Party occurred, setting back the national territorial agenda for nearly a decade. This was a period of recentralisation of political power, and also a period of Magyar national resurgence. Estimates of ethnic reidentification made for the period 1950–80 indicate that after decades of population decline, the dampening of Slovak nationalism during the 1950s resulted in a 're-Magyarisation,' indicating that the re-Slovakisation programme had gone too far (Tables 8.3 and 8.5).

Table 8.5 Estimates of ethno-national reidentification, Czechoslovakia 1950–80 (absolute number reidentifying, in 1000s)

Ethno-national communities Total	Czech	Slovak	Ruthen	Pole	Magyar	German	Other
1950–61	72	−123	−23	−12	106	−20	—
1961–70	81	−67	1	−8	5	−12	—
1970–80	73	−18	−10	−9	−25	−14	3
Czech Republic							
1950–61	76	−41	−2	−11	−2	−20	—
1961–70	100	−68	−4	−7	−3	−12	−5
1970–80	76	−49	−2	−12	−3	−12	1
Slovakia							
1950–61	−4	−82	−21	−1	108	—	—
1961–70	−19	1	5	−1	8	—	5
1970–80	−3	30	−8	3	−22	−1	1

Note: Ethno-national population size was estimated for each year in Czechoslovakia on the basis of natural change and migration statistics. During the year in which the census is taken, these estimates are revised in accordance with the results of the census. The need for revision is caused by errors in the collection of vital statistics, and national reidentification during the intercensal period. The error factor is taken into account by examining the adjustment of the total population, since reidentification was not a factor in the size of this population. This error estimate was distributed proportionally according to the size of each ethno-national community. The remainder was treated as a rough estimate of the ethno-national reidentification that occurred between the censuses.

Source: 1950–61: Demografie 1966, 273. A similar estimation procedure was used to derive 1961–70 and 1970–80 figures using Czech Republic 1985a, 62, 429 and 630.

During the 1960s, the Slovak national communists were re-habilitated, as was their national territorial programme . The push for greater sovereignty in Slovakia increased, as did the pressure for

Slovakisation of the population and socioeconomic equalisation between the republics. The Slovaks were successful on all counts, though Slovak nationalists remained dissatisfied that the improved status of Slovaks and Slovakia was not greater.

Political liberalisation in Prague during the 1960s allowed for greater federalisation of the state, and the restructuring of the state as a binational federation was the one part of the Action Programme to survive the Warsaw Pact invasion in 1968. While this political restructuring granted the Slovaks greater control over decision-making in Slovakia and a more equal voice in Prague, it was not the symmetrical federation that Slovak nationalists had demanded. The failure to create a Czech political structure to parallel the one in Slovakia meant that the all-union political institutions concentrated in Prague served as the Czech government, with Slovaks and Slovakia still placed in a subordinate position. In addition to this, during the early 1970s some degree of recentralisation occurred, and this clearly moved the state in a direction opposite from the ideal envisioned by Slovak élites (i.e. a confederal Czecho-Slovakia).

None the less, the Slovak nationalists were afforded enough autonomy to enable them to restructure ethnic stratification in Slovakia in order to ensure Slovaks a dominant position. The 'Slovaks first' political agenda of the nationalists during the interwar years was continued after a brief hiatus in the early 1950s. Czech dominance did not appear to extend to Slovakia, where the Slovak language became established as the *de facto lingua franca* of the republic, and the language of upward mobility.

Socio-economic equalisation between the two republics and between Czechs and Slovaks was the third goal of Slovak nationalists, and of the Communist Party which saw equalisation as the key to solving the 'national problem' (Kaiser, 1993). According to three measures of socioeconomic development (urbanisation, educational attainment and occupation structure) tabulated by republic and nation, equalisation was clearly evident from the 1960s to the 1980s. For urbanisation and occupation structure, a trend toward equalisation occurred, but Slovaks and Slovakia continued to lag behind Czechs and the Czech Republic. Within Slovakia, the southern region populated primarily by Magyars lagged even further behind, indicating that investments made for interregional and international equalisation went primarily to Slovak-populated areas. This is of course another measure of the restructuring of ethnic stratification that was taking place in Slovakia during the postwar period. For educational attainment, equality between the two republics and between Czechs and Slovaks was attained, and the Slovaks actually had a higher rate of educational attainment than the Czechs. However, as with urbanisation and occupation structure, the Magyars of southern Slovakia continued to lag behind, again indicating relative neglect of this region and minority (Kaiser, 1988, 198–236).

This interregional and international equalisation did not 'solve the national problem' in Czechoslovakia, and indeed socio-economic development and equalisation in Slovakia coincided with rising Slovak nationalism. Two reasons for this are apparent. First, equality is an extremely difficult objective to attain, because there are numerous ways of measuring comparative status, just as there are numerous measures of comparative status (i.e. political equality, socio-cultural equality, economic equality, etc.). It would be impossible for any two national communities to be equals across all possible variables. Beyond this, since a group's comparative status is a matter as much of subjective feeling as of objective measurement, a group may continue to feel relatively deprived and unequal even if a process of equalisation is well under way. In a recent survey of national sentiments in Czechoslovakia, 64 per cent of respondents in Slovakia disagreed with the statement 'The resources of the federation are equally distributed between the Czech lands and Slovakia', and only 10 per cent agreed (Deis, 1992, 10).

Second, and more significantly, indigenous nationalists do not have equalisation as their goal, but rather seek to attain a dominant political, socio-cultural, and economic position in their homelands. In the case of Czechoslovakia, the equalisation programme as it was implemented measured success across nations as well as regions, and the only two nations that mattered were the Czechs and Slovaks. The programme encouraged Slovak nationalists to enhance their own status in Slovakia; Slovaks became equalised with Czechs in the state overall, while at the same time each nation became more dominant within its own respective homeland. This relationship between international equalisation in the state overall and growing indigenous dominance at home was a common feature in all three socialist federated states (Kaiser, 1988, 1990, 1993).

THE DISINTEGRATION OF CZECHOSLOVAKIA

Slovak national separatism has been a long-term process during which Slovak nationalists attempted to establish themselves and their nation in a dominant position within their homeland. The events since 1989, ultimately resulting in the dissolution of Czechoslovakia and the establishment of two national states, cannot be understood as solely a reaction to liberal winds blowing from the east, but must be seen as the culmination of societal processes at work for much of the past seventy-five years. Czechoslovakia had by the 1980s become two relatively ethnically homogeneous nation-states, and independence in Slovakia was the final step in this long-term process of separation or divorce. As a final consideration in this chapter, I shall briefly sketch the critical events of the late 1980s and early 1990s leading to the 'Velvet Divorce' of 1992–1993, and also consider the ethno-territorial conflicts that remain to be resolved in the Czech Republic and Slovakia.

The Velvet Divorce

It is somewhat ironic that throughout most of the history of Czechoslovakia the relationship between Czechs and Slovaks was one of Slovak nationalist pressure for greater independence and Czech resistance to it, but that Slovak independence was actually pressed more forcefully by Czech than by Slovak political élites. Nevertheless, the events leading to the dissolution of the state conform to the historical pattern more closely than might at first appear. Slovak political élites initially pressed for greater sovereignty in a confederal Czecho-Slovakia, a goal of Slovak nationalists for most of the past seventy-five years. In particular, the Slovak nationalists demanded the restructuring of the state as a 'symmetrical federation', and also demanded that more powers be ceded to each republic. A compromise appeared to have been reached in April 1990, when the state was renamed the 'Czech and Slovak Federative Republic', and was restructured as a union of two equal sovereign republics, each of which was to gain much greater decision-making authority within its own territory (Cutler and Schwartz, 1991, 526).

In 1991, Slovak political élites began to press for greater independence than was provided for in the CSFR. They argued in favour of the explicit right to secede, which was not included in the Constitutional Amendments of 1990, and also attempted to further weaken the central government. The Czech political élites categorically refused to agree to further confederalization of the state, preferring outright independence of the two republics to a confederal arrangement. The inability of the Czech and Slovak political élites to reach a compromise on the degree of con-federalism in the new state continued during the following year, ultimately leading to a decision to separate peacefully in a process that has been labelled the 'Velvet Divorce', The Czech Republic and Slovakia became independent states on 1 January 1993.

According to public opinion polls taken during the period leading up to the agreement to separate, a majority of Czechs and Slovaks did not favour the break-up of Czechoslovakia (Table 8.6). However, there was also no majority in favour of retaining the dual federation, and in each republic a plurality of the population favoured the position of its nationalists (i.e. Czechs favoured a more unitary state,

Slovaks a more confederal Czecho-Slovakia). The two communities were clearly at odds with regard to their vision of a future Czechoslovakia, as their nationalist élites had been since the creation of the state in 1918. In addition, the percentage favouring separation increased dramatically between the summer and autumn of 1992, and by September 1992 the vast majority of respondents felt that the split was inevitable.

Table 8.6 Public opinion surveys on the future of Czechoslovakia, November 1991–September 1992

November 1991
Responses to the statement: *Czechoslovakia should be split into two independent states* (%)

	Czech Republic (n = 1209)	Slovakia (n = 1360)
Strongly agree	5	10
Agree somewhat	8	13
Neutral	9	19
Disagree somewhat	22	23
Strongly disagree	56	35

Source: Deis, 1992, 9.

Summer 1992
Percentage who favour

	Czech Republic (n = 603)	Slovakia (n = 562)
Unitary Czechoslovakia	38	14
Dual federation	19	27
Federation with more than two republics*	18	8
Confederation	3	30
Separation	16	16

* This option refers to the proposal to restructure the Czech Republic into Bohemian and Moravian Republics in a tripartite federation with Slovakia. Some favoured an alternative proposal of adding a Prague and Silesian Republic to this Tripartite Federation.

Source: Pehe, 1992, 37.

September 1992

	Czech Republic (n = 577)	Slovakia (n = 505)
Percentage for split	46	41
Percentage against split	45	46
Percentage who consider split inevitable	>80	>80

Source: Pehe, 1992, 37.

By law, a referendum was required for the legal separation of the two republics. However, with the inconclusive results of the surveys, and the growing sense that divorce was inevitable, the political élites from each republic concluded that a referendum would solve nothing, and would almost certainly do more harm than good. Thus, the decision to separate was made on 25 November 1992 by the Czechoslovak Federal Assembly, and the dissolution of Czechoslovakia took effect on 1 January 1993.

Slovakia

A recent study of ethnic conflict in Yugoslavia described the restructuring of the former Socialist Republics into nationalistic states as examples of 'constitutional nationalism' which 'envisions a state in which sovereignty resides with a particular nation, the members of which are the only ones who can decide fundamental questions of state form and identity' (Hayden, 1992, 656). This is comparable to the concept of 'ethnic democracy', which Smooha and Hanf define as 'a democracy in which the dominance of one ethnic group is institutionalised'. This 'constitutional nationalism' or 'ethnic democracy' is clearly evident in Slovakia today.

The Slovakisation of life in Slovakia, which was certainly apparent in the pre-independent republic, is likely to become much more aggressive in independent Slovakia. The Declaration of Sovereignty adopted on 17 July 1992 proclaimed sovereignty over Slovakia in the name of the Slovak nation and its right to determine for itself 'the path and form of our national and state life'. While the declaration also states that the rights of 'all citizens, nations, national minorities, and ethnic groups will be respected by the Slovak nation' (Obrman, 1992b, 25), this formulation clearly establishes the Slovaks as 'first among unequals' in Slovakia. The Slovak Constitution, which came into effect on 1 October 1992, also clearly signals that 'Slovakia for the Slovaks' is to be the foundation upon which the nation-state will be constructed. As a clear example of this, the preamble to the constitution, which originally read 'We, the citizens of the Slovak Republic', was rewritten as 'We, the Slovak nation' in the version that was adopted. Again, while ethnic minorities were granted some cultural autonomy, these rights 'must not endanger the sovereignty and territorial integrity of the Slovak Republic or cause discrimination against the rest of the population' (Mates, 1992, 39).

The group made most anxious by Slovakia's new status is obviously the Magyars of southern Slovakia. The Magyars and their political representatives were the strongest voice in opposition to the Slovak nationalist push for confederalism, and were also strongly opposed to outright independence for Slovakia. This is not surprising, given the fact that a more independent Slovakia would be a more anti-Magyar place. Several anti-Magyar policies have already been implemented, including the removal of Hungarian language signs in southern Slovakia, and the refusal to enter Hungarian names in birth registeries (Fisher and Reisch, 1993).

The Magyars and their political representatives have advocated territorial autonomy for Magyars in southern Slovakia, in order to help ensure that their rights as an ethnic minority are respected (Reisch, 1992). This desire for greater control over territory in order to control the fate of the Magyar population in Slovakia (i.e., national territoriality) was interpreted by Slovak nationalists as an attack on the territorial integrity of Slovakia not only by the Magyars of southern Slovakia but also by Hungary, which is seen as a threat to the viability of the Slovak nation-state. This perception of a Hungarian threat was reinforced by Magyar nationalists, who view all of the territory lost under the Treaty of Trianon as an integral part of 'Greater Hungary'. Hungary has taken an active interest in the treatment of Magyars in southern Slovakia, and there were concerns that Hungary might vote to block Slovakia's entry into the Council of Europe. This did not occur, but Hungary did abstain from the vote in protest over the status of Magyars in Slovakia (Pataki and Fisher, 1993). Given the vast disparity in the way each national community in Slovakia perceives its past relationship with the ethnic other, its present status, and its future in an independent Slovakia, the dispute between Slovaks and Magyars over their proper place in Slovakia is certain to grow more intense, and will almost unavoidably become a source of interstate tension and potential conflict between Hungary and Slovakia.

The Czech Republic

The one major 'national problem' faced by the Czech republic historically – the status of Germans in Sudetenland – had been more or less definitively resolved by the end of the 1940s with the expulsion of all but a handful of Germans from the state. Demographically, the Czech Republic became a nation-state, and during the postwar period the general trend has been toward the further decline of indigenous ethnic minorities and their reidentification to the Czech nation (Tables 8.2 and 8.5). This is particularly the case with the German population that remained, which is an aging population that is experiencing a natural decrease, and is also intermarrying at a very high rate with Czechs. Over the course of generations, the children of these Czech-German couples are becoming Czechised, further reducing the German population (Kaiser, 1988, 353–354). In addition, while the German population in Germany that traces its ancestry to the Sudetenland has lobbied for the right of return, or at least for compensation for lost property and land, the 1992 Czechoslovak-German Friendship Treaty declared the existing borders inviolable, and that the two states had no territorial claims against each other. The issue of compensation or the return of property was not addressed by the Treaty, but Vaclav Havel stated that he was opposed to it, because 'if we were to return all their property, it could start a new cycle of injustice' (Obrman, 1992a, 21).

One additional potential ethno-territorial problem has surfaced in recent years: the so-called Moravian Question (Dokulil, 1992, 84; Obrman, 1991). While the indigenous Slavic population of Moravia has historically been treated as part of the Czech nation, and it is extremely difficult to gauge the degree of Moravian self-consciousness as a separate and distinct nation, there has been a minor movement for greater autonomy in Moravia and Silesia in recent years. During the late 1980s, there was a proposal to divide the Czech Republic into two (Bohemia and Moravia) or three (Bohemia, Moravia and Silesia) federal units within the borders of the historic regions that carried these names.

This movement for greater autonomy appears to be more regionalism than nationalism, although for some the argument in favour of Moravian autonomy is posed in national territorial terms (i.e. 'we are a nation deserving of our own sovereign control over our homeland'). The 1991 census results published figures for self-declared Moravians and Silesians for the first time. Nearly 1.4 million people, or about 13 per cent of the total population in the Czech Republic, declared themselves to be Moravians by nationality, and another 44,446 (0.4 per cent) declared themselves to be Silesians (Table 8.2). This reduced the Czech demographic dominance in the republic from 95 per cent of the total population to 81 per cent, and made Moravians the second largest 'national' community in the state.

The desire to reconstruct Czechoslovakia as a tripartite federation may also have been an effort to dilute the political strength of the Slovaks at a time when they were pushing for a more confederal arrangement in a dual polity. This is certainly how the movement for Moravian autonomy was interpreted by Slovak nationalists.[7] However, the issue of Moravian autonomy has not gone away with independence, and was the one issue holding up the adoption of the new Czech Constitution. The issue of territorial autonomy for Moravia and Silesia was not resolved in the constitution as finally adopted. According to Mates (1993, 57):

> The constitution states that the Czech Republic is to be divided into municipalities and larger self-governing units – regions or lands . . . Deputies from Moravia and Silesia have demanded that both regions be given the status of 'land' and the right to establish their own representative bodies. The constitution is ambivalent on this point; it does not specify how many lands or regions the Czech Republic should have.

The Czech political élites are clearly concerned that the creation of self-governing Moravian and Silesian Lands will begin a new process of federalisation that may result in the disintegration of the Czech Republic, and are therefore strongly opposed to it. On the other hand, the Moravian 'nationalist' representatives refused to vote for the constitution as written (Mates, 1993, 57). This may be the leading edge of a new round of unitarist–separatist tension and potential conflict in a state that appeared, at least up until 1991, to be an ethnically homogeneous nation-state.

CONCLUSION

The fate of Czechoslovakia was affected to a great extent by ethno-territorial conflicts at both levels discussed in this chapter. In the interwar period (1918–1938), Czech political élites attempted to solve the ethno-territorial problem associated with Slovakia (a level one conflict) by assimilating the Slovaks into a Czech or Czechoslovak nation. They were unsuccessful in this endeavour, and in fact the Czechisation programme proved counterproductive, since it raised the level of Slovak nationalism and separatism. It had the same catalytic effect on the Ruthenians to the east. The level two conflicts within the state, and particularly those with the formerly dominant German and Magyar national minorities, were also exacerbated during the interwar period, due to the restructuring of ethnic stratification to favour the Czechs and Slovaks and to exclude, subordinate or attempt to assimilate (e.g. re-Slovakisation of Magyars) these groups. The growing ethno-territorial conflicts in the state certainly facilitated the conquest and dissolution of Czechoslovakia after 1938.

During the postwar period, level two ethno-territorial conflicts were minimised. The borderlands were ethnically cleansed through the expulsion of ethnic others. This was particularly true with regard to the German population of Sudetenland, but also was attempted with a lesser degree of success with the Magyars of southern Slovakia. In the east, the Ruthenian/Ukrainian population and homeland were incorporated into the Ukrainian Union Republic, although some Ruthenians remained in Slovakia in a region considered to be part of their ancestral homeland. This made Czechoslovakia a much more binational duality, and the focus of the national problem during the postwar period was on the relationship between Czechs and Slovaks (i.e. a level one conflict). Slovak nationalists were relatively successful in gaining a more dominant position within Slovakia and a co-equal status with the Czechs during this time period. The revolutionary changes begun in 1989 provided a further impetus for the national separatism already in evidence in Slovakia, and ultimately resulted in the dissolution of Czechoslovakia into two nation-states.

Each state (particularly Slovakia) is being restructured around the idealised image of the nation-state envisioned by nationalists, which leaves little room for the accommodation of ethnic others. This ethno-territorial exclusiveness, clearly evident in the 'constitutional nationalism' of Slovakia (and also in the former republics of Yugoslavia and the Soviet Union), is having the most serious effect on the one large minority remaining in either of the two states – the Magyars of southern Slovakia. Their demand for territorial autonomy in the face of rising Slovak nationalism is almost certain to emerge as the next serious ethno-territorial conflict facing Eastern Europe.

Czechoslovakia serves as an excellent case study of territorial nationalism and the unitarism–separatism tension found in most multinational, multi-homeland states. The utility of federalism as an instrument in ethno-territorial conflict management, and its limitations, are clearly visible in the socio-political history of Czechoslovakia. In the aftermath of the break-up of the socialist federated states (Yugoslavia, Czechoslovakia, USSR), there has been a tendency – particularly on the part of members of the dominant nations in these three states (Serbs, Czechs, Russians) – to blame the federal structure for the disintegration of these multinational, multi-homeland states. In some ways, this is an accurate assessment, since the federal structure based on ethno-national homelands did promote the nationalisation process, and encouraged the development of a sense of spatial exclusiveness among members of the titular groups. However, it is also true that the federal system, and the limited territorial and cultural autonomy allowed each national community in its homeland, helped the central authorities manage their 'national problems'. The real fault of the socialist federal system was that it did not evolve sufficiently, and was not flexible enough to meet the needs of the increasingly nationalised indigenes in these three states. If the federal system had been viewed as an instrument in conflict management, rather than as a solution to the national problem, then it may have been designed flexibly enough to reflect changes in the relationship between centre and republics over time.

NOTES

1. On the other side of the border, some Slovak nationalists did claim that their dominance of 'Great Moravia' prior to the Hunga-

rian conquest gave their quest for independence during the nineteenth century a historical legitimacy, and this could have led to a type two ethno-territorial conflict between Slovaks and Czechs over the status of Moravia. However, this never became a serious point of contention between the two groups.

2. This future project of remaking Slovaks into Czechs was favoured over the ceding of territory to Austria or Germany in order to reduce the number of Germans in the state. As perceived by Masaryk (1969, 385–387), the Czech right to retain their historic lands was greater than the right of Germans in these regions to self-determination.

3. According to Miroslav Hroch (1985, 44), the nationalisation of the masses in Bohemia toward a Czech consciousness began as early as the revolution of 1848–49, and was much more advanced than among the Slovaks. See also Cohen (1981). However, the degree to which a Czech national consciousness penetrated the Moravian countryside prior to independence is more questionable, and the issue of a separate Moravian 'nation' is an issue that has re-emerged in the independent Czech Republic (see above).

4. The rise of a nationally conscious mid-level intelligentsia, and especially the nationalisation of school teachers and an 'enlightened peasantry', is frequently cited as a critical element in the successful nationalisation of the masses (e.g. Hobsbawm, 1990; Weber, 1976; Hroch, 1985; Kaiser, 1993).

5. The actual reason that the USSR desired control over this region was less ethno-national reunification, and more geopolitical; the acquisition of this territory gave the USSR a border with Hungary for the first time (King, 1973, 30).

6. The official term for this 'ethnic cleansing' of the Sudetenland in Czechoslovakia has been 'population transfer', though Vaclav Havel in a speech immediately preceding the Czechoslovak-German Friendship Treaty referred to it as an 'expulsion' of Germans from Czechoslovakia, and this word was used in the preamble of the Treaty (Obrman 1992a, 20).

7. Not surprisingly, the 'federation with more than two republics' option in the Summer 1992 survey was the future alternative that Slovaks supported least (Table 8.6).

REFERENCES

Breuilly, J. 1982. *Nationalism and the state*. Manchester: Manchester University Press.

Cohen, G. 1981. *The politics of ethnic survival: Germans in Prague, 1861–1914*. Princeton: Princeton University Press.

Connor, W. 1972. Nation-building or nation-destroying? *World Politics* 24 (3): 319–355.

Connor, W. 1986 The impact of homelands upon diasporas. In *Modern Diasporas in International Politics*, edited by G. Sheffer. London: Croom Helm.

CSFR. 1992. *Scitani Lidu, Domu a Bytu k 3. 3. 1991*. Praha: Federalni Statisticky Urad.

Cultler, L. and Schwartz, H. 1991. Constitutional reform in Czechoslovakia: *E duobus unum? The University of Chicago Law Review* (58): 511–553.

Czechoslovakia. 1921. *Recensement de la population dans la Republique Tchecoslovaque le 15 fevrier 1921*. Prague: Polygrafie.

Czechoslovakia. 1931. *Resultats preliminaires du recensement de la population dans la Republique Tchecoslovaque du 1er decembre 1930*. Prague: Politika.

Czechoslovakia. Ustredni Komise Lidove Kontroly a Statistiky. 1965. *Scitani lidu, domu a bytu v Ceskoslovenske Socialisticke Republice k 1 breznu 1961*. Praha: Ustredni Komise Lidove Kontroly a Statistiky.

Czechoslovakia. Federalni Statisticky Urad (FSU). 1971. *Scitani lidu, domu a bytu k 1 prosinci 1970 v CzSSR*. Praha: Listopad.

Czech Republic. Cesky Statisticky Urad. 1982. *Scitani lidu, domu a bytu 1980*. Praha: Listopad.

Czech Republic. 1985a. *Vyvoj Spolecnosti CzSSR*. Praha: Listopad.

Czech Republic. 1985b. *Historicka Statisticka Rocenka CzSSR*. Praha: Listopad.

Czech Republic. 1989. *Statisticka Rocenka Ceskoslovenske Socialisticke Republiky 1989*. Praha: SNTL.

Deis, M. 1992. A study of nationalism in Czechoslovakia. *RFE/RL Research Report* 1 (31 January): 8–13.

Demografie. 1966. Pohyb obyvatelstva v CzSSR podle narodnosti 1950–65. *Demografie* 8 (3): 366–372.

Demografie. 1981. Narodnosti slozheni obyvatelstva podle scitani lidu 1950–1980. *Demografie* 23 (4): 360–364.

Dokulil, M. 1992. Ethnic unity and diversity in Czechoslovakia. *International Social Science Review* 67 (2): 76–86.

Fisher, S. and Reisch, A. Will Hungary block Slovakia's entrance into the Council of Europe? *RFE/RL Daily Report*, no. 116 (22 June).

Hayden, R. 1992. Constitutional nationalism in the formerly Yugoslav republics. *Slavic Review* 51 (4): 654–673.

Hobsbawm, E. 1990. *Nations and Nationalism since 1780*. Cambridge: Cambridge University Press.

Hroch, M. 1985. *Social Preconditions of National Revival in Europe*. Cambridge: Cambridge University Press.

Janics, K. 1982. *Czechoslovak Policy and the Hungarian Minority 1945–1948*. New York: Columbia University Press.

Johnson, O. 1985. *Slovakia 1918–1938. Education and the making of a nation*. New York: Columbia University Press.

Jurecek, Z. 1968. Narodnostno slozeni obyvatelstva. *Demografie* 10 (2): 97–109.

Kaiser, R. 1988. *National territoriality in multinational, multi-homeland states: a comparative study of the Soviet Union, Yugoslavia and Czechoslovakia.* PhD dissertation, Columbia University.

Kaiser, R. 1990. The equalization dilemma in Yugoslavia. *Geoforum* 21 (2): 261–276.

Kaiser, R. 1991. Nationalism: the challenge to Soviet federalism. In *The Soviet Union. A New Regional Geography?*, edited by M. Bradshaw. London: Belhaven Press.

Kaiser, R. 1993. *The Geography of Nationalism in Russia and the USSR.* Princeton: Princeton University Press.

Kelly, D. 1992. Woodrow Wilson and the creation of Czechoslovakia. *East European Quarterly* 26 (2): 185–207.

King, R. 1973. *Minorities under Communism.* Cambridge, MA: Harvard University Press.

Kolossov, V. 1992. *Ethno-territorial conflicts and boundaries in the former Soviet Union.* Durham: University of Durham International Boundary Research Unit (IBRU), Territory Briefing 2.

Leff, C. 1988. *National Conflict in Czechoslovakia.* Princeton: Princeton University Press.

Magocsi, P. 1978. *The shaping of a national identity: Subcarpathian Rus', 1848–1948.* Cambridge, MA: Harvard University Press.

Masaryk, T. 1969. *The making of a state.* New York: Howard Fertig.

Mates, P. 1992. The new Slovak Constitution. *RFE/RL Research Report* 1 (43): 39–42.

Mates, P. 1993. The Czech Constitution. *RFE/RL Research Report* 2 (10): 53–57.

Obrman, J. 1991. The issue of autonomy for Moravia and Silesia. *RFE Report on Eastern Europe* (12 April): 13–22.

Obrman, J. 1992a. Czechoslovak Assembly affirms German Friendship Treaty. *RFE/RL Research Report* 1 (21): 18–23.

Obrman, J. 1992b. Slovakia declares sovereignty; President Havel resigns. *RFE/RL Research Report* 1 (31): 25–29.

Obrman, J. 1993. Havel challenges Czech historical taboos. *RFE/RL Research Report* 2 (24): 44–51.

Pataki, J. and Fisher, S. 1993. Czechs and Slovaks join the CE, Hungary abstains from Slovak vote. *RFE/RL Daily Report*, no. 123 (1 July).

Pearson, R. 1983. *National Minorities in Eastern Europe 1848–1945.* London: Macmillan.

Pehe, J. 1992. The referendum controversy in Czechoslovakia. *RFE/RL Research Report* 1 (43): 35–38.

Pehe, J. 1993. Law on Romanies causes uproar in Czech Republic. *RFE/RL Research Report* 2 (7): 18–22.

Reisch, A. 1992. The difficult search for a Hungarian-Slovak accord. *RFE/RL Research Report* 1 (42): 24–31.

Seton-Watson, R. 1965. *A History of the Czechs and Slovaks.* Hamden, CT: Archon Books.

Slovenska Socialisticka Republika. 1983. *Scitanie l'udu, domov a bytov 1980.* Bratislava: Slovensky Statisticky Urad.

Smith, A. 1981. States and homelands: the social and geopolitical implications of national territory. *Millennium: Journal of Studies* 10 (3): 187–202.

Smith, G. 1990. Nationalities policy from Lenin to Gorbachev. In *The Nationalities Question in the Soviet Union,* edited by G. Smith. London: Longman.

Srb, V. 1975. 30 let populacniho vyvoje socialistickeho Ceskoslovenska. *Demografie* 17 (2): 97–104.

Statisticheskiy Komitet Sodruzhestva Nezavisimykh Gosudarstv (SNG). 1992. *Itogi Vsesoyuznoy Perepisi Naseleniya 1989 Goda.* Moskva: Statkom SNG.

Steiner, E. 1973. *The Slovak Dilemma.* Cambridge: Cambridge University Press.

Weber, E. 1976. *Peasants into Frenchmen.* Stanford, CA: Stanford University Press.

Williams, C. 1986. The question of national congruence. In *A World in Crisis? Geographical perspectives,* edited by R. Johnston and P. Taylor. Oxford: Blackwell.

Williams, C., and Smith, A. 1983. The national construction of social space. *Progress in Human Geography* 7 (4): 502–518.

Wynne, W. 1953. *The population of Czechoslovakia.* Washington: US Government Printing Office (Bureau of the Census, International Population Statistics Reports, Series P-90, No. 3).

PART III

Federations in the Making?

CHAPTER NINE

Spain: a Federation in the Making?

Montserrat Guibernau

Spain has been one of the last Western European countries to achieve democratic rule. After forty years of Franco's dictatorship, the 1978 Constitution offered a new political framework within which the Spaniards could organise their lives. One of the major issues faced by the new regime was the national question, which was particularly acute in Catalonia and the Basque Country. The Autonomous Communities System was created to solve this problem by radically transforming the centralist nondemocratic socio-political system inherited from Francoism. The lack of violence in the transition to democracy, and the almost immediate acceptance of Spain by Western organisations such as NATO and the EC, together with the rapid activation of the economy, have prompted the emergence of a highly dynamic Spain opposed to traditional patterns. Today, Spain is a country struggling to overcome a chronic backwardness and willing to catch up with its European neighbours. The lack of bloodshed in the 1989 East European revolutions, the multinational character of the former USSR and the wish to initiate democratic rule have instigated many to look to Spain as a model and way forward. However, any comparison should not ignore the fact that well before 1975 Spain had a capitalist economy. In contrast, Eastern European countries are caught up in the processes of bringing democracy about while at the same time they are experiencing a painful transition from planned to market economy.

This chapter concentrates upon the question of whether the Autonomous Communities System will act as a federalising agent leading to the transformation of the Spanish state, or whether it will stand as a pragmatic solution to the Catalan and Basque active demands for decentralisation. This claim for decentralisation was made acute during the Franco regime when the national question and the struggle for democracy were inseparable. In what follows, I explore the process that led to the democratisation of Spain. In so doing, I concentrate upon the 1978 Constitution's sections dealing with the definition and structure of Spain, and study the Catalan Socialists' position towards federalism and the debate it prompted with their Spanish counterparts. Finally, some observations are made about the changing nature of the Spanish state in the light of further European integration.

The tension between centralisation and some form of cantonalism or federalism (Pi i Margall) has been a constant problem faced by Spanish rulers. The joint rule of Ferdinand and Isabella (*Reyes Católicos*) over Castile and Aragon from 1479 put two very different areas under the same monarchs. As Elliott argues, the gulf between the two was made still wider by their differing political traditions and institutions. Although each possessed parliamentary institutions (*Corts*), the Castilian Corts had never attained legislating power and emerged from the Middle Ages as isolated and weak, while those of Catalonia, Valencia and Aragon shared the legislative power with the Crown and were well buttressed by laws and institutions which derived from a long tradition of political liberty (Elliott, 1963:7). Thus, apart from sharing common sovereigns, neither Castile nor the Crown of Aragon underwent any radical institutional alteration.

However, in practice the equality between Castile and Aragon did not long survive the death of Ferdinand the Catholic and a widening gap between Castile and all its territories, including the states of the Crown of Aragon, began. A radical change in the Castilian policy towards Catalonia took place when Philip IV (*Felipe IV*) appointed the Count Duke of Olivares as chief minister in March 1621. His objective was to create a powerful absolutist state and in order to do so, diversity should be replaced by unity. The increasing tension between Castile and Catalonia had its climax in the Revolt of the Harvesters (*Revolta dels Segadors*) in 1640 which would acquire a particular significance in the Catalan nationalist literature. It has been argued that as early as 1640, the Catalans led what can be considered one of the first nationalist revolutions. They united against the harsh treatment received from Castile, emphasised their difference from Castilians and, if they did not object to the figure of Philip IV as their king, it was on condition that he acknowledge the Catalan institutions, law and customs, since monarchy had a pactist character according to the Catalan Constitutions (Vilar, P. 1987:217 ff.).

Catalonia maintained its rights and liberties until 1714, when on 11 September after a massive Franco-Spanish attack that followed a siege of 14 months, Barcelona surrendered. Philip V (*Felipe V*) ordered the dissolution of the Catalan institutions – *Consell de Cent* (Council of one hundred), *Diputació* and *Generalitat* – and the Catalans suffered brutal repression. Catalan was forbidden and Castilian was proclaimed as the official language. On 19 January 1716, Philip V promulgated the *Decreto de Nueva Planta*, a new ground plan for the centralised government of Catalonia and its integration with the rest of Spain. This involved the practical disappearance of the Catalan aristocracy – only very few were absorbed into the Spanish nobility. This fact, together with other processes such as the demographic recovery of Catalonia, the existence of a free *pagesia* (land-owning farmers and peasants) entrenched in their properties, and the Catalan *menestrals* (artisans, shopkeepers, workshop owners) who combined individualism, familism, commitment to hard work and respect for the methodical accumulation of wealth through savings, was the basis for the transformation of Catalonia into an industrial society. The process of industrialisation that took place in Catalonia in the nineteenth century was accompanied by major social changes along patterns similar to those that were happening in other industrialising Western European countries and resulted in the creation of a sharp contrast between Catalonia and the rest of the Peninsula, with the exception of the Basque Country. This originated a very peculiar scenario in which the most economically developed part of a country, Catalonia, found itself politically subjected to an anachronistic and backward state, Castile, that held political power. Although differences have diminished, Catalan nationalists claim that this is still the case today (see Vilar, 1977)

By the end of the nineteenth century, the influence of Romanticism favoured demands for Catalan autonomy, first in the form of regionalism and later in demands for a federal state. Catalan nationalism did not emerge as a unified phenomenon: diverse political ideologies and cultural influences gave rise to different types of nationalism, from the conservative nationalism of Balmes to the federalism of Pi i Margall, the Catholic nationalism of Torres i Bages, or the Catalan Marxism of Andreu Nin, among many others (see Bilbeny, 1988 and Colomer, 1984).

Catalonia would enjoy a certain degree of autonomy during the First Spanish Republic under the administrative government of the *Mancomunitat* (1913–1923), suppressed in 1923 after the *coup d'état* of Miguel Primo de Rivera, and the *Generalitat* (1931–1938), (government of Catalonia) restored in the Second Spanish Republic and abolished by Franco's decree of 5 April 1938. After Franco's dictatorship, Catalonia would recover the *Generalitat* (1977) and have a new Statute of Autonomy (1979).

CLASHING IMAGES

Opposing conceptions of the nation and the state were at stake in the Spanish Civil War (1936–39). The Francoists put forward a highly centralised and uniform image of Spain. The Republicans defended a moderately diffused image of a Spanish state that allowed Catalans and Basques to enjoy a certain degree of political and cultural autonomy. As Llobera points out, it should be made absolutely clear that the centralist vision of the state was not a monopoly of the extreme Spanish right, but was typical of the whole political spectrum. The main difference was, of course, that while the democratic parties were prepared to compromise and accept part of the demands of autonomy made by Catalans and Basques, the Fascists were not (Llobera, 1990:16).

The separatist disease of Basques and Catalans had to be cured once and for all. The immediate effects of the Francoist victory over Catalonia entailed not only the suppression of all Catalan political institutions and laws, but also the prohibition of the Catalan language and all sorts of symbolic elements (flags, anthems) of the Catalan identity (see Benet, 1973).

The Francoists, 'nationals', fought to impose a closed 'image' of Spain, an image that emphasised unity and condemned all forms of diversity. Their nationalism emerged as a reaction against modern ideologies such as socialism and anarchism which where threatening the traditional socio-political structure of Spain. The Second Republic had already implemented some progressive policies and was working in the construction of a state within which national minorities were taken into account and conferred a substantial degree of cultural and political autonomy. Francoism used a particular form of nationalism to stop the Spanish path towards modernisation and sustain the traditional structures defended by large conservative Catholic sectors. National-Catholicism used tradition to enhance the power of a right-wing political regime.

National minorities such as the Catalans filled the word nationalism with a radically different content. For them, to be nationalists signified the will to be recognised as different and have the right to express this difference in political as well as in cultural terms. A fundamental distinction between the nationalism instilled by the state and the nationalism of a nation without its own state springs from their different access to power. The state imposes the rules of the game and defines the rights and duties of its members. Furthermore, when it comes to national minorities, the state has the power to acknowledge their existence, allowing them to develop their own specific culture and providing them with sufficient economic and political resources to realise the achievement of various degrees of autonomy. But the state also has the power to decide on the eradication of difference. Thus, a Fascist state such as that in Francoist Spain could easily ignore the nationalist claims of the national minorities it included, while a democratic state would find it harder to silence the different voices emerging within itself while continuing to be defined as democratic. However, the degree of recognition enjoyed by national minorities within modern democratic states is not at all consistent. All states see a potential threat in acknowledging diversity within their territory, and almost all states develop some more of less subtle policies in order to increase the cohesion of the nation and legitimise their existence.

After the Civil War, the reaction of the Catalans faced with a repression that penetrated all their day-to-day activities turned into passive resistance. They had been defeated. Their country was destroyed and they were living in precarious conditions. They had to confront the presence of a Spanish army and an imported Castilian-speaking bureaucracy. The official public sphere was occupied by the new regime. But the strength and capacity to convince of those who had achieved power by force was always incomplete. The same intense force exerted by the 'nationals' to erase difference contributed to the construction of a clear-cut distinction between 'us', the Catalans, and 'them', the Francoists (identified with the Castilians). The subjection the Catalans had to endure in the public sphere increased a 'non-spoken agreement' between them and encouraged a particular sense of solidarity; a feeling that arises only in situations of high risk and shared danger. The Francoist regime and its officials were perceived as a common enemy for all Catalan people regardless of social class, since to be 'a Catalan' was enough to arouse the suspicion of the regime. Only some sectors of the upper Catalan bourgeoisie saw the Francoist victory with relief and supported the new Fascist ideology which would protect their interests.

THE SPANISH TRANSITION TO DEMOCRACY

The transition to democracy that began after the death of Franco can be seen as an attempt by the political class of Francoism to disentangle the problem of synchronising Francoist institutions with the requirements of a modern society. During the 1970s, the profound dislocation between the social and political spheres became increasingly alarming and highlighted the political system's inability to solve the multiple problems facing Spanish society. Yet, although Francoism endorsed significant changes in trying to adapt to the new scenario, it proved obsolete and ill-suited to run a society that had experienced dramatic transformations since 1939. Spain was no longer a rural country. Heavy industrial zones were concentrated in Catalonia and the Basque Country; industrialisation advanced irreversibly. A demographic explosion took place in the 1960s and, together with great internal migrations, led to the growth of urban areas. A new middle class emerged and some sectors of the bourgeoisie that had once supported Franco now pushed for reforms. With the Spanish economy practically isolated, these new sectors saw the importance of 'facing outwards', perceiving Spanish integration in the European Community as an urgent need. With one million unemployed and inflation standing at 30 per cent in 1975, the inadequacy of Francoist policies became patently clear (see Solé Tura, 1985).

Illiteracy decreased from 50 per cent in 1931 to 11 per cent in 1981 (Tezanos, 1989:106). Furthermore, the strong Catholicism which was once the main legitimating force of the Francoist regime was in decline, thus giving rise to a new secular society. All these changes need to be seen in the context of a new international political environment within which Spain could be fully accepted only if it adhered to Western democracy. It was essential to create a new political system capable of changing Spain's image as homogeneous, conservative, Catholic and identified with Castile. The Spanish archetype contained in National Catholicism had to be urgently replaced. The isolation imposed upon Spanish society after 1939 was being gradually eroded. The impact of communication technology and the industrialisation of Spain made it impossible to stop the images and voices of democracy. New values and life-styles challenged the outdated political and social structures of Spain. All these factors converged and led to disillusionment with Francoism in large sectors of Spanish society, which in turn generated a crisis of authority. Increasing pressure was exerted upon the regime by the still illegal unions and political parties. Change was unavoidable.

Rupture or reform were the two options faced by Spaniards after Franco's death in 1975. The political establishment opted for reform, but as Cebrián points out, the outcome was a democratic break with the past (Cebrián, 1982:13–24). In the light of the Francoist law, the regime prompted its own historical suicide by opening the way to democratic rule. The break was initiated from above. As a result, a peculiar situation arose: although the Francoist regime had disappeared, the public administration and institutions of the state remained intact. In such a context, Solé Tura argues that the transition to democracy could only succeed by a combination of three factors (1985:80). First, institutional stability arising from the leading role played by King Juan Carlos I in backing the reforms. Second, the attitude of the various political factions engaged in attempting to reach a consensus over the terms under which the transition should be made, once the political reform was sanctioned by the Spanish people and the first democratic elections were held in 1977. Finally, the active mobilisation of large social sectors of the population in favour of the democratisation of Spain, in contrast to the primarily restrained attitude of the Catholic Church and the Army. A process of disentanglement of what according to Franco's political last will was 'tied up and well tied down' reached a turning point in 1978 when Spaniards ratified the new democratic Constitution. It was at this moment that the need to substitute a 'culture of resistance' with a 'culture for democracy' emerged (Abellán, J. L. 1982:33).

Probably the most dangerous legacy of Francoism was the intensification of the national minorities question, an issue embittered by the inexorable centralism of the regime. After almost forty years of division and resentment between the 'winners' and the 'losers' of the Civil War, the pressures increased for what the Left and some progressive Catholic groups called 'national reconciliation'.

THE 1978 SPANISH CONSTITUTION

The 1978 Spanish Constitution was the product of the consensus achieved between the main political parties that arose from the first democratic elections. The need to obtain the support of both Francoist reformists and anti-Francoists generated endless discussions in the writing of the Constitution and even contributed to a lack of precision and incoherence in some parts of the text. Nevertheless, for the first time Spain would have a Constitution that was not the consequence of the opposition of one single political force against the others, and although there were some limits and deficiencies, the political model advanced by the Constitution 'was not exclusive or divisive, but an integration model' (Solé Tura, 1985:84). The radically conservative character of the Spanish nationalism defended by Francoism was questioned by the 1978 Constitution, which not only aimed at the transformation of Spain into a democratic state, but also admitted the existence of national minorities within its territory.

The Preamble to the Spanish Constitution acknowledges the will of the 'Spanish nation to protect all Spaniards and all the peoples of Spain in the exercise of human rights, their cultures and traditions, languages and institutions'. Article Two, probably the most controversial in the whole text, exemplifies the tension between the unity of Spain and the social pressure to recognise historic nations such as Catalonia, Galicia and the Basque Country: 'The Constitution is founded upon the indissoluble unity of the Spanish nation, the common and indivisible *patria* of all Spaniards, and recognises and guarantees the right to autonomy of the nationalities and regions integrated in it and the solidarity among them'.

By emphasising the indissoluble unity of Spain, while recognising and guaranteeing the right to autonomy of the nationalities and regions, the Constitution put forward a radically new model of the state that rejected Francoist centralism. But even more importantly,

Article Two attempted to reconcile two opposing conceptions of Spain at stake during the Civil War. 'Unity' had to be preserved, although it was dramatically challenged by the recognition of the existence of 'nationalities and regions' within Spain. As Colomer asserts, this had the effect of acknowledging the diverse 'group consciousnesses' resulting from particular historical events (1984:351). As Solé Tura notes, it is highly controversial and juridically ambiguous to stress the unity of a 'nation' at the same time as accepting the existence of 'nationalities' within it (1985:101). In this context, the reference to 'the Spanish nation' as the 'common *patria*' of all Spaniards seems implicitly compatible with the existence of other 'little *patrias*' such as Catalonia or the Basque Country. This poses a question faced not only by Spain but also by the United Kingdom and Belgium among other democratic nation-states containing national minorities: how far can a nation-state go in promoting the cultural differences and political aspirations of national minorities existing within its territory without undermining its own power and risking fragmentation?

THE AUTONOMOUS COMMUNITIES SYSTEM

The right to autonomy for the nationalities and regions forming Spain materialised into what is called the Autonomous Communities System (*el Sistema Autonómico*). Yet, while Catalonia, the Basque Country and Galicia, which had enjoyed statutes of autonomy during the Second Republic, could immediately attain full autonomy, other regions had to fulfil a five year 'restricted autonomy' period. Once full autonomy is achieved, however, the Constitution makes no distinction between the seventeen Autonomous Communities. Instead, it equalises nationalities with a strong sense of identity based upon common culture, language and past (Catalonia, the Basque Country, Galicia), with newly and sometimes artificially created 'communities' (Madrid, Cantabria, La Rioja).

The Autonomous Communities System responded to pressure exerted primarily by the Basque Country and Catalonia. Both Catalans and Basques felt that they had not only the right but also the power to press for a political solution to their claims for self-determination. However, what some saw as a solution was seen by others as a threat to the integrity of the 'Spanish nation'. These groups included large conservative sectors of the Army, the Administration and former Francoists. For them, it was extremely risky to recognise the existence of 'nationalities' as well as 'regions' within Spain. Even today there is no common agreement about what the term 'nationality' means, especially when some nationalist politicians who belong to these 'nationalities' refer to them as 'nations' and use the term 'Spanish state' while avoiding the expression 'Spanish nation', arguing that there is no such thing.

Once the new model of the Spanish state was established by the Constitution, the implementation of the Autonomous Communities System became a pressing matter. The question arose of whether it would turn into a simple administrative decentralisation device or would symbolise the acknowledgement of particular cultural and political aspirations of national minorities that could eventually lead towards a federalist structure. As Molas puts it, 'the endorsement of self-government is an abstract idea, and it is necessary to specify not only the degree of real power conferred on Catalonia but also the content of self-determination' (1982:16). The Socialist leader Joan Reventós was ever more concerned about the temptation of reducing the recognition and guarantee of political autonomy of the nationalities and regions to mere rhetoric, since he felt that this would pose a serious threat to the future stability of Spain (1979:53).

The Constitution set down the basis for a new agenda which established how national minorities should be treated. Since 1978, however, conflict between the autonomous communities and the central government has been ranging to the point where such conflict seems to be a necessary forerunner to negotiations and agreements between both political institutions. A constitution that strives to reconcile unity within the state's territory with a fair amount of cultural and political autonomy to the nations it contains faces tension and conflict. This is so because the clash between two entities which seek the same objective, that is the creation and enhancement of the nation, is inevitable. The Spanish state endeavours to create a nation in order to gain legitimacy and avoid reducing its relationship to its citizens to a merely political form of interaction. In many ways, the autonomous Governments act as states. In Catalonia and the Basque Country, for example, they provide services in education, health, culture, housing, local transport and agriculture. They have even recuperated the autonomous police force they enjoyed in the Second Republic (*Ertzaina* in the Basque Country, *Mossos d'esquadra* in Catalonia); a body charged with different responsibilities from those of the National Police (state's police) or the *Guardia Civil*. The central state holds exclusive jurisdiction over defence, the administration of justice, international relations and general economic planning, among other matters included in chapters 149 and 150 of the Constitution.

Each Community has a regional legislative assembly consisting of a single chamber. Deputies are elected on the basis of proportional representation and usually the leader of the majority party or coalition assumes the presidency of the Community. The President heads a regional executive of ministers in charge of departments which mostly, but not always, follow the Spanish state's pattern (see Brassloff, 1989).

But is this sufficient to imply that Spain is a federation in the making? Giner and Moreno adduce three major premises to show that Spain is not to be classified as a federation (1990:187).

(a) The Spanish Senate does not have the character of a 'House of Territorial Representation' (as it is referred to in Article 69.1) in the same way as the US Senate or the *Bundersrat*.

(b) The Constitution defines the provinces as local organisations. However, they occupy an intermediate position between the autonomous communities and local governments (city council). This contributes to a certain degree of discrimination between uniprovincial autonomous communities that have fully absorbed the role of the former province, and some multiprovincial communities that maintain this intermediate administrative body regarded in many cases as a state's control apparatus.

(c) The open-ended nature of the Constitution concerning the division of powers and responsibilities which the Autonomous Communities may assume does not entail a federal distribution of power. A further point refers to the creation of the Autonomous Communities model while preserving former centralist administrative bodies such as the *Diputaciones*.

The strongest argument against defining Spain as 'a federation in the making' stems from the definition of what a federation is. In Gagnon's view, 'federalism implies a commitment to a contractual arrangement between political units that decide to create a new political space' (1993:17). The new model of state adopted by Spain in 1978 was the outcome of a vertical decision to solve the national question; an endemic problem exacerbated by forty years of centralism. The areas that became Autonomous Communities did not intervene, as such, in the writing of the Constitution. In some cases they were not even 'conscious' of forming a community or did not have the will to become one.

King argues that federations are contractual 'because of the assumption that any contracting party remains as free to withdraw from, as it was to enter into, such an association' (1982:108). This implies that federations consist of 'sovereign states'. In the case of Spain such freedom does not exist and blatantly contradicts the 'indissoluble unity of the Spanish nation' emphasised in Article Two of the Constitution. To illustrate this point we turn to the controversy generated by the Catalan Socialists (PSC or Socialist Party of Catalonia) when, in its fifth PSC-PSOE Congress, it put forward the idea of creating a federal state: 'We Catalan Socialists think it necessary to advance in the formulation of the Autonomous Communities System as a state of federal inspiration'. The PSC's leader Raimon Obiols defended federalism, but he also recognised that within Spanish socialism there is a tension between federalism and centralism, the latter being strongly influenced by the Jacobin and statist ethics impregnating left-wing French culture (*La Rosa*, 1991).

Jordi Solé Tura, former Minister of Culture and major socialist ideologist, points to the technocratic neo-centralism of the Spanish state and the political hegemony of nationalism within the Autonomous Communities as two political factors that could interfere with the Spanish path to federalism. Both elements, he argues, reflect continuity of the conflict between the state and the nationalities and regions, and also imply ambiguity concerning the concept of nation within the territorial basis of the state (1985:15). In Solé Tura's view, the Left cannot fall for nationalist ambiguities, that is, it cannot either be ambiguous about the model of state or cultivate the logic of an exterior enemy. The Left cannot be nationalist but 'it has to be strongly national, have profound roots in the collectivity, express the feelings and aspirations of all popular sectors, and reflect the anxieties and hopes of the majority of the population'. Solé Tura condemns the tendency of Catalan and Basque nationalists to develop particularism and elevate sporting, cultural or political rivalries to the category of symbols which define the national essence. The outcome of this is a conflict-based relationship with the 'central power', a relationship in which negotiation and agreement are always preceded by conflict and where conflict acquires relevance above all other subjects (1985:178).

The federalist proposal of the PSC encountered some hostile reactions among the PSOE (Spanish Socialist Party). Alfonso Guerra, then vice-president of the Spanish government, argued that 'the 1978 Constitution does not favour the configuration of Spain as a federal state' (*La Vanguardia*, 1987). Gregorio Peces Barba, a prominent figure within the PSOE's élite, stressed that: 'federalism implies the existence of sovereign states which decide to unite in order to create a single state. In Spain, this is not the case because there are no previous sovereign states' (*El País*, 1987). Objections to the federalist project stemmed from some sectors which argued that the transformation of Spain into a federation would require the reform of the Constitution. Further opposition to the federalist proposal came from Catalan nationalist parties such as the CiU (Convergence and Unity). They regarded a possible federalisation of Spain as a tool to eradicate the difference between historically rooted communities such as Catalonia and newly and sometimes artificially created ones. Their attitude was against the famous 'coffee for everyone' (*café para todos*) policy implemented by minister Clavero Arévalo in the early 1980s. Additional concerns arise from the two-faced character of federalism as an organisational principle that could either develop in the direction of centralisation or lead to greater differentiation and various degrees of independence (Kriek, 1992:11), the second path being specifically forbidden by the Constitution.

Solé Tura supports the thesis that 'Spain is not and cannot become a federal state without modifying the 1978 Constitution'. However, according to him, 'what is important is not the name, but the thing. The crucial issue is that the Spanish state ends up working as a federal state.' He adds: 'this is perfectly possible within the present constitutional framework' (1988:154 and Molas, 1992:17–36). Yet he fails to acknowledge that under these circumstances, the federalism inspiring the functioning of the Autonomous Communities System depends entirely upon the political will of the party in office since the open-ended character of the Constitution allows different and even contradictory readings. For instance, after the first regional election (1980), the Catalan president Jordi Pujol pursued a policy of a rapid transfer of powers from the central state to the *Generalitat* (Catalan Government), a process facilitated by Adolfo Suárez, Prime Minister and protagonist of the Spanish transition to democracy. Suárez's party needed the support of the CiU to attain a majority in the Spanish Parliament. A radical shift took place after the attempted *coup d'état* in 1981. The new Prime Minister, Leopoldo Calvo Sotelo, yielded to the pressure of Spanish conservatives and halted the transfer of power to the Autonomous Communities. The new centralist policy reached its climax with the endorsement of the *Ley Orgánica de Armonización del Proceso Autonómico* (Organic Law for the Harmonisation of the Autonomous Communities Process, or LOAPA) which was sanctioned by the votes of the party in government, the Democratic Centre Union (*Unión del Centro Democrático*, or UCD) and the PSOE.

The Autonomous Communities System may develop all its potential and end up operating as a federal state, as Solé Tura argues. But, as Brassloff points out, 'at the very last, federalisation would involve a revision of Title VIII in order to allow the Senate to function as a House of full regional representation, and to give increased taxation powers to the Autonomous Communities' (1989:44). The lack of federalist provisions in the 1978 Constitution and the reluctance of some sectors to open a path that could eventually lead to the fragmentation of Spain need to be contrasted with a powerful trend able to push in the opposite direction; this is the impact of further European integration upon the political, economic and cultural patterns of the member states.

The claim that the state is an 'independent authority' or a 'circumscribed impartial power' accountable to its citizens, a notion that, as Held argues, lies at the centre of the self-image or ideology of the modern state, is today fundamentally flawed (1991:200). The nation-state is caught up in profound processes of transformation prompted by alterations in the conditions of its existence *vis-à-vis* a changing world economy and international order. Nation-states have lost aspects of their sovereignty and are forced to face patterns of increasing global interconnections. The nationalism of minorities and the proliferation of supranational organisations such as the European Union are transforming the nature of the state.

The future shape of the Union has not yet been decided, and the prospective role of nations without a state, such as Catalonia or the Basque Country, completely depends on it. Llobera distinguishes between three possible frames for the new Europe: centralised federalism (all powers exerted by the centre), confederalism (general government subordinated to constituent states) and federalism (general and regional government within clearly defined spheres) (1993:17–30). In this context, a federalism understood as the pact of equal independent members where the principle of subsidiarity is applied could generate a 'Europe of the Regions'. This is a construction cherished by many who oppose the emergence of a European super nation-state.

A decentralised federal democratic Europe would not only respond to sound economic arguments, but would also offer an adequate framework within which nations without their own state could preserve and develop their culture. The Catalan nationalists of the CiU defend the idea of a 'Europe of the peoples'. In the 1990 election, the Scottish National Party's slogan was 'Independence in Europe'. As McCrone points out, this recognises the limited character of a sovereignty that would inevitably be circumscribed by Europe (1992:214). However, the minorities' willingness to gain, while simultaneously renouncing to a certain degree, sovereignty occurs just at the time when states such as the United Kingdom are particularly reluctant to lose further sovereignty to Europe. At present, the degree of autonomy, cooperation and subsidiarity that will constitute the European Union remains uncertain. What can be taken for granted is its tremendous capacity to influence the functioning of the member states and consequently impinge upon the future unfolding of the Spanish model. The factors that prompted the initiation of a process of unity between a limited number of European nation-states did not include a grasp of the aspirations and claims of the national minorities that would benefit from a federalist European structure cutting across state boundaries. Rather, it was state weakness, not strength, which forced many politicians, economic interest groups and social movements, to advance in the direction of unity. The need to increase competitiveness in a rapidly changing techno-economical environment is already encouraging the creation of industrial areas such as the *Route des Hautes Technologies de l'Europe du Sud* (Euroregion: Catalonia–Languedoc–Roussillon–Midy Pyrenees) that transcend state boundaries. The Single European Market is likely to favour an economical structure that, in the long term, will probably transform the political one. If this were the case, nation-states would progressively need to be re-defined and regional institutions to gain control. The situation of federalism would stem from the need to decentralise a gradually obsolete nation-state system.

To sum up, the 1978 Constitution prevents Spain from becoming a federation since the unity of Spain is presented as a primary value. The 'nationalities and regions' forming Spain are given a certain degree of autonomy by the Constitution but they are not 'sovereign states'. They did not take part in the writing of the Constitution and lack the right to decide whether to remain within or withdraw from the political space created by it.

The present member states of the European Union have become, at the same time, both too small and too large to deal effectively and democratically with geopolitical changes taking place at the global and local levels. A successful movement towards an ever closer federal Union will impact upon the socio-political structure of the EU members. In such a context, substantial changes could affect the 1978 Constitution and make possible a Spanish federation which otherwise would seem unlikely in the foreseeable future.

ACKNOWLEDGEMENTS

I would like to thank Anthony Giddens for his comments on an earlier version of this chapter as well as Ernest Gellner, Salvador Giner and Josep R. Llobera for their suggestions and advice. This chapter is based on my PhD thesis, *Nationalism in stateless nations: the case of Catalonia*, for which I received financial support from King's College, Cambridge, and the CIRIT (Generalitat de Catalunya).

REFERENCES

Abellán, J. L. 'La función del pensamiento en la transición política' in Cagigao, J. L. *et al.*, *España 1975–1980: Conflictos y logros de la democracia* (Editorial J. Porrúa Turanzas: Madrid, 1982)

Benet, J. *Catalunya sota el règim franquista* (Edicions Catalanes de París: París, 1973)

Bilbeny, N. *La ideologia nacionalista a Catalunya.* (Laia/L'entrellat: Barcelona, 1988)

Brassloff, A. 'Spain: the state of the autonomies' in Forsyth, M. (ed.) *Federalism and Nationalism* (Leicester University Press: Leicester, 1989)

Cebrián, J. L. 'La experiencia del período constituyente' in Cagigao, J. L. *et al.*, *España 1975–1980: Conflictos y logros de la democracia* (Editorial J. Porrúa Turanzas: Madrid. 1982)

Colomer, J. M. *Espanyolisme i catalanisme: la idea de nació en el pensament polític català 1939–1979* (L'Avenç: Barcelona, 1984)

Constitutión Española: edicion comentada (Centro de estudios constitucionales: Madrid, 1979)

Elliott, J. H. *The revolt of the Catalans: a study in the decline of Spain (1598–1640)* (Cambridge University Press: Cambridge, 1963)

El País, Madrid, 30 August 1987

Gagnon, A. G. 'The political uses of federalism' in Burguess, M & Gagnon, A. G. *Comparative Federalism and Federation* (Harvester Wheatsheaf: London, 1993)

Giner, S. and Moreno L. 'Centro y periferia: la dimensión étnica de la sociedad española' in Giner, S. (ed.) *España: Sociedad y Política* (Espasa Calpe: Madrid, 1990)

Held, D. 'Democracy, the Nation-State and the Global System' in Held, D. (ed.) *Political Theory Today* (Polity Press: Cambridge, 1991)

King, P. *Federalism and Federation* (Croom Helm: London, 1982)

Kriek, D. J. *Federalism: the Solution?* (HSRC Publishers: Pretoria, 1992)

La Rosa, Barcelona, November 1991

La Vanguardia, Barcelona, 14 September 1987

Llobera, J. 'Catalan identity: the dialectics of past and present' in *Critique of Anthropology*, vol. 10, no. 2 & 3, winter 1990

Llobera, J. 'Els canvis a Europa i la crisi dels models clàssics: el futur de les etnonacions dins d'una Europa unida' *Sisenes Jornades. El Nacionalisme Català a la fi del segle XX*. Reus, 1992 (Edicions de la Revista de Catalunya: Barcelona, 1993)

McCrone, D. *Understanding Scotland: the Sociology of a Stateless Nation* (Routledge: London, 1992)

Molas, I. 'Introducción' in Gerpe Landín, M. *et al.*, *Comentaris Jurídics a l'estatut d'autonomía de Catalunya* (Edicions 62: Barcelona 1982)

Molas, I. 'Actualitat del federalisme' in *Debat*, no. 16, September 1992

Ponències V. Congrés PSC-PSOE, 11–12, 13 December 1987

Reventós, J. 'Comunidades Autónomas' in *Perspectivas de una España democrática y constitucionalizada* (Ciclo de conferencias pronunciadas en el Club Siglo XXI, curso 1978–1979) (Unión Editorial, S.A.: Madrid, 1979) vol. III

Solé Tura J. *Nacionalidades y nacionalismos en España: Autonomía. Federalismo. Autodeterminación* (Alianza Editorial: Madrid, 1985)

Solé Tura J. 'Una lectura autonomista i federal del model d'Estat constitucional' in Armet, Ll. Molas, I. et altri. *Federalisme i estat de les autonomies* (Edicions 62: Barcelona, 1988)

Tezanos, J. F. 'Modernización y cambio social en España' in Tezanos, J. F. *et al.*, (eds) *La Transición Democrática Española* (Editorial Sistema: Madrid, 1989)

Villar, P. *La Catalogne dans l'Espagne moderne* (Flammarion: Paris, 1977)

Villar, P. *Història de Catalunya*, vol. III by Batlle, C. (ed. 62: Barcelona, 1987)

CHAPTER TEN

Federalism and the Transformation of the South African State

Jenny Robinson

INTRODUCTION

The possibility of federalism in South Africa has been strongly – and violently – contested. As one of the key platforms of the Zulu nationalist Inkatha Freedom Party (IFP) and of various right-wing Afrikaner parties as well as the liberal Democratic Party, it formed a nexus for a variety of moral and political dilemmas in the recent negotiations process.[1] The final outcome of the negotiated transitional Constitution is, I would suggest, a protofederalist state, with strong internal dynamics likely to promote, rather than undermine, a federal form of government.

As with Apartheid and the struggle to overthrow the Apartheid regime, South African federalist arguments were strongly mediated by their connections with Western moral and political projects. Indeed, as the postcolonial literature has suggested, relations between the West and other places leave subjects and theories transformed by these interactions. This is no less true in the case of South African political discourse. Informed by an enlightenment tradition of equality and liberty for all, the anti-Apartheid movement has been shaped by and has in turn shaped the politics of the West. Even the Apartheid regime, portrayed as outcast and distinctive in its racist political progammes, was dependent upon the rationalities and strategies of modernising states everywhere. Indeed, far from being the only 'word' on racism, Derrida's (1985) formulation of Apartheid as racism's 'last word' suggests a linkage between the darker sides of Western modernity and the Apartheid state. Far less crucial to our understanding of both the West and South Africa, federalism none the less presents a similar set of complex interconnections between Western thought and South African political debates.

As the representative of the modernist struggle for nationalist liberation – of the extension of Western democratic rights without reference to race – the African National Congress (ANC) faced, in its hour of victory, the prospects of an ethnicisation of the post-Apartheid state. Initial reactions, based upon the theorisation of Apartheid in Marxist and national liberation terms, understood these ethnic challenges to be simply the products of Apartheid, and thus morally inappropriate as foundations for a future, non-racial South Africa. And yet in turning to federalism as the basis for their claims to sovereignty and political power, ethnically based organisations (and others) invoked a rationality of government with a respectable Western political and moral pedigree. Thus a local morality, which rejected the validity of Apartheid racial categories, confronted a Western-inspired federal moralism. Together with a growing pluralism in political theory and practice in the West, South African political debates were substantially disrupted and had to be reformulated.

And yet, the particular history of federalist debates in South Africa in turn raises some important questions for the analysts of federalism elsewhere. Inextricably linked to a politics of power and of violence in South Africa, the discourse of federalism in general seldom investigates its own complicity in power relations. Through an analysis of the South African case, I will suggest that federalist discourse is necessarily linked to, and constitutive of, power relations. And while I have found the work of Chantal Mouffe of value in trying to make sense of new forms of politics, I am not as certain as she seems to be that 'To accept with Foucault that there cannot be an absolute separation between validity and power (since validity is always relative to a specific regime of truth, connected to power) does not mean that we cannot distinguish within a given regime of truth between those who respect the strategy of argumentation and its rules, and those who simply want to impose their power' (Mouffe, 1993: 15). For both strategies (argumentation and force) were clearly in evidence – on all sides – during the negotiations phase. The South African case would seem to indicate that a 'strategy of argumentation', in the liberal, respected form in which Mouffe intends it as a foundation for radical democracy, bears little relationship to the complexities of political power relations, and the intertwining of discourse, power and violence, as a review of the debates over federalism in South Africa will reveal.

The chapter will first sketch the historical and geographical aspects of state power which set the background to debates over a federal form for the post-Apartheid state. The second section will provide an overview of the negotiations process itself. The body of the chapter will discuss in some detail the positions of the different political parties on federalism, and the concluding section will offer an assessment and interpretation of the future of federalism in South Africa as well as some reflections on federalist theory from the South African experience.

FEDERALISM AND THE GEOGRAPHY OF STATE POWER BEFORE NEGOTIATIONS

The coincidence of race and space which Apartheid policies sought to create over the past five decades (and segregationist policies before this) formed the backdrop to the lengthy negotiations about the appropriate form of state for a post-Apartheid government. Not only the non-democratic character of the state but also the architecture of the state apparatus was brought into question as various parties to the negotiations sought to gain maximum advantage from the constitutional settlement. Thus, the geography of the Apartheid era was to play a key role in determining the possibilities for the spatiality of the post-Apartheid state. Long predicted by geographers, the 'spatial fix' of Apartheid has therefore been an important force in the transition. And one of the more obvious ways in which the influence of spatiality has been evident in the period of transformation to date has been in the arguments for and against a federal structure for the post-Apartheid state.

The geography of colonisation laid the foundations for the emergence of a unified state across the area which is today South Africa. British state-building strategies, in conflict with Boer Republics and in concert with a wide range of colonial efforts to subjugate indigenous populations, gave rise to the initiative to unify the British holdings in the region with the defeated Boer Republics, and the Union of South Africa was formed in 1910. It is here that the tradition of federalist positions in South African parliamentary politics is usually understood to have begun. As strategies to protect various regionally-based interests and identities, these were mostly connected to the Anglo-Boer divisions which had a clear territorial form, especially in the case of Natal, with a majority of English-speaking whites (Welsh, 1989).

While somewhat autonomous Provinces emerged as a compromise from the Union constitution debates (although this autonomy was to be severely eroded over the ensuing decades), the familiar racially fragmented geography of Apartheid South Africa began to take shape with the passing of the 1913 and 1936 Land Acts, declaring much of South Africa for the exclusive ownership of white citizens. Although elements of regional distinctiveness and provincial self-interest shaped the relations between the Provinces and the central government, with some more or less serious secessionist arguments in the Natal Province over the declaration of the Republic, the relations between African areas, or 'Bantustans' in Apartheid parlance, and the centre were directed by the policies of the central government. Moving on the front of territorial segregation at a national level, the Apartheid government of the 1960s sought to create independent homelands in its efforts to deal with political crises and the problem of maintaining minority power. Thus the Apartheid state, far from being a monolith, was territorially fragmented in important ways. And this legacy of 'balkanisation', while never gaining international legitimacy, was to have some important implications for the shape of the post-Apartheid state. While there were certainly variations in the docility of homeland leaders under Apartheid, in the years of late Apartheid considerable differences in the political allegiances of homeland leaders emerged. Between the Transkei (ANC supporting) and Bophuthatswana (which offered sustained resistance to re-incorporation into the new South Africa), for example, there was a wide gulf. Most importantly, though, it was this pre-existing political geography which provided the territorial power bases for the mobilisation of federalist positions in the negotiations. Together with historical and Apartheid-induced concentrations of various racial and ethnic groups in particular parts of the country, at least some elements of the territory-nation or ethnic group pairing so crucial to ethnonationalist arguments for federation or secession would seem to have been present. However, the limitations of this linkage will emerge in the following discussion.

Another of the legacies of the Apartheid state which played a large role in arguments for federalism in the negotiations phase, and before, was the growing centralisation of the state. By the time Mandela was released from prison, there were no elected Provincial governments, and Provincial Executive Authorities were appointed by the central state. All urban African government had been concentrated in central state hands in the early 1970s, and various efforts to implement elected bodies with limited powers in African urban areas had been rejected by popular organisations. Inter-municipal cooperation had none the less been implemented at a metropolitan scale, with wealthy white and poor, unrepresentative black councils forming Regional Services Councils to deliver services across the cities. These have seen a measure of infrastructural development in African areas, but were also rejected for their foundations in an illegitmate and divided system of urban government. They represented part of a government tactic to devolve responsibility for the provision of services in urban areas (which served as a focal point for anti-Apartheid opposition) without decentralising autonomy to local bodies (Seethal, 1991).

Intiatives by the reforming Apartheid state to reshape the political and economic boundaries within the country led some analysts to forecast a revival of federalist or regionalist solutions (Cobbett *et al.*, 1986). These projections were based on the Buthelezi-led KwaZulu-Natal Indaba of the early 1980s (which entailed efforts by a coalition of homeland and capitalist forces to find an independent political settlement in the KwaZulu/Natal region), and the creation by the government of development region boundaries to cross-cut homeland areas, drawing them into functional economic regions. Here a capital-logic argument was offered to suggest that a new 'spatial fix' was being sought to regenerate Apartheid capitalism. These development regions have certainly played an important role in re-imagining the internal political geography of South Africa: the nine post-Apartheid Regions bear a strong resemblance to these divisions, and decision-makers took territorial economic integration as a key factor in deciding on their form (Muthien and Khosa, 1994). The shift from homeland to regional power bases which the analysts of this reform initiative forecast was not without prescience in view of the outcomes of negotiation. But as we shall see, it is the emergence of a new regional politics, rather than the persistence of many Apartheid and homeland politicians and power bases, that is most likely to be the outcome of the new constitutional arrangements.

It is also in the horizons limiting the possibilities for imagining the form of the state that we need to look for explanations of the particular outcome of contemporary federalist debates in South Africa. The ethnicisation and balkanisation of the South African state by the Apartheid regime led to a strong non-racial and state-centralist opposition movement. Reformulating the federalist project and distancing it from the past divisive policies of the government required some careful theorising on the part of its proponents. None the less, it can be argued that these reformulations seldom strayed far from some of the assumptions which underpinned the old order. As MacDonald (1992) suggests, proponents of power-sharing and federalism relied upon notions of the ethnic or racial group which essentialised these individual and communal qualities, enshrining them as political pre-givens. While the opponents of this position wrestled with the dilemma of a meaningful, if historically and politically constituted ethnic/racial identity, the search for a reformulation of the left's dismissal of ethnic identity as politically relevant came to be a crucial part of the transition in both politics and theory. The articulation of positions respecting various cultural traditions, fewer references to the value of one 'South African' culture, and a distinct effort to highlight traditional and minority cultures during electioneering were evidence of this reformulation of the political place of ethnicity. The idea of a 'rainbow nation' perhaps captured something of this initiative (*Work in progress*, 1993). However, unlike this more cultural politics, or the shift from a centralist politics to the compromise of a 'strong, but slim' state by the ANC, the issue of fragmenting political power along the lines of ethnically weighted territorial divisions had to be more formally negotiated, and was one of the main reasons for the protracted and dangerously violent nature of the negotiations process. The following section provides a background to the negotiations process, and a brief synopsis of its dynamics. The place of deadlocks over the issue of regional powers is described, before the details of the various arguments mobilised around federalism are explored in section four.

THE STAGING OF NEGOTIATIONS

The setting, causes and actors

Explanations for the breakthrough in what was one of the world's most intractable political conflicts between the white minority government and the black opposition in South Africa circulate at a popular and intellectual level in approximately the following form. The growing internal political and economic (organic?) crisis was pushing the state into an increasing reliance on force to contain opposition movements, whose successes included brief attainment of localised powers in some black urban areas, which became effective 'no-go' areas for the state forces in the late 1980s. However, these gains proved difficult to translate into real power, and the capacity of the opposition for governance and the maintenance of order and services was minimal. At the same time, international economic and political isolation of the Apartheid regime, politically supported by a relatively strong international anti-Apartheid movement, was reported to be taking its toll on the Government and business. In addition to a declining economy and the internal contradictions and failures of state-directed political reforms pursued through the 1980s, the shift in the international political climate of the late 1980s and the end of the Cold War increased the pressure on both sides of the political conflict to seek a settlement. With the ANC's sources of support in the Eastern Bloc drying up and the international significance of Southern African regional conflicts declining, the opportunity to pursue an internal negotiated settlement was seized. De Klerk's assumption of position as President and leader of the ruling National Party (NP) apparently fortuitously accelerated this emerging shift in regime strategy (O'Meara, 1994).

The negotiations, once entered into, did not proceed smoothly. Without international supervision or mediation (except for one abortive attempt rather late in the day), each side (or more correctly, all the different players) attempted to mobilise whatever resources they had at their disposal to advance their position. A key aspect of the negotiation process, then, was the attempt to 'level the playing field' since one party to the negotiations, the Government, had the enormous resources of the state to disburse as it wished, while the

ANC had access to mass mobilisation and a huge international legitimacy. In addition, rather than declining with the progress of negotiations, violent political conflict continued during the four years of negotiations. While it is glib to assert, as some popular commentators are wont to, that this conflict is simply the expected by-product of transition, it is important to assess the significance of violent conflict within the political process of negotiation. Of course all sorts of local political and other dynamics affected the course of violence in particular places, and initiatives to contain conflict and promote peace and reconstruction have been exceptionally difficult to implement effectively. But the place of violence in the course of debates over federalism was particularly important, and is considered below.

A further observation made by commentators on the negotiations has been the importance of individuals in shaping particular outcomes and of the personal relationships struck during the course of the negotiations. To some activists and radical observers, the familiar and easy relations between the chief negotiators of the state and the ANC seemed to smack of élite pacting and even betrayal of the mass of supporters. However, to other analysts these relation-ships, and the style and culture of negotiations, augured well for the stability of the country and for the power sharing phase which was to follow the first general election. In the context of federalist debates, one commentator has suggested that it was a behind-the-scenes conference between members of different parties and organisations, hosted by a business forum, which led to a breakthrough in thinking about federalism (Humphries *et al.*, 1994) and enabled a face-saving agreement on the shape of the future state. Many aspects of the story of negotiations in general and agreements on federalism in particular are therefore publicly unknown, and while some useful research has already been conducted, important parts of this period of South Africa's history will probably remain unknowable, relegated to the realm of hearsay, or will be only selectively discussed by insider participants for whom political niceties govern their revelations. As always, then, but rather sadly in the case of this world-historic tale of transformation, our stories of even contemporary history can be only partial.

A brief synopsis of the negotiations process[2]

After Mandela's release from prison, it was more than 18 months before the first formal negotiating forum convened. Prior to this parties had disagreed over the form which negotiations should take – whether they should take place prior to the election of a Constituent Assembly (the NP and the IFP) or after (ANC, PAC). By the time a compromise had been found and the Convention for a Democratic South Africa (CODESA) sat for the first time, it was December 1991. But then the first obstacle appeared in the form of Buthelezi, who demanded that the IFP, the Zulu King and the KwaZulu homeland administration should all have representation at the forum. In the event, he stayed away but the IFP sent a representative. Further contests over leaving the possibility of a federal state open emerged later in the proceedings, but Friedman (1993) argues that the breakdown in the Codesa II talks occurred because of quite large differences in the positions of the two major parties over the form and pace of change – even though the final breakdown was presented in the media as taking place as a result of a difference of a few percentage points in the majority required to amend certain constitutional principles.

Bilateral talks between the ANC and the NP paved the way for further multiparty negotiations to begin in April 1993, where the details of the transitional government and constitution were thrashed out – although the IFP and the Conservative Party (CP) withdrew as a result of disputes over process. A broad compromise on the timing and nature of the transitional arrangements was arrived at during this 'Multi Party Negotiating Forum' (MPNF), but it was the position of the federalist parties which remained unresolved until very close to the election. A behind-the-scenes conference had brokered the initial proposal for regional powers – a compromise between a federalist and a centralist position which set out concurrent powers for regions and the centre and which saw powers for regions entrenched in the constitution. None the less, Humphries *et al.* (1994) suggest that the IFP never won as many concessions in terms of federalism as it had initially demanded, but agreed to participate in the elections when its demands for the status of the Zulu monarch to be constitutionally entrenched were met. They conclude that 'some of (the federalist) theories were adopted by IFP strategists when they conformed to their goals, but that they were not wedded to them. The goal remained a regional power base, as immune as possible from ANC control. The theories were a dispensable means' (p. 175).

The following section outlines the various 'theories' of federalism or regional government which were proposed by the different parties during the constitutional negotiations. Whether or not these theories were simply dispensable means to the end of meeting the clear interests of different political parties is a question certainly worth addressing. I shall argue that alongside the contest for political power between political parties with more or less identifiable *interests*, the role of federalist and other *discourses* of contemporary state power in shaping the political outcomes of negotiations and resultant power relations also needs to be assessed.

THE HORIZONS OF THE POSSIBLE: FEDERALIST DISCOURSE AND GOVERNMENTAL POWER

The task of governing modern societies is truly complex, and for a party facing the prospect of governing in a country celebrating liberation, with widespread high expectations, it is particularly onerous. The ANC's election slogan, 'Ready to Govern', represented the culmination of four years of intensive policy research and preparation for a dominant role in the government of the country. And yet in the euphoria of liberation and the installation of a new state, it is appropriate to recollect that in their efforts to liberate and govern, modern states often find that the web of state power proves to be disabling. In the South African situation there are a number of emergent reasons why a government of liberation might not be able to fulfil its ambitions. This is not only because those in power have a relative freedom from the immediate voice(s) of the population, nor because the position from government is always a distinctive institutional location, not reducible to the positions of other social agents. It is also because the form and tasks of modern government enmesh the population in routines and practices which are potentially both enabling and constraining, both liberating and subjecting. The micro-powers of modern society, then, are likely to be as double-edged in a society in transition as they are elsewhere.

But it is not only the discourses and practices of social regulation which shape the political and social order, and the human possibilities of those who live in it. It is also, I would suggest, the broad character of government and state form that powerfully frame modern society. The idea of the modern state itself offers a good example of the way in which widespread and seemingly formal political practices and institutions sustain particular power relations. And here I would argue that the domain of the internal territorial and hierarchical organisation of the modern state also has significant consequences for the constitution of power relations. Discourses concerning state form, then, and in this case the division of responsibility and sovereignty between different tiers of government, signify a horizon of the possible organisation of contemporary/ modern society. Of course these discourses are internally contested but, as the negotiations in South Africa suggest, there is a substantial area of agreement about the practice of governance which underpins the creation of a modern state.

Despite the apparently enormous political differences among the different parties to the negotiations, and of course the significantly different consequences for different parties should sovereignty be devolved to regional governments or particular regions secede, the notion of statehood, the concept of the territorial decentralisation of state powers, and the rhetorical justifications for government at whatever scale were similar across the pro- and anti-federalist positions. Similar sets of concerns were apparent, then – concerns of state – in addition to the particular concerns of groups who perceived the possibility of gaining advantage in a complex set of political manoeuvrings during the course of the negotiations, or who came from quite different political traditions. A detailed analysis of the discourse of statehood in general must await another opportunity: of interest here is the discourse of federalism, and the resultant proto-federalist form of the post-Apartheid state.

Before an interpretation and a critique of the place of federalist arguments within the South African political negotiations are offered, elements of the different arguments for and against federalism mobilised during the course of the negotiations process in South Africa will be presented. Different arguments were not held uniquely by specific parties, nor did each party have only one argument for federalism. But each was more strongly associated with a particular position, which will be used as a basis for organising this section of the chapter. The ANC, most concerned with strong states and more inclined to a centralist and socialist position, will be discussed first, followed by the general liberal and Democratic Party concern with limiting central state power in the interests of democracy. The Inkatha Freedom Party and the National Party had ethnic-territorial interests in some kind of federal arrangement, and their positions will be discussed together. The final outcome of the constitutional negotiations in terms of regions and federalism will be assessed at the end of this section.

Central and strong states

Against the various balkanisation and consociational strategies of the Apartheid state, it was the virtues of unification and of the transformation of racially-based inequalities through strong central state action which attracted the ANC and other oppositional organisations. Regional government was seen as important, but mostly in terms of enhancing the efficiency of government to deliver in different parts of the country, and to meet the different needs of particular communities. A healthy suspicion of racially-based motivations for autonomous or sovereign regional government was apparent, along with concerns that Apartheid homeland or Bantustan governments would retain powers through a more federal dispensation. In Burgess's (1993) terminology, then, federalism as ideology was strongly suspected as serving particular political interests, and not being useful in furthering the political aims of the ANC or addressing the need to fundamentally transform Apartheid society. And it was largely in response to the emergence of a strong initiative for federalism and regionalism from the NP and IFP that the ANC was pushed into developing a coherent regional policy. But as Humphries *et al.* (1994) remark, this regional position was not simply imposed from outside: internal differences between regions within the ANC and a strong belief in participatory government also contributed to its formulation of a Regional Policy.

In the introduction to their document outlining its regional policy, the ANC noted that 'The ANC approach to regions is that of building and re-uniting – not redividing – a nation' (African National Congress, 1993). It continues to note that it is 'involved in the process of knitting together the state again after the nightmarish dismemberments created by apartheid' (p. 3). It makes a plea for 'soft boundaries' rather than entrenched relations between regional, local and national government and argues that the final decisions about regional powers should be made by the democratically elected Constitutional Assembly and not be entrenched as a result of the constitutional negotiations. Its preference was for concurrent powers between regional, local and central governments, with overriding powers for the central government, citing the case of Germany.

Concerns about efficient spatial redistribution and about the negative impact of competition between regions led to a cautious approach on fiscal decentralisation. As it notes, 'The level of inequality in the country compromises the extent to which account-ability can be based on a direct relationship between payment of taxes and receipt of public services' (p. 10). None the less, it was concerned that an equitable and institutionalised framework for redistributing national resources among regions should be established. Whereas pro-federalist organisations were asking for residual powers to be vested in regions, the ANC document was clear that such powers would vest in the central government, and it offered a list of areas in which regions might have constitutionally entrenched powers. Table 10.1 compares these ANC proposals with the powers conferred on regions within the current (post-Apartheid) South African constitution. The ANC argued that these powers are comparable with arrangements in Germany.[3] The concerns of the ANC then were with effecting development, equality and efficient government and with preventing the resurgence of territorially based ethnic politics, against which it had been struggling for a long time. And while devolution of powers was widely seen to enable participation by local people in appropriate policy making for their area, the decentralisation of the state *per se*, rather than the creation of generally democratic forms of government, was not seen as a way of achieving this (Sutcliffe, 1993).

Table 10.1 Comparison of ANC proposals for regional powers with those subsequently entrenched in the new South African constitution

ANC Proposed Regional Powers (1993)	Legislative Competences of Provinces as outlined in the new Constitutions
Imposition of taxes within guidelines	Agriculture
	Abattoirs
Airports	Airports (not national or international)
	Animal control and diseases
Horse racing and gambling	Casinos, racing, gambling and wagering
	Consumer protection
	Cultural affairs
Education (not tertiary)	Education (not university and technikon)
Environment	Environment
Health services	Health services
Housing	Housing
	Indigenous law and customary law
	Language policy (subject to relevant section of the constitution)
	Local government (subject to relevant section of the constitution)
Markets and pounds	Markets and pounds
	Nature conservation (excluding national and marine resources)
	Police (subject to relevant section of the constitution)
	Provincial public media
Punishment of contraventions of regional law	Provincial sport and recreation
Transport, including harbours, airports and roads	Public transport
Town and regional planning; industrial and other development in the region	Regional planning and development
Traffic control	Road traffic regulation
Roads	Roads
	Soil conservation
	Tourism
	Trade and industrial promotion
Works and undertakings	Traditional authorities
Town and Regional planning	Urban and rural development
Welfare	Welfare services
All other matters delegated by Parliament	

Source: SA Government Gazette, No. 15550, 3 March 1994.

Limiting political power

The Democratic Party (a liberal white parliamentary party) had as one of its antecedents the Progressive Federal Party, which had seen federalism as a key policy proposal. It was influenced by a long tradition of liberal thinking in South Africa which saw a federal arrangement as a possible 'second best' option for all parties which, in a classical liberal sense, seemed to therefore stand out as the 'best' option, avoiding the perils of one group's imposing its perspective on opponents (Simkins, 1986; Welsh, 1989). The DP's reasons for proposing federalism centred around issues of greater democracy, greater citizen participation in government, the dispersal of centralised power and the possibility of accommodating the 'linguistic, cultural, geographic and political pluralism' present in South Africa (Kriek, 1992). The DP was also concerned that an overconcentration of power could lead to 'tyranny', and during its election campaign, it mobilised its concern with a possible over-concentration of power in the ANC's hands and saw strong regional government as one important way of preventing this (Welsh, 1994).

Checks and balances on central authority were seen by the DP as crucial to maintaining liberal freedoms in the new South African state. Its role as liberal watchdog, then, was to be reinforced by various strategies, including a justiciable bill of rights, separation of the executive, the legislature and the judiciary, and the creation of two houses of Parliament, one elected on a regional basis. As it notes, 'It is accepted modern constitutional practice that a necessary check and balance on the activities of the one house of Parliament is another, differently composed chamber of Parliament' (DP Submission to the Technical Committee on Constitutional Issues (TC on CI), Vol 1, 15 June 1993). The DP strongly rejected the notion that regions should be delimited on ethnic grounds, but felt that community interests, economic viability and administrative effectiveness were important reasons for the regional organisation of society.

As David Welsh wrote (1993: 76), reflecting something of an emergent liberal consensus, 'The need for an effective and coherent central government is undoubted; but the need for brakes on the centre and mechanisms for maintaining a pluralist dispersal of power is equally undoubted'. The example of the German system, which South African commentators increasingly felt combined both of these apparent 'needs', was once again mentioned.

Ethnicity and state power

The Inkatha Freedom Party (IFP) made arguably the strongest stand in favour of federalism, and used both legal and political federalist discourses in its arguments for a federal position. Together with conservative Afrikaans organisations it appealed to the rights of ethnic communities to sovereign power and cited numerous cases around the world in support of its position. One of the fundamental differences between other political parties and the IFP/Conservative position was its insistence on 'residual' powers for regional government, that is, that all powers except those specifically invested in the central government should reside in the regional state. It also insisted that federalism be established and entrenched in the constitution during the negotiations phase prior to the election of either a new government or a Constitutional Assembly. It noted in one of its submissions to the Technical Committee (TC on CI) that failure to do this 'would, in the South African context, be a sure recipe for civil war and disaster' (IFP Submission to TC on CI, Vol 1, 12 July 1993). It also campaigned for separate constitutions for the sovereign regional governments, to be ratified only at that level. In order to accommodate the clear differences between different regions, it advocated a situation of 'assymetrical federalism'. KwaZulu/Natal would then be able to have strong autonomy in its relations with the centre while other regions could relate to the centre as in a unitary state.

The reasons advanced by the IFP for the federal arrangements included those given by other parties, e.g. efficiency, checks and balances and increased democracy. But it also cited the virtues of minority protection and the possibility of enabling an 'institutional expression of the cultural and social diversity of a given territory'. Unlike other parties, it promoted the ideal of the US system in its proposals, and a legal 'expert' (Mario Ambrosini) assisted in drawing up its position papers (Humphries *et al.*, 1994). However, it also warned that it was the 'strength of political events taking place on the ground' that determined the suitability of one system over another, rather than a technical decision. The threat of secession was added to that of civil war as it noted, strangely for a region in the midst of a decade-long civil war, that 'the people of regions such as KwaZulu/Natal have achieved a great deal along the path of racial harmonization which is now expressed in a true commonality of interests . . . (and which) justifies the recognition to such a community of the right to self-determination . . . Theoretically they would have the right to UDI' (IFP Submission to the TC on CI, Vol. 1, 12 July 1993, Annexure A). This claimed 'veto power' (Welsh, 1993: 71), the ability to jeopardise the possibility of a peaceful and consensual transition from Apartheid, not only won Inkatha the enhanced powers of regions (discussed below) but also played a crucial part in the elections settlement (rather than 'result'[4]), out of which the IFP emerged with a clear majority in the Kwazulu/Natal region (Hamilton and Mare, 1994).

Exiting from the formal negotiating process in the face of resistance to its demands for sovereign regional powers and an elevated role for the Zulu king, the IFP, and to a lesser extent the Afrikaner organisations, continued to influence the negotiations largely through the threat (and reality) of violence and disorder which their non-participation entailed. Only the day before the elections the Government enacted an amendment to the newly-agreed consitution in which the IFP wrested further concessions from the ANC and the NP on the issue of the powers of the traditional Zulu king. It was around this issue of the 'traditional' powers of the king and the extent of his kingdom which raised contention about the selective reinterpretation of history. The territory claimed by Buthelezi and the king was much larger than any which was decisively controlled by the Zulu nation historically, and historians were drawn into the political debate (Hamilton and Mare, 1994). None the less, the King's powers were be entrenched for the entire KwaZulu/Natal region. Events subsequent to the elections have seen a split between Buthelezi and the King, and some success on the part of the regional ANC in wresting the king from Buthelezi's influence and articulating Zulu traditionalism as part of the heritage of all Zulu people in the region, not only those who supported Inkatha. Buthelezi's ascendance to the national cabinet as Minister for Home Affairs will also pose some logistical problems for him in retaining his regional political base.

At the beginning of March 1994, a provision for the establishment of a Volksraad to investigate Afrikaner claims to a territorial homeland was also added to the new Constitution, along with numerous changes which extended and further entrenched the powers and functions of regions. Regional powers now included competence (rather than 'concurrent competence' with Parliament) to pass legislation within areas prescribed (see Table 10.1) and subject to certain constraints, such as effective national performance, minimum standards and national economic policies.

The Constitution now also included specific comments on the rights of communities to self-determination:

'Constitutional Principle 34:

1. This Schedule and the recognition therein of the right of the South African people as a whole to self-determination, shall not be construed as precluding, within the framework of the said right, constitutional provision for a notion of the right to self-determination by any com-

269

munity sharing a common cultural and language heritage, whether in a territorial entity within the Republic or in any other recognised way.

2. The Constitution may give expression to any particular form of self-determination provided there is substantial proven support within the community concerned for such a form of self-determination.

3. If a territorial entity referred to in paragraph 1 is established in terms of this Constitution before the new constitutional text is adopted, the new Constitution shall entrench the continuation of such territorial entity, including its structures, powers and functions' (Government Gazette No. 15550, 3 March 1994).

Unlike the IFP and Conservative Afrikaans groups (discussed below), the National Party emphasised the values of power sharing arrangements in protecting minorities against 'domination' along with other strategies such as 'the decentralisation of power, the imaginative devolution of authority, constitutional checks and balances, the requirement of consensus on contentious matters, systems which are conducive to consensus and a strong independent judiciary' (F.W. de Klerk, April 1990, quoted in Cilliers, 1992). Its input to the negotiation process also stressed the values of preserving community or group rights and identities, and emphasised that geographical diversity within South Africa had to be recognised, and that federalism was an appropriate vehicle for doing this. As Humphries *et al.* (1994: 148) comment: 'Well before Codesa, the NP had discovered, as it did on many other issues, that its traditional attitude to regional government made little sense if it was going to lose control of the centre. Since demographics offered the NP a strong prospect of controlling at least one region, the Western Cape, it became a keen advocate of federalism.' An election strategy which appealed to Coloured voters and re-included them in the fold of Afrikanerdom from which they had been excluded during Apartheid years proved successful – for reasons which are still being hotly debated – and the NP did win a strong majority in the Western Cape (Giliomee, 1994). However, like the ANC, the NP was not convinced that a formal federalist position was appropriate since, as Humphries *et al.* point out, it maintained an interest in sharing power at the central government level. But winning control of at least one regional government, these authors suggest, was seen by the NP as enabling it to push for enlarged regional powers after the election.

Although an alliance was formed between the IFP, the CP and various black homeland organisations (the Freedom Alliance), the Afrikaner organisations articulated a somewhat different position from the IFP. With a stated confederalist position, the Conservative Party and other Afrikaner groups centred their demands around a 'volkstaat' (a 'people's or folk state'). Clearly the problem of geography was against these organisations, as Afrikaans people were scattered throughout the country. Efforts to construct a territory in which Afrikaners formed a majority were tortuous, and the question of the citizenship rights of black people remaining in the volkstaat was never quite resolved. Proposals included that black residents would vote only for national government and not for the regional government, which was to remain in Afrikaner hands. This was of course rejected by the ANC, but negotiations about a volkstaat continued until close to the election date.

In April 1993, the Afrikaner Volksfront was launched, an alliance of a number of right-wing Afrikaner groupings. Split over the question of participation in the elections and a more or less hardline stance on the demand for an independent volkstaat, most parties in the AVF refused to participate in the elections. But one grouping emerged, at the last minute, willing to participate in the elections: the Vryheid's Front (Freedom Front) led by Constand Viljoen who was previously an army general. It did so on the strength of the provision made in the amended constitution for the establishment of a Volkstaat Council to explore the possibility of a volkstaat through constitutional means. Those who insisted on a confederal alternative did not participate in the elections but did not substantially pursue their threats to violently disrupt the proceedings.

Van Rooyen (1994: 104) estimates that the Freedom Front won some 27 per cent of Afrikaans votes at a national level and 41 per cent at regional level, and concludes therefore that less than half of the Afrikaner population supported self-determination. None the less, the arguments made by the right wing for self-determination were couched in terms of the 'right of self-determination which is a universally accepted right in general international law' (CP submission to TC on CI, Volume 14, 8 June 1993). Drawing on the work of Arend Lijphart (who had also influenced NP thinking), the CP argued that when power sharing or pluralism broke down, the alternative was 'territorial splitting in order to create more homogenous units'. It raised the spectre of Bosnia-Herzogovina as it suggested that ethnic mixing was a recipe for civil war. Referring to the USSR forming the 'Confederation or Commonwealth of Independent states', it proposed an adapted form of this model for South Africa. Its submission to the TC on CI was an extremely long document which outlined in considerable detail its case for an ethnically-based and independent state within an economic and negotiated union (based on treaties) with the rest of South Africa. A long history of the Afrikaner Volk and their struggles as a nation was included, together with numerous references to situations of ethnic conflict and academic interpretations of these. It suggested that efforts to reach a consociational solution (after Lijphart) were doomed to fail since, 'the hard arithmetic is simply that a majority is a majority is a majority. And the majority within South Africa's colonial borders is black. It is an illusion to believe that a way can be found to rule such a deeply divided society in a way that one group will not be dominated by others.' Like the IFP, it threatened the horror of civil war if its demands for a separate state within a confederation were not met.

Despite the strong resonances of Apartheid logic in this and other submissions, and the clearly racial (rather than ethnic) basis to its argument, some of the demands of the white right wing were accommodated in the settlement. As van Rooyen (1994: 105) notes, 'the ANC's recognition of the threat posed by scorned ethno-nationalism, and the mutual agreement between the major parties that Afrikaner self-determination could be effectively accommodated within the existing constitution, have left the back door open for the possible creation of a tenth province, the volkstaat'. Indeed, the fears of the international examples cited by the CP and others in the debates, together with the cases much closer to home (in Angola and Mozambique) of minority, ethnically-based groups leading to the catastrophic failure of post-independence governments, meant that the ANC was from early in the negotiations process mindful of this potentially disruptive force. Government ministers from these two neighbouring countries spoke publicly at ANC conferences of the problems posed by a 'small crocodile' which could certainly grow into a 'big crocodile' and cause the havoc and destruction seen in these Southern African civil wars. Thus not only formal legal, political and academic discourses of federalism, devolution of state power and ethnic rights, but also the common understandings of recent world and regional events played their part in shaping the outcome of negotiations in South Africa.

CONCLUSION: REFLECTIONS ON FEDERALISM, ETHNICITY AND POWER

Very differently from other parties, then, the IFP and various conservative Afrikaner parties made their arguments for sovereign regional or independent government on the basis of ethnic or racial identity and history, more or less neatly aligned to particular territorial divisions. And it was in these proposals that the influence of federalism as an ideology and as a political project served an important legitimating function for parties whose aim seemed to be to survive the transition from Apartheid without losing the powers which that political system had granted them. But these are complex issues, and the contextual meaning of ethnic politics within South Africa, given the legacy of Apartheid, makes assessing the agendas of these organisations particularly difficult. For in an international context there is certainly a growing legitimacy for ethno-nationalist claims to autonomous rule, and for secession. It is difficult to assert in any nationalist movement that the 'nation' has not been constructed through the creative and sometimes instrumentalist use of history (Smith, 1981), and indeed efforts to promote a 'South African' nation must also be so understood. In a period in world intellectual history when it is freely acknowledged that all political identities are constructed and are constantly being transformed, it would seem churlish to admit some identities as real and others as simply fabrications and therefore politically reactionary.

From a radical democratic perspective, though, it is the extent to which particular political identities rest upon the exclusion and destruction of other identities, refusing to engage with or accept and tolerate the existence of alternative political identities which provides a basis for assessment (Mouffe, 1993). The space for a critical appraisal of various efforts to construct political identity can then be preserved. But politics is about more than identity and also concerns the power relations and the vision of society which organisations promote. It is widely acknowledged that the political practices of the IFP rest upon clientelist relations, traditional authorities and a violent effort to draw Zulu-speaking people into the politics of ethnicity. None the less, the prolonged civil war in the KwaZulu/Natal region between IFP and ANC supporters means that a mutual intolerance between the ANC and the IFP does exist on the ground. The prioritisation of an ethnic identity, instead of a toleration for the multiple identities which most political agents create for themselves is, however, a crucial difference between the national liberation movements and ethnically-based organisations. Although one could interpret the appeals to ethnic identities on the part of the ANC before and during the election campaign in a cynical fashion, it could also be argued that the generally democratic perspective it adopts has a tendency to enable the incorporation of multiple political identities and encourages the expression of pluralism. But it is this proliferation of political identities in the post-Apartheid context which has led to the fragmentation of political power along federal lines in the new state form, in ways that have been strongly framed by the institutional and discursive context in which they have been mobilised.

The manipulation of ethnic nationalism and of federalism in the pursuit of the maintenance of Apartheid-derived powers, and the resultant persistence of power relations which are far from democratic, would seem to be grounds for presenting the promotion of federalism as being related directly to particular forms of power and subjectivity which in the post-apartheid context could be interpreted as profoundly anti-democratic. In many senses, then, this reminds us of the difficulty of ascribing normative values to federalist proposals independently of the political context in which they are being supported (King, 1993). And I would argue that the failure to foreground this political context also alerts us to the potential role of federalism itself as a normativising discourse, whose specific relation to power, and particularly to ethnic power and territorial politics, usually passes unexamined.

On the basis of the analysis of the South African case, then, I would argue strongly against Burgess's (1993) and others' assertion that one can separate a process of federalism from the institutional arrangements of federation, as if 'federalism' were simply the unlimited variety of everyday cleavages in society. The fact that these 'federal' charateristics of society mobilise in support of the territorial fragmentation of the institutions of the state highlights federalism as first and foremost a political project clearly associated with transforming the character of state power and with asserting certain types of political subjects as central. The concepts and ideas of federalism have given to certain political projects an identity and a legitimacy – at the same time as they have arguably provided the institutional means for resolving intractable conflicts created by the production of particular political identities. But it is the particularity of the subject identities involved in federal arrangements that should alert us to federalism's intrinsically political character. For it is ethnic groups and territorially based communities that find some relief in the federal position. Groups indentified on the basis of a wide variety of social cleavages, perhaps age, gender, class or sexuality, or groups dispersed across territories, find federalism of no use. In this last case, conservative political theorists and practitioners (including the National Party in South Africa, as evidenced in the power sharing elements included in the new Constitution) have devised 'consociational' systems to accommodate ethnic cleavages. Rather than promoting a pluralist solution to political problems, then, federalism restricts the nature of the political terrain and is instrumental in re-shaping it in ways which disadvantage some, and empower others.

Thus while federalism does not have moral value in its own right, and assumes the meaning of those who pursue a federal solution as the means to secure their own advancement, it can also be thought of as a discourse linked in to the particular limiting political practices and ideas of the modern state. The nexus of states, nations and territories thus forms a crucial framework for the place of federalism in any political situation. This is not to suggest that federalism is a moral evil, but rather, that it has a particular relationship to the politics of different places, at least partially shaped by the discourse of federalism itself.

One analyst of federalism posed the question as to whether South

Africa is a 'federal country'. That is, following arguments along the lines of Burgess (1993), do we find here the socio-territorial cleavages which seem to promote or facilitate federalist solutions (Welsh, 1993)? The various federal aspects identified by different participants in the debate have included: regional identities, ethnic identities, regional interests, political style. None the less, observers noted that various social cleavages were not clearly territorialised, and that regionalism would be creating or fostering as much as it would be responding to various territorial or regional economic and political interests (Heymans, 1993). Thus not only does a federal solution empower particular political identities and organisations and disempower others, but it is also likely to generate new forms of political identity, not least territorial ones. Thus gender issues, and the mobilisation of political organisations around the rights of women have failed to be strongly insitutionalised in the new state form in South Africa, despite an unprecedented level of women's organisation and representation during the negotiations. federalism and consociationalism have, however, institutionalised and enhanced the political powers of certain ethnically based political groups[5] and have also set the stage for the emergence of new, powerful territorially-based groups. For the proto-federalist settlement which has emerged not only contains more federalist elements than the negotiators realised, according to Humphries et al. (1994), but also set in place the opportunity for an even greater decentralisation of powers and autonomy.

New regional prime ministers (of all political parties) were pressurising for their proper powers to be instated almost as soon as they had taken office. Bureaucratic delays in passing enabling legislation and in organising diverse personnel into functioning regional administrations were being criticised by regional ministers as undermining their authority and capacity. As a power base for the emergence of important regional interests and identities, the new regionalised state form is likely to increase pressures on the central state to decentralise decision-making and financing. The future of federalism in South Africa is by no means determined as yet, but all indications are that this form of state is likely to remain influential, as concept and as institutional framework. However, whether it functions to undermine post-Apartheid efforts at reconstruction and development, or to reinforce the ethnic and racial identities that anti-apartheid movements opposed for so long, remains to be seen.

ACKNOWLEDGEMENTS

I owe a great debt of thanks to Richard Humphries for his helpful discussions of federalism in South Africa, and for making available to me documents of the Technical Committee on Constitutional Issues. Doreen Atkinson was also helpful, and without Graham Smith encouraging me to write the article, it would never have even been conceived! Richard Ballard let me use newspaper articles collected for our Honours classes, and the discussions during these classes were always stimulating and certainly helped me think through these issues in new and exciting ways.

NOTES

1. Of course these kinds of political debates, especially when they involve the loss of life and the contestation of political principles long struggled for, such as the struggle for a unified and non-racial democracy in South Africa, are also deeply moving at a personal level. Engaging with these debates has been, for me, unexpectedly difficult. Having a deep moral abhorrence of the Apartheid order and of those who used the system to their own advantage, and being personally involved in the politics of the region most affected by violent conflict over the rights of some to rule by force, clientelism and, of course, ethnic identity, has made analysis of the federalist debate very difficult for me. Not that this influence of social location or political position is unusual – more usually it simply remains unstated.
2. I have relied quite heavily here on the very useful record and analysis of the negotiations until the end of Codesa II contained in Friedman (1993). The negotiations were lengthy and involved much that was technical and complex. Clearly the brief summary offered here is simply to provide a background for readers un-familiar with recent South African history.
3. The references to Germany reflect the results of a study tour which a number of ANC officials undertook to examine the German political system. Apparently it was this visit which caused a number of key consitutional negotiators from the ANC to become more open to the provision of greater entrenched regional powers. Even so, the final agreements on regional powers reflect a stronger position for regions than that presented in this document (Humphries *et al.*, 1994).
4. Very controversially, a behind-closed-doors settlement of the election results in the KwaZulu/Natal region left the IFP with 50.3 per cent of the vote in the regional parliament, a clear majority.

Extensive election fraud and intimidation were reported by observers and election officials in the Northern areas of KwaZulu/Natal – but a formal contestation of the result, initially proposed by the Southern Natal ANC region, was shelved as a result of national pressure, and the 'negotiated' election result stood (Hamilton and Mare, 1994).

5. Within the South African context the linkage between race, ethnicity and class also implies that at least some of those who stand to benefit from the accommodationist strategies such as federalism and power sharing are the old élite. As MacDonald (1992: 724–5) notes, 'in South Africa the fusion of the economic and the ethnic . . . convert(s) vetoes from defensive mechanisms of the weaker into weapons of the stronger, entrenching inequality and raising questions about the stability and consensus that consociationalism is said to promote . . . Moderation, therefore, begins where Apartheid left off.'

REFERENCES

African National Congress. 1993. *ANC Regional Policy*. Centre for Development Studies: University of the Western Cape.

Burchell, G., Gordon, C. and Miller, P. (eds) 1991. *The Foucault Effect: Studies in Governmentality*. London: Harvester Wheatsheaf.

Burgess, M. 1993. Federalism and Federation: a Reappraisal, in M. Burgess and A. Gagnon (eds) *Comparative Federalism and Federation*. London: Harvester Wheatsheaf, pp. 3–14.

Cilliers, J. 1992. The National Party and Federalism, in Kriek, D., Kotze, D., Labuschagne, P., Mtimkulu, P. and O'Malley, K. (eds) *Federalism: the Solution?* Pretoria: HSRC, pp. 239–266.

Cobbett, W., Glaser, D., Hindson, D. and Swilling, M. 1986. South Africa's Regional Political Economy: a Critical Analysis of Reform Strategy in the 1980s, in South African Research Services (ed) *SA Review* 3. Johannesburg: Ravan.

Derrida, J. 1985. Racism's last word *Critical Inquiry* 12: 290–299.

Friedman, S. 1993. *The Long Journey: South Africa's quest for a negotiated settlement*. Johannesburg: Ravan.

Giliomee, H. 1994. The National Party's Campaign for a Liberation Election, in Reynolds, A. (ed) *Election '94 South Africa: The Campaigns, Results and Future Prospects*. Cape Town: David Philip, pp. 43–72.

Hamilton, G. and Mare, G. 1994. The Inkatha Freedom Party, in Reynolds, A. (ed) *Election '94 South Africa: The Campaigns, Results and Future Prospects*. Cape Town: David Philip, pp. 73–88.

Heymans, C. 1993. Regional interests and identities: an uncertain transition?, in Friedman, S. and Humphries, R. (eds) *Federalism and its Foes*, Johannesburg: Centre for Policy Studies, pp. 90–97.

Humphries, R. and Shubane, K. 1992. *A Delicate Balance: Reconstructing Regionalism in South Africa*. CPS Transition Series, Research Report No. 24.

Humphries, R., Rapoo, T. and Friedman, S. 1994. The shape of the country: negotiating regional government, in Friedman, S. and Atkinson, D. (eds). The small miracle: South Africa's Negotiated Settlement, Johannesburg: Centre for Policy Studies, Raven Press, pp. 148–81.

King, P. 1993 Federation and representation, in M. Burgess and A. Gagnon (eds) *Comparative Federalism and Federation*. London: Harvester Wheatsheaf, pp. 94–101.

Kriek, D. 1992. The federation plans of the Democratic Party, in Kriek, D., Kotze, D., Labuschagne, P., Mtimkulu, P. and O'Malley, K. (eds) *Federalism: The Solution?* Pretoria: HSR, pp. 231–238.

MacDonald, M. 1992. The siren's song: the political logic of power-sharing in South Africa. *Journal of Southern African Studies* 18, 4: 709–725.

Mouffe, C. 1993. *The Return of the Political*. London: Verso.

Muthien, Y. and Khosa, M. 1994. Divided We Fall, *Indicator SA*, Winter Vol II, 3:27–33.

O'Meara, D. 1994. (Manuscript) 'Slouching towards the Rubicon'. Paper presented at the African Studies Seminar Series, University of Natal, Durban.

Seethal, C. 1991. Restructuring the local state in South Africa: Regional Services Councils and crisis resolution *Political Geography Quarterly* 10: 8–25.

Simkins, C. 1986. *Reconstructing South African Liberalism*. Johannesburg: South African Institute of Race Relations.

Smith, A. 1981. *The Ethnic Revival*. Cambridge: Cambridge University Press.

Sutcliffe, M. 1993. Natal: more of a concept than a region? in Friedman, S. and Humphries, R. (eds) *Federalism and its Foes*. Johannesburg: Centre for Policy Studies, pp. 185–194.

Van Rooyen, J. 1994. The white right. in Reynolds, A. (ed) *Election '94 South Africa: The Campaigns, Results and Future Prospects*. Cape Town: David Philip, pp. 89–106.

Welsh, D. 1989. Federalism and the problem of South Africa, in Forsyth, M. (ed) *Federalism and Nationalism*. London: Leicester University Press, pp. 250–279.

Welsh, D. 1993. Federalism and South Africa: The future is not yet written. in Friedman, S. and Humphries, R. (eds) *Federalism and its Foes*. Johannesburg: Centre for Policy Studies, pp. 56–76.

Welsh, D. 1994. The Democratic Party, in Reynolds, A. (ed) *Election '94 South Africa: The Campaigns, Results and Future Prospects*. Cape Town: David Philip, pp. 107–116.

Work in Progress, 1995. *The New South African Identity Crisis*, 93. SARS (South African Research Services).

CHAPTER ELEVEN

'Arrested Federalisation'? Europe, Britain, Ireland

James Anderson

Arguments about how the European Union could or should develop tend to polarise around positions for or against a 'federal Europe'. Substantial 'federalisation' is already perceived in the transfers of sovereignty over some economic matters from member states to the EU as a whole, and further moves in that direction are widely anticipated. Despite opposition from defenders of existing state sovereignty, these developments have encouraged the imagining of federal scenarios to solve the problems of conflicting nationalisms in the United Kingdom and, particularly, in Ireland. It is argued that reconstructing the over-centralised British state on federal lines would recognise the diversity of its regional political cultures. It could be a way of accommodating pressures for devolution or 'buying off' demands for independence in Scotland and Wales. It could help address the problems of a 'pre-modern' and absolutist conception of sovereignty as the indivisible preserve of the Westminster Parliament – problems of an 'archaic' constitution and the lack of a written one. But others see it as the 'slippery slope' to the 'break-up of Britain'.

However, it is in Ireland that the problems of conflicting nationalisms have been most acute, and it is here that the limitations of the British state and constitution have been most exposed, both historically and in recent decades. Northern Ireland is now the most problematic part of the ramshackle 'United Kingdom of Great Britain and Northern Ireland', an entity whose very title hints at dis-unity, or at least a regional diversity which might be better accommodated in a federalised state. Some Irish nationalist supporters of a re-united Ireland also see a federalised state as the best solution to nationalist conflict, although in their case it is a federal Irish state independent of Britain. A federal or confederal Ireland would recognise Northern Ireland's distinctiveness – partitioned from Southern Ireland since 1920 with a built-in majority supporting the British unionist tradition – but the recognition would be within an Irish rather than a British framework. Joint British-Irish sovereignty has been suggested as a 'balanced compromise', but the Irish and British governments are instead seeking general cross-border agreement on 'North–South institutions'. These, they claim, would not involve 'federation', or 'unification', or impinge on existing state sovereignties, but not everyone is convinced.

Europe, Britain and Ireland thus appear suitable cases for federalisation but there is considerable opposition to the treatment. This chapter looks at its prospects in these related contexts, on both empirical and theoretical grounds. The first section outlines the strong pressures both for and against federalisation, historically and today. It suggests that these conflicting pressures may in the future result in 'compromise' or 'intermediate' outcomes which stop well short of formal federal structures, whether characterised as 'partial' or *de facto* but not *de jure* federalisation. The second section lends this idea some theoretical support. Rather than simply focusing on the main 'actors' involved – the EU and state institutions, governments or nationalist movements – it focuses more on the 'stage' on which they have to operate. With the recent acceleration of globalisation it seems that the ground is shifting underneath established political institutions, practices and concepts, including the concept and practice of federalism. Historical analogies of a 'new medievalism' and a 'postmodern unbundling of territorial sovereignty' suggest that contemporary developments are both encouraging federalisation and at the same time working against its full realisation. The partiality of territorial 'unbundling' points towards processes which for want of a better term we might call 'arrested federalisation'.

FOR AND AGAINST FEDERALISATION

It is widely believed by supporters and opponents that the EU is promising/threatening to become a federal European 'super-state', the state 'writ large', a 'United States of Europe'. In some versions the existing member states will become like the 'states' in the United States of America or the 'provinces' in the Canadian federation; in other versions a 'Europe of the Regions' will see regions and regionalisms displacing nation states and nationalisms. It is argued that the logic of the Single European Market and of global competition, particularly against the other two major economic blocs dominated by the USA and Japan, will necessitate ever-closer economic and monetary union and that political union will inevitably follow. The argument is quite powerful. Independant state sovereignty over important economic matters such as imports and exports has already been ceded to the EU as a collective, and its activities can be interpreted as further undercutting existing state authority.

For instance, to further integration, sub-state regionalism is being encouraged by the EU's central supra-national institutions – the European Parliament, the Committee of the Regions, and particularly the European Commission – and this serves to legitimise regional and sub-state nationalist movements within member states. Thus in the early 1990s the Commission proposed that the 'Committee of the Regions' should act as the 'upper house' of the European Parliament. The proposal was later watered down by the Council of Ministers representing the member states, and the Committee has only a consultative role in narrowly-defined 'regional' matters. Nevertheless, Commission officials believe that its role will be progressively enhanced because regionalism is increasingly important 'on the ground', and because the Committee provides a political platform for a growing number of important regional politicians from 'federalised' states such as Germany and Spain (Anderson and Goodman, 1995). The Single Market has the effect of encouraging regions to seek more political autonomy: regional pressure groups, such as the campaigns for a Scottish, for a Welsh and, in England, for a Northern Assembly, argue that regional autonomy is urgently required to prevent further peripheralisation because of increased competition from the stronger 'core' economies in the unified Market. But unsurprisingly, it is the more prosperous and politically autonomous regions – on the continent rather than in Britain – that have taken the lead in forging new inter-regional groupings, most notably but not only the 'four motors' of Catalonia, Lombardy, Baden-Wurtemburg and Rhone-Alps. Elected regional bodies are established features of political life in four of the five largest EU states and in several of the smaller ones, the United Kingdom and the Irish Republic being notable exceptions.

The implications of European integration can therefore be seen as two-fold, encouraging federalisation both of states in a federal EU and of sub-regions within those states. However, the 'post-nationalist' vision of a federal 'Europe of the Regions' replacing the 'Europe of States' seems highly improbable. Nationalism is far from 'dead', and if we agree with Nairn (1977) that it is basically a response to uneven development, then the continuing generation of unevenness, in both spatial and functional terms, by globalisation, including its highly selective 'internationalising' of the state (see e.g. Cox, 1992), can be expected to generate and regenerate national responses and nationalisms. A fully federal 'United States of Europe' based on existing nation-states is only slightly less improbable than the 'postnationalist' vision, and partly because of these same types of unevenness. Material interests vary across the different member states and each has its own particular sets of interests to defend or further. Therefore, while it seems increasingly implausible that individual member states would find it in their interests to opt out of the EU, to 'go it alone', it also seems highly unlikely in the forseeable future that they would simply agree to 'sink their differences' in a federal state, and not least because the pace of cultural unification has not been at all commensurate with the pace of economic union. Perhaps equally important is the related point that the EU impinges strongly on state sovereignty in some policy areas (e.g. in the economic field) and very weakly or not at all in others (e.g. some aspects of social policy).

While the Commission has some autonomy from the member states, it is the latter, and particularly the larger states, that determine the pace and direction of integration. They are unlikely to 'commit suicide', or simply dissolve themselves into a federal super-state, though they are being changed by the integration process and sometimes despite themselves. The union is more a case of selective confederation which allows more independence to the constituent units. The EU will continue to encourage sub-state regionalisms and nationalisms because its over-arching 'umbrella' increases the viability of smaller units, such as 'an independent Scotland in Europe' to quote the Scottish nationalists. But while likely to continue to stimulate interest in federal solutions, the EU itself may in the future turn out to be less potent as a 'model' of federalisation.

Federalism in British and Irish history

A fully federal UK or a federal Ireland also seem improbable outcomes, despite a long history of federal ideas and the contemporary problems of two overly-centralised states whose boundaries spectacularly fail to match those of nations. If federalism accommodates difference in unity, the multinational but unitary United Kingdom has long been a particularly suitable case for treatment. It encompasses distinct Scottish, Welsh, Irish, and English identities imperfectly bound together by a wider but incomplete sense of Britishness. England, with over 80 per cent of the total UK population, is very much the political 'centre' (though there is increasingly a case for confining that term to the South-East of England). Scotland, Wales and Northern Ireland are politically its 'peripheries' and they differ markedly not just from the 'centre' but from each other. Even the designations of the different territories – 'kingdom', 'principality', 'region', or 'province' – lack uniformity and general agreement. Northern Ireland has always had its own separate civil service, education system and judiciary, and from 1921 to 1972 it also had its own parliament, though in 1974 this was replaced by 'direct rule', in effect rule by a British colonial governor. Wales, by contrast, is a 'principality'; and Scotland, like England, is a 'kingdom' which has retained many of the trappings of a separate state (e.g. its own state church, its own legal and education systems). Whereas England is administered by the specific departments of state – Education, Employment, Environment, etc. – the 'peripheries' are administered via their 'own' sections of *central* government – the Scottish, Welsh and Northern Ireland Offices. The Scottish Office was established in 1886; in contrast the Welsh Office was set up in response to nationalist pressure in the 1960s.

This *ad hoc* character of the UK reflects its different histories. The English kingdom developed from its South-East 'core' region between the tenth and fifteenth centuries; it incorporated Wales and Ireland by conquest mainly in the sixteenth and seventeenth centuries, and Scotland through a merging of crowns in 1603 and a negotiated union of parliaments in 1707. There were also major differences in how the three 'peripheries' developed economically. Scotland and Wales (or at least Central Scotland and South Wales), along with north-eastern Ulster around Belfast, shared fully in the economic benefits and political 'glories' of the Industrial Revolution and the British Empire, whereas much of Ireland, including much of Ulster, did not. This 'uneven development', and a legacy of political, religious and cultural discrimination, particularly against Roman Catholics and Gaelic traditions (e.g. Irish language speakers had declined from about 50 per cent to 10 per cent of Ireland's population since the Union with Britain in 1800), were the underpinnings of the partitioning of Ireland in 1920.

The resulting United Kingdom of Great Britain and Northern Ireland seemed a relatively successful example of state integration up to the 1950s. Indeed it was much to the surprise of pundits and politicians that in the 1960s substate nationalisms re-emerged as a serious political force. Within little over a decade the fragmentation of the multi-national British state was being discussed as a serious possibility, as were federal scenarios both to halt and to hasten the process.

The Scottish National Party (SNP) and Plaid Cymru (PC) in Wales had almost ceased to exist in the 1940s and 1950s. In the 1951 General Election PC put up just four candidates who averaged only 6 per cent of the vote in their four constituencies, while the SNP had only two candidates and they got only about 10 per cent of the vote in their respective constituencies. By contrast, in 1974 the SNP stood 71 candidates. Its percentage share of the total vote in Scotland rose from only 1.3 per cent in the 1945 General Election to over 30 per cent in October 1974 (only 6 percentage points behind Labour), and the party won 11 seats. In Wales Plaid Cymru's share of the vote increased from 1.1 per cent in 1945 to over 19 per cent in 1970. In both cases support fell back, but it remained at much higher levels than before the nationalist resurgence. The main Britain-wide parties were forced to accept at least part of the nationalists' agendas, including the resurrected possibility of federalisation.

This issue goes back to the eighteenth century and the union of the Scottish and English parliaments in 1707, though for the past hundred years Ireland has provided the main focus. Ideas of a federal British state, and a federal British Empire centred on Westminster, were first seriously mooted in response to Irish demands for 'Home Rule' in the late nineteenth century. Federalism then was mainly a unionist answer to Irish nationalist separatism, though later it would come to be more a nationalist answer to the unitary state supported by unionism. In the 1870s the Irish Home Rule Party of Isaac Butt argued that federalisation would prevent the break-up of the Empire. With the same objective still prominent before World War I, Winston Churchill advocated a federal UK with Wales, Scotland and the English regions as well as Ireland having their own parliaments; these, together with parts of the (white) Empire such as Canada and Australia, were all to come under a federal 'imperial parliament' at Westminster in what had become known as 'Home Rule all round' (see Jay, 1989).

However these federal schemes were thwarted, largely by English Conservative defenders of Westminster sovereignty as absolute and indivisible. They blocked attempts to establish a highly circumscribed and limited form of Irish self-government in the three 'Home Rule crisis' periods of 1886, 1892 and 1912. Partly motivated by the fact that Irish nationalist success would encourage other 'Home Rule' movements in the Empire (particularly in 'jewel in the crown' India where a nationalist movement had recently been established), right-wing Conservatives and others actively encouraged sectarian opposition from the Protestant minority in Ireland (and especially in Ulster) under the slogan 'Home Rule is Rome rule'. To block the large Irish majority favouring 'Home Rule', they encouraged the threat of armed opposition. This in turn encouraged Irish nationalists to arm and it led directly to the creation of the Irish Republican Army, the 'troubles' in the shape of an armed struggle against British rule in Ireland, and the partition of the country in 1920.

Two 'Home Rule' parliaments were established, one for Southern Ireland in Dublin and one for Northern Ireland at Stormont in Belfast; and the Government of Ireland Act 1920 also provided for a 'Council of Ireland' to be made up of an equal number of representatives from each. The Council, seen as an all-Ireland parliament in embryo, was to deal with matters affecting the whole island, promote North–South relations and take immediate control of certain functions or issues which straddled the border such as the railway system. But shunned by Northern unionists, the Council never met. Britains's temporary expedient of partition became permanent, with a quasi-federal 'Stormont' in an otherwise very centralised state, and British acquiescence in the continuation of a Protestant ascendancy in Northern Ireland.

The Dublin parliament later declared itself fully independent, while Northern Ireland retained a significant degree of *de facto* self-rule until 1972, when 'Stormont' was closed down and replaced by 'direct rule' from the 'sovereign' parliament at Westminster. The 'troubles' had re-emerged in 1969 because of systematic anti-Catholic discrimination over nearly fifty years of one-party unionist rule (which generally equated 'Catholic' with 'disloyal Irish nationalist', itself something of a self-fulfilling equation). Westminster had ignored unionist misrule, and the 'Stormont' regime was incapable of reforming itself in response to mainly, but not exclusively, Catholic demands for 'civil rights'. Then unionist inability to respond to belated British pressures for reform completed the change from a high degree of autonomy and *de facto* federalisation to 'direct rule' on the colonial model. That, and twenty-five years of armed conflict, hopefully now being brought to a close by the IRA's ceasefire of 1 September 1994 followed by the Loyalist ceasefire, is (in an admittedly over-simplified 'nutshell') the main context in which federal solutions have again been mooted in Ireland and Britain.

A federal UK?

Nationalists in Wales and Scotland now have raised hopes that their own separate campaigns for 'self-rule' will be furthered by some restoration of 'self-rule' in Northern Ireland and perhaps some loosening of Westminster's 'absolutist' sovereignty in relation to North–South institutions in Ireland and the developing EU context. Conversely, however, many Northern Irish unionists argue that their own 'self-rule' as an integral part of the UK should be no greater and no different from that granted to Scotland and Wales; and, like their allies on the right wing of the British 'Conservative and Unionist' Party, they oppose any new arrangements for the 'political peripheries' which might weaken the UK's territorial integrity.

The problem here is that federalisation could hasten or halt 'disintegration'. Allowing limited regional autonomy can reduce separatist pressures, as for example in Spain (see chapter nine), where the harsh 'centralism' of Franco did so much to stimulate Basque and Catalan nationalisms. In Britain there is a similar argument that the 'centralism' set in train by Mrs Thatcher's Conservative governments has given separatists an easy and popular target to mobilise against, just as her harsh response to IRA hunger-strikers revived the flagging political fortunes of Provisional Sinn Fein in the early 1980s. But while 'centalism' can be counterproductive for its adherents, so too can federalism as a 'safety valve' for separatist pressures. Attempts to 'buy off' Scottish and Welsh separatism and 'modernise' the British state could conceivably hasten the UK's dismemberment. Rather than reducing separatist pressures, a federal structure might simply provide a stronger institutional base for separatist mobilisation, as the provincial assembly and administration in Quebec provides Quebec nationalists with a base for opposing Canadian federation (see chapter two). In short, neither federal nor unitary state forms can guarantee territorial integrity, and it depends on the particular historical and geographical circumstances whether federalisation would help or hinder separatist demands for independence. Hence, rather than federalisation being a matter of abstract principle, it is a matter of debate around complex issues 'for and against', whether the objective is the maintenance or the transformation of the territorial *status quo*. (And the matter is further complicated by more mundane political considerations, for example electoral calculations about the Labour Party in England needing the present level of representation of Scotland and Wales at Westminster for it to have the possibility of again forming a government.)

Federalisms for Ireland

In Ireland the issues are even more complex than in Britain because there are two states and several quite different federal scenarios, including Northern Ireland in a reformed United Kingdom, the North in a re-united federal or confederal Ireland, even North and South within a 'federation of the British (and presumably Irish) Isles'. Northern Ireland's full integration either with Britain or with the rest of Ireland is unlikely, because these mutually exclusive positions would completely negate each other and alienate either Irish nationalists or unionists. Unitary states do not 'fit' the reality of geographically mixed national identities and a border unusually permeable by European standards.

Some element of federalism can therefore seem a very attractive option, though since partition it has mostly been proposed by Irish nationalists with unionists generally hostile. Before the country was partitioned, Eamon de Valera, the Sinn Fein leader, proposed the alternative of Irish federation and he continued to support it, as did other prominent nationalist leaders (Bowman, 1983). When the 'troubles' re-erupted in the late 1960s, Jack Lynch, the Irish Taoiseach, suggested a federation with two provincial legislatures and a new Council of Ireland as the federal parliament; and in 1971

Provisional Sinn Fein advocated a federal Ireland based on the four historic provinces (the six county North reverting to the nine county Ulster). Sinn Fein later abandoned this four-part scheme as unrealistic, but two-part federal and confederal scenarios were revived by the New Ireland Forum organised by then Taoiseach Garret FitzGerald in 1983–4. Although nothing came of its specific proposals, the Forum was important in helping bring about the Anglo-Irish Agreement of 1985, an international treaty which contains elements of confederation and joint sovereignty, despite government claims that sovereignty was unaffected. The Agreement, uniquely for the UK, gives another state, the Irish Republic, a legitimate role in the internal affairs of a part of the UK, a definite though limited breach of sovereignty as the exclusive preserve of one state. It established an Intergovernmental Conference framework for all aspects of North–South cooperation with regular ministerial meetings and a joint secretariat.

Since 1985 the economic and political pressures for North–South cooperation and institutions have increased substantially. The traditional nationalist goal of a unitary 'united Ireland' is widely seen as unrealistic in the immediate future, partly because of the North's continued dependence on the massive financial 'subvention' from Britain's tax-payers. Northern nationalists, however, want 'parity of esteem' for their 'Irish identity' within Northern Ireland, and they want it guaranteed by North–South institutions and Dublin government involvement. On the economic front, the formal completion of the Single Market in 1992 has greatly increased the pressures for cross-border economic integration: in business circles a 'one island economy' is now widely seen as imperative to avoid a further peripheralisation of both parts of Ireland, and something requiring a political-administrative North–South framework (see Anderson, 1994; Anderson and Goodman, 1994).

Thus the establishment of North–South institutions is a central issue in any settlement, and to be effective they would necessarily involve modifications to state sovereignty. But what form of institutions, and how are they to be achieved? A Council of Ireland has twice been ruled out by unionist opposition, initially in the 1920s and again in 1974 when it fell as part of the 'Sunningdale Agreement' wrecked by the loyalist 'Ulster Workers' Strike' of 1974. Joint sovereignty by Dublin and London over the North has been discussed in Labour Party circles (O'Leary et al., 1993) and has the merit of accommodating the national aspirations of both Irish nationalists and British unionists without either group having to be a disadvantaged minority, whether nationalists in a purely Northern Ireland context or unionists in the whole of Ireland. So is it third time lucky for a Council, combined perhaps with joint sovereignty? Is a federal solution at long last a possibility?

Despite strong pressures, there are several reasons why it may not happen. Firstly, federalism is no panacea, nor is it necessarily even an attractive option. Federations may contain the seeds of their own destruction and can require very cumbersome and costly mechanisms to ensure functioning stability. These problems are generally compounded in federations with only two 'partners' who can become locked into a continual conflict, and perhaps especially where there is a marked assymetry in their sizes. Both conditions would occur in Ireland, where the South has roughly double the population of the North. One potential outcome is captured by the Quebec separatist description of Anglophone and Francophone Canada as 'two scorpions in the same bottle'.

Secondly, as with the EU and Britain, the pressures for and against federal solutions may result in outcomes which stop short of formal federalisation. One advantage of partial and *de facto* federalisation over formal *de jure* federalism is that it allows the two governments to maintain that sovereignty has not been affected, and it presents unionist opponents with less explicit or clear-cut targets to mobilise against. Since the arrival of the Single Market, unionists have little option but to publicly accept the need for economic cooperation with the South, but they deny that it has or should have any political dimension or implications. The implausibility of this separation of 'economics' from 'politics' is highlighted by the fact that in the 1960s unionists used to argue against economic cooperation on the grounds that it would inevitably lead to political reunification. Nevertheless they still oppose any revision to traditional British sovereignty as leading towards a unitary all-Ireland state. Adherence to absolute sovereignty rules out compromise and is arguably what has made the unionists' Northern Ireland such a political disaster. But despite the twenty-five years of bloodshed, unionists show little sign that they have learned from this particular mistake, and to placate them both governments insist that 'North–South institutions' would have no effect on sovereignty. However, the ability of Northern Irish unionists to block change is now markedly less than it was early this century. The wider setting is now provided by integration in the EU rather than the British Empire. State sovereignty is much more problematical than it was in the period up to 1920, and especially so in the EU. Adherence to the British conception of sovereignty as absolute and indivisible is increasingly out of line with contemporary global developments.

THE SHIFTING 'STAGE' OF TERRITORIALITY

The ground seems to be shifting underneath established political arrangements and concepts, including federalism. The contemporary 'shrinking of the world' or 'time-space compression', which Harvey (1989) suggests is the greatest transformation in geographic space since the Renaissance, is altering the nature of territorial sovereignty. The 'medieval to modern' transformation of politics was associated with a radical transformation in how people experienced and represented space and time, and now we may be experiencing similarly radical political changes for analogous reasons. The EU, it is suggested, might be neither an emerging federal 'super-state' nor simply a traditional intergovernmental collection of sovereign states, but a new arrangement reminiscent of the overlapping authorities and multiple loyalties which existed in medieval Europe – a 'new medievalism' (Bull, 1977). If the transition from 'pre-modern to modern' involved sovereignty over everything being 'bundled' together in territorial 'parcels' called nation states, then contemporary changes may involve a 'back to the future' or 'modern to postmodern' transition in which territoriality is now being 'unbundled'. Ruggie (1993) argues that this 'unbundling' has gone further in the EU than anywhere else and that in consequence the EU can be seen as 'the world's first postmodern international political form'. A historic shift away from the territorial sovereignty of nation states towards multiple and partial sovereignties – because of globalisation and the increased importance of regional and ethnic identities – may be simultaneously encouraging and 'arresting' federalisation.

There are problems with historical analogy – since medieval times sovereignty has been democratised and 'nationalised', the contemporary world lacks the universality of medieval Christendom's social and moral order, and the term 'postmodern' comes with confused and confusing epistemological 'baggage'. Nevertheless, ideas of 'new medieval' and 'postmodern' territorialities are useful in signalling the possibility of radical transformations, not just to states and the other 'actors', but to the time-space of the 'stage' on which they have to operate.

Contemporary globalisation and increased differentiation in the availability and applicability of 'space annihilating' communication technologies are rendering geographic space increasingly complex, variable and 'relative'. Conventional representations of states and politics based on a conception that space is 'absolute and homogeneous' are increasingly detached from reality. For example, in some situations involving 'foreign' multi-national companies it is increasingly difficult to find one fixed viewpoint or perspective from which to make sense of territorial sovereignty or to maintain the conventional dichotomy between 'foreign' and 'domestic', a dichotomy based on an 'absolute' conception of space. Ideas about federalism also generally reflect such a conception, and there is often an assumption that existing state forms will be replaced either by the state 'writ large', as in a federal 'United States of Europe', or 'writ small', as in separate 'regional governments'. In this 'Gulliver fallacy' the only real change is one of scale in homogeneous space (as with the two societies which Gulliver met in his Travels, one a society of giants the other of midgets, but both exact replicas of human society). There is a failure to recognise that political processes and institutions at different levels are qualitatively (not just quantitatively) different (Walker, 1993, 133–4).

An 'absolute' conception, as in Euclid's geometry and Newton's physics, is seriously counterproductive if we want to understand how the 'ground' of 'time-space' is now shifting under established political arrangements. Instead we need to see space as 'relative', as in Einstein's physics where things exist in a world of four dimensions – one of time as well as three of space – a world of 'time-space'. Contrary to the 'Gulliver fallacy', federalisation may neither replace nation states with a 'United States of Europe' nor with federations based on sub-state regional governments.

A 'new medievalism'?

In 1977 Bull speculated about 'a secular reincarnation of the system of overlapping or segmented authority that characterised medieval Christendom'. This, he thought, might arise because of, among other things, a growth of transnational corporations and networks, a 'regional integration of states', as in the European Community, or 'a disintegration of states' because of sub-state nationalist and regionalist pressures 'from below' – all developments now arguably further advanced than in 1977. Crucially, according to Bull, a return to 'overlapping authority' is most likely where the pressures 'from above and below' achieve partial and ambiguous changes, diffusing but not clearly relocating sovereignty. The situations to look for include an intermediate 'stage where, while one could not speak of a European state, there was real doubt . . . as to whether sovereignty lay with national governments or with the organs of the "community"' similarly, 'the disintegration of states would be theoretically important only if it were to remain transfixed in an intermediate state' in which sub-state nationalisms or regionalisms substantially undermined but did not succeed in replicating existing state sovereignty (Bull, 1977, 264–267).

Thus to debate Europe's future in terms of a federal 'United States of Europe' or an inter-governmentalism of independent states is perhaps to miss the point. Maybe the 'future' has already arrived, maybe 'this is it', neither a continuation of the modern system of states nor a federal state in embryo, but something quite different from both, an 'intermediate' form which is distinct in its own right rather than merely 'transitional'. A return to 'overlapping authority and multiple loyalty' does not involve anything as clear-cut as the replacement of existing states by scale replicas, macro-regional or microregional. On the contrary, it would happen where the pressures 'from above and below' altered territorial sovereignty in more partial and ambiguous ways.

Furthermore, there are other contemporary developments suggestive of a 'new medievalism', such as the emergence of other newly important world 'actors' such as 'global cities' and the recent mushrooming of transterritorial, functionally-defined networks. As Strange (1994) points out, states may be losing some of their autonomy, not because power has been 'lost upwards' to other political institutions such as the EU, but because it has 'gone sideways' to economic institutions and global market forces, and in some respects has 'gone nowhere' as economics outruns politics and political control is simply lost.

'Unbundling territoriality'

All these developments are consistent with the idea that sovereignty, having been 'bundled' into modern territorial states, is now being partially 'unbundled'. In medieval or pre-modern Europe political sovereignty was shared between a wide variety of secular and religious institutions and different levels of authority – feudal knights and barons, kings and princes, guilds and cities, bishops, abbots, the papacy – rather than being based on territory *per se*, and the territories were often discontinuous, with ill-defined and fluid frontier zones rather than precise borders. The rise of the modern state, and what distinguished it from medieval predecessors, was a 'bundling' of sovereignty over all aspects of social life into territorial state 'parcels'.

An 'unbundling' of territoriality may be a key to understanding the contemporary spatial reorganisations of politics and states. The medieval to modern transformation of politics was bound up with 'a radical reconstruction of views of space and time' (Harvey, 1989, 242). For example, medieval painters had seen their subjects from different sides and angles rather than from a single, fixed viewpoint, but Renaissance paintings differed radically following the invention of perspective from a single fixed point. For Ruggie (1993, 159) there was an analogous and related transformation of political space which '. . . came to be defined *as it appeared from a single fixed viewpoint*. The concept of sovereignty was merely the doctrinal counterpart of the application of single-point perspectival forms to the spatial organisation of politics.' Conversely, the present

291

'unbundling' of territorial sovereignty can be interpreted as a reversion to multiple perspectives, a 'reconstruction of views of space' which has been anticipated by cubist paintings that again showed things from different sides and angles.

Thus in a 'multiperspectival' European Union, relations between the (at present) twelve member states can no longer realistically be seen as simply involving twelve separate, single viewpoints. The twelve sometimes act as a collectivity which has its own singularity; the central institutions which were set up by the states, particularly the European Commission and Parliament, are now also to some extent 'actors' in their own right; and in defining their own interests each of the twelve states increasingly takes into account or 'internalises' at least some of the interests of the other eleven as well as the views of the central institutions (Ruggie, 1993, 168–174).

The 'unbundling' process is however markedly selective and partial, and this partiality militates against any simple alternative 're-bundlings' at different geographical scales. Accelerated globalisation underlies the 'unbundling', and as we have seen it also makes it increasingly important to differentiate between various policy areas. State territoriality is becoming less important with respect to some areas of economic and social life, but for others the modern nation state with its sovereignty defined by (often the same old) territorial boundaries seems as firmly rooted as ever, and in some aspects of social policy state powers are increasing.

Although a new form, the EU is still territorial; and in many respects 'singular sovereignty' remains dominant, whether exercised by the member states (e.g. in deciding education policies) or by the EU as a political collective (e.g. in negotiations about world trade). 'Fortress Europe', from the viewpoint of an intending immigrant, can display exactly the same unfriendly 'singularity' as a conventional territorial state. On the other hand, the EU's 'democratic deficit' is at least partly due to the diffuseness and lack of 'singularity' in its decision-making structure, particularly the powerlessness of its central parliament.

Thus ideas of 'new medieval' and 'postmodern' territorialities highlight the possibility of radical but partial shifts in the underlying 'time-space' of politics. Such changes to the political 'stage', and the possibility of 'compromises' between conflicting pressures and 'actors', both support the conclusion that formal federalism is unlikely, whether for Europe, Britain or Ireland. Rather than being a model for federal solutions, the EU and its 'unbundling' of territorial sovereignty may be a model of 'arrested federalisation'. The partiality of territorial 'unbundling' seems to be simultaneously encouraging federalisation and working against its full or formal realisation.

REFERENCES

Anderson, J. (1994) Problems of interstate economic integration: Northern Ireland and the Irish Republic in the Single European Market, *Political Geography*, 13, 1, 53–73.

Anderson, J. and Goodman, J. (1994) Northern Ireland: dependency, class and cross-border integration in the European Union, *Capital and Class*, No. 54, Autumn 1994.

Anderson, J. and Goodman, J. (1995) Euro-regionalism and national conflict: the EU, the UK, Ireland North and South, in *Development Ireland*, P. Shirlow (ed.), Pluto, Dublin.

Bowman, J. (1983) *De Valera and the Ulster Question*, Oxford University Press, Oxford.

Bull, H. (1977) *The Anarchical Society*, Macmillan, London.

Cox, R. W. (1992) 'Global Perestroika', in Miliband, R. and Panitch, L. (eds), *Socialist Register*, 26–44, Merlin Press, London.

Harvey, D. (1989) *The Condition of Postmodernity*, Basil Blackwell, Oxford.

Jay, R. (1989) Nationalism, federalism and Ireland, in *Federalism and Nationalism*, M. Forsyth (ed.), Leicester University Press, Leicester.

Nairn, T. (1977) *The Break-up of Britain: Crisis and Neo-nationalism*, London: New Left Books.

O'Leary, B., Lyne, T., Marshall, J., Rowthorn, B. (1993) *Northern Ireland: Sharing Authority*, Institute for Public Policy Research, London.

Ruggie, J. (1993) Territoriality and beyond: problematizing modernity in international relations, *International Organisation*, 47, 1, 139–174.

Strange, S. (1994) The power gap: member states and the world economy, Chapter 3 in F. Brouwer, V. Lintner and M. Newman (eds), *Economic policy making and the European Union*, Conference proceedings, London European Research Centre, University of North London, 14 April, Federal Trust.

Walker, R. B. J. (1993) *Inside/Outside: International Relations as Political Theory*, Cambridge University Press, Cambridge.

CHAPTER TWELVE

Postscript: Federalism in the Post-Cold War Era

John Agnew

In what appears now as a very different historical era, Kenneth C. Wheare's *Federal Government* (1st edition 1946; 4th edition 1963) served to introduce the postwar generation in the English-speaking world to the comparative politics of federalism. That book was a major step forward for its time. It shifted attention from the law of constitutions to the practice of federalism. It saw federalism as an evolutionary political arrangement rather than a fixed formula for the territorial division of governmental powers. The balance of power between central and regional units could change over time. Wheare (1963, 236) pointed out that among a group of states that could be labelled as 'classic' federations – the United States, Switzerland, Canada and Australia – Canada, with the least federal constitution was the one where 'the strict application of the federal principle' appeared to be the strongest. The United States and Switzerland, heretofore the favourite examples of advocates of federalism, were knocked off their constitutional pedestal.

In the present era Wheare's basic method of comparing cases to arrive at an understanding of the practices of federalism still has much to commend it. Every one of the chapters in this book follows the implicit logic of comparing its particular case to others so as to indicate its specific features. The approach also lends itself to the possibility of generalisation. Is each case totally unique or are there tendencies across a set of cases? Wheare noted, for example, the emerging tendency among federations for 'general' (central) governments to expand their powers at the expense of regional ones.

In this postscript to a set of studies that 'revisit' Wheare's 'federalist problematic' in the mid 1990s, I want to provide two services to the reader. One is to discuss how much the context for examining federalism has changed. In this book and in much of the contemporary writing on federalism, the federal form of governance is firmly tied to the management of inter-ethnic conflict. Previously differences of language, religion or nationality were not privileged relative to other considerations such as dissimilarity of social institutions or forces of geographical separation such as mountain barriers or great distance between communities. Discussion of federalism is today related much more strongly to the 'politics of identity' than was formerly the case (on potential problems with the concept of identity when used in comparative studies see Handler, 1994). Why has this happened? Does it make sense?

In the past federalism was also usually looked at as one end of a constitutional polarity whose other end was defined by 'unitary' or totally centralised governance. This is less so today. Now the emphasis is on how a federal division of governmental powers can intersect with other institutional arrangements – such as con-sociationalism and arbitration – to produce hybrid forms of government. In this context, what has been happening 'on the ground' around the world in the achievement and practice of federalism? Certainly, by Wheare's standard things have not been going so well. But perhaps this standard, in drawing largely on the past experience of the four 'classic' cases, derives from a number of historical-geographical experiences that are irrelevant to the problems of governance in a wide range of other settings or the classic cases themselves today. Imposing 'models' of federalism drawing from the experience of the four cases (in particular, the United States) has been largely unsuccessful (e.g. Central Africa, Nigeria, Malaysia). Using them as the norm for judging practice may well be equally misleading. In the United States today American federalism is questioned for its inability to guarantee representation in State legislatures and the US Congress for under-represented minority groups such as African-Americans. One of the quintessential 'established' federalisms has its own problems with 'identity politics'.

Second, what generalisations about the forms and practice of federalism, if any, does the comparative approach embodied in this book reveal? Are there any tendencies across the cases surveyed in this book that are similar in generality to that of Wheare noted previously concerning the expansion of central government to the disadvantage of regional governments? The organisation of the book reflects a number of tentative generalisations: federations in crisis, the break-up of socialist federations and federations in the making. But to what extent does the content of the case studies back these up?

THE NEW CONTEXT FOR FEDERALISM

Federalism and identity politics

It is widely remarked that the world has experienced a remarkable upsurge in the politics of place and group identity over the past twenty years. This has coincided with the increased permeability of state boundaries to flows of capital, goods and people and the collapse of the Cold War geopolitical division of the world that effectively 'froze' political borders for forty-five years. These coincidences have not gone unremarked. Many of the chapters in this book allude to them. For example, some commentators have argued that the importance of an 'intermediate government' at a regional level has increased because of the crisis of the Keynesian welfare state and the relative decline of Fordist production principles (e.g. Trigilia, 1991). From this point of view people's 'imagined communities of fate' are increasingly regions and localities rather than entire states. The activity of the US Civil Rights movement and decolonisation movements around the world also stimulated an enhanced sense of alternative but submerged group identities other than those attached to established nation-states. Together with vastly increased flows of migrants from poorer to richer countries, this has encouraged the flowering of a complex 'group identity politics' in many countries, to which conventional state institutions have had trouble in responding (e.g. Young, 1989; Torres, 1991). Finally, the collapse of the former Soviet sphere of influence in East-Central Europe and the disintegration of the Soviet Union itself have produced an explosion of ethnic conflicts that surprised even the most astute of commentators.

This is the context in which discussion of federalism has revived. As a territorial strategy for decentralising governmental powers, federalism is recommended as a means for managing inter-group conflicts that might otherwise escalate in violence and lead to a proliferation of mini-states without much viability (except as tax havens, perhaps) in the contemporary world economy. But what is the likelihood of this happening? Has the 'danger' of ethnic conflict to which federalism is posed as one element of a solution been exaggerated? In this context, is federalism an appropriate response?

In the first place, the geographical extent and intensity of ethnic conflict can be exaggerated. The apparent increase in 'tribal' conflicts at the end of the Cold War has led to speculation that the existing system of states is under threat of imminent disintegration. But apart from the former Soviet Union and Yugoslavia and some states in Africa there are few candidates for violent ethnic secession. Indeed, as Gurr (1994) reports, the end of the Cold War did not initiate a global outbreak of ethnic disputes. Secondly, federalism, in the form of greater regional autonomy, does appear to be a relatively successful strategy for defusing serious conflicts. Gurr (1994) points to Spain, Canada and Czechoslovakia (pre-1992) as providing examples of successful negotiated regional autonomy. The dilemma is that the demands of groups for recognition of a right to autonomy rest on a primordial claim to a particular identity as originating in the distant past and exercising a 'full-time' or total hold over individuals. Yet the social and spatial boundaries of ethnic groups can change over time. A good example of this would be the rapid depoliticisation of Catholic identity in the Netherlands in the 1960s after a period of fierce differentiation from the Protestant majority (see, e.g., Bakvis, 1981). Federalism institutionalises what may be 'temporary' or partial group identities as permanent ones. The territorial nature of the federal solution inscribes difference and ensures its reproduction.

Norms of federalism

Federal constitutions entrench divisions of powers between central and regional governments. Where the boundaries of the regional units match the boundaries of the main concentrations of the relevant ethnic, religious or language groups federalism is an effective means of managing conflict. In the 'classic' cases where federalism emerged as a response to ethnic division – Switzerland and Canada – the matching was very close, although not without problems as chapter two on Canada shows to great effect. Elsewhere, however, federalism, as McGarry and O'Leary (1994, 111–112) recount, 'has a poor track record as a conflict-regulating device in multi-national and polyethnic states, even where it allows a degree of minority self-government'. Only the constant renegotiation of the division of powers 'as a result of technological advances, economic transformations and judicial interventions' and the use of 'supplemental consociational practices' at both central and regional levels can ensure a degree of stability. Spain and Canada offer different examples of this kind of federal metamorphosis. Even then, as the Canadian case suggests, secession cannot be ruled out.

In terms of conventional usage most cases of federalism applied in polyethnic settings, such as in India or South Africa, are examples of 'quasifederalism.' In these cases the central governments have a final power unavailable to other governmental units that can be used to coerce acceptance of strict limits on regional autonomy. But, if anything, federations involving only two ethnic groups have been the most fragile of the lot. As McGarry and O'Leary (1994, 112) suggest, 'With the possible exception of Belgium, there is not a single case of successful federalism based upon dyadic or two-unit structures. Even the Belgian federation technically has four sub-units, even if it is built around a dualist ethnic division, and the EC has helped to sustain the unity of Belgium.'

This pessimism reflects the application of norms of federalism that see it as a 'pure' form of territorial governance without accommodation to the peculiarities of specific settings. From this point of view federalism is a particular legal form to which all places confessing it must conform. Otherwise they are all 'quasifederal' or *really* unitary. Particularly when the legal form of federalism is that of the early United States, as it usually is in most academic writing, there is an assumption of an *a priori* cultural homogenisation. This is because in American constitutional history the only legitimate approach to minorities has been to regard their members 'as abstract individuals like everyone else' (Piccone, 1991, 32). Reflecting this, the argument of the US Civil Rights movement, at least that of the dominant wing led by the Rev. Martin Luther King, was essentially an appeal to equal treatment of blacks irrespective of where they lived in the United States. The historic tension between 'federation' and 'nation', at work since the founding in the late eighteenth century, has made it impossible for the American central government to recognise minorities as political entities since their recognition would imply giving them a quasi-nation status incompatible with the increasingly clamorous claim to an over-arching nation-in-the-making that reached its highest point with the New Deal of the 1930s.

American federalism has acquired a peculiarly territorial concept of itself as federation has, at least ideologically, given way to nation. Federalism is increasingly seen as a geographical mechanism for aggregating individual preferences and organising political representation without attention to the non-geographical affiliations, such as ethnicity, religion, gender, sexual orientation and other group identities, upon which so much recent American political discourse has been based. This was manifested in the outcry in 1993 against the nomination of Lani Guinier as the head of the Civil Rights Enforcement Division in the US Department of Justice. In a number of articles in American law journals Ms Guinier had argued forcefully for proportional representation in elections and guaranteed minority representation in municipal and other legislatures (Guinier, 1994). These positions were widely seen as departing from the purely territorial and non-group character of American federalism. The multiculturalism implicit in Guinier's perspective is antithetical to the nature of contemporary American federalism.

Consequently, the legal form of American federalism is not a good model to hold up either for 'imitation' elsewhere or as a standard for judgment about other 'federal' arrangements. It is the result of a peculiar historical experience. A danger in proposing federalism as a strategy for managing ethnic and other group disputes is that the

American model with its powerful cultural-assimilationist element will serve as the standard for judging other federalist arrangements. Not surprisingly, they fail to live up to the model. The model is not doing so well at home (see, e.g., Kull, 1992).

TENDENCIES OF FEDERALISM

The chapters in this book suggest a number of tendencies in the current forms and processes of federalism around the world. First of all, there is no universal form of federalism. Every case considered in this book has a mix of general and specific characteristics. In Canada, for example, it has been one regional unit, Quebec, that has stimulated most attempts at revising governmental practice. Yet Quebec, like regional units elsewhere, has its own problems with minority groups who challenge its right to govern part of its territory without their active consent. Federalism is a whole range of institutional arrangements involving a balance in the distribution of central and regional governmental powers. This is why using a particular model to judge particular practices is singularly inappropriate.

A second tendency is somewhat less obvious. The drawing of regional boundaries intrinsic to federalism tends to reify and reproduce the group differences to which federalism is itself a response. The cases of the former Soviet Union and Yugoslavia, both federalist in many respects prior to their recent disintegration, are instructive in this regard. In each case boundaries between the basic federal units were drawn with respect to the distribution of the major ethnic groups. In each case this left significant minorities in most of the regions but the majority in each could act as if it was the master of the others because the federal division of powers legitimised its hegemony. This laid the basis for the open expression of hostility once the heavy hand of the central government was removed, most clearly with the Serbs of Croatia and Bosnia. But it also meant that with the collapse of the communist parties that provided the major links between centre and periphery there was a ready-made alternative in a nationalism based on the claim to ethnic hegemony within a historic territory, i.e. the territory established under federalism (Kaldor, 1993). The break-up of the socialist federations, therefore, an important focus of the book, originated in part in the legitimising of ethnic identities provided by federalism.

Apparent in many of the chapters is a third tendency deserving of identification. This is the 'second best' quality of federalism in many situations. It is never what anyone really wants because it usually involves sharing institutions and power precisely with *those* people, a neighbouring group, who are most despised and/or feared by the group in question. Sometimes federalism has been imposed from outside (as in 1960s Nigeria), sometimes it has been a way of playing groups off against one another (as in Tito's Yugoslavia, and Stalin's Soviet Union) and sometimes it has been the product of inter-group negotiation (as in contemporary South Africa and in many historic examples). Rarely, if ever, has federalism inspired great political feats or revolutions.

A theme emerging from some of the chapters and underlying the selection of cases in the first section of the book, particularly the chapters on Canada, Belgium and Nigeria, is the tendency of federations to be in 'perpetual crisis'. In one sense this is not surprising. Not only is federalism usually not everyone's first choice, but by its nature federalism has a built-in disequilibrium between the imposition of common values and standards by the central government and the jealous protection of local powers by the regional units. This tension is not new. The American Civil War of 1861–65 was all about this. It was Abraham Lincoln in his 272-word Gettysburg Address of 1863 who gave the 'Federalist' view its most eloquent and succinct expression. His characterization of the United States as a singular rather than a plural noun represented his solution to the inherent contradiction between the sovereignty of the States and the national union that had dogged the country since the Declaration of Independence (see Wills, 1992). The growth of 'big' (usually central) government in most federal states – not even Switzerland is immune – has only exacerbated this sense of persisting constitutional crisis.

Finally, there is no necessary relationship between the growth of identity politics based on ethnicity or locality and the emergence of federalism. Federalism is only one among a number of ways in which identity politics can be managed. McGarry and O'Leary (1994) identify eight different methods of conflict regulation – from genocide and forced population transfer to federalism and consociationalism – and federalism is by no means the most frequent response. Indeed, given federalism's relative rarity and its incidence of failure the fact that experiments in federalism continue to be proposed and practised, as in contemporary Italy, Russia, Ireland and South Africa for example, says something about its appeal. It promises a rational, clean-edged approach to managing conflict and encouraging political participation. It is an Enlightenment doctrine *par excellence*. In the context of the explosion of identity politics this is precisely its main problem.

CONCLUSION

The mystery, then, is why federalism persists in both practice and attraction. On the one hand, it offers a fixed, reliable territorial solution to inter-group conflict. On the other hand, many groups are not sufficiently concentrated and the potential imbalance of centre and periphery is so great that it should hold little appeal. Its secret, irrespective of its eighteenth century patrimony, however, is that it holds out the promise of continued plurality and multiplicity in a world in which homogeneity, either local or global, appears as the only alternative. Wheare (1963, 244–5) captured this sentiment well in his classic book when he wrote:

'One of the most urgent problems in the world today is to preserve diversities either where they are worth preserving for themselves, or where they cannot be eradicated even if they are not desirable, and at the same time to introduce such a measure of unity as will prevent and facilitate co-operation. Federalism is one way of reconciling these two ends.'

After the Cold War federalism still deserves the attention the chapters in this book give it.

REFERENCES

Bakvis, H. (1981). *Catholic Power in the Netherlands*. Kingston, Canada: McGill-Queen's University Press.

Guinier, L. (1994). *The Tyranny of the Majority: Fundamental Fairness in Representative Democracy*. New York: Free Press.

Gurr, T. R. (1994). Peoples against states: ethnopolitical conflict and the changing world system. *International Studies Quarterly*, 38: 347–77.

Handler, R. (1994). Is 'identity' a useful concept? in J. R. Gillis (ed.) *Commemorations: the Politics of National Identity*. Princeton, NJ: Princeton University Press.

Kaldor, M. (1993). Le radici della guerra. *L'Indice*, giugno: 47–50.

Kull, A. (1992). *The Color-Blind Constitution*. Cambridge, MA: Harvard University Press.

McGarry, J. and O'Leary, B. (1994). The political regulation of national and ethnic conflict. *Parliamentary Affairs*, 47: 94–115.

Piccone, P. (1991). The crisis of liberalism and the emergence of federal populism. *Telos*, 89: 7–44.

Torres, G. (1991). Critical race theory: the decline of the universalist ideal and the hope of plural justice – some observations and questions of an emerging phenomenon. *Minnesota Law Review*, 75: 993–1007.

Trigilia, C. (1991). The paradox of the region: economic regulation and the representation of interests. *Economy and Society*, 20: 306–27.

Wheare, K. C. (1963). *Federal Government*. 4th edn. London: Oxford University Press.

Wills, G. (1992). *Lincoln at Gettysburg: The Words that Remade America*. New York: Simon and Schuster.

Young, I. M. (1989). Polity and group difference: a critique of the ideal of universal citizenship. *Ethics*, 99: 250–74.

Index

Numbers in bold indicate a map or table